TWENTIETH-CENTURY
IRISH DRAMA

TWENTIETH-CENTURY IRISH DRAMA

MIRROR UP TO NATION

Christopher Murray

Manchester University Press

Manchester and New York

distributed exclusively in the USA by St. Martin's Press

Copyright © Christopher Murray 1997

Published by Manchester University Press
Oxford Road, Manchester M13 9NR, UK
and Room 400, 175 Fifth Avenue, New York, NY 10010, USA

Distributed exclusively in the USA
by St. Martin's Press, Inc., 175 Fifth Avenue, New York, NY 10010, USA

British Library Cataloguing-in-Publication Data
A catalogue record for this book is available from the British Library

Library of Congress Cataloging-in-Publication Data
Murray, Christopher
    Twentieth-century Irish drama : Mirror up to nation /
Christopher Murray.
        p.   c.m.
    Includes index.
    ISBN 0-7190-4156-2. — ISBN 0-7190-4157-0 (pbk.)
    1. English drama—Irish authors—History and criticism.
2. English drama—20th century—History and criticism. 3. Ireland—
Intellectual life—20th century. 4. Ireland—In literature
I. Title.
PR8789.M87   1997
822'.91099415—dc20   96-27486
                                                                  CIP

ISBN 0 7190 4156-2 *hardback*
     0 7190 4157-0 *paperback*

First published 1997

01   00   99   98   97   10   9   8   7   6   5   4   3   2   1

Set in Dante and Tiffany Demi
by Koinonia Ltd, Manchester
Printed in Great Britain
by Biddles Ltd, Guildford and King's Lynn

For Kathleen, Paul, Felicity
and Chris, with love

If we write plays that are literature, and find people to like them, it will be because that strong imaginative energy, which is needed to fill with life the elaborate circumstance of a play, has not often come except as from a Sinai to some nation wandering as in the wilderness; ... Our daily life has fallen among prosaic things and ignoble things, but our dreams remember the enchanted valleys.

W. B. Yeats, 'The Irish Literary Theatre, 1900'

Contents

Acknowledgements — *page viii*

Introduction — *1*

1 Yeats's theatre of the heart — *13*

2 Lady Gregory: coming to terms — *37*

3 Synge: ironic revolutionary — *64*

4 O'Casey: in search of a hero — *88*

5 Into the twilight:
Robinson, Johnston, Carroll — *113*

6 Shades of the prison-house:
Shiels, D'Alton, Molloy, Behan — *138*

7 Revolutionary times:
'A Generation of Playwrights' — *162*

8 'A Modern Ecstasy': playing the North — *187*

9 'A National Dream-life':
the contemporary drama — *223*

References — *249*
Index — *269*

Acknowledgements

The roots of this book go far back in my life. Many of those people who first encouraged me in the study of theatre and drama are now, alas, dead. I should nevertheless like to express my indebtedness to Jeremiah Murphy, Patrick Diskin and Patrick Brennan late of University College, Galway, and to the late Frank J. Bailey, the young director from whom I first came to understand the art of theatre. Likewise Traolach Ó hAonghusa, director with *An Taibhdhearc* in the early 1960s, helped me to appreciate at first hand both the fun of performance and its power.

Alois M. Nagler, who died in 1993, was my mentor and teacher at Yale University. His enthusiasm for theatre of all nations was such that it was from him, strangely, that I learned to see Yeats as a man of ideas to put alongside Craig and Appia. Back in Ireland, I was initiated in 1970 into the teaching of Irish drama by the late Roger McHugh, first Professor of Anglo-Irish Literature and Drama at University College, Dublin (UCD). I came to appreciate Roger's experience as theatre historian, critic and scholar, and owe him a debt for his confidence in me.

At UCD I owe many others a word of appreciation also. Denis Donoghue gave me my head when he saw that all I was any way good for was talking about drama. His successor Seamus Deane gave me every encouragement, and honoured me by asking me to edit the section on early Irish drama for the *Field Day Anthology of Irish Writing*. I owe a major debt to the late Augustine Martin for his unstinting support as Professor of Anglo-Irish Literature and Drama. Thomas Kilroy became a dear friend from whose expertise I benefited a great deal over the years. Maurice Harmon invited me onto the Board of *Irish University Review* in 1977 and thereby opened up for me a whole new world of scholarship and bibliography. I should also like to thank the following for years of friendship and support: John Barrett, Andrew Carpenter, Terry Dolan, Brian Donnelly (who read the chapter on the North and offered much advice that I adopted), Alan Fletcher, Anne Fogarty (who commented helpfully on the Introduction), Joseph Long, Gerardine Meaney (who read and advised on two chapters), and Anthony Roche.

Acknowledgements

Other friends and colleagues also listened patiently over the years and I should like to thank them here for their encouragement. They include Kevin Brophy, Pat Burke, Brenna Clarke, Peter Denman, John Devitt, Martin Drury, Ger FitzGibbon, Paul Hadfield and Lynda Henderson of the badly missed *Theatre Ireland,* David Krause (who kindly read the O'Casey chapter in advance), and Riana O'Dwyer (who read two chapters and offered useful comments).

The International Association for the Study of Anglo-Irish Literature (IASAIL) has also brought me much benefit. Through its conferences and committees I have become indebted to many who have taken an interest in my work. In particular I must mention Csilla Bertha (Debrecen), Carla de Petris (Rome), Joris Duytschaever (Antwerp), Jacqueline Genet (Caen), Derry Jeffares (Stirling), Heinz Kosok (Wuppertal), Mária Kurdi (Pécs), Carla Locatelli (Trent), Ann Saddlemyer (Toronto), Masaru Sekine (Tokyo) and Wolfgang Zach (Graz).

The Irish Theatre Archive was part of my life in the 1980s, and I gained much from lectures and committee work attended. In particular I enjoyed discussions with the late Cyril Cusack, Séamus de Búrca, Maureen Hurley, John McCormick, Richard Pine and Joseph Woods.

The Synge Summer School twice offered me invaluable stimulation as lecturer and tutor. To its founder and director Nicholas Grene I express my deep appreciation. I have been helped also by Kevin O'Byrne and Saor-Ollscoil na hÉireann, by Noelle Clery and by Chris Morash for invitations to speak on Irish drama at their annual summer schools. The Association of Teachers of English (ATE) have likewise provided me with a stimulating audience on numerous occasions, for which I should like to thank chairperson Bertha McCullough.

In the actual writing of this book I was greatly helped by the library staff of University College, Dublin. In particular, I should like to thank Máirín Cassidy, Monica Cullinan and Madeleine O'Dwyer. The National Library of Ireland has also been a valuable resource, and I should like to thank the director Dr Pat Donlon and staff, especially Dónall Ó Luanaigh. The library facilities of Trinity College, Dublin, have likewise been indispensable over the years, and I should like to express my appreciation to the librarian, Mr Peter Fox, and his staff, especially Charles Benson and Áine Keegan.

My research on Behan was helped by Riobárd Mac Góráin, Seán Ó Briain, Padraic Ó Siocrú, and above all by Séamus Paircéar, to whom I extend heartfelt thanks. Gary McKeone offered useful information on the Field Day Theatre Company. At the Abbey Theatre I began research useful to me at the invitation of Lelia Doolan in 1972, and ever since I have been made welcome there. I should like to thank the manager Martin Fahy on behalf of the National Theatre Society Ltd, and to thank also those who have shown me much courtesy and kindness over the years, in particular Máirín Woods, Tadhg Crowley, Deirdre McQuillan, Tony Hardiman and Lucy McKeever.

Acknowledgements

I am indebted to Professor Don Cruickshank, Chairman, Board of Studies, UCD Drama Centre, for standing in for me as Director during a term's leave of absence in 1994 which enabled me to get on with the book. I express my appreciation to the Board for their support and to Dr Fergus D'Arcy, Dean, Faculty of Arts, for a small grant from Faculty towards expenses. Professor J. C. C. Mays deserves my gratitude for relief from some examination duties which allowed me to concentrate on the book.

The School of Irish Studies Foundation provided an award in 1994 which assisted me with travel expenses. I am grateful to the Foundation and express my appreciation in particular to the late Seán J. White, secretary, and Professor Kevin B. Nowlan, chairman.

I wish to thank Bernard Laughlin, curator, Tyrone Guthrie Centre, for allowing me to spend several valuable weeks at Annaghmakerrig, Co. Monaghan, where I managed to kick-start the book in a most appropriate setting.

My students, too, over many years, have offered great stimulation. I have often felt that they give back anything I can offer with renewed point, meaning and clarity. I thank them for their attention and youthful inspiration, and hope that a future generation of students may likewise be able to transform what I stumble to say into wider meanings and more challenging issues. This process, after all, is what teaching, that two-way path to knowledge, is all about.

Finally, to my long-suffering family, who have lived for years with the inconvenience of masses of clippings, papers, files and books overwhelming the very dining-room of our house, goes my deepest appreciation for their forbearance and indulgence. The dedication is for them, along with my thanks.

Introduction

The fascination of the national movement for me in my youth was,
I think, that it seemed to be an image of a social ideal which could
give fine life and fine art authority.

W. B. Yeats, 'Journal' (1909), in *Memoirs* (1972)

Beginnings

If you take the road northwest from Kinvara in County Galway and
go up the Doorus peninsula you will if you persist through rugged
terrain reach a youth hostel confusingly called Duras House. This
was the birthplace of the modern Irish theatre. A more unlikely
setting for such an event would be hard to find. It is certain that the
young foreigners who sit around the place nowadays, tending their
bikes or frowning over ordnance survey maps, have little awareness
that here is the spot where Lady Gregory and W. B. Yeats planned
the foundation of the Irish Literary Theatre in the late summer of
1897. And yet, when one looks around the locality with more attention the appropriateness of this birthplace is less questionable. To
the north are an ancient stone ring fort side-by-side with St Ciaran's
Bed, a shrine which was the site of an all-night vigil in July; to the
south a megalithic tomb; to the east the ruins of a seventeenth-
century church where the Frenches and their descendants the de
Basterots, old Catholic families, were buried; and to the west lies St
Colman's Church, completed in 1819 on land donated by James de
Basterot of Duras (the first Catholic church to be built in the west of
Ireland since the late Middle Ages), while a mile or two away is
Aughinish Tomb, reputed to be one of the beds used by Diarmuid
and Gráinne in their flight from Fionn MacCumhaill. Christian and
pagan remains lie cheek by jowl; myth and history are intermixed. It
is a landscape inscribed with thousands of years of culture.

Since Doorus is in the northern part of the barony of Kiltartan, it was not far, as the crow flies, from Lady Gregory's estate at Coole and the Gregorys knew the then Count de Basterot well. 'He had been my husband's warm friend, and always in the summer time we used to go and spend at least one long day with him – we two at first, and then later I went with my son and the boy and girl friends of his childhood. They liked to go out in a hooker and see the seals showing their heads, or to paddle delicately among the jellyfish on the beach. It was a pleasant place to pass an idle day' (Gregory 1972, p. 18). It still is.

That famous day in September 1897 was wet, however, when Edward Martyn, accompanied by Yeats, called at Duras House, where Lady Gregory was staying. Martyn came armed with his new play *Maeve* for Lady Gregory to read, she adds in her *Diaries* (1996, p. 152). There could be no thought of going for a walk, much less of venturing on or even in the sea. 'We sat there through that wet afternoon, and though I had never been at all interested in theatres, our talk turned on plays', Lady Gregory continues. Yeats told her there seemed no opportunity in London to stage the plays Edward Martyn and himself had written, in particular *Maeve* and *The Countess Cathleen*. 'I said it was a pity we had no Irish theatre where such plays could be given. Mr. Yeats said that had always been a dream of his. … We went on talking about it, and things seemed to grow possible as we talked, and before the end of the afternoon we had made our plan.' They would organise a theatre in Dublin and once a year stage Irish plays on Irish themes, in direct opposition to the colonialist tradition. 'We will show that Ireland is not the home of buffoonery and of easy sentiment, as it has been represented, but the home of an ancient idealism' (Gregory 1972, p. 20). Thus was created the modest plan which was to find fruition first in the productions of the Irish Literary Theatre between 1899 and 1901 and subsequently in the formation of the Irish National Theatre Society in 1903, out of which developed after December 1904 the limited company popularly known as the Abbey Theatre. It is a reasonably familiar story, too well documented to need retelling here (Robinson 1951; Hunt 1979).

Suffice it to say that with the initial staging in 1899 of Yeats's *The Countess Cathleen* and Martyn's *The Heather Field* (in preference to *Maeve*, staged the following year), plays both poetic and realistic, a common purpose was formulated to locate and give voice to the

Introduction

soul of a people. Articulation of a focalised theme and the search for an appropriate style (in production) were to become the two defining preoccupations of this literary theatre. The early writers, Yeats, Martyn, George Moore (especially in *The Bending of the Bough*, 1900), in however amateurish a fashion showed how authentic Irish experience might be recast as vision, the dream of an alternative reality. Representation, mirroring of reality, was from the outset to be bound up in dreams and symbols. Production style was likewise to have its base in realism but to aspire to something beyond naturalism, something poetic and transcendent. That step towards an ideal theatre could not be taken until after 1901, until the hopeless involvement of the Frank Benson Shakespearean Company from England was dispensed with and the Fay brothers led the way towards an authentic, literally cottage-industry style of realising the Irish imagination on stage.

Aesthetics and politics

The extent to which the dramatic movement was implicated in cultural nationalism needs fully to be recognised. This book is located within the confines of that interaction. The starting point here is the assumption that in the Irish historical experience drama (the creation of texts for performance) and theatre (the formation of the means of production and conditions of reception of drama) were both instrumental in defining and sustaining national consciousness. Martin Esslin says in *An Anatomy of Drama* that theatre is 'the place where a nation thinks in front of itself' (1978, p. 101). But before a people can do this it must have an awareness of itself *as* a nation. The poet Seumas O'Sullivan reports on the fervent reception of the Yeats–Gregory collaboration *Cathleen Ni Houlihan* in 1902: 'I was with Arthur Griffith, and I can still see his face as he stood up at the fall of the curtain to join in the singing of what was then our national anthem – and would to God it was still our national anthem – "A Nation Once Again"' (1946, p. 121). The words of Thomas Davis's song looked forward to the day when 'Ireland, long a province' will become 'a nation once again' (Griffith 1916, p. 60). The mood is optative, the tense future. The process of becoming is what receives emphasis. No man in 1902 was to be so much a part of this process as Arthur Griffith, destined to be founder and president of Sinn Féin and ultimately president of the Irish Free State (for a tragically brief

[3]

time). As a journalist Griffith at first supported and then fought against the Irish National Theatre Society, making Synge's [In] the Shadow of the Glen (1903) his casus belli. Griffith, like Maud Gonne, believed that the function of the new theatre movement was to contribute towards national liberation. Yeats had to differ. Whereas he shared, and made the dramatic movement he headed share, the national aspiration, Yeats tried to draw a sharp line between politics and art.

This was no easy task for a writer who had repeatedly said that all great literature is national. Neither was it an easy task for a man in love with the incendiary Maud Gonne. Yeats's integrity in the battle to maintain the autonomy of art within a cultural revolution is beyond reproach. His defence of Synge, in 1903, in 1905 and especially over the Playboy riots in 1907, crystallised the aesthetic by which the Abbey was entitled to be regarded as important. Only if the theatre preserved the right of the artist to create in freedom could it meaningfully contribute to the process of national self-definition. Of course, the situation was enormously complicated by Annie Horniman's facile belief that it was possible to omit politics altogether. Miss Horniman, a spiritualistic Englishwoman with a modest fortune which she used to patronise poetic drama, having generously provided the Abbey Theatre building in 1904 interfered constantly in its management until finally withdrawing her annual subsidy in 1910. Hearing that the cast of The Playboy was hissing back at certain quarters of the audience she was furious: 'it must be clearly understood that I will not allow my theatre to be used for political purposes. ... I am fighting for us to stand above all low political spite on either side. ... From the very first and ceaselessly I have held firm to the position that I will have no politics' (Hogan and Kilroy 1978, p. 161). But Yeats recognised that 'politics are our national passion' (1962a, p. 241). What he did not want and fought valiantly to exclude was anything based on mere 'opinions'. He could only steer a course between art and propaganda by insisting on the artist's personal vision.

Here Yeats divorced himself from Davis's cultural nationalism. A national theatre, he wrote in 1903, was not a dramatisation of The Spirit of the Nation, which favoured mere rhetoric rather than poetry ('patriotism transformed into a personal emotion by the events of life'), and if that form of cultural nationalism were followed Ireland would not produce a theatre which would reflect the life of the country 'as the Scandinavian theatre reflects Scandinavian life' (Yeats 1962a, p. 115). Synge proved a test case. In 1904 Yeats described him as 'truly a National writer, as Burns was when he wrote finely' (p. 157). Moreover, national literature 'is the work of writers who are moulded by influences that are moulding their country, and who write out of so deep a life that they are accepted there in the end' (p. 156). The idea is identical with the declaration in the manifesto of the Irish Literary Theatre that the central purpose was 'to bring upon the stage the deeper thoughts and emotions of Ireland' (Gregory 1972, p. 20). It is not a million miles from Joyce's aim to forge in the smithy of his soul the uncreated conscience of his race.

In his *Nation and Narration* (1990) Homi Bhabha includes and approves Ernest Renan's essay, 'What is a Nation?', to which Yeats also referred approvingly in 1900. Writing in the second number of *Beltaine*, Yeats placed a distance between the glorification of the Celtic race by Edward Martyn and George Moore and his own preference for Renan's endorsement of a living tradition embodied in speech, literature, institutions and examples of history: 'It is these that make nations and that mould the foreign settler after the national type in a few years; and it is these, whether they were made by men of foreign or of Celtic blood, that our theatre would express' (Yeats 1975, p. 202). What distinguished Yeats from the run-of-the-mill nationalists was his acceptance of Renan's notion that 'It is good for everyone to know how to forget' (Bhabha 1990, p. 16). A perpetual sense of grievance kindled only a low emotional flame. For art to flourish there had to be a rising above obsession with the past. Bhabha himself underlines the implications. 'Being obliged to forget becomes the basis for remembering the nation, peopling it anew, imagining the possibility of other contending and liberating forms of cultural identification' (p. 311). But Bhabha is talking mainly about the role of fiction in the construction of national consciousness; in Ireland it was drama rather than fiction which assumed this role, a dynamic being needed for a culture with strong roots in oral tradition and public rhetoric. (In Shakespeare's day, too, it was the theatre, above all, which created national consciousness.) In Ireland the writer tends to look for a live audience. Thus Irish novelists from George Moore through Joyce to John McGahern and John Banville have turned at least once to the theatre as the place where a shift from private to public discourse can take place. To some degree also it can be said that Brian Friel's success as playwright is implicated in his exploitation of short-story techniques, fictional procedures; transferred to the open space of theatre, where a collective response can negotiate terms of belief, identity and freedom. Narration becomes dramatisation, in this context; in Ireland the nation is staged rather than told.

Whenever the 'cultural heritage' has a living relationship to the 'real life of the people', Georg Lukács argues, it is characterised by 'a dynamic, progressive movement in which the active creative forces of popular tradition … are buoyed up, preserved, transcended and further developed'. Indeed, the best modern writers 'are an organic product of the development of their nation' (Taylor 1980, pp. 53–4). The point is that Yeats's idea was both traditionalist and progressive and it was this strange blend which lent itself to a nationalist dynamic. The fusion may be seen in the wording of his 'Advice to Playwrights Who are Sending Plays to the Abbey Theatre', written some time before 1910: 'A play to be suitable for performance at the Abbey should contain some criticism of life, founded on the experience or personal observation of the writer, or some vision of life, of Irish life by preference, important from its beauty or from some excellence of style' (Gregory 1972, p. 62). This emphasis on 'criticism' smacks of Matthew Arnold on poetry. But it lifts the idea of drama out of any imputation of turning its back on the realities of Irish life. Whether in poetry or prose, whether mythic or naturalistic, the drama would engage with the conditions of Irish experience. Art for art's sake was not on the agenda. It is fair to say that this broadly defined aesthetic of engagement was the one firmly established in the modern Irish drama. It had its exclusive side as well as its dynamic: it probably kept Samuel Beckett firmly out of sympathy with the current of the Irish drama after O'Casey's Dublin plays.

Nationalism becomes a problematic concept in Irish culture after 1922. There are those who would say it means nothing but trouble, and there are those who would say it means nothing. But in the light of what happened in Eastern Europe and the USSR from 1989 on, not to speak of the emergence of African states from colonial rule in the 1960s, it would be folly to underestimate the enduring power of nationalism. Tom Nairn faults nationalism as a disease, as inescapable as 'neurosis' in the individual (1977, pp. 347, 359). Shaw held a similar view. But a more recent commentator, John Hutchinson, argues that cultural nationalism does not die but mutates. It stands

Introduction

for 'an evolutionary vision of the community' (1987, p. 30). There is always a drive to re-create the nation so that it will rise to the forefront in world progress: it is geared up with economic development. However, it seems quite plain that in the Irish experience 1922 was a watershed. After that date writers and intellectuals left aside any role as singers of the 'Soldiers' Song' and adopted a critical stance to the new state (Goldring, 1993, p. 169). The community which Hutchinson sees evolving was more like the artists' alternative abode, a new dream, in contrast to the dystopia achieved through independence. The legacy of the civil war was division. Partition made nationalism a suspect ideology, to which a writer like Brendan Behan fell victim but from which most writers in the Republic simply turned aside in apathy, embarrassment, or both. In addition, censorship and a severe moral climate of repression created an unprecedented divide between writers and society in Ireland from the 1930s on. Although he was speaking of the Gate and not of the National theatre, Micheál MacLiammóir's gloomy acceptance that he and Hilton Edwards had changed nothing in the theatre speaks for Irish drama and society in general: 'We remained, as Ireland herself remains, wayward and conceivably amusing figures at odds, not merely with the dramatic force at work in other countries, but often with the country itself, and, it may be with our own selves' (1961, n.p.). It was not until the 1960s and the arrival of Friel, Murphy, Leonard and other representatives of a new generation that something like the old energy and power of engagement were restored to the Irish theatre. One thus cannot speak of absolute continuity or an unbroken tradition in the history of modern Irish drama. Rather, one must accept that there were discrete phases, governed and animated as the case might be by forces mainly political and only in a highly ironic sense nationalist. Artistic values often had a hard time of it during these phases, notably between the death of Yeats in 1939 and the opening of the new Abbey in 1966.

Recently, Seamus Heaney has commented in general terms on the interrelationship between North and South in the context of cultural nationalism:

> The political arrangement which incorporated Northern Ireland into the United Kingdom of Great Britain and Northern Ireland was not one allowed for in the envisaging minds of the writers of the Irish Literary Revival. Yeats, Synge and Lady Gregory constructed an imagined place that gave eternal life to Gaelic country people of the west and their

[7]

Anglo-Irish lords and ladies, while Joyce made a divine comedy out of the urban tumult of Dublin. So, both Joyce and the Revivalists, in their different ways, prepared cultural paths for the political fact of Irish independence; and indeed when that independence came it included only those constituencies whom the writers of genius at the turn of the century had written into the imaginative record. The Irish Free State was from the start coterminous as a demographic and geographic entity with the textual Ireland of Joyce and the Revivalists – the Ireland, that is, of urban Catholicism, rural peasantry and those of the Protestant ascendancy and professional classes who were prepared to stay on after the Union Jack came down. (1995, pp. 194–5).

Obviously, the outbreak of violence in Northern Ireland in 1969 revived Irish nationalism as an issue in ways which cut clean across the new ideology of pragmatism, secularisation and economic progress which had turned the Republic's attention more towards the European Economic Community than towards any but a token interest in the North. The drama of this period inevitably found models in O'Casey and St John Ervine; the past was revisited in search of forms through which to order and find meaning in the present. Here, to be sure, Hutchinson's notion of a cycle in cultural nationalism proves fruitful. And the emergence of the Field Day Theatre Company in 1980 raised all over again questions of politics and aesthetics considered necessary for the exploration of language, history and identity in the context of Ireland's relationship with and to England.

Procedures

We have noted above the contradictions which arose between Yeats's aesthetic programme and the rather narrow nationalism of those, like Griffith, who saw the Abbey as having a propagandist function. It would also be possible to consider the work of Padraic Colum (1881–1972) as significantly emblematic of this struggle. *The Land* (1905) is a paradigm of modern Irish drama. Concerned with family conflicts arising from a turning point in Irish social history, the Wyndham Land [Purchasing] Act of 1903, this play stood, one reviewer said, 'in a definite, luminous relation to the Ireland in which we all live and move' (Hogan and Kilroy 1978, p. 31). It deals not only with the great Irish theme, passion for the land, on the dramatic agenda since Edward Martyn's *The Heather Field* (1899), but also with emigration as betrayal. 'The nation, men of Ballyhillduff, do you ever think of it at all? Do you ever think of the Irish nation, that is waiting all this time to be born?' (Colum 1963, p. 47). The speaker here is described as 'struggling with words', the perpetual condition of the Irish playwright. The relationship between actuality and possibility is seen as complex; drama becomes a two-sided mirror, with dream on the other side. Colum's aesthetic of social reflection is also a vehicle of provocative idealism.

Thus, in Irish drama the mirror does not give back the real; it gives back *images* of a perceived reality. The play as mirror up to *nation*, rather than to nature in Hamlet's sense, results in a dynamic in process: you have to stop it in freeze-frame to distinguish what happened (history) from what might yet happen (politics). The thing is fluid and proleptic. Therefore a prescriptive approach to the relations between art and society in Irish drama is unfruitful. An open, pluralist form of dramatic criticism seems preferable. Drama helps society find its bearings; it both ritualises and interrogates national identity. The task of criticism is to map this process descriptively and, in the present case, historically.

Instead of attempting a comprehensive history of the modern Irish drama, which would call for several volumes, this book is organised in two ways, by authors and by themes. In the first part the work of Yeats, Lady Gregory, Synge and O'Casey is each given a chapter by way of emphasising their significance as founders of a tradition. O'Casey, indeed, may be said to dominate the history of Irish drama after Independence, for his demythologising stance in the Dublin 'trilogy' initiates the stance taken by Irish playwrights after him. They are all nothing if not critical. The second half of the book begins with Lennox Robinson, a figure torn between the earlier and the later forms of Irish drama. Robinson began as a protégé of Yeats, under whose shadow his timid spirit was artistically blighted. Alongside Denis Johnston and Paul Vincent Carroll, Robinson serves to give definition to the new Ireland. Johnston's intellectualism, a major contribution to the Irish theatre, was applied to assessing the fruits of violence in the new Free State. In a comic style reminiscent of Shaw, Johnston represented Irish society perpetually revising a text, always hoping to re-create history, and in the attempt always taking an ambivalent view of violence. The early Joycean, Catholic *non serviam* is heard in the theatre for the first time with Carroll. But that gesture soon becomes redundant. There was no place for Carroll in the theatre of the 1940s and what

MacLiammóir called the 'fatal fifties' in Ireland (1964, p. 57). A new conformism permeated Irish culture at this time, summed up in Roger McHugh's amusing review of *The Righteous Are Bold* (1946) in *The Bell*. When Nora went into her demonic fit at the end of Act I, spat at and then broke the holy statue, McHugh overheard a young woman in the audience say, 'it's all right, mother, I have my eyes shut tight; I'm not looking at all'. Audiences were not looking for any real manifestation of evil in the age of de Valera; society had its eyes shut tight. They didn't open them again until the 1960s. The riches of the period after 1960 are such that I had a major problem in organisation of material. If I were to give individual chapters on Friel, Murphy, Leonard, Keane and Kilroy, as they deserve, the book would have expanded beyond my wildest dreams; therefore, because there have been several publications in recent times which have already provided assessments of these authors, I thought it best to tackle the problem by decades and thematically. I am aware that this is not entirely satisfactory, but I hope the attempt will be seen to have its merits.

Central to my approach, in any case, is Raymond Williams's idea of the artist as one who provides a structure of feeling: 'not an unformed flux of new responses, interests and perceptions, but a formation of these into a new way of seeing ourselves and our world' (1968, p. 11). It is by their structure, their form, that the better writers articulate their obsessions and fears and thereby communicate these with such force as to speak for the community at large. Thus Tom Murphy could remark in interview in 1980: 'You reflect things in drama because you absorb them, not because you decide to reflect them.'

The chapter on the North is the only occasion when the book goes outside the Republic for its material, but the venture hardly requires justification given the importance of the North as subject since 1969. Within that chapter a three-part structure is followed so that the drama of the North itself is kept separate from that of the South in relation to the same issue (the extended war between 1969 and 1994), and a third section devoted to Field Day tries to argue for a synthesis or a drama of North-and-South. The whole history of suffering dealt with by way of art presents a huge difficulty here. I find that what Philip Larkin told a mother who had written a novel about her son, who had been killed in an accident, very useful: 'I can quite see that to "play about" with the kind of subject matter you

Introduction

have taken would seem heartless, frivolous, even untrue ... and yet in literature it somehow has to be done – one might almost say that it's the mixture of truth and untruth that makes literature' (Motion 1993, p. 271). As in personal tragedy so in national; and so I call the chapter 'Playing the North'. The final chapter, on the contemporary scene, is necessarily limited in scope but the aim is, as throughout the book, to show how Irish drama continues to take seriously the task of holding the mirror up to that constantly changing, fascinating, bewildering, infuriating, indefinable entity, the nation.

Bibliographical addendum

The list of works cited, appended at the back of the book, stands jointly as source references and as bibliography. At the same time, for the benefit of students, I should like here to comment on some texts basic to the history of twentieth-century Irish drama.

E. H. Mikhail's *An Annotated Bibliography of Modern Anglo-Irish Drama* (1981) is still the best available. In *Anglo-Irish Literature: A Review of Research* (1976), edited by Richard J. Finneran, the chapter on the modern drama by Robert Hogan, Bonnie K. Scott and Gordon Henderson supplies wide-ranging bibliographical information, updated in *Recent Research on Anglo-Irish Writers* (1983), also edited by Finneran. A third updated edition fell through in 1990. It is some compensation that a section on Irish drama is included annually in Charles A. Carpenter's bibliography published in the summer issue of the journal *Modern Drama*. Carpenter's *Modern British Drama* (1979) also contains a section on Irish drama, as will *The Annotated Bibliography for English Studies*, forthcoming from ESSE.

Although, to date, no study of Irish drama has looked in detail at the interrelations of history, politics and performance in the way I find rewarding, the earliest books have undoubtedly blazed the trail. Cornelius Weygandt, the first in the field, insisted in *Irish Plays and Playwrights* (1913) that Irish playwrights were 'more resolutely native' than the 'most national dramatists of other countries have been' (p. 14). Although awkwardly put, his point is entirely valid. Ernest Boyd's two studies, *The Contemporary Drama of Ireland* (1918) and *Ireland's Literary Renaissance* (1922), both excellent introductions to the first phase of the Irish dramatic movement, stress that politics gave rise to the literary renaissance and that 'the spirit of the race' informed Irish literature thereafter (Boyd, 1922, p. 10). The first chapter of Andrew E. Malone's *The Irish Drama* (1929) is entitled 'The Need for Irish National Drama'. The note of celebration is quite strong here, but Malone finally declares that the time had come for a widening of themes and opportunities. The Abbey theatre should become one with the theatres of Europe. Here Malone misunderstood completely the way Irish society was to develop in the 1930s, closing down avenues left and right (mostly left) for intellectuals and creating a Catholic hegemony which writers were bound to counter in local, traditional terms (if they didn't simply skip the country like O'Casey and Beckett). By the time Peter Kavanagh's book on the Abbey appeared in 1950 the deadliness of Irish culture was apparent and Kavanagh could only mourn the betrayal of Yeats's ideals. Una Ellis-Fermor's revised edition in 1954 of her *The Irish Dramatic Movement* (1939) consolidated these earlier studies and established the canon of Irish drama for many years. It is still an influential book, even if it suppressed the political factor in Irish drama. Later studies, Robert Hogan's *After the Irish Renaissance* (1967) and D. E. S. Maxwell's *The Irish Drama 1890–1980* (1984) in particular, have helped to expand the canon without addressing the political question. Katharine Worth's *Irish Drama of Europe from Yeats to Beckett* (1978) extended the frontiers of dramatic criticism in an exciting new direction and has enabled us to view the Irish tradition as closely linked to the European. Anthony Roche's *Contemporary Irish Drama* (1994) has, in a sense, built upon this approach by making Beckett the arbiter of Irish drama since Behan. It is perhaps time now to go back to the earlier emphasis.

In addition, Robert Hogan and his collaborators have provided in the six volumes to date of their documentary history, *The Modern Irish Drama* (1975–92), the source materials for a full understanding of the period up to 1926. Finally, I should mention the history of anthologies of Irish drama, from Curtis Canfield's two influential volumes, *Plays of the Irish Renaissance 1880–1930* (1929) and *Plays of Changing Ireland* (1936), down to the three recent volumes, Brendan Kennelly's *Landmarks of Irish Drama* (1988), Coilin D. Owens's and Joan N. Radner's *Irish Drama 1900–1980* (1990), and John P. Harrington's *Modern Irish Drama: A Norton Critical Edition* (1991). These anthologies take their place alongside the critical works already cited as moulders of the canon.

1

Yeats's theatre
of the heart

O silver trumpets, be you lifted up
And cry to the great race that is to come.
Yeats, *The King's Threshold* (1903)

Seminal playwright

As the twentieth century draws to a close a question mark still
seems to hang over Yeats's standing as playwright. To a lot of
people Yeats's status as lyric poet overwhelms the question, as if
there could be no room for serious consideration of Yeats in any
other guise. To many Irish people, in particular, Yeats as playwright
presents difficulties they are unprepared to surmount: the verse by
its mythological and esoteric references makes demands they would
prefer not to have made in the theatre. Some would plainly claim
that Yeats was a mere amateur in the theatre who made impossible
demands on actors and audiences alike (everybody knows the story
of Yeats's wish to rehearse Abbey actors in barrels). Others would
decry what they see as Yeats's remoteness from ordinary life and
everyday concerns; he was not a man to take a pint with the lads, it
is averred by cognoscenti of the indissoluble link in Irish literature
between alcoholism and genius. All of this negativity, gleaned by the
present author from years of patient listening during intervals at the
Peacock Theatre and from attending to dramatic enthusiasts holding the answer to the ever-recurring crisis in Irish playwriting, is
greatly surprising in view of the written testimony in favour of Yeats
the dramatist. Una Ellis-Fermor (1954), Peter Ure (1963), Leonard E.
Nathan (1965), James W. Flannery (1976), Liam Miller (1977),
Katharine Worth (1978), A. S. Knowland (1983) and Karen Dorn
(1984) are but some of the critics who have painstakingly answered
all of the obvious reservations paraphrased above. In addition,

directors such as Lennox Robinson, Katharine Worth and Jim Flannery have spent years demonstrating the theatrical variety and inventiveness of Yeats's plays on the stage. Flannery's successful annual Yeats Festival held at the Abbey between 1989 and 1993 should have been enough, one might have thought, to secure Yeats's reputation as man of the theatre unchallenged in his own country. And yet the bias remains.

There is a cruel irony in all of this. Of the twenty-six plays in *Collected Plays* (1952) only a handful could be called in any degree inaccessible; *The Shadowy Waters* and *The Unicorn from the Stars* (far more accessible, actually, thanks to Lady Gregory's assistance, than the original *Where There is Nothing*) would be the least forthcoming, perhaps. But even plays that have behind them a wealth of symbolic and esoteric lore, such as *The Only Jealousy of Emer* or *The Player Queen* or *The Cat and the Moon* or *The Herne's Egg*, all have tremendous verve and theatrical life. It is never as necessary to know the philosophy behind the plays as it is to know Yeats's *A Vision* when reading the poems from 1919 on. All is embodied in terms as broadly theatrical as melodrama, pantomime and farce; the plays epitomise performance values. A second irony is that Yeats strove to be a kind of Fiddler of Dooney, an artist of the people, a Homer of modern times. He did not entirely relish the aura of sage which descended on him in later years. As playwright, in particular, he wanted to enter the imagination of the people, having installed there images and codes for self-understanding and for expansion of consciousness.

It has also to be borne in mind that when Yeats went to Stockholm to collect the Nobel Prize for Literature in 1923 he chose to present himself as a man of the theatre rather than as a lyric poet:

> I have chosen 'The Irish Theatre' for my subject, that I may commend all those workers, obscure or well-known, to whom I owe much of whatever fame in the world I may possess. If I had been a lyric poet only, if I had not become through this Theatre the representative of a public movement, I doubt if the English committees would have placed my name upon that list from which the Swedish Academy selects its prize-winner. (Yeats 1961b, p. 552)

Yeats's address was entitled 'The Irish Dramatic Movement' and it was a combination of the argument that 'players and painted stage took all my love' ('The Circus Animals' Desertion') and the argument that the movement derived from a political situation: 'The modern literature of Ireland ... began when Parnell fell from power in 1891. A disillusioned and embittered Ireland turned from parliamentary politics; an event was conceived; and the race began, as I think, to be troubled by that event's long gestation' (p. 559). That 'event' was, of course, 1916 and the consequent achievement of Irish independence.

Yeats's enterprise as playwright may thus be seen as fundamentally political. Had his career not coincided with the resurgence of cultural nationalism in the 1890s it is unlikely it would have realised its full potential. Philip Edwards (1979) has plausibly argued that the Irish dramatic movement arose out of the wider European cultural nationalism of the nineteenth century. For all his dislike of Ibsen's prose plays Yeats saw himself as replicating in Dublin Ibsen's valiant attempt to found a Norwegian National Theatre in Bergen: 'The theatre of Scandinavia was the nearest approach to an ideal theatre in modern Europe. It was the only theatre whose plays were at once literary and popular' (Yeats 1975, p. 155). Moreover, Yeats's reading of Shakespeare led him to translate or transform Shakespeare's success with the history plays into a model for the creation of modern national consciousness. In that regard, 'Yeats is a consequence of Shakespeare. His work to create an Irish national spirit, and a national literature and drama, could not have come into existence except as a counter to the results of the earlier English nationalism' (Edwards 1979, p. 211). Yeats's own comments in 'A General Introduction for my Work', written in 1937, show what Edwards's claim means. Here Yeats concedes his love-hate relationship with English culture and the dynamic supplied by a sense of history: 'No people hate as we do in whom that past is always alive ... Then I remind myself that ... all my family names are English, and that I owe my soul to Shakespeare, to Spenser and to Blake, perhaps to William Morris, and to the English language in which I think, speak, and write, that everything I love has come to me through English; my hatred tortures me with love, my love with hate' (1961a, p. 519). Thus the whole venture of becoming the voice of the emerging Irish nation was for Yeats a personal as well as a cultural drama of maturation.

Yeats may be called the seminal figure in the growth of modern Irish theatre and drama, not just because he had the energy, skill and authority to establish and maintain the Abbey Theatre but because it was he who first formulated the role of the Irish dramatist as shaman, as the necessary outsider/insider with the power to bring wholeness and self-knowledge to a community. Yeats had what James Flannery (1976), following Francis Fergusson, calls an 'idea of the theatre' which was both enabling and enduring. He made serious theatre possible in Ireland, where before his time commercialism and mere diversion ruled the roost. He knew instinctively that the public domain was where his art should flourish: 'I need a theatre; I believe myself to be a dramatist; I desire to show events and not merely tell of them ... and I seem to myself most alive at the moment when a room full of people share the one lofty emotion' (1966, p. 415). In addition, Yeats was preoccupied with the nation, or the race as he preferred to call it, in its emergence from nineteenth-century confusion into full realisation after 1916. 'We are trying to put upon the stage in playing as in playwriting the life of this country, not a slavish copy of it as in a photograph, but a joyous, extravagant, imaginative image as in an impressionist painting' (1975, p. 366). Yeats was firmly of the view that the way to give voice to national consciousness was through sincere expression of individual experience: by a kind of synecdoche related to the very process of theatre itself (where the partial world we see on stage represents the world at large) the solitary writer created the microcosm which challenged and transformed the world-view, the episteme, held by the audience, itself a fragment of the community at large. Thus theatre was no idle business but the moulder of the people's very souls.

While not denying that Yeats's plays reach out to Europe, as Katharine Worth (1978) has argued, and have roots in French symbolism which extend in due course to fructify in the minimalist plays of Beckett, I wish to limit this discussion to Yeats's involvement with home affairs, with questions of Irish identity, history and consciousness. The markers thus put down by Yeats were to guide such diverse playwrights as the later O'Casey, Brian Friel (for example, *Faith Healer*), Tom Murphy (*Bailegangaire*), and Tom MacIntyre (*passim*).

It is possible to divide the plays chronologically into three stages. In the first group, up to 1903, where folklore is the base, the general theme is the consolidation of the self. In the second group, from 1904 to 1919, based on myth, there is the triumph of art. In the final group, to 1939, where the Noh influence is modified, the emphasis is on the irony of history. All three phases indicate how Yeats positioned himself *vis-à-vis* the world, to supply what he was to call a theatre of the heart, 'understanding heart, according to Dante's definition, as the most interior being' (1962a, pp. 252–3).

Early and middle plays

Yeats's first staged play was *The Land of Heart's Desire* (1894), produced by the Independent Theatre, London's answer to the *Théâtre Libre*. The title of the play is significant. This 'land' was never for Yeats a place but rather a site for struggle. Shaw, who shared the playbill on this occasion with Yeats, had his own 'land of heart's desire' to chart in his plays, a socialist utopia. Yeats had no such goal. In *The Land of Heart's Desire* the destination is the world of the *Sidhe*, the fairy world, seen as simultaneously menacing and liberating. Mary Bruin, the bride who on May eve invites a fairy child into her cottage, in effect rather prefers to die than to endure the boredom and materialism of peasant life. But the play presents Mary's situation as a choice leading to life at another level rather than resulting in death. The play exploits this ambiguity. The power of the fairies is evil and yet at the same time their music is beautiful; the priest's warning is timely and perceptive and yet what he sees as Mary's 'duties' in the home can also be seen as intolerable misery. As the fairy child says (1966, p. 206):

> For if you hear him you grow like the rest;
> Bear children, cook, and bend above the churn,
> And wrangle over butter, fowl, and eggs,
> Until at last, grown old and bitter of tongue,
> You're crouching there and shivering at the grave.

By means of this ambiguity the stage space becomes a site for debate and the play establishes a critique of conventional Irish marriage in the form taken up later by Synge in *The Shadow of the Glen* (1903). In this regard, the presence of the priest on stage makes Yeats's critique a challenge to Irish Catholicism. He needs to do this if the world of the fairies is to have superior force. The play is thus a miniature *Doll's House*, although heavily disguised as a quaint piece of dramatised superstition. The point of the ending is that Mary is not dead but a changeling. As Peter Alderson Smith (1987, p. 185) says, 'She has exchanged this life for a better one.' That Yeats is actually a lot closer to Irish folklore in his subject-matter than to Ibsenist social drama goes without saying, and yet when Yeats reviewed Douglas Hyde's *Beside the Fire* in 1891 he could not keep Ibsen out of the discussion: 'Here at last is a universe where all is large and intense enough to almost satisfy the emotions of man. Certainly such stories are not a criticism of life but rather an extension, thereby much more closely resembling Homer than that last phase of "the improving book", a social drama by Henrik Ibsen' (Welch 1993, p. 68). As Yeats admitted of Ibsen in his *Autobiographies* (1961b, p. 279), 'neither I nor my generation could escape him because, though we and he had not the same friends, we had the same enemies.'

As stated in the Introduction, Yeats took a firm stand against propaganda in literature and was always on the side of artistic freedom in the theatre. This is not to say, however, as Christopher Innes claims (1992, p. 359), that 'the subject of Yeats' drama is art'. Such a view unfairly condemns Yeats to the ivory tower so convenient to popular prejudice. Yeats is constantly aware of a borderline, variously conceived, over which the audience is enticed to step in imagination and which posits a dangerous alternative to 'reality'. In other words, the plays are invitations to perceive the world as binary, experience as dialectic. Shadow rivals substance; mythology challenges history; the dream constantly opposes responsibility. This formal opposition, intensely compressed into a brief and sudden action, may or may not have political overtones. But it will always have cultural implications (be these religious or historical), which if ignored restrict the impact of the plays to elitist, self-enclosed performance.

The folk tale was the basis of Yeats's dramaturgy. There is, he claimed, 'something of an old wives' tale in fine literature. The makers of it are like an old peasant telling stories of the great famine or the hangings of '98 or from his own memories. He has felt something in the depth of his mind and he wants to make it as visible and powerful to our senses as possible' (1961a, p. 276). At the same time the tale was invariably given a subversive cast. It did not, as conventional tales do, reinforce community norms, values and beliefs; it interrogated and opposed them. The dialectic is often obscured in Yeats by the incantatory verse but the unorthodoxy is nevertheless crucial to the effect. Thus *The Countess Cathleen* was certain to cause controversy when it was first staged in Dublin in 1899. It must be borne in mind that this is a play about famine; it confronts the greatest catastrophe in modern Irish history. Yet it coolly indicates that Catholics have a price in crisis time, and are willing to sell their souls to save their skins. Further, Yeats shows how the lady of the manor, the good Countess and Lady Bountiful herself, redeems the souls of all her tenants by selling her own (infinitely more valuable) soul and yet, in the last reel as it were, gets off scot-free, since God 'Looks always on the motive, not the deed' (1966, p. 167). This is not so much death-bed conversion, which would be melodrama, as outrageous casuistry, turning the tables (of the law) on the pious. Frank Hugh O'Donnell was right to be outraged. 'Out of all the mass of our national traditions it is precisely the baseness which is utterly alien to all our national traditions, the barter of Faith for Gold, which Mr. W. B. Yeats selects as the fundamental idea of his Celtic drama!' (Gregory 1972, p. 261). Yeats's anti-Catholicism, whereby he showed 'that the Gaels of Erin have and had only the thinnest veneer of Christian religion and civilisation', was also detailed and deplored (p. 263). No doubt James Joyce saw through Yeats's iconoclasm and thus refused to sign the student protest against the play. In a note not printed until the 1907 edition of *The Countess Cathleen* Yeats commented: 'The greatest difficulty before the creator of a living Irish drama has been, and to some extent still is, the extreme sensitiveness of a nation, which has come to look upon Irish literature not as a free play of the mind over the surface and in the depths of life, but as a defence delivered before a prejudiced jury, who have heard a very confident advocate on the other side' (1966, p. 177). One sees what Yeats meant when he said in '*Samhain*: 1903' that the task was 'to make the theatre a place of intellectual excitement – a place where the mind goes to be liberated' (1962a, p. 107).

There is a moment in the middle of *The Countess Cathleen* which goes far to define the nature of Yeats's early plays. An old woman steps forward to sell her soul to the demon merchants and as she takes her money she says, in the conditioned way of peasant to moneyed superior, 'God bless you, sir' and then screams in pain. The merchant comments: 'That name is like a fire to all damned souls' (1966, p. 145). The scream affects those around the old woman, frightening them, making them change their minds. And then the Countess comes to save them by her sacrifice. The scream is the key. The drama is a form of shock, a palpable touching of the heart. With the shock comes revelation and a heightened awareness. In this play the scream is allayed by the Countess, whose own suffering, stoically endured, soon puts that of the peasantry in the shade. Her sorrow is meant to be in measure of her consciousness of the evil all around her; it is actually not all that convincing. As icon of Ascendancy altruism the Countess is a poor argument for the settlement of the land question. Yeats obviously built up this image from an idealised Maud Gonne, to whom the play was dedicated, while he (over various revisions) built up his own counterpart as the poet Aleel, her rejected lover. The climax of the play, the Countess's death and immediate deliverance from the jaws of hell, marks Aleel's abandonment of passivity, symbolised by the mirror he shatters, but this effect is marred by Yeats's emphasis on the Countess's apotheosis: 'It is the soul of one that loves Ireland' (1962a, p. 142). The central feeling of the play, deriving from the reality expressed through the old woman's scream, is dissipated. But in subsequent plays where the feeling arises from the hero's or heroine's experience such dissipation does not happen. *The Hour Glass* (1903), also a much-revised play, likewise deals with spiritual crisis and salvation, although this time the scream comes from the hero himself, the Wise Man brought face to face with the folly of his atheism. The Wise Man comes to realise his true self, his soul, through terror. A nerve is likewise touched by Cuchulain in *On Baile's Strand* (1904) and by Deirdre in *Deirdre* (1906) as each comes to appalled awareness of transgression and betrayal. The pain of such recognition is communicated to the audience as real and as the climax of a process.

Yeats himself was inclined to dismiss *The Countess Cathleen* as no more than 'a piece of tapestry', and commented that as the Countess sold her soul but was not herself transformed the play lacked tragic power (1961b, p. 417). It is hard to quarrel with this assessment: in Yeats's better plays a change takes place within the hero. Yeats was soon made aware that stronger stuff was needed for the Irish stage. The actor Frank Fay said in a review, 'In Ireland we are at present only too anxious to shun reality. Our drama ought to teach us to face it. Let Mr. Yeats give us a play in verse or prose that will raise this sleeping land' (Hogan 1970, p. 53). Yeats obliged by giving Fay's new-formed dramatic company *Cathleen Ni Houlihan* (1902). Written in prose, it was much indebted to Lady Gregory for the concreteness of its language. Its success was also much indebted to Maud Gonne, who played the leading role of the old woman who visits the peasant household just as the 1798 rebellion begins. The household is, in fact, preparing for a wedding and the effect of the play is to transfer the allegiance of young Michael Gillane from bride and from family to the cause the old woman tells him of. This is done in such a way that Michael is as mesmerised by the old woman as Mary Bruin was by the fairy child, which allows Richard Ellmann (1948, p. 131) to make the point that *Cathleen Ni Houlihan* is 'a powerful rewriting of the theme of *The Land of Heart's Desire* in terms of nationalism'. Moreover, the action reflects back upon its own purpose: the process Michael undergoes as he listens to the stories and songs of the old woman is the same process which the audience undergoes in attending to the play. He is changed utterly. As in a dream he exits to join the revolution. The old woman is then described as having been renewed or rejuvenated, having 'the walk of a queen' (1966, p. 231), that is to say her goddess-like aspect is revealed (as in Virgil, *et vera incessu patuit dea*, when the hero recognises Venus by her walk). Maud Gonne was described as 'the very personification of the figure she portrayed on stage' (Nic Shiubhlaigh 1955, p. 19). Since the old woman was already a personification of Ireland, as the title indicates, Maud Gonne was the personification of a personification. The whole thing is completely theatrical, at one remove from the realism it superficially resembled, and that is what made it excellent propaganda. Its incendiary quality was to become a source of worry to Yeats in later life ('The Man and the Echo'), but its effect cannot be denied: it was a clarion call to the republican cause. It thus reversed completely the nature of the Countess Cathleen's sacrifice and instead made Cathleen the catalyst for change in the young man.

Adrian Frazier (1990) makes an interesting case for the view that by 1903, when Annie Horniman appeared on the scene and promised a theatre in Dublin, Yeats began to backtrack from political drama. Certainly that lady made no secret of her desire for an art theatre in which politics should have no place. Yeats in part agreed, since he wanted to secure a theatre in which extreme nationalists would not be able to call the tune, but of course he was too much the pragmatist to accept her prejudice absolutely. In the fullness of time he was able to tell Horniman: 'I understand my own race and in all my work, lyric or dramatic, I have thought of it. If the theatre fails I may or may not write plays – but I shall write for my own people – whether in love or hate of them matters little – probably I shall not know which it is' (Wade 1954, p. 501). Horniman never fully understood Yeats's dual commitment to art and to country. There was to be a positive link between Yeats and 1916. Referring to *Cathleen Ni Houlihan,* Declan Kiberd remarks: 'As a poet, [Yeats] invents an ideal Ireland in his imagination, falls deeply in love with its form and proceeds to breathe it, Pygmalion-like, into being. It is hard, even now, to do full justice to the audacity of that enterprise' (1995, p. 202). Conor Cruise O'Brien, however, is simply appalled at what he sees as the play's 'powerful influence on the development of Irish nationalism in the following fourteen years', leading to the Easter Rising (1993, p. 63).

In the meantime, to be sure, Yeats edged away from *Cathleen Ni Houlihan*, which caused a little embarrassment when application had to be made to Dublin Castle for a patent for the Abbey. In briefing Horace Plunkett, who acted in support of the patent, Yeats wrote in July 1904 that *Cathleen Ni Houlihan* 'may perhaps raise a difficulty ... It may be said that it is a political play of a propagandist kind. This I deny. I took a piece of human life, thoughts that men had felt, hopes they had died for, and I put this into what I believe to be sincere dramatic form. I have never written a play to advocate any kind of opinion and I think that such a play would be necessarily bad art, or at any rate a very humble kind of art. At the same time I feel that I have no right to exclude for myself or for others, any of the passionate material of drama' (Kelly and Schuchard 1994, pp. 622–3). This is known as playing safe with the authorities. Yet Yeats had already wrestled with this question in '*Samhain*: 1903', where he declared that if forced to write nothing but 'drama with an obviously patriotic intention, instead of letting my work shape itself under the casual impulses of dreams and daily thoughts', he would have quickly lost the power to write movingly on any theme. 'I could have aroused opinion; but I could not have touched the heart' (1962a, p. 116). The 'heart' is thus, once again, Yeats's main target. 'Opinion' was a dirty word, something newspapers offered (and possibly Bernard Shaw). *Cathleen Ni Houlihan* was proudly in the opening bill when the Abbey opened its doors on 27 December 1904, although some unknown party 'solemnly begged' Yeats to withdraw it 'for fear it would stir up a conspiracy and get us all into trouble' (Gregory 1972, p. 36).

Yet Yeats's real investment in the new theatre was *On Baile's Strand*, also in the opening bill. Here he was moving in a new direction, into Celtic myth. He had made the transition the year before with *The King's Threshold*, much admired by Annie Horniman (who was responsible for the terrible costumes) since it had for theme the autonomy of the poet in society. In fact, that play is highly political in its claim for the artist a role as shaper and even begetter of social values. In spite of *The Shadowy Waters* (1904), dramatising a pilgrimage and a love story that is all dreams and no responsibilities, the venture into myth was a major step forward. It allowed Yeats to combine allegory and psychological symbolism. Yeats later defined myth as 'one of those statements our nature is compelled to make and employ as a truth though there cannot be sufficient evidence' (1962a, p. 392). The idea is uncannily close to T. S. Eliot's 'objective correlative', which has been so useful a term in twentieth-century literary criticism. Moreover, in praising Joyce's use of myth in *Ulysses*, 'making the modern world possible for art', Eliot gave credit to Yeats as innovator. 'It is a method already adumbrated by Mr. Yeats, and of the need for which I believe Mr. Yeats to have been the first contemporary to be conscious' (Kermode 1975, p. 177). From 1903 on, Yeats's plays relate closely, though indirectly, to his personal experience. Myth gave him the means of developing a successful form of theatre of the anti-self, a theatre of masks. Thus as Richard Ellmann (1948, p. 166) puts it, the five plays which Yeats wrote between 1903 and 1910 'are filled with this sense of guilt at having separated himself from "the normal active man"'.

On Baile's Strand and *Deirdre* are the best, the most accomplished, of these early mythic plays. In the former the mighty Cuchulain is being tamed by the crafty high king, Conchubar, and forced to leave his former, anarchic ways to subordinate his will to the king's authority. He is urged to forget his old love Aoife, a wild and dangerous woman, and to settle down in decent bourgeois fashion. Cuchulain, ageing, is torn between the wisdom of this advice and the passion which will always draw him to worship this destructive goddess. Now Aoife is his bitter enemy and seeks revenge for his deserting her. The plot shows how this is achieved, so that Cuchulain unwittingly kills their son. In Conchubar Cuchulain confronts his opposite, the man of reason, but each has a shadow character in the Fool and the Blind Man, opportunists whose actions effectively parody the serious concerns of the main characters. We see here Yeats edging towards a complex modern form of art, tracing the fluidities of selfhood. 'You are but half a king and I but half,' Conchubar tells Cuchulain, 'I need your might of hand and burning heart,/And you my wisdom' (1966, p. 491). The Fool and Blind Man are also symbiotic but at the same time each is an ironic projection of the personality of their social superiors. Yeats divided himself into four parts, four masks as he would later say. The play confronts a mass of feelings, 'heart-mysteries' as Yeats says elsewhere ('The Circus Animals' Desertion'), but bitterness and rage are chief among them.

Deirdre, an equally well-structured piece, classically concentrates on the climax of the love story: 'One woman and two men; that is the quarrel/That knows no mending' (1966, p. 378). The triangle is beautifully self-sufficient, the knowing Musicians being helpless as a Greek chorus to intervene. Conchubar's jealous passion meets Deirdre's fierce loyalty to Naoise once the lovers fall into the king's power. Lennox Robinson, who directed many of Yeats's plays at the Abbey, commented (1942, pp. 59–60): 'Yeats used to say about Deirdre's performance, "red-heat up to Naisi's death, white-heat after he is dead".' In spite of its brevity, this version is the best of the many adaptations of the Deirdre legend, largely because Yeats stayed true to Conchubar and his fierce, obsessive passion. Even at the end, after Deirdre's death, Conchubor is not broken and can cry out against his enemies (p. 388):

> Howl, if you will; but I, being King, did right
> In choosing her most fitting to be Queen,
> And letting no boy lover take the sway.

The integrity of this is magnificent. Endurance triumphs over guilt. Yeats's procedure here, in part resulting from his discovery of Nietzsche in 1902, is in line with his combative stance over Synge's work. It did not matter that what was represented on the stage was not typical of everyday life: myth expanded consciousness. 'The misrepresentation of the average life of a nation that follows of necessity from an imaginative delight in energetic characters and extreme types, enlarges the energy of a people by the spectacle of energy' (1962a, p. 191). Thus Yeats forged a link between his own art, based on personal experience, and the moral life of the nation.

This interest in myth allowed Yeats to develop a tragic idea which turns loss into glory. It is a romantic theory, nevertheless with roots in Greek tragedy, whereby the mythic becomes specially symbolic. (It is no accident that Yeats's prose version of *Oedipus the King* (1926) is among the best of the century.) Among its features is a concentration of form so that each play is perceived as 'a moment of intense life' ('First Principles', 1962a, p. 153). In the essay 'The

Tragic Theatre' (1910) the effect is declared to be to move the audience 'by setting us to reverie, by alluring us almost to the intensity of trance'. It is a novel idea, and one which gives a special quality to Yeatsian drama: the play becomes a shared experience: 'We feel our minds expand convulsively' (1961a, p. 245). The mind becomes a platform for a drama about power.

Moreover Yeats's tragic idea was carried over into his adaptations of the Japanese Noh form undertaken after he left Dublin in some disgust in 1913. By this time Annie Horniman had decided that the Abbey was far too political for her taste and had withdrawn her annual subsidy. The Abbey then developed along comparatively more commercial lines, favouring realism over anything resembling Yeats's poetic symbolism. The Abbey company had to make money through touring in the United States, where the reception of Synge's *Playboy* offered a sharp series of reminders that the fight for artistic freedom in the Irish theatre was by no means over (Gregory 1972, pp. 97–135; Nic Shiubhlaigh 1955, pp. 108–39). Yeats's disillusion with Dublin was compounded by the city's failure to provide an art gallery to house the Hugh Lane collection; he left and settled in England for several years. His enthusiasm for the Noh drama should be seen in the context of his general disappointment with Ireland and the Abbey. As he wrote in his 'Open Letter to Lady Gregory' in 1919, the success of the Abbey as a 'People's Theatre', where realism flourished, was to him 'a discouragement and a defeat'. This is not what he had hoped would develop. 'You and I and Synge', roll the magnificent sentences so often quoted, 'not understanding the clock, set out to bring again the theatre of Shakespeare or rather perhaps of Sophocles. ... We thought we could bring the old folk-life to Dublin, patriotic feeling to aid us, and with the folk-life all the life of the heart ... but the modern world is more powerful than any propaganda or even than any special circumstance, and our success has been that we have made a Theatre of the head' (1962a, pp. 250, 252–3). The venture into Noh plays was an attempt to sidestep this unwelcome reality.

As I have made clear elsewhere, Yeats's discovery of the Noh form in 1913 through Ezra Pound proved mainly a reinforcement and refinement of ideas Yeats had already developed in the theatre (Sekine and Murray 1990, pp. 1–21). Only the use of dance was something Yeats had not yet considered as a feature of performance (although there is, indeed, a dance at the end of *The Land of Heart's*

Desire). So far as the drama is concerned, the translations Pound put before him excited him through their lyric beauty, creation of place on stage through language and ritual alone, and their unembarrassed use of the supernatural in the plot. The main point about *Four Plays for Dancers* (published 1921) is that they are dream plays. In each, *At the Hawk's Well*, *The Only Jealousy of Emer*, *The Dreaming of the Bones* and *Calvary*, the story is at one remove from the audience, persuaded that all is taking place in some space beyond the real, in 'the deeps of the mind' (1961a, p. 224). In a sense, these plays are plays-within-plays, and should not be considered naturalistically. If properly played they are extraordinarily beautiful and moving.

For two of the plays Yeats carried forward his interest in the Cuchulain myth, which he now combined with his growing fascination with the psychological meaning of mask: 'The poet finds and makes his mask in disappointment, the hero in defeat' (Yeats 1959, p. 337). In *At the Hawk's Well* (1916), the only one of these plays to be staged at this time, the subject is the young Cuchulain's initiation into his tragic destiny as warrior; in *The Only Jealousy of Emer* the story takes up where *On Baile's Strand* left off, with the apparent death of Cuchulain fighting the waves. Yeats's personal concerns are transformed into symbols and mythic situations, especially in *The Only Jealousy*, which exorcises anxieties following Yeats's marriage in 1917 (Jeffares 1988, p. 235). Unaware of such details, T. S. Eliot (who was in the audience for *At the Hawk's Well* in Lady Cunard's drawing-room), said that in becoming more Irish Yeats 'became at the same time universal' (Kermode 1975, p. 252). It may be questioned, however, if this is true of *The Dreaming of the Bones*, 'Yeats's most imaginatively telling parable for his own nation' (Bloom 1970, p. 309).

Here myth blends into and is overwhelmed by history. In the play on which *Bones* is based, *Nishikigi*, which the Cuala Press published in 1916 with three other Pound/Fenellosa translations and Yeats's introduction, a simple love story is told with a happy ending. As a dream play, it concerns the encounter between a wandering priest and a couple who are, in fact, spirits, although this is not apparent. They relate a story of rejected love, death and remorse. Through the priest's pity and prayers their souls are released and the lovers unified in eternity. In Yeats's version the Young Man who encounters a strange man and woman at night-time near the ruined Abbey of Corcomroe in County Clare is no priest but an Irish-

[26]

speaking peasant on the run from the failed Rising in Dublin: 'I was in the Post Office, and if taken / I shall be put against a wall and shot' (1966, p. 764). The strangers, who offer to lead the Young Man safely across the mountain, are discovered to be Dermot McMurrough and his adulterous lover Dervorgilla, through whose agency the Normans were invited to Ireland in AD 1169, thus originating Ireland's subjugation to England. In Irish history, this event has the status of myth. Lady Gregory had already explored the inexorable guilt attached to it in *Dervorgilla* (1907). Yeats, however, by juxtaposing this story with the failure of the 1916 Rising is doing something entirely different. The climax of the play arrives when the lovers dance in plaintive appeal to the Young Man for the forgiveness which would release their guilty spirits from torment and allow their love fulfilment. Unlike the priest in *Nishikigi*, the Young Man, having first recognised the subjects of the story and then recognised his guides as their ghosts, refuses: 'never, never / Shall Diarmuid and Dervorgilla be forgiven' (p. 775). The lovers drift away unappeased.

Yeats wrote *The Dreaming of the Bones* in 1917 after he had finished 'Easter 1916'. Where the latter expressed an ambivalent response to 1916 and asserted that 'Too long a sacrifice / Can make a stone of the heart', the play is inherently pro-1916. Indeed, Yeats feared that it was 'only too powerful politically' (Wade 1954, p. 626). He also indicated that the play suggested a parallel between Germany's treatment of Belgium in 1914 and England's former treatment of Ireland (Wade 1954, p. 654). The play is very much about a haunted landscape; its desolation is used to argue the price of British occupation. This is, no doubt, strange territory for Yeats to patrol, but no stranger, after all, than *Cathleen Ni Houlihan*. He is as concerned in the play, moreover, with the notion of 'dreaming back', or purgation after death, which forms the basis of many of his final plays, as he is with politics. If anything, he uses the politics to reinforce the tragic plight of those caught in a web of timeless remorse. By setting a play about the walking dead at night-time and beside a ruined abbey Yeats evokes an atmosphere of fear and foreboding. The whole incident (flight, encounter, request, temptation, refusal), while firmly related to the Young Man's point of view, is framed within the Musician's narrative and lyrics. This mediating device emphasises fear and racial memory as the two poles of the play's disturbing experience. The narrator's feelings become ours: 'Why does my heart beat so?' ... 'Why should the heart take fright?' ... 'My rascal heart is proud/Remembering and remembering' ... 'My heart ran wild when it heard' (1966, pp. 762–76). This emphasis on the heart's response induces involvement at an emotional rather than an intellectual level. David Pierce speculates that in his refusal to help the lovers the Young Man 'turns his heart into a stone' (1995, p. 194). Opposing 'the living stream' of liberation he shows himself fanatic in the way Yeats foresaw the fate of Maud Gonne and other patriots. Certainly, the lovers react 'as though their hearts/Had suddenly been broken' (1966, p. 775), and this unites the audience with them. And yet, alienated though he is, the Young Man heroically holds the stage at the end; his point of view cannot be dismissed. The play thus involves its audience very effectively in a dilemma.

The Dreaming of the Bones was not staged until 1931, when it was 'enthusiastically received' (Wade, 1954, p. 788). This was at the Abbey, to which Yeats actively returned when he settled in Dublin in 1922. He had never really left Ireland.

Later plays

When the wars were over and he was appointed senator in the new Free State Yeats the Nobel Prize winner assumed the mantle of national bard. The difficulty for him now as playwright was to find some way of making a truce between the aristocratic Noh form and the unashamedly democratic Abbey form. He found his way through by writing in prose. The success of his version of Oedipus the King (1926) both surprised and encouraged him. Likewise, his prose version of The Only Jealousy of Emer, under the title Fighting the Waves (1929), proved successful. Yeats came to the conclusion that he must accept the conventions of the proscenium stage: 'I have gone over to the enemy'. If this necessity was depressing it was also in some respects liberating, since Yeats could now mask esoteric ideas with realism. 'I can be as subtle or metaphysical as I like without endangering the clarity necessary for dramatic effect' (1966, pp. 1009–10). He found it possible, consequently, to present both Words upon the Window-Pane (1930) and Resurrection (1934), in prose, at the Abbey. Of course, one must not forget the opening of the Peacock Theatre, the Abbey's annexe, in 1927, where Yeats hoped to build up a ballet company with the help of Ninette de Valois. Even though that ambition was not quite realised, the hope of an experimental space at the Abbey was now sustainable. Moreover, although he returned to dramatic verse in the mid-1930s, to end his career as he had begun, Yeats retained the tone and emphasis newly elaborated by means of his accommodation both with the new Ireland and the new, government-subsidised Abbey. The tone and emphasis were ironic, harsh and violent.

It is necessary to see this work in the context of Yeats's attitude towards the Abbey. Frank O'Connor, who was very close to Yeats in the 1930s, testifies that he wanted 'a living theatre. If he had been younger and in better health he would have come to the theatre himself and insisted on it.' Yeats was fighting for a tradition. 'His sense of urgency is evident in the dispute over the production of *Coriolanus*. It had just been produced in Paris in coloured shirts and caused a riot. Yeats demanded that we produce it in coloured shirts among our European classics, in the hope that, as in France, a Dublin audience might riot and he could defend the message of the play as he had defended the message of *The Playboy of the Western World* and *The Plough and the Stars*' (O'Connor 1971, pp. 151–2). In the event, Hugh Hunt's production in 1936 was not controversial, but Yeats was very keen to do something to meet the competition being so stylishly offered by MacLiammóir and Edwards at the Gate Theatre. His own new plays, accordingly, were provocative and experimental. Ireland had opted for modernity, and this was something Yeats could not forgive. Denis Donoghue sums up this final phase well. 'So far as the Abbey was concerned, the only available audience was the middle class, coming straight from their counting houses. Yeats had to drive them beyond themselves, or fail in the attempt. I think his last plays, and notably *The Herne's Egg*, are canes for punishing the bourgeoisie which had let him down' (1974, p. 32).

The key to Yeats's last plays, which are among his best, lies in his conviction that Western society in general was not only in sharp decline but imploding: the age of anxiety and of the Second Coming was nigh. Ireland, convulsed by violence and bloodstained by civil war, could hardly hope to escape mere anarchy. In general, the attitude Yeats embodied at this time was a refusal to go gentle into that good night, to rage, indeed, against the dying of the Celtic twilight. Therefore, bitterness and (favourite word) scorn were to mark the individual's response to the modern world. For his own part, Yeats looked to the eighteenth century for a model of individual comportment: 'I seek an image of the modern mind's discovery of itself, of its own permanent form, in that one Irish century that escaped from darkness and confusion.' Thus Yeats declared in his introduction to *Words upon the Window-Pane*, a play which aggressively elevates Jonathan Swift and his politics over Lilliputian modernism. Simultaneously, Yeats sought 'some identification of my beliefs with the nation itself' (1962a, pp. 344–5). Some of these later plays brought together history and the contemporary, rather in the manner of *The Dreaming of the Bones*. Some returned to myth, but in a parodic and grotesque form akin to that neglected but fascinating anticipation of theatre of the absurd, *The Player Queen* (1919).

Irony is the governing style of these later plays. It permeates the very stance of the plays themselves towards an audience, which is being mocked while it is being offered versions of popular fare. Nowhere is this more apparent than in *Words upon the Window-Pane*, where the realistic setting and chatter of people arriving to attend a seance are merely the framework for a play-within-the-play, a story of Swift, Vanessa and Stella told in an intense and tragic style totally unwelcome to the audience on stage. The whole Swift episode is received as an intrusion, and the seance is regarded as a failure: yet the reality of Swift's suffering is ironically of greater moment than the trivial pursuits of his impatient eavesdroppers. Thus two styles collide effectively, Abbey realism and Noh intensity. Dr Trench, in some respects a version of Yeats himself, asks before the seance starts if the intrusive spirits went through 'the same drama' at two previous sessions. The reply confirms the idea: 'Yes – just as if they were characters in some kind of horrible play' (1966, p. 943). Mrs Henderson, the medium, conjures up Swift and Vanessa (Stella remains silent), so that the dead take over the stage. In his introduction to the text, Yeats praised the acting ability of May Craig as Mrs Henderson and then made the large claim: 'mediumship is dramatisation' (1962a, p. 365). This allows us to see the play as metatheatre. It is all about performance (for Mrs Henderson may be a fraud, which is to say she may be masked). And yet the suffering which filters through Mrs Henderson has all the shock and immediacy of reality. The paradox of this event foregrounds the inner drama. The 'moment of intensity' which we overhear is the moment when Swift rejects love definitively, and must live forever with the consequences. No such passion is possible in the modern setting.

[30]

If it can be said that *Words upon the Window-Pane* is vestigially a Noh drama (without the climactic dance), then *Purgatory* is Noh drama turned inside out. In its bleakness it is waiting for Beckett. It is a ghost play, once again, with an inner drama set 'in the deeps of the mind', but there is no music, no colour, no splendour of costume and no dance. It is also a history play, a palimpsest of past and present tragic events. The dead interlock with the living. In *Words upon the Window-Pane* Dr Trench explains why it is a spirit might intrude on a seance. 'Sometimes a spirit re-lives not the pain of death but some passionate or tragic moment of life. ... If I were a Catholic I would say that such spirits were in Purgatory' (1966, p. 944). In *Purgatory* the Old Man explains the process of 'dreaming back' in just such Catholic terms (he was, after all, educated by a priest), which are simpler than Yeats's official theory in *A Vision* (1937). The Old Man speaks of the 'souls in Purgatory' coming back to 'familiar spots' to 're-live/Their transgressions' over and over (1966, p. 1042). The setting is significant also. Yeats tends to inter-nalise landscape in his later plays: the Noh form facilitated this move since no scenery is allowed, except for a painted pine tree as back-ground. For *Purgatory* there is only '*A ruined house and a bare tree in the background*': each is a potent symbol of history and the individual conscience. The purpose of the spirit's revisitation is expiation, but as the Old Man poses the problem it depends whether the original injury or transgression was done to the self or to others: if the latter, 'There is no help but in themselves/And in the mercy of God' (1966, pp. 1042–3). The major irony of the play is that although the Old Man knows this he vainly tries to help his mother at the cost of killing his own son. He acts on the premise that his mother's crime was against others because she, an aristocrat, married a groom who went on to dissipate the property and burn down the Big House. The Old Man's motive is not revenge; he is the victim of a tragic error. At the same time, one must not believe all he says. *Purgatory* is presented from the Old Man's point of view, which is demonstrably unstable and even sectarian: in the class structure which underlies his elegy for the Big House it is likely that grooms like his father were Catholics (Torchiana 1966, p. 361).

The text allows the voice of the Boy to be heard, however, and that is important to the meaning of the play. 'What's right and wrong?/ My grand-dad got the girl and the money' (1966, p. 1043). Yeats knew well that an Abbey audience in 1938 would be likely to approve the Boy's sentiments: it was an age when 'money's rant is on' ('The Curse of Cromwell'). He allows the Old Man to stifle this voice brutally in the name of ethnic cleansing, lest the boy should live to pass 'pollution' on (p. 1049). Unlike the case of the Countess Cathleen all those years earlier the Old Man's motive does not cancel the wrong done, but is 'a fresh addition to the links of consequence' (Ure 1963, p. 111). The power of *Purgatory* lies in this appalling revelation of culpability. The belief that his mother's soul has been 'purified' by the murder of the boy is shown to be an illusion. The returning hoof beats signify the Old Man's failure, which he must endure as his burden or 'mask'; his mother could not put off the mask of sexual pleasure in which she played out her wedding night.

The effective horror of *Purgatory*, Yeats's *Heart of Darkness*, lies in the madness of its deluded hero, whom Yeats nevertheless admires. He had not forgotten how Coole House had been allowed to fall into decay following Lady Gregory's death in 1932. He had, most recently, written *Words upon the Window-Pane* at Coole and dedicated it to Lady Gregory. Big Houses were very much on his mind, as emblems of cultural change. Not for Yeats the pragmatic solution of Lennox Robinson, who had argued in his play *Killycreggs in Twilight* (1937) that the Anglo-Irish must accept defeat gracefully in modern Ireland and, intermarrying, start anew. On the contrary, *Purgatory* was a provocative call to the Abbey audience to wake up to the full consequences of Irish freedom. Mother Ireland had been traduced and could never again be entirely at peace. Thus it is far too bland to describe *Purgatory* as 'a moral parable on the fate of modern Ireland' (Moore 1971, p. 51). It is a tragedy incorporating a social cataclysm. It is also, as Eric Bentley has said (1969, p. 97), 'pure theatre'. As a ghost play it strikes terror into the heart.

Purgatory had its premiere at the Abbey on 10 August 1938 in a double bill with a revival of *On Baile's Strand*. The plays go well back-to-back, being contrasting episodes in heroic endeavour. The occasion was a special Abbey Festival and so the Yeats plays were intended as representative work. *Purgatory* proved controversial on theological grounds, and Yeats was pleased to have a Catholic priest (Rev. Terence Connolly, SJ) as public opponent, just as he had had Cardinal Logue as opponent to *The Countess Cathleen* almost forty years earlier. All Yeats had to say in interview was that his plot was his meaning and that Ireland was littered with ruined houses of the kind he portrayed in his play. 'Sometimes it is the result of poverty, but more often because a new individualistic generation has lost interest in the ancient sanctities' (Torchiana 1966, pp. 357–8).

Seeing *On Baile's Strand* on stage again pleased Yeats. He was stirred by Cuchulain because 'he seemed to me a heroic figure ... creative joy separated from fear' (Wade 1954, p. 913). Fear was perhaps rather more in supply in the late 1930s than was joy. Yet for Yeats, 'Joy is the salvation of the soul' (Wade 1954, p. 876). Somehow, as in his poetry during this period (for example, 'Lapis Lazuli'), joy had to be wrung from defeat: no small order, admittedly, in a play such as *Purgatory*. In this spirit, in an attempt to write a play which might reconcile his later tragic mode and this belief in joy, Yeats began his last play, *The Death of Cuchulain*. Like Ibsen's *When We Dead Awaken* (1899), it is an important summary. 'My "private philosophy" is there but there must be no sign of it; all must be like an old faery tale' (Wade 1954, p. 917). From start to finish Yeats pitched his dramatic camp in this land of heart's desire.

The use of a prologue in prose, in which an Old Man as director of the play addresses the audience directly and mocks Yeats's own pose as 'old-fashioned' author, marks a return to an idea he had for *The King's Threshold*, over thirty-five years earlier. Now he mocks himself and his dramaturgy and yet ironically sets about reasserting the place of poetry / drama in society.

The revenge play, which is what the basic structure of *The Death of Cuchulain* enacts as Aoife and Maeve converge on a burnt-out case, is undercut by a counter-structure which dissolves the revenge into a travesty. The Blind Man cuts off Cuchulain's head for 'twelve pennies' (1966, p. 1060). The Blind Man is modern man, whose values are solely materialistic. Like the play itself, a palimpsest of *On Baile's Strand*, the Blind Man is an ironic representation. He had appeared already as the Fool in *The Herne's Egg* and the Old Man in *Purgatory*. He may be on top now but he is anti-heroic. The only way the Blind Man can penetrate the world of myth is by violence, by using the knife with which he cuts his food. He is but the tool of determining history. He transforms Cuchulain's head into negotiable currency (coinage Yeats helped to design in 1928). Yet when Emer dances to mourn Cuchulain's death and curse his destroyers the Blind Man is elided from the text completely. He does not really feature in the heroic world; he is no more than its antitype, the beast slouching towards Bethlehem to be reborn.

Emer's dance is the climax of the play. It is a fusion of love and hate and thus a repudiation of the seductive dances which provide the climaxes of *Four Plays for Dancers*. The complexity of the dance is a great challenge to the director, since the dancer must express, as the prologue says, 'upon the same neck love and loathing, life and death'. Yeats strangely yields the text to the dancer here, to the poetic possibilities of the human body: 'where there are no words there is less to spoil' (1966, p. 1052). Is he paralleling Aoife's abandonment of the stage to the Blind Man? If so, he allows the dancer to resurrect Cuchulain. This is moving close to the 'philosophy' Yeats wanted to disguise in the play: 'To me all things are made of the conflict of two states of consciousness, beings or persons which die each other's life, live each other's death' (Wade 1954, p. 918). Here he tries to *show* this idea rather than state it. Thus Sylvia C. Ellis has rightly emphasised that 'while the *function* of the dance may be interpreted through words ... and will play a crucial part in narrative significance, the *meaning* may be grasped as the logic of choreography alone' (1994, p. 267). In the course of Emer's dance she moves as if in adoration and triumph before Cuchulain's severed head. Then she stands listening. *'There is silence, and in the silence a few faint bird notes'* and the stage darkens slowly (1966, p. 1062). As in the poem 'Cuchulain Comforted', the bird notes signify Cuchulain's successful passage into immortality. The dance then leads into what one might call the redemption of the world of squalor. The scene changes to a modern fair, with street-singers in ragged clothes. If this is an extension of Cuchulain's dream it is far from Stephen Dedalus's glib definition of history as the nightmare from which he was trying to awake (Joyce 1960, p. 42). It is more the Yeatsian foul rag-and-bone shop of the heart placed on stage for the last, most celebratory time.

In this last episode the play folds in upon itself. Instead of a song from the mouth of the Street-Singer Yeats provides a reported song, which 'the harlot sang to the beggar-man' (1966, p. 1062). It is a dialogue repeated: a dialogue to which the Street-Singer was audience and is now the relayer to the actual audience of *The Death of Cuchulain*. The first fifteen lines of this song must thus be taken as being within quotation marks. Their point is that a bridge can after all be made between Emer and this offstage harlot. The modern harlot, whether or not she has the walk (or dance) of a queen, embodies an image of beauty just as energising. There is acceptance here of modernity. Yeats celebrates the continuity of Emer-like anger, even though the age is now debased. The seven lines which follow, however, appear to be in the voice of the Street-Singer, invested with Yeats's own late style. He wishes to know, among other things, what the source of the revolutionary spirit of 1916 was: a sudden application of the play's meaning to modern Ireland's political rebirth. 'What stood in the Post Office / With Pearse and Connolly?' (1966, p. 1063). The remaining lines of the play provide the answer (although it helps to glance aside at 'The Statues' also). It was Cuchulain who stood beside Pearse and Connolly, who 'went out to die calling upon Cuchulain' (1961a, p. 515). As testament, a statue of Cuchulain by Oliver Sheppard was erected in the GPO (an emblem too strong, it will be recalled, for the character in Beckett's *Murphy* (1938), who dashes his head against Cuchulain's buttocks). The actual event, the Rising, is still perceived as ironic, as generating an oxymoronic terrible beauty. But such, Yeats insists, is reality. It is made up of what one both loves and loathes. It is as if the 1916 Rising were the play-within-the play here.

Yeats's final lines, then, blend into the actual art-work in Dublin's GPO, a real piece of sculpture in a real place symbolically commemorating a real if ambiguously heroic event. Yeats claims his own part in enabling this transformative process, which was also a performance process. It was he, as poet, who 'thought Cuchulain' until that image entered the public consciousness. Because the text abolishes its authority in favour of oral tradition or the songs of the people, which record folk experience as reality, Yeats can end the play with the inference that, like Homer, he has imaginatively moulded a nation. The death of the author is the life of the imagined community. In returning to the Cuchulain myth for his last play Yeats clearly wished to make this claim. He cared, as Eliot has said, 'more for the theatre as an organ for the expression of the consciousness of a people, than as a means to his own fame or achievement' (Kermode 1975, p. 256). By showing Cuchulain's continuity, his resurrection, Yeats was asserting that the true heart never dies, the heart of a nation, and he was asserting this by means of the ideal medium: for the theatre is itself a form of re-presentation, of circularity, the public heartbeat of emotional re-circulation. The Yeatsian theatre has as its ambition, through 'emotion of multitude', the creation of *cor unum*.

In addition to his historical achievement in creating a national theatre for Ireland Yeats has left a double legacy. He has influenced the development of modern Irish drama by providing a powerful alternative to realism. True, there have been few poets in the Irish theatre since, but those few, such as Austin Clarke, Donagh McDonagh and more recently Tom MacIntyre and Sebastian Barry, have inherited Yeats's dedication to formal experiment. Moreover, once the concept of 'poet' in the theatre is widened, as it must be when Synge arrives on the scene, to include writers using prose, the Yeatsian dedication to language, to a theatre of the word, becomes obvious. People sometimes complain about this, and deplore the literary emphasis in Irish drama; it is a distintinctive feature and must be celebrated as such. But the other legacy is larger and less obvious. Yeats said more than once that his ambition was to bring together reality and justice in his work. That is, he impressed on all those around him the necessity for the truth in art, truth to experience above all. That insistence on verisimilitude has stayed with the Irish drama ever since. Perhaps, as it was part of modernism itself, and is to be found in the great dramatic tradition extending from Ibsen and Strindberg well into the twentieth century, that insistence on truth would have entered the Irish dramatic movement in any event. But it is doubtful if its significance and seriousness would have been so embedded had it not been for Yeats's artistic conscience and his authority. Therefore, it is characteristic of Irish drama in the twentieth century that it constantly goes beyond the proximate into the shadowland, where, paradoxically, truth is to be tracked down in the theatre. Irish drama is always binary; there is always a play within the play. By such means is the sometimes deceptive mirror held up to the elusive nation.

2

Lady Gregory:
coming to terms

Lady Gregory knows the soul of our people & expresses it as no one else does. Through the surface of triviality, of selfish avarice, of folly which often jars on one, she never ceases to see & to express in her writing that deep passion which *only heroic* action or thought is able to arouse in them, & when once aroused makes them capable of sacrifice for ideals as no other people on earth are.

Maud Gonne to W. B. Yeats (1905) in White and Jeffares (1992)

Introduction

Lady Gregory is entitled to be assessed as writer on her own merits. In her autobiography *Seventy Years* she comments, 'If I had not met Yeats I believe I should still have become a writer' (1974a, p. 390). Yet when a writer is lauded by such as W. B. Yeats, who provided mummifying tributes to Lady Gregory in verse and prose alike, she tends to stiffen into monumental awesomeness like a building, like Coole House itself or the Abbey Theatre. Both buildings, ironically, are gone. The house at Coole was shamefully demolished in 1940; the old Abbey was demolished after a fire in 1951. Lady Gregory's fate was not dissimilar. Her work has disappeared from the repertoire of the modern Abbey. There is no Lady Gregory Summer School as there are Yeats and Synge Summer Schools. Not a page of her works is prescribed for Irish students of English. A pat on the laurelled head from Yeats does not do Gregory justice.

Historically it happened that Gregory's involvement in theatre resulted from Yeats's inspiration and enthusiasm. When they first met for any length of time, in the autumn of 1897, it was in Duras House, County Galway, where Edward Martyn brought Yeats to talk to her about the possibility of establishing an Irish theatre. Up to this point Gregory was interested mainly in Irish folklore and dialect. As Yeats elaborated his dream of an Irish theatre to be based in Dublin the idea caught her imagination: 'things seemed to grow possible as we talked' (1972, p. 19). Yet it was her dynamism which propelled Yeats's idea, got the right kind of social and financial backing, and even found a way to sidestep the law which prohibited the establishment of a new theatre in Dublin.

Likewise, when a patent had to be obtained for the newly founded Abbey Theatre in 1904 it was granted in Lady Gregory's name and not in Yeats's or even in Miss Horniman's. Thereafter, Gregory became one of the three controlling directors of the Abbey and remained one until her death in 1932. During all that time she gave more energy than anyone else to 'the endless affairs of the Abbey Theatre, almost crushing out, as it seems, other interests; the effort to maintain discipline, the staging, the reading of plays, the choice of plays, the quarrels among players, the suspicion of politicians and of the authorities, anxieties about money' (1974a, p. 411). Many of the details of this expenditure of energy are available in the fascinating record of correspondence between Synge, Yeats and Gregory edited by Ann Saddlemyer under the Yeatsian title *Theatre Business* (1982). But that account stops at the death of Synge in 1909. Gregory had over twenty years' active service to go. The highlights thereafter include her fight in the summer of 1909 to have Shaw's *The Shewing-Up of Blanco Posnet*, banned by the Lord Chamberlain in London, staged at the Abbey where the Lord Chamberlain's writ did not run. In Dublin, the Viceroy took upon himself the role of arbiter in such matters. Thus Lord Lieutenant Aberdeen, seriously embarrassed by Gregory's challenge to his authority, tried to put a stop to the production. He met more than his match. She who had fought for Synge's *Playboy* to be heard in 1907 was not about to give in to pressure from the king's man now. 'We did not give in one quarter of an inch to Nationalist Ireland at *The Playboy* time, and we certainly cannot give in one quarter of an inch to the Castle' (1972, p. 90). *Posnet* went on in defiance of Dublin Castle, and Gregory directed it herself, winning the admiration and friendship of Shaw by her stand (McDiarmid, 1994). It was a famous victory. Equally famous was the support she gave to the Abbey players during the first tour to America in 1911–12, when they ran into extraordinary opposition from Irish-Americans over *The Playboy*. In spite of a death threat she worked fearlessly to ensure that the play was not banned and the tour destroyed, even though the players were all arrested on an obscenity charge in Philadelphia. When things were looking their blackest Gregory would call on one more wielder of municipal power or influential newspaperman and in the end the sky would lighten again. The tour was a triumph. Teddy Roosevelt became a public defender of the Abbey Theatre. The philanthropist lawyer John Quinn saw off the ridiculous obscenity charge. The genius of Synge and the appeal of the Abbey plays in general and their style of production were to influence the 'little-theatre movement' in the United States and inspire writers such as Eugene O'Neill to create a new American drama. Some of Gregory's own plays were included in this and subsequent Abbey tours up to 1914, and so she made her contribution on more than one level. Later on she was to ensure the production of O'Casey's *The Plough and the Stars* (1926) at the Abbey on the same basis as she and Yeats had fought originally for the reception of Synge. When the government representative on the Abbey board looked like insisting on damaging cuts to the play Gregory strongly and successfully opposed him, as, of course, did Yeats. She confided to her *Journals* when the production was under threat: 'If we have to choose between the [government] subsidy and our freedom, it is our freedom we choose' (1987, p. 39).

Gregory was at least as entitled as Yeats, therefore, to be credited with the moulding and protection of that very fertile idea of a theatre in Ireland planted at Duras House in 1897. That idea germinated to produce countless new writers and offered the emerging nation a cultural means of formulating its own identity.

Similarly, the point can be made that if Yeats had a lot to teach Lady Gregory about poetry and literature she also had much to contribute to his development as a playwright. It was she who wrote most of *Cathleen Ni Houlihan* and *The Pot of Broth*, two of his most popular plays. (The former has now been included under her name by the editors of *Lady Gregory: Selected Writings*, Penguin, 1995.) She contributed dialogue to several other Yeats plays, including his only full-length play *Where There is Nothing* – not that that is much to boast about – and co-wrote the version eventually staged at the Abbey, *The Unicorn from the Stars* (1907). Her service was not something Yeats denied, even if he made her sound like a bullying matron at times. He paid handsome, indeed chivalrous, tribute when he published his *Collected Plays* in 1922 and thereafter. And yet, dedications aside, the plays which Lady Gregory wrote in part or in more than part continued until 1995 to be published under Yeats's name alone. Her contribution to his art as dramatist remains even yet not fully measured.

At the same time, Gregory's interest as playwright must be separated from this question of collaboration with and reference to W. B. Yeats. It may be taken as read, for the purposes of this chapter, that she learned much from working with him and that together, and with the assistance of Synge, they created the Irish dramatic movement. Indeed, Yeats (1961b, p. 571) said as much to his audience in Stockholm when he was presented with the Nobel Prize for Literature in 1923. The point worth pursuing from here on is what kind of writer Lady Gregory was and, further, why she should claim our attention today, one hundred years after her co-founding of the Irish Literary Theatre. The dismissive comments of Gogarty, Joyce and Moore have long since been themselves dismissed and Gregory is recognised as 'as much a rebel as any one of her detractors' (Kopper 1976, p. 138). The problem now is one of coming to terms with a writer too easily venerated and too little read, not to mention staged. In this respect it is startling to note one woman's final assessment in a book still widely used. Una Ellis-Fermor concluded her chapter on Gregory in the revised edition of *The Irish Dramatic Movement* with the pronouncement that Gregory's contribution was 'characteristically feminine': it provided 'the means or the medium by which men [sic] of genius could realize themselves' (1954, p. 162). Forty years later this anti-feminist view seems woefully inadequate. Part of the problem lay in Gregory's own gospel of service. It only goes to show that nice guys come last.

Nationalism and language

It is best to approach Gregory's career as writer as in itself a coming to terms. It has to be recalled that she was born, like Synge, into a land-owning Ascendancy family, the Persses, Unionist to the core. Owning a large estate in south Galway called Roxborough, the Persses were not regarded by the people, the tenantry, as beneficent. In fact, they benefited from the famine of 1845–47. The Persses believed entirely in the British Empire and acted accordingly, in token whereof the IRA burned the house down in 1922. (My great-grandparents worked on the estate and were subjected to the *droit de seigneur*.) Independence of mind was something Isabella Augusta Persse was born with, however, and once she married out of the Persses and into the Gregorys in 1880 she began to develop the sense of Irish history which, paradoxically, was to make her a republican. Through her work she was to exorcise whatever guilt was accrued by her Anglo-Irish connections. Coole was not burned by the IRA.

Gregory's development, however, was a slow process. Sir William Gregory, whose estate at Coole adjoined Roxborough, was a seasoned and sophisticated diplomat and former governor of Ceylon: a man of the world who led his young wife into the salons of London's intelligentsia, where her lively mind sharpened itself among some of the best talkers of the day. She travelled to Italy with Sir William and then to Egypt, where she began to write by championing the revolutionary Arabi Pasha. Gregory's association with Wilfrid Scawen Blunt, up to his ears in the cause of Egyptian Home Rule, heightened her own liberal sentiments. It is somewhat disappointing, in this regard, that Edward Said makes no mention of Lady Gregory in his fascinating *Culture and Imperialism*, while devoting a large section to the anti-colonialism of W. B. Yeats (1993, pp. 265–88). At an intellectual level, Gregory was at least as much an opponent of colonialism as was Yeats, and from an earlier date. Ann Saddlemyer has provided abundant evidence for this view in her article, 'Augusta Gregory, Irish Nationalist' (1977). Gregory's problem was, indubitably, that she was immersed in the very culture she opposed. It was not until her husband died in 1892, and she edited both his autobiography and a book on his grandfather, that Gregory began to come to terms with British colonialism in Ireland. When eyebrows were raised and she was accused of supporting Home Rule for Ireland (to which she was actually opposed at this time) she replied that it was impossible for anyone to study Irish history 'without getting a dislike and distrust of England' (1972, p. 41). History and nationalism were thus the first things Gregory as a writer confronted and was forced to deal with. Compromised as she was by her position as landlord at Coole her task was not easy. Sean O'Casey, coming from the other side of the tracks, recognised the problem when he wrote to her in 1928 (1975, 1, p. 233) that 'you had to fight against your birth into position & comfort as others had to fight against their birth into hardship & poverty, & it is as difficult to come out of one as it is to come out of the other'. But come out Lady Gregory certainly did.

Her coming to terms with Irish history propelled Gregory into cultural nationalism and the Irish language. Under the chapter heading 'The Changing Ireland' in *Seventy Years* (1974a, p. 306) she says: 'I think it was in 1896 that I suddenly became aware of the change that had come about in Ireland in those first years after Parnell's death.' In the upstairs-downstairs world of Roxborough and Coole the servants were Catholic and Irish-speaking (i.e. bilingual). Having absorbed a raw version of Irish military history from this source Gregory was now fired to learn the language of the dispossessed people and to read Irish literature for herself. The main inspiration came from Douglas Hyde (1860–1949), who had founded the Gaelic League in 1893 for the 'de-Anglicisation' of Ireland. One hundred years later Hyde's achievement stands out clearly as a cultural project of enormous significance (Dunleavy 1991). The 'Irish condition' cannot be understood if Hyde is ignored. A Gaelic scholar, poet and translator, Hyde was in due course to become the first President of the Irish Free State. He was a Protestant from the same landed class as Gregory and shared a similar altruistic view of cultural nationalism. The Irish language was dying: all through the nineteenth century, especially following the establishment of the National School system in the 1830s, when Irish was banned and children punished for using it at school, English became the imposed vernacular. The acquisition of English may have made good sense politically and even sociologically but the suppression of Irish was cultural genocide. Brian Friel dramatises this tragic situation in *Translations* (1980). From the Famine onwards British policy in Ireland (with a little help from the 'Gregory clause') favoured emigration as a solution to the problem of subsistence; the learning of English became an imperative by imperialist design. As happens in such circumstances, the learning of Irish became a revolutionary reflex. Not that Hyde had a political agenda: on the contrary, he wished to keep politics out of the Gaelic League and instead to awaken and foster a widespread awareness among all classes of the beauty and value of the Irish language *per se*. For all that, when Gregory described her early involvement with the Gaelic League and outlined its aims she was not blind to the implications: 'That does not sound like the beginning of a revolution, yet it was one. ... Our Theatre was caught into that current, and it is that current, as I believe, that has brought it on its triumphant way' (1972, p. 50). She meant, of course, a cultural revolution. Her approval of Hyde's movement paralleled her own hopes of creating a theatre which would be at once national and artistic.

In *Poets and Dreamers* (1903) Gregory makes the startling claim: 'I hold that the beginning of modern Irish drama was in the winter of 1898, at a school feast at Coole, when Douglas Hyde and Miss Norma Borthwick [who taught Gregory Irish] acted in Irish in a Punch and Judy show' (1974b, p. 136). She goes on to point out that one of Hyde's plays, *Casadh an tSúgáin*, was included in the bill offered by the Irish Literary Theatre during its final outing at the Gaiety Theatre in Dublin, 'the first Irish play ever given in a Dublin theatre'. Gregory was working with Hyde at this time, translating, expanding from scenarios for plays, and collaborating generally. It is important to bear in mind how the Irish language was at first part of the dramatic movement in this way. Otherwise it is difficult to understand the tradition fully. It is difficult, for example, to appreciate Brendan Behan's irony in first entitling *The Quare Fellow* (1956) 'The Twisting of Another Rope', after Hyde's *Casadh an tSúgáin* (translated by Lady Gregory as *The Twisting of a Rope*, 1903), recording a pastoral ritual Behan was working to subvert. The Hidden Ireland is encoded in the Irish language, as Synge knew before Gregory and as both of them were encouraged by Hyde to find imaginatively liberating. Perhaps this is why, in the patent for the Abbey Theatre, writing in Irish is prioritised (Holloway 1967, p. 42). At the same time, it would be misleading to imply that the Abbey in its early days did much for the Irish language: it did nothing, because it was *de facto* dedicated to the cultivation of new drama in English. But that drama drew much of its inspiration from the speech of the people, which was in the west of Ireland still either Gaelic or a form of English imbued with the patterns of Gaelic (cf. Knapp, 1987).

The Abbey Theatre, then, at least while Yeats was alive, embodied a literary rather than an Irish language movement. Consequently, translation was a form and a process of more practical interest to Gregory and Synge than was the thing-in-itself, the Irish language. Here again Douglas Hyde was an important influence. For Hyde had translated Irish folk stories, *Beside the Fire* (1890), and Irish poetry, *Love Songs of Connacht* (1893), into a dialect form, and thereby gave a lead which Gregory and Synge could follow. To use the dialect properly, i.e. artfully, it was necessary to know the Irish language, for otherwise artificiality and a bogus imitation were bound to result. Gregory saw instantly that Hyde's translations provided a model for her use. All around her in south County

Galway and north County Clare the native Irish were speaking a form of English heavily indebted to Irish grammar and syntax. From her interest in Irish folklore (evidenced in her collections *Poets and Dreamers*,1903, and *A Book of Saints and Wonders,* 1906) Gregory gained an intimate knowledge of the speech-forms around Gort, which she used for all her works and which became known as the Kiltartan dialect, from the name of the townland nearby. It was in that dialect she wrote her first major work, *Cuchulain of Muirthemne* (1902), a version of the Ulster cycle of Irish sagas. Not knowing the old Irish of the original transcriptions, Gregory used available translations to form a basis. Her achievement was to discover a new language which had at once dignity and a popular, if synthetic, flavour. Synge, not one to praise lightly, wrote from Paris to say he was reading *Cuchulain* 'with intense delight. ... I had no idea the book was going to be so great. What puny pallid stuff most of our modern writing seems beside it! Many of the stories, of course, I have known for a long time, but they seem to gain a new life in the beautiful language you have told them in' (Gregory, 1974a, p. 403). Synge rightly assessed *Cuchulain* as literature rather than scholarship. As such its influence on Synge himself as well as on Yeats (for the Cuchulain plays in particular) was immense. Synge said to Lady Gregory in 1904 that her *Cuchulain* was still part of his daily bread (1972, p. 75). His own *Deirdre of the Sorrows* was to butter a whole hunk of that homemade bread a few years later.

Gregory followed up with *Gods and Fighting Men* (1904), using the same dialect to re-tell more literary romances surrounding Finn Mac Cumhaill and the Fianna. Each of these books was critically well received. When she began to write plays in 1902, Gregory thus had no qualms about using the Kiltartan dialect again. Since the plays literally depend on this language, which after all was an important experiment in the modern theatre, it is necessary here to describe its main features. A fuller account may be found in Hugh Kenner's *A Colder Eye* (1983, pp. 74–7). On the broader question of Hiberno–English analyses and commentaries are available in P. W. Joyce's standard work, *English as We Speak it in Ireland* (1910), and in the special issue of *Irish University Review* edited by T. P. Dolan (1990).

The first characteristic is simplicity. As the Irish language is concrete so Lady Gregory's dialect avoids abstractions, and will make use instead of circumlocutions. It strikes the ear as quaint but natural. Today, when the concept of the natural is itself contaminated, we perhaps have a problem with this. But dialect is a form of poetry. For Yeats poetry was a special language, the antithesis of journalism. Yeats never stopped believing in the high style, even after Ezra Pound impressed on him the need to approximate poetry and living speech; the Druidic notion of poetry as magic utterance was too strong to relinquish. Gregory's notions of language were devoid of any such esoteric content. Gregory simply wished to provide a medium to allow the simple speech of Irish country people to have its effect on a stage.

Irish is also rich in imagery and racy, if formulaic, idioms and proverbs. Often these images and proverbs are limited in range and are repeated somewhat emptily, but they are invariably rooted in racial rather than personal experience. One could compare writers such as Tomás Ó Crohan and Maurice O'Sullivan and their popular autobiographical books about life in remote West Kerry earlier this century, *An tOileánach* (1929) and *Fiche Blian ag Fás* (1933), translated as *The Islandman* and *Twenty Years A-Growing*. Here one may find support for the belief that English based upon native Irish speech (in this case translated) can display a richness and a liveliness not found in so-called normal English usage. That richness is what Gregory tried to render dramatic. An example will be given below.

A third feature is the syntax of the language. Unlike standard English, Irish allows the most emphatic word precedence in a sentence. Or the word to be emphasised can be foregrounded by use of the verb 'to be', for example, 'it is she [who] would cry her fill, and it is I [who] would cry along with her'. In Irish such locutions lend accuracy and vividness to the discourse; in English they appear as redundancies or illiteracies. So it is with all dialects, however. Archbishop Trench was one of the first to point out in the last century that what grammarians call errors can be viewed as linguistic strengths (1898, pp. 233–5). Irish lacks a relative pronoun and so English speech based on Irish usage omits it likewise, as in the example above from *Cuchulain of Muirthemne* (1970b, p. 112). Irish also lacks a perfect or a pluperfect tense. Thus one cannot say in Irish 'he is gone' or 'he had gone'; one must say 'he is/was after going'. Gregory, no less than Synge, exploits this circumlocution endlessly, including all sorts of variations and inversions. More than Synge, however, Gregory uses what has become known as 'the Kiltartan infinitive' to express a subordinate clause, e.g., 'Och! if she knew to-night, Naoise *to be* under a covering of clay ...'. In standard

English that would read, 'If she knew tonight that Naoise is under a covering of clay.' The dialogue of Gregory's plays is saturated in this usage, sometimes contorted to an extraordinary degree, e.g., 'I to stoop on a stick through half a hundred years, I will never be tired with praising!' (*Gaol Gate*), or, 'To open me to analyse me you would know what sort of a pain and a soreness I have in my heart' (*The Workhouse Ward*). In standard English each of these sentences would begin with 'if', introducing an adverbial clause.

A final feature to be cited is the tendency in Irish to use co-ordinate clauses where subordination would be demanded in standard English. This, however, is a syntactical feature not confined to Irish: the King James Bible is written in this style also. It results in a narrative form peppered with conjunctions. Whenever Gregory has reason to use the high epic tone, as at the end of *Gaol Gate* or *Dervorgilla* or *Grania*, the rhythms fall into this quasi-Biblical pattern. In a sense Gregory regarded dialect as emblematic, recording the Bible of the poor, and thus as somehow inspired or visionary.

It is likely that Gregory's language is a major reason for her unpopularity in Ireland today. Where Synge's language can still be accepted as powerful and credible Gregory's language seems artificial and embarrassing. As will follow from the comments above, this negative view can be regarded as hasty and unjust. If anything, Gregory's language is more authentic than Synge's. She was less interested in gilding the lily. But the truth of her language, its fidelity to a particular region, refers to an age and a culture now long gone. English has triumphed over Irish in popular culture, in spite of an official government policy to make the learning of Irish compulsory in primary and secondary schools. To a generation which annually applauds Irish prowess in the Eurovision Song Contest, or which sees the language of Roddy Doyle proclaim the new Ireland from the top of the (British) best-seller lists, or which joyfully celebrates with Irish soccer fans doing a Mexican wave and singing *olé, olé, olé!*, the Kiltartan dialect has to sound as if from another and despised world. Nationalism and modernity here clash head-on. This is a great pity, because Gregory's language, if traditional, is by no means merely quaint. It is alive, strong and penetrating, as even the shortest of quotations can show:

> MRS TULLY If they do get him, and if they do put a rope around his neck, there is no one can say he does not deserve it!

Lady Gregory: coming to terms

MRS FALLON Is that what you are saying, Bridget Tully, and is that what you think? I tell you *it's too much talk you have,* making yourself out to be such a great one, and to be running down every respectable person! A rope, is it? It isn't much of a rope was needed to tie up your own furniture the day you came into Martin Tully's house, and you never bringing as much as a blanket, or a penny, or a suit of clothes with you and I myself bringing seventy pounds and two feather beds. And now you are stiffer than a woman would have a hundred pounds! *It is too much talk the whole of you have.* A rope is it? I tell you the whole of this town is full of liars and schemers that would hang you up for half a glass of whiskey.

(emphasis added, *Spreading the News*, Gregory 1970–1, 1, p. 221)

Here we have the living speech of a small, well-observed community whose veneer of tolerance is being comically stripped away. Like Jane Austen, Gregory concentrates on the manners and morals of the small-town life she knew intimately. Again like Austen, there is a 'regulated hatred' (*Emma*) in the niceness of the observation, an awareness of a certain amount of malice underlying the *bonhomie* of close neighbours. It is because Gregory is tolerant of this subterranean intolerance that she is a great comic artist. Access to that art is through her language, which unlike Austen's is purely dramatic: there is no room for a narrator's voice slyly decoding a conversation, which advances cumulatively by cut and thrust of word and phrase steeped (as in the passage above) in the recollection, the history, of characters who treasure details as weaponry. 'It's too much talk you have', Mrs Fallon first levels at Mrs Tully and then at the community at large. The fact of the matter is that the talk is the play and the play is all talk. As Gregory put it, 'what is the substance of drama but conversation clipped and arranged?' (1974a, p. 412). In one of her best one-act plays, *The Workhouse Ward*, a character who must have the company of a man whom he fights with everlastingly says, 'All that I am craving is the talk'. Gregory thereby defines in one sentence not only the basis of her own drama but of Irish drama in general. This is why it is beside the point to say that her language is old-fashioned. It is how that language is mobilised that is important. It is not mobilised to luxuriate in local colour or anything approaching stage Irishry. On the contrary, one of the aims of the whole dramatic movement which Gregory helped set up was 'to show that Ireland is not the home of buffoonery and of easy sentiment, as it has been represented' (1972, p. 20). There was an energetic corrective employed. Gregory never went for easy buffoonery; she is the least sentimental of Irish playwrights. The whiplash of truth underlies the homely speech she employs. Thus the mistake is to take Gregory's language as harmless dialect. It can draw blood, and therein lies its dramatic potential.

Theatricality

In an attempt to rescue Lady Gregory from the cul-de-sac into which history now seems to have driven her, some contemporary critics (Kohfeldt, Young) suggest that she is more a literary than a theatrical writer. This is an approach which at least has the merit of paying Gregory the attention she deserves, following the pioneering work done by Coxhead and Saddlemyer. But it is worrying because even if feminist criticism continues to take an interest in Gregory, a disservice is being done when a dichotomy is created between drama as literature and drama as performance. To be sure, if the plays are not being performed it is difficult to sustain discussion in this area, apart from the historical or optative modes one might advance. Yet it is unwise to quit the field just because the winds are contrary. Lady Gregory was not a novelist as Jane Austen was, solely and completely; she did not work in secret or in isolation. Her achievement was that she came forward into the spotlight, got involved in theatre, and wrote her plays to be performed. In a note to *Bogie Men* (1912) she referred to the Irish people's 'incorrigible genius for myth-making, the faculty that makes our traditional history a perpetual joy' (1970–1, 1, p. 260). This genius for myth-making or fantasy obviously implies a love of make-believe, of invention, of 'play'. From the first short piece of hers to be staged, *Twenty-Five* (1903), Gregory's plays depended on this histrionic quality for their effect. It is an intrinsic part of her body of work, which totals forty-two plays in all, including translations, thirty-six of which were staged between 1903 and 1927. Therefore, the rest of this chapter will attempt to show how significant the idea of performance is in Gregory's work, and, further, how the role of women in her plays must be assessed in relation to that idea.

In *Twenty-Five* the scenario is as simple as can be. A lover returns from America to find his fiancée married. To help her financially he plays a game of cards with her husband and deliberately loses a large sum of money as if its loss meant nothing to him. The pretence lends pathos to his departure. The use of a game here, at the heart of the play, underlines the performance element. Strangely enough, it was regarded at the time by the actor W. G. Fay as rather dangerous, inasmuch as it might give the impression that the Irish National Theatre Society was encouraging gambling and emigration (Robinson 1951, pp. 28–9). Such timidity indicates how careful Gregory, of all writers, had to be. She agreed to reduce the sum lost at cards to a less startling amount. But it is the game as metaphor which is significant. She uses a card game again in *Damer's Gold* (1912), a play about a miser who overcomes his obsession when he loses all to a devil-may-care neighbour, in spite of the beady eyes of his relatives upon his gold. Damer is liberated to go gambling at the race track. The game and the risk involved awaken Damer to the joys of spending rather than hoarding. The allegorical quality of Gregory's imagination is seen here. In *Shanwalla* (1915) the plot revolves about a racehorse of that name which is interfered with so that he loses a big race. The real interest in the play, however, centres on the passions aroused by the possession and protection of the horse; the performance element, likewise, has nothing to do with the race itself but with the skulduggery and murder which precede it and with the trial scene which follows it.

But Gregory did not usually need a game or a sporting image to kickstart her plays. It was far more usual for her to construct and develop a play around an illusion which, like the game of cards or the racehorse, acts as a catalyst to transform peace into chaos. In *Spreading the News* (1904) a false report of murder and adultery grows from the simplest of misinterpretations until a whole community is involved in seemingly inextricable misunderstandings. The 'performance' of the new Removable (*sic*) Magistrate, fresh from governing the Andaman Islands (a British penal colony) and convinced he knows how to handle these suspects also, is absurdly inadequate in unravelling the errors triggered by Irish myth-making. The whole farce depends on split-second timing and cumulative, unrelenting pursuit of a non-existent crime, or what Ellis-Fermor (1954, p. 141) calls 'the nice adjustment of successive misconceptions'. In this kind of work every character must play the game; there is no room for a consciousness which through doubting the validity of the rules of the game arrests it. It is rather like Ben Jonson's *Bartholomew Fair* (1614) in that respect, and indeed Gregory's Magistrate is a bit of a Justice Overdo with political overtones. It may be recalled also that in *Bartholomew Fair,* Jonson's metaphor for teeming life, there is a puppet theatre which the Puritan opponent of its joys is rudely brought to respect and let thrive. Gregory, an admirer of Jonson, virtually puts that puppet theatre on stage every time. We are not required to find psychological depth to the characterisation; we are invited to delight in the totality of the illusion. A dementia pervades and energises the plot. We may see this in play after play: *The Jackdaw* (1907), *Hyacinth Halvey* (1906) and *The Full Moon* (1910), for example. Pretence, created and sustained by the characters themselves against all the odds, lies at the heart of each of these short, ingenious pieces.

Gregory seemed to think that tragedy was easier to write than comedy, and she gives the impression that she stuck to comedy because it was needed at the Abbey as light relief. Writers sometimes sustain themselves by such illusions. There is no case for regarding Gregory as having a tragic vision as such. The fact that she saw the story of *Spreading the News* at first as tragedy but that it came out as comedy, as she says in her note on that play (1970–1, 1, p. 253), is an important indicator. Her gift was to look on life and to find it amusing. She had her serious side, of course, but that is hardly enough to create tragedy. In *The Gaol Gate* (1906) there is a vacuum where the tragic hero ought to be. *Grania* (1910) replaces catharsis (most effectively) with bitterness and irony. These are the only two of her plays in which Gregory even attempted the tragic form. Therefore it is best to characterise her imagination as essentially comic, unlike Yeats's, which was essentially tragic.

As Ann Saddlemyer remarks (1970–1, 1, p. vi), in the comedies 'can be traced the themes and framework of all of her plays'. Therefore it is quite in order to view Gregory's plays as a whole as embodying performance in ways seen already in *Twenty-Five* and subsequent plays. *The Rising of the Moon* (1907) is clearly more serious in intent than this material. And yet the climax, in which a Fenian escapee is protected by a police sergeant, depends upon the latter's ability to convince his own men that he is best left alone to catch the Fenian. It depends, in short, on acting ability. Moreover, the Fenian (simply called Man in the text) impersonates an itinerant ballad singer and it is in that guise that he stirs atavistic feelings in the Sergeant. He even assumes a name: 'I'm one Jimmy Walsh, a ballad-singer' (1970–1, 1, p. 60). As such, he claims to know the wanted man well and describes him in epic terms. Here is myth-making with a difference: 'There isn't a weapon he doesn't know the use of, and as to strength, his muscles are as hard as that board (*slaps barrel*).' The dramatic point here is that the wanted Man's picture is pasted on the barrel. The action grows in suspense the more the barrel is used. It is when the two men are sitting on it back-to-back (like two characters in Beckett) and the Sergeant joins in the Man's patriotic song that one suddenly sees that they are mirror images of each other: 'Sergeant, I am thinking it was with the people you were, and not with the law you were, when you were a young man.' The dichotomy between people and law eventually makes the law a pretence. The Sergeant fails in the 'performance' of his duty but in doing so he performs a patriotic act. Its nature is summed up in the image of the Sergeant hiding the Man's wig and hat behind his back when his colleagues enter and his disguising the Man's hiding place behind the barrel. This is all very neatly done and the idea of collusion is rendered complete when the Sergeant turns to the audience at the end to ask, because he has passed up the chance of a reward, 'I wonder, now, am I as great a fool as I think I am?' (1970–1, 1, p. 67). Made complicit in the Sergeant's act the audience can only approve. It is a dangerous moment as people and law confront each other: depending on the quality of the perform-ance and the nature of the audience a powerful interchange can take place. In 1907 extreme nationalists objected because the play showed a policeman in too kindly a light, while unionists objected because it showed a policeman as a traitor. Between those two poles of re-sponse *The Rising of the Moon* lays its theatrical fuse.

The Image (1909) was a personal favourite among Gregory's own plays. Here the whole question of representation is comically dramatised. When two whales are beached beside a small town it is agreed that the revenue should go to pay for some public amenity. The people decide on a statue but cannot decide on a subject. A crazed mountainy man suggests Hugh O'Lorrha, a name he has just seen on a piece of driftwood found on the shore, and immediately the people appeal to the folk-memory of Peggy Mahon, the oldest inhabitant, who claims to remember O'Lorrha well but is slow to produce a biography. The question of how O'Lorrha might be sculpted is then combined with old Peggy's defence of the 'image' or 'shadow' of her dead husband, which she has kept in her heart for something like eighty years. When she tells of this image she is mocked for having wasted her life, and so the idea of a secret if groundless hope is developed. Viewed as an allegory of creativity, what the play seems to be saying is that the inner image must be kept inviolate and if it is revealed rather than transformed or transmuted it will be lost. Coppinger the stonemason has no idea how to realise the statue of O'Lorrha; designs sent down from Dublin for the suitable representation of public monuments merely reinforce his fear of failure. The mountainy man, Malachi, is outraged when he sees the designs and curses the men who would put up a statue like themselves 'and ugly out of measure' (1970–1, 2, p. 170). When Peggy Mahon is pressed for more details on O'Lorrha she launches into a folktale with O'Lorrha as hero 'at the time of the giants' (p. 174). He is, in fact, 'nothing but a name on the wind'. With that the whole project collapses, and the expected revenue from the two whales vanishes when one is swept back out to sea and the other is stolen by Connemara men. All that remains is the promise of copious talk on the subject in the future. The play shows the irreconcilability of dream and experience, while the Irish fidelity to the dream image is at once celebrated and mocked.

Gregory expanded the notion of performance when she turned to the idea of writing history plays for the Abbey Theatre. She wrote three such full-length plays, which are folk histories rather than history plays in the modern sense of political allegory. Cheryl Herr (1991), in her edition of historical melodramas played at Dublin's Queen's Theatre in the 1880s and 1890s, has shown how much of popular culture found its way into the form. Lady Gregory's efforts, *The White Cockade* (1905), *Kincora* (1905) and *The Canavans* (1906), all in three acts, followed by the one-act *Dervorgilla* (1907), were more educational in aim and omitted all the trappings of romance, intrigue and sensationalism which were the stock-in-trade of the Queen's melodramas. The Abbey stage, small, shallow and with little space behind or above the stage, was not suitable for a form which, as Brecht was later to demonstrate when he undertook history plays such as *Mother Courage* and *Galileo*, is epic in nature and requires epic treatment in performance. In such company Gregory's history plays have little place. They are of interest mainly as essays in identity which make use of disguise, replacement and unmasking. *The White Cockade* concerns James II in Ireland, his defeat at the Boyne and his attempted desertion of the Irish forces. In a key scene Patrick Sarsfield saves James's life by assuming his identity and acts the part so effectively that Williamites turn their coats and join the

Jacobites. Subsequently, James is discovered in a barrel as he is being rolled away in secret to ship for France. This farcical incident was based on a little play in Irish by Douglas Hyde, which Gregory translated as *King James* (in *Poets and Dreamers*, 1903). The point of it is that the image of James as a coward lived on in the popular imagination. In Gregory's play, the focus is finally on Sarsfield, doomed to go on fighting for such an unworthy leader. It is the idea of the 'image' over again, this time in historical guise. In *Kincora* there is a greater attempt at depth of characterisation, the main character being the Danish Gormleith, who marries Brian Boru and in an ambivalent way both betrays him and creates his finest hour at Clontarf. In *The Canavans* a man impersonates Queen Elizabeth during the Munster wars of the 1590s and thereby persuades even his own brother of the power of illusion. Although a light piece, in a comic vein, *The Canavans* cleverly explores the link between performance and power, which is one of Gregory's most fruitful themes. In *Dervorgilla* the action develops in the opposite direction: where in *The Canavans* impersonation is enabling, in *Dervorgilla* the protagonist has authority so long as she is incognito, but as soon as her real identity (as betrayer of Ireland) is discovered her status in the community at Mellifont suddenly dissolves. Gregory is interested in exploring how, depending on the investment of faith provided by a community, in an instant the self that is up can be down, and vice versa. This process is in itself a version of the relationship of audience to actor on stage.

Finally, under the heading of performance, some mention must be made of Gregory's translations of Molière. She translated four comedies in all, which were staged at the Abbey between 1906 and 1926. They were all written in the Kiltartan dialect. The experiment has been examined by both Mary FitzGerald (1987) and Waffia Mursi (1987), so there is little need here to go into detail about the plays, entitled by Gregory *The Doctor in Spite of Himself, The Miser, The Rogueries of Scapin* and *The Would-Be Gentleman*. What needs to be emphasised is that the association with Molière makes clear once again the genuinely theatrical nature of Gregory's imagination. It is similar to Molière's, although not, of course, either as inventive or as profound. The resemblance lies in the quality of the humour. Indeed Gregory says the decision was taken to stage Molière's plays at the Abbey because 'they seemed akin to our own' (1972, p. 60). The plays she chose were not the darker, more ambivalent ones, and not the plays which explore religious and political authority, but plays close to the simple, peasant life which she herself favoured. It is important to note that for the three plays staged before 1910 and published in that year as *The Kiltartan Molière*, the stage business was imported from the *Comédie Française*. This means that for Gregory the exercise was not an academic one by any means; it was an attempt to broaden the Abbey repertoire by providing versions of highly theatrical comedies. Accordingly, it was the performances of these plays Gregory herself comments on. For example, she praises Arthur Sinclair as the mischievous Scapin in the production directed by Synge in 1908: 'he [Sinclair] was wonderful, he seemed a Manannan in disguise playing with mere mortals, such an easy consciousness of inexhaustible power' (1974a, p. 420). That last phrase indicates what Gregory demanded from comic performance. It is significant too that she should here relate Sinclair's performance to Manannan Mac Lir, the Proteus of Irish mythology. In *The Jester*, a 'wonder' play written in 1919 but never staged, the magical master of ceremonies who is the Jester is revealed at the end to be none other than Manannan himself. He corresponds in some ways to Shakespeare's Puck in *A Midsummer Night's Dream*, but one should be aware that the Puck in turn is derived from the Irish *pooka*, or mischievous spirit. Gregory was trying to embody in her own work this mischievous spirit, or rather that of the *cleasaí* or jester. There is something international about this trickster figure, who is highly theatrical in function, as Alan Harrison (1989) has shown and as the director Augusto Boal (1979) has fruitfully explored in his 'theatre of the oppressed'. Even if one were to agree, therefore, with Saddlemyer (1966, p. 98) that Gregory was 'more akin in spirit than in technique' to Molière, that should not rule out the acceptance of Gregory's theatricality. In 1910, after all, Shaw called Gregory both a 'born playwright' like Molière and 'one of the most remarkable theatre talents of our time' (Laurence and Grene 1993, p. 63).

Moreover, this performance motif may be seen in a broader sense as an expression of the Abbey itself and even of Ireland. Both the Abbey and the Irish national movement were founded on dreams awaiting enactment. Gregory insisted that 'one must touch a real and eternal emotion' if one is to come into contact with the life of the country (1972, pp. 57–8). This was her aim: to give voice to the Irish soul. It may sound pretentious when so expressed but it would be wrong to consider Gregory's studies of Irish 'performance' as no more than the amused response of a superior observer. Rather, they provide fables of identity. The comedies, the histories and even the adaptations form part of this process. There is nothing patronising about either style or tone; Gregory was, one might say, merely performing a service.

Among Gregory's last plays, following the successful *Would-Be Gentleman* (which one Dublin reviewer endearingly said had been written for Barry Fitzgerald), was an adaptation of one of the greatest of all comedies, *Don Quixote*, under the title *Sancho's Master* (1927). Here once again dream and pretence combine thematically. Yet as the title suggests it is not the realist Sancho but the dreamer Quixote who is hero, for all his folly. Gregory politicises this dream when in Act III Quixote prepares to sally forth again recklessly: 'Freedom is best. It is one of the best gifts heaven has bestowed upon men. The treasures that the earth encloses or the sea covers are not to be compared to it' (1970–1, 4, p. 288). There is something Quixotic about all of Gregory's comic characters, image-makers and image-chasers all. The lure of freedom is the other side of that dream, even in 1927 with independent Ireland in being.

Feminism and identity

There is no disputing the fact that Lady Gregory has a special place in the ongoing feminist debate and the attempt to reread her texts. It is clear that those who have best championed her work are women: Una Ellis-Fermor, Ann Saddlemyer, Elizabeth Coxhead, Mary Lou Kohfeldt and, most recently, Lucy McDiarmid and Maureen Waters. Shaw and O'Casey were among the first to appreciate Gregory's greatness but neither undertook a study of her work. That task was, oddly enough, left to the women to do.

Odd and yet somehow appropriate. For leaving aside the cliché about the hospitality at Coole, making sure Yeats had his sherry and biscuits at the appointed time and so on; leaving aside also the barmbracks in the Abbey green-room, the poor man's Coole, and the idiotic notion put about that Gregory was some kind of Irish Queen Victoria a bit astray in her dominions, it remains to be said that in her plays as a whole there is a special place for women. The nurturer, as it were, strikes back. It may be agreed that hers is a gender-based art: 'her political unconscious was matriarchal' (McDiarmid and Waters 1995, p. xli).

Yet Gregory was no radical in favour of women's emancipation (1974a, p. 58). The people she most admired were all strong men, not women: Parnell, Roosevelt, Shaw, Collins, de Valera and, in a rather different way, Yeats. She had little in common with radical women such as Countess Markiewicz or Maud Gonne. They were never invited to Coole. She stood up to Annie Horniman, the formidable patron of the Abbey, but she never admired her. Indeed, Gregory seemed to find Horniman somewhat ridiculous.

During the war of independence Gregory wrote a long poem, 'The Old Woman Remembers', which Sara Allgood delivered as a monologue at the Abbey in 1923. The old woman was, in a sense, Ireland herself, brooding on the Irish rebellions over a period of seven hundred and fifty years. She is also, by the same token, Lady Gregory herself. Ireland as woman was, of course, at the centre of the play she co-wrote with Yeats, *Cathleen Ni Houlihan* (1902). In 1919 Gregory acted the part of the old woman in that play when the actress Maire Nic Shiubhlaigh was unavailable. 'What is wanted but a hag and a voice?', she queried disarmingly (1978, p. 55). It is tempting to see this identification as the key to Gregory's role as dramatist, giving voice to the spirit of Ireland (Kohfeldt 1985, p. 237). Moreover, when one turns to the plays women either have the key roles or are significantly silenced. The spirit of Ireland is thus feminised.

In *Spreading the News* (1904) the whole frantic business of misrepresentation and false accusation of murder is rooted in the gossip of Mrs Tarpey, who, being somewhat deaf, hears only fragments of conversation and so spreads news based on false premises but embroidered by others before returning to her for further re-processing. Thus she is the fulcrum of the whole mechanism. If it is the men who take action and enforce the law it is the woman who holds the secret. That empowerment is very significant in Gregory's work. In *The Gaol Gate* (1906) a mother and her daughter-in-law are joint chorus to the heroism of son/husband who dies in another man's place rather than inform against him. It is they who will clear his good name and confer public honour on him. They have the power to give him new life. In *The Workhouse Ward* (1908), the whole question of the deliverance of Mike McInerney depends on his sister's good will; she is empowered to bring him home but refuses when he insists on the company of his mortal enemy. In *The Full Moon* (1910) it is a madwoman who shows Hyacinth Halvey the way out of his trapped existence. In *The Image* (1909) it is the old woman Peggy Mahon who holds the key to the identity of Hugh O'Lorrha, mythical though that name is. It is noteworthy how in this play women are sidelined when action is to be taken. When it comes to a vote on how to spend the money from the two whales neither of the two women in the play is consulted, even though Mrs Coppinger is respected for her intelligence and reading skills. The situation was, of course, realistic. Gregory often found herself in that position.

In the history plays the woman is similarly marginalised and yet the one with knowledge or quasi-magical power. In *The White Cockade* (1905), when Sarsfield pretends to be King James he fools everybody except an old aristocratic lady, regarded as mentally unstable, who knows the real king instantly by touch. In *The Canavans* (1906) it is Antony's disguise as Queen Elizabeth which effects his and Peter's release from prison: farcical though the episode is it emphasises the iconic power of Elizabeth to turn the heads of her subjects. (Yeats was to explore similar territory in *The Player Queen*, 1919.) The portrayal of Gormleith in *Kincora* (1905) is more complex. Two versions of the play exist. In the first version Gormleith is demonised as a Dane who betrays Brian Boru; in the revised version staged in 1909 she is much tamed and offset with a wandering, visionary woman (the Beggar Girl) who persuades Brian all Ireland is at peace while Gormleith insists that war is necessary and peace dangerous. The revised version followed upon the *Playboy* riots and the premature death of Synge, who had helped Gregory with the first version (Saddlemyer 1982, p. 55). Gregory was now, like Gormleith herself, angry at the complaisant majority (the 'trader' whom Yeats was later to mock more bitterly). The Amazonian Gormleith is caught out and subdued in the play and in the revised version is made to accept responsibility for her treachery. Political and sexual treachery are equated. Gormleith has to listen to Brian's pious prayer for God's mercy on 'every woman's vain changing heart' (1970–1, 2, p. 90) before seeing him off to the battle of Clontarf. Gregory sees women as obliged to accept obloquy so long as they bring about some form of political, social or moral good. As troublemaker and opponent of Catholic passivity, Gormleith enables Brian to unify warring factions and establish a form of Home Rule (Hawkins 1990).

The portrayal of Gormleith suggests that Gregory saw women as sexually guilty. This consorted, no doubt, with her inherited imperialist ideology, which included a stern, male-dominated theology. (Gregory was a great one for quoting the Bible.) More of this kind of guilt is seen in *Dervorgilla* (1907) and *Grania* (unstaged, written 1909–10). In each case the woman is guilty of infidelity and must pay. It is indeed strange that Gregory as playwright was captive to the same standard morality as Arthur Wing Pinero and *The Second Mrs. Tanqueray* (1893). Dervorgilla's adulterous affair with Diarmuid, King of Leinster in the early twelfth century, supposedly led to the Norman invasion of Ireland and hence to British occupation. It is a case of *cherchez la femme* for the roots of Ireland's ills. Yeats was to write on the same theme in *The Dreaming of the Bones* but in a romantic/philosophical vein remote from Gregory's interests. Gregory has nothing to do with all of this; she could always tell an Irish dancer from a Japanese dance. Her *Dervorgilla* is set in broad noonday and simply confronts the aged Dervorgilla with the consequences of her youthful action. Forgiveness is not on the agenda. Dervorgilla lives in secret at Mellifont Abbey, and once her identity is known she is held accountable for the British presence locally and for the death of an innocent Irishman at their hands. Dervorgilla has to accept the responsibility, and the loss of respect gained from the next generation around her: 'the swift, unflinching, terrible judgment of the young!' (1970–1, 2, p. 110). Here Gregory was herself expiating the guilt-by-association incurred as a descendant of the colonisers. In a sense, Gregory wore black all her life after 1892 because (like Chekhov's Masha) she was in mourning for her life.

Although remaining professionally unstaged *Grania* is a play which has attracted increasing critical attention over the years. Ellis-Fermor faulted it on technical grounds and then gave it eight pages of her chapter on Gregory. Coxhead disagreed with the technical criticism and defended the play as a love triangle 'in which a woman is ousted from an emotional relationship between two men' (1966, p. 137). To Kohfeldt (1985, p. 213) *Grania* represented a new venture by Gregory, a 'heroic attempt to explore her own personality'. More recently Maureen Waters (1995) has interpreted the play as articulating a feminist voice. To all of this may be added the minority male voice of Hazard Adams (1973, p. 61): 'When all is said, this play is a study of a woman'.

So, who is this woman? Her story as one of the great lovers of Irish mythology, second only to Deirdre, was told in Gregory's *Gods and Fighting Men* (1904). The most immediate point to note (in contrast to the Yeats–Moore version of this story) is the elision of Diarmuid's name from the title. This was to be a play where the spotlight was to fall on the woman and not on the man. In her note on the text Gregory compares the character to the more glamorous Deirdre and expresses a preference for Grania: 'Grania had more power of will' (1970–1, 2, p. 283). The main question Gregory found the material posing was why Grania would return to Finn at the end. Her answer in the play is that Diarmuid finally turns against Grania and towards Finn: 'That would be a very foolish man would give up his dear master and his friend for any woman at all. (*He laughs.*)' (1970–1, 2, p. 42). It is in the last four pages of her text that Gregory's originality is most clearly exhibited. In bitterness Grania rejects love as an illusion. Whereas in the tale as told in *Gods and Fighting Men* (p. 308) one reason offered for Grania's decision to go with Finn at the end is 'because the mind of a woman changes like the water of a running stream', Gregory now makes Grania transfer this variability to the man. 'It is women are said to change, and they do not, but it is men that change and turn as often as the wheel of the moon.' The charge made by Brian against Gormleith is answered. The woman is finally empowered to realise herself, in the face of the public mockery which greets her as Finn's prize. When she makes her final exit she silences the laughter of the men. This is completely the opposite point made at the end of Synge's *Deirdre of the Sorrows*. It provides a revolutionary, if harsh, representation of woman's choice, an escape from the aesthetics and ideology of Victorian high romance. But it involves self-injury and debasement, as if Gregory still felt that in any circumstances the woman, descendant of Eve, had to pay for guilt thrust upon her by a male. Guilt over her love for Blunt may have been a factor here.

In no other play does Gregory explore so seriously the relations between the sexes. At the same time, *Grania* seems unfinished, inasmuch as the homoerotic area of the play, coded in the conventions of epic as male bonding and chivalry, is not integrated with the heterosexual main theme. The play remains a fascinating curiosity rather than an idea fully and dramatically realised. In other plays Gregory presented woman as idealised; that was her means of resolving the problem of empowerment. Woman was to be the spiritualising force intervening in a male-dominated, violent and fallen world. The obverse was a witch. Gregory kept her witches for her wonder plays, which are not exactly children's plays but which occupy a theatrical territory at one remove from realism, in a realm once defined by Charles Lamb as 'beyond the diocese of the strict conscience' (1964, p. 296). In *The Golden Apple* (1920), dedicated to Shaw, whose own last plays may owe something to Gregory, there is an interesting version of the witch. The witch's daughter, Pampogue, wishes to marry but her mother is against a human alliance. 'There is not a woman of my race that had not a king under her feet! But as to yourself, I will give you no leave at all to wed any man of Adam's race' (1970–1, 3, p. 103). In the nature of all fairytales the witch is destroyed and Pampogue is released: to be the possible helpmate of the king's steward. The last word, ironically, goes to the man in search of a wife as servant: 'I might be looking for a companion for myself. It's a lonesome thing to be housekeeping alone!' (1970–1, 3, p. 169).

A variation on this orthodox role for woman as servant is found in *Shanwalla* (1915), *Aristotle's Bellows* (1921), *The Story Brought by Brigit* (1924) and *Dave* (1927). Here one discovers within the domestic setting the woman as saint and inspirer of men. Gregory unequivocally endorsed for Irish society the Victorian idea of woman as the angel in the house. It was certainly to be a dominant cultural idea in the new state and was to find its way indirectly into the Irish constitution of 1937 and the ideology underpinning Irish society up to recent times. In *Shanwalla*, which is no more than a melodrama about a racehorse and a nasty murder, the wife is not only saintlike in life but also literally saintlike after she is murdered: she comes into court as a ghost and gives evidence against the villain. This makes clear the position of woman in the society Gregory saw around her. It is the woman who is attacked and killed, not her husband the farmhand minding the horse, and not the local bigwig who is the owner of the horse. It is interesting to note that Bride Scarry is not allowed to speak in court herself: her evidence is mediated through a man.

In *Aristotle's Bellows*, which is a wonder play but also a kind of political allegory, the Mother (she has no other name) is the seat of wisdom and good sense while her stepson Conan is a scholar in pursuit of a magical cure to change all that is wrong with the world. Mother's philosophy is: 'It's best make changes little by little the same as you'd put clothes upon a growing child' (1970–1, 3, pp. 266–7). After a series of attempts to change things with the magic bellows all returns to the status quo and Conan accepts Mother's wisdom. Adams (1973, p. 94) cites this ending as evidence of Gregory's conservatism: she had no Utopian ideals. This is perhaps to miss the point. Gregory was writing *Aristotle's Bellows* while Ireland was being torn apart through the war of independence (1919–21), followed by the civil war (1922–3). Gregory's *Journals* provide horrific details of the outrages around Gort. She held on while her old home at Roxborough was burned by the IRA in 1922 and the fate of Coole hung in the balance. She liked to quote her own lines from *Kincora* at this time: 'I will make an end of quarrels' (1970–1, 3, p. 74). Gregory wanted change all right, and an end to violence and destruction. She looked to women somehow to be the agents of that change. In an unpublished article, cited by Saddlemyer (1977, p. 35), Gregory called for a republic or a 'commonwealth'.

The *Story Brought by Brigit* (1924) can be seen as Gregory's prayer for peace. As a play, it is of its time. Saint Brigit turns up in Jerusalem just as Jesus is about to be captured and put to death. She is a bystander and witness; she mediates what is essentially a passion play. The use of dialect and even the *caoine* at the Cross give a strange effect, and if one reads the play as a piece of folklore it has a surrealistic quality. Brigit or Brigid (also Brid or Bride, as in *Shanwalla*) was not only a seventh-century Irish saint but a pagan goddess also (Ó Catháin 1995). In Irish folklore, as Gregory herself testifies (*Visions and Beliefs*, 1920), Brigit was known as 'Mary of the Gael' and fostered the child Jesus in Ireland for a time. She was thus a mediatrix, a source of the divine. To this day Saint Brigit's day, the first day of February, being also the first day of spring, is a special day in the Irish calendar with its roots in ancient rituals more pagan than Christian. Gregory's play is an attempt to knit into Irish culture, through the local witness of Brigit, the overcoming of imperialism by Christianity. Because the occupying Romans stand for the British in Ireland the play has an unexpected political animus. A Roman sergeant says, 'a little Rising now and then is no harm at all. It gives us an excuse to get rid of disturbers and to bring more of our armies in' (1970–1, 3, p. 310). When writing the play in September 1923 Gregory recorded in her *Journals* (1978, p. 474), 'I keep wondering what Christ would do were he here now'. She was thus writing symbolic allegory, declaring that the woman's role in the last stages of colonised Ireland was simply to make God manifest in a redeemable world. Her source for such a train of thought lay deep in Irish folklore.

Dave, although only one act, is a far better play which gets this frankly religio-political purpose across in more dramatic terms than *Brigit* does. The germ of *Dave* lay in the idea of a woman, later called the Servant of Poverty, who flashed into Gregory's awakening mind in March 1925, as she describes in her *Journals* (1987, p. 8): 'Another good night, awakening sometimes but happily and without pain. [Lady Gregory was suffering from breast cancer.] And suddenly I seemed to get the play clearly (*Dave*), a ragged woman coming into the house through a storm, faints, believes when revived she is in Heaven and so brings the others something to the mind of "dwellers in that high country." It seemed to flatten as I wrote it down this morning, yet I think it is the framework I want.' When she finished the play Lennox Robinson, playwright and fellow-director at the Abbey, persuaded her to drop this stranger figure and to make the woman of the house, Kate, prove the catalyst to transform the boy Dave from brutalised servant to inspired man of action. In the event, this works very well.

Dave was Gregory's last play. Like a lot of her work it is vulnerable to the sophisticated criticism of modern times. It wears its heart on its sleeve in a manner calculated to attract superior smiles. It has, however, the kind of integrity which need fear no such response. It has been called 'a modern miracle play' (Coxhead 1966, p. 180). That may be so but its championing of woman as the spiritual regenerator of brutalised and colonised Ireland is where the real force of *Dave* lies. It is Gregory's legacy epitomised. To quote Kohfeldt (1985, p. 291), 'In some ways she gives a better picture of what motivated her entire life in the twenty pages of *Dave* than she gave in the 560 pages of her autobiography'. When Gregory herself saw *Dave* on stage at the Abbey in May 1927, in a triple bill with *The Rising of the Moon* and Shaw's *Fanny's First Play* (1911), she could accept that her life's work as co-creator of a theatre and as creator of a drama of liberation had borne fruit. 'I did feel proud and satisfied – a theatre of our own, Irish plays, such a fine play by our countryman [Shaw] – company playing it so splendidly, all our own – "Something to have lived to see!"' (1987, p. 187). She had come to terms with who she was and with her calling as artist.

That same year, 1927, Gregory sold off Coole House and lands to the Irish Department of Forestry, having in 1920 sold most of the estate to her tenants. In every sense she had paid her dues to Ireland and to history. Her heart was with the people, not with what she dismissively called the *ancien régime*, a 'banished society' (1978, p. 610). The Department of Forestry eventually returned to the people the woods, walks and gardens of Coole as a public amenity. To walk there now is to be aware of the absence of Coole House itself and all it signified in Irish literary history. Yet that vacancy is perhaps after all the most honest monument, to use an Irish bull, to the author of *The Image* and other plays. Her absence from the contemporary Irish stage is another matter, one with which there will in time have to be a coming to terms.

3

Synge: ironic revolutionary

I am with Synge in thinking that the Irish should do their own Ibsenizing; and in fact all your successes have been nothing else than that.   *Shaw, Lady Gregory and the Abbey* (1993)

Synge as radical

Although undoubtedly one of the 'last romantics', with a strong conservative streak, Synge was also in his own way a true radical. That is, Synge endorsed primitivism and was within an ace of idealising tradition in plays which provide what William Empson (1935) in another context termed 'versions of pastoral', and yet Synge was subversive. If art, as I believe, is energy in pursuit of form then Synge's whole artistic project was the celebration of energy directed towards forms of freedom. Again and again, the six plays move to the point of emancipation, where a marginalised figure finds voice and gesture to revolt against oppressive circumstances. This voice may, as at the end of *Riders to the Sea* (1903), appear to be mere resignation to a higher order but in fact it is always a declaration of independence, and in Synge's greatest play, *The Playboy of the Western World* (1907), it is manifestly revolutionary. In view of the attack on Synge by the nationalists there is a great irony here. For Synge's agenda, just as much as theirs, was emancipation.

Whereas Synge was, undoubtedly, a complete artist in the sense in which we habitually regard Keats or Joyce, it may be misleading to see Synge altogether through Yeats's eyes. In *A Vision* Yeats put Synge into Phase 23 as the Receptive Man alongside Rembrandt: 'When out of phase … he is tyrannical, gloomy and self-absorbed. In phase his energy has a character analogous to the longing of Phase 16 to escape from complete subjectivity: it escapes in a condition of explosive joy from systemisation and abstraction' (1962b, p. 164).

Synge: ironic revolutionary

From his early tendency towards morbid self-pity Synge 'had to undergo an aesthetic transformation, analogous to religious conversion, before he became the audacious, joyous, ironical man we know' (p. 167). According to Yeats, this transformation came about through Synge's experience of the Aran Islands (intermittently, 1898–1902). But one would have to say that Synge's record, *The Aran Islands* (1907), is as full of morbidity as it is of joyousness: Synge read into the landscape his own romantic melancholy, and the landscape gave him back examples of the co-existence of death and endurance, material hardship and spiritual wonder, desolation and transcendence. The Aran Islands were for Synge a two-way mirror, of his and the nation's soul. It is a mistake to see Synge as Yeats rather enviously does as without contradictions, entire in himself, 'Passionate and simple', 'that rooted man', and so on (Yeats 1950, pp. 149, 369). For Synge was as riddled with contradictions as anyone else. Just because he was silent it did not mean he had all the answers. His letters to Molly Allgood, of which Yeats would have known nothing, reveal a man in turmoil, anxious, unsure, jealous and self-pitying, not at all the heroic figure Yeats mythologises. Similarly, I would argue, Synge was by no means only the self-absorbed aesthete Yeats imagined, who 'had no life outside his imagination' (1961a, p. 329). In so far as Synge was in conflict with himself, his class, his religion, and aspects of Irish life he found detestable, he struggled to reconcile what he termed (in the preface to the *Playboy*) 'reality' and 'joy'. To do so he had to find a style. That style was founded on ironic detachment. It provided Synge with the means of a social critique as well as the occasion of artistic fulfilment. It is not true, then, as Yeats asserted (1961a, p. 319), that Synge was 'unfitted to think a political thought'. On the contrary, 'the nature of the nation was Synge's fundamental concern' (Cairns and Richards, 1988, p. 78).

It happens that historically Synge flourished during a time of transition in Ireland, when there was, in Roy Foster's phrase, 'a failure, on many levels, of political inspiration and direction' (1988, p. 434). Synge died five years before the outbreak of the First World War and seven years before the 1916 Rising; he wrote during a period when settling the land question took priority over the Home Rule issue, which was to gather momentum in 1912, as Shaw's new preface to *John Bull's Other Island* (1904) aptly underlined (1963, 2, pp. 433–42). It was doubly difficult for Synge to make the bridge between art and politics which Yeats, in his competent way, was publicly constructing for himself from the early 1880s on. Synge was far more a member of a unionist, Ascendancy family than Yeats (Foster 1993, pp. 198–9). His people were landlords in Wicklow and Mayo; one brother was a land agent involved in evicting poverty-stricken tenants in the 1880s, another was a missionary in China in the best imperialist tradition. The Synge household in Dublin was strongly Evangelical and had close connections with Trinity College, then a bastion of the Protestant establishment, and the Church of Ireland. John, the youngest of four children, was to be the black sheep (although this was a strictly relativist term: Synge always had his family allowance and the family home to return to). From the time he was fourteen, having read Darwin, Synge rejected his mother's low-church religion and declared his atheism, at least to himself and his private writings. Synge's biographers make clear the political implications of this apostasy, which was, indeed, life-long (and was reciprocated by his family's never once attending a performance of a Synge play):

> The Protestant minority, which saw itself succumbing to historical forces too great to cope with, no longer felt the assurance which its position of privilege had given it in Ireland for centuries. Fearful of the rising power of the Catholic masses and the loss of their lands, they were losing also the power of reasoned criticism which had animated the best of Anglo-Irish culture in the past. Like a threatened aristocracy they rallied behind their barricades of class supremacy and forced their members into rigid adherence to their own traditions and beliefs. By his disbelief Synge was dissociating himself from his own people.
>
> (Greene and Stephens 1959, p. 10)

In his fragmentary autobiography Synge himself revealed how his religious rebellion was followed by his adoption of Irish nationalism: 'Soon after I had relinquished the Kingdom of God I began to take a real interest in the kingdom of Ireland. My politics went round from a vigorous and unreasoning loyalty to a temperate Nationalism. Everything Irish became sacred' (1968, 2, p. 13). His good friend Stephen MacKenna remembers Synge's Anglophobia: 'There were few men who ever had a deeper hatred of the English, he thought that as a people they were heavy, stupid, bovine, who "had achieved a great literature by a mystery." The English influence in Ireland he thought absolutely bad and regretted that the Irish people had lost their national characteristics through it' (1982,

p. 149). But being alienated from an already alienated (if supreme) minority did not position Synge within nationalist circles. Indeed, such was his independent temperament that he had little in common with the organisers of national committees or their tactics. While in Paris in 1897 he took an interest in *L'Association Irlandaise*, founded by Maud Gonne to support Irish independence, but quickly and characteristically backed off in alarm, and wrote to Ms Gonne a letter of resignation in which he said: 'I wish to work in my own way for the cause of Ireland, and I shall never be able to do so if I get mixed up with a revolutionary and semi-military movement' (Greene and Stephens 1959, p. 63).

Synge's way was not Yeats's way. Both men prioritised art, and each was equally determined to make self-expression the core of his aesthetic. But Yeats liked to adopt people for a cause, and having adopted them insisted on their paying such dues as he thought necessary to his own self-esteem. Synge was far more independent; his genius needed no bolstering from others (Foster 1993, p. 211). It is now believed doubtful that it was Yeats who first advised Synge to give up Paris and to live on the Aran Islands as one of the people: a story Yeats first told in his preface to Synge's *Well of the Saints* (1905). Yeats said: 'Give up Paris. You will never create anything by reading Racine, and Arthur Symons will always be a better critic of French literature. Go to the Aran Islands. Live there as if you were one of the people themselves; express a life that has never found expression' (1961a, p. 299). Yeats says this happened six years before 1905, whereas Synge first visited Aran in the summer of 1898; later on, Yeats changed the year of his conjuration to 1896. We have here what Mark Mortimer (1977) has called 'an inappropriate myth'. Whereas it is engaging to imagine Yeats as a Molly Ivors figure wagging a finger at Synge cast as Gabriel Conroy, it seems likely, as Nicholas Grene has argued (1982, p. 2), that Yeats was preaching to the converted. Synge was already deeply involved in studies in Celtic literature. He had learned Irish while a student at Trinity College (1888–92), something Yeats never did. Synge's uncle, the Revd Alexander Synge, had been a Protestant missionary on Aranmore in the 1850s (there is a monument to him beside Kilronan), and Synge may well have felt drawn to Aran as much on account of this curious family history as for linguistic and cultural reasons. All Yeats did was to reinforce Synge's own peculiar sense of mission. But it is necessary to understand, at the same time, that between 1898 and 1902 Synge spent most of each year in Paris and only six weeks at a time in Aran. He believed in maintaining a distance from his subject matter, and whereas there is no question but that the experience of Aran was artistically crucial it was in Paris that Synge encountered the two currents of modernism which steered his development: naturalism and symbolism. It was after 1902 that Synge's major plays were written. It was also when his essays on Connemara and Mayo were written, as a result of a commission jointly undertaken by Jack B. Yeats and himself. These articles reveal as clearly as anything Synge wrote how keen his political eye actually was.

Synge often illustrates in these articles the subsistence economy which kept the western peasants captive. In one essay ('The Village Shop') he analysed the dependency of the small farmer and his family on the capitalist economy managed by a local shopkeeper who was also a sort of banker: 'the shops are run on a vague system of credit that is not satisfactory. ... The people keep no passbooks, so they have no check on the traders ... [and] it is likely that the prices charged are often exorbitant. What is worse, the shopkeeper in out-of-the-way places is usually the only buyer to be had for a number of home products ... so that he can control the prices both of what he buys and what he sells, while as a creditor he has an authority that makes bargaining impossible' (1968, 2, pp. 329–30). Such huxterism lies behind the genial facade of the O'Flaherty shebeen in *The Playboy of the Western World*, where self-interest is the final and imperative consideration of proprietor and community alike. Synge does not apportion blame, yet he is not blind to the controls exerted by the dominant ideology, partly religious (Fr Reilly) and partly legalist ('the juries ... selling judgments of the English law', 1968, 4, p. 105). Collaboration with such hegemony forms the basis of Synge's searing irony.

In a letter to John Quinn in 1905 Yeats remarked: 'We will have a hard fight in Ireland before we get the right for every man to see the world in his own way admitted. Synge is invaluable to us because he has that kind of intense narrow personality which necessarily raises the whole issue' (Wade 1954, pp. 447–8). Synge's 'way', therefore, was somehow to 'raise the whole issue' of independence in its manifold cultural forms.

Synge: ironic revolutionary

Synge and Ibsen

It is commonly believed that, because of comments made in his prefaces, Synge had no interest in Ibsen and the modern movement in naturalism. Commentators have thereby too easily been thrown off the scent. For Synge, like George Moore, Bernard Shaw, Edward Martyn and Padraic Colum at this time, fell very much under the influence of Ibsen (Setterquist 1951). But it was a classic case of 'the anxiety of influence': Synge disowned Ibsen, reviled naturalism and set out to establish his own individual style. His plays are best understood, then, as variations upon the Ibsenist drama of revolt.

A firm indication of what this means may be gained from Synge's first completed play, *When the Moon Has Set* (1900–03). It was a two-act play when Synge read it at Coole in September 1901; it was cut to one act during 1902–3. In neither form was it acceptable to Yeats for production. Even after Synge's death Yeats was adamant that *When the Moon Has Set* should be left in obscurity, and he forbade publication. 'It is just the kind of work which some theatrical experimenter with no literary judgment or indifferent to literature would be glad to get' (Synge 1968, 1, p. 155n.). It was, accordingly, suppressed until Ann Saddlemyer included it in the definitive edition of Synge's plays for the *Collected Works* in 1968. The two-act version was not published until 1982, when it was edited by Mary C. King. These editions are highly valuable recoveries of a key text. For Yeats felt he had rescued Synge from an unpromising start: 'It was after its rejection by us he took to peasant work'. But, in effect, Yeats was occluding Synge's real dramatic origins.

Synge's nephew Edward Stephens has described *When the Moon Has Set* as a 'dramatization of his [Synge's] own life under a thin disguise of fiction' (Carpenter 1974, p. 147). Use in the play of passages from Synge's fragment of *Autobiography* verifies this claim. This use of autobiography for the purposes of drama links Synge straight away with the Ibsen of *Brand* (1865) who said 'Brand is myself in my best moments' (Meyer 1974, p. 262). Act IV of *Brand* was reasonably well known in Dublin after 1900; Edward Martyn, in particular, laboured to make Ibsen's procedures acceptable. As dramatist, Synge followed in Ibsen's footsteps. In his private life Synge had been refused marriage by Cherry Matheson because of his atheism; this happened more than once, impressing on Synge the forces towards conformity at work all around him. (Ms Matheson had the sympathy of Synge's mother.) Such was his independence of

[69]

spirit, however, not to mention his stubbornness, that Synge would not revert to Christianity in any form (Ms Matheson was a member of the Plymouth Brethren) even for the sake of true love. In *When the Moon Has Set* there is a background and a foreground story which coincide and relate to Synge's own history. In one the story is of the destruction of a love affair through religious prejudice; in the other the overcoming of a reprise of this same situation in the next generation. In the background story the atheistic landowner Colm (or Columb) Sweeney (or Sweeny) has just died, his life blighted because of the refusal of his Catholic fiancée; in the foreground story Colm Sweeney, nephew and heir to the dead man and a would-be writer, is attracted to the religious sister who nursed his uncle in his last illness. Sister Eileen, equally attracted, fights off Colm's advances, and a repetition of the former story seems inevitable. One thinks of Ibsen's *Ghosts* (1880), which Synge had seen in Antoine's production in Paris in March 1898 (Mercier 1994, p. 205). But joining the two stories and exerting a major influence for change is the uncle's fiancée, Mary Costello, whose bitter denunciations of the clergy who ruined her life reinforce the younger Colm's overtures to Sister Eileen. The reference here is to the one-act version published in the *Collected Works* (vol. 3); the earlier and fuller two-act version keeps Mary offstage, indeed in a mental home. In both versions she is a powerful signifier, but more so by her presence in the one-act version, where her denunciation of the clergy, à la Yeats's Crazy Jane thirty years later, expresses the central thesis of the play: 'It's well I know you've no call to mind what the priests say, or the bishops say, or what the angels of God do be saying, for it's little the like of them knows of women or the seven sorrows of earth.' Mary Costello's fate prefigures the possible history of Sister Eileen. The play builds to the moment of choice.

Sister Eileen must choose either to leave her religious order and marry Colm or to refuse to obey her natural impulses, as Synge puts it, in favour of obedience to her religious vows. Synge couches the choice in terms of a dialectic between nature and conformity. If Sister Eileen obeys Colm's direction she will be making a spiritual choice of a more profound kind than religious orthodoxy provides: 'You realize that the forces which lift women up to a share in the pain and passion of the world are more holy than the vows you have made' (1968, 3, p. 175). This siren song was to be given rather greater force and credibility in the mouths of Martin Doul and

Christy Mahon but it is interesting to see here its radical, subversive origin, even if the style is lacking in Synge's saving grace of irony. Sister Eileen, of course, makes her choice for nature and impulse, in order to complete Synge's contrived thesis. Exiting at this point Sister Eileen re-enters after what must be one of the fastest costume changes in theatrical history, having abandoned her nun's habit and being now dressed 'in a green silk dress which is cut low at the neck'. In the two-act version it is made clear that this was Mary Costello's wedding dress. Sister Eileen's line as she re-enters is thus a sign, a re-dressing: 'Colm, I have come back to you.' History has been redeemed by her courageous apostasy, as Colm's reply indicates: 'You are infinitely beautiful, and you have done a great action. It is the beauty of your spirit that has set you free.'

Crude (and humourless) though it is, this celebration of freedom is the key to Synge's drama. Art made possible what life itself declared impossible. The politics of Synge's work emerges here. In his plays there is always a choice to be made. This choice is in the broadest sense revolutionary. When Nora Burke goes off with the Tramp in *The Shadow of the Glen* she chooses to be his common-law wife in defiance of her husband's high moral tone. Synge altered his source, the story narrated in *The Aran Islands*, to make that point. Although her future is as uncertain as that of Ibsen's Nora (*A Doll's House*, 1879) she is not alone: 'you've a fine bit of talk, stranger, and it's with yourself I'll go' (1968, 3, p. 57). It's a going into exile Irish style, with the *non serviam* declared more flamboyantly by Stephen Dedalus, but in Synge's version of the revolt the going is into nature and away from society. Such, it turns out, is the dialectic of Synge's drama generally. He constantly polarises the life of the settled, bourgeois community and the life of the open roads, or the sea, or the wilds of Alban (Scotland), where intensity of being is valorised. On the one hand are the values of safety, orthodoxy, fear; on the other danger, ecstasy, love. Here Synge ironises the commonplace dialectic of life versus death so that life becomes life-in-death and death becomes death-in-life. This is not escapism, even in *When the Moon Has Set* where irony is pretty thin on the ground. In introducing the two-act version of that play Mary C. King (Synge 1982, p.12) says that the ending is 'committed to an escape from history into an aesthetically harmonized universe'. To hold such a view is to admit the possibility that all of Synge merely aestheticises revolt. But, arguably, the only play of which this charge may validly be made is

Deirdre of the Sorrows. This play attempts to find a form to accommodate the dying Synge's awareness that his love for Molly Allgood (a Catholic half his age) would so be destroyed by disease that social convention, opposed to such a misalliance, would appear to be affirmed by nature. In the other plays it is more persuasive to see the final choice enacted as a defiance of history itself. Hugh Kenner puts the case in a nutshell (1983, p.120): 'Synge, it may be, handled but the one story six times, a story of setting out and then dying, in which those who set forth have chosen better than those who choose to stay.' It is necessary to add, however, that the seventh story, the double story told as admonishment in *When the Moon Has Set*, is prologue to this theme. Its Ibsenist address is unmistakable.

It can readily be countered that Synge referred dismissively to Ibsen in both the preface to *The Playboy of the Western World* and the preface to *The Tinker's Wedding*. But if one looks at what he actually says there it amounts to no more than two assertions: because Ibsen dealt with 'problems' in society Ibsen is obsolescent, if not obsolete; and Ibsen, like Zola, lacked linguistic colour and provided only 'joyless and pallid words' when 'dealing with the reality of life'. Sifting these comments one can say that Synge was no utilitarian in his art and wanted to avoid topical issues and discussion, which Shaw (1891) had claimed was the innovative element in Ibsen's drama. But Ibsen, it is now realised, was a great deal less of a sermoniser or utilitarian than Shaw happily believed: the proof lies in the continuing relevance for audiences today of *A Doll's House*, *Hedda Gabler* and even (in spite of the syphilis metaphor in the age of AIDS) *Ghosts*. Shaw was convinced that in time *A Doll's House* would be 'as flat as ditchwater' when *A Midsummer Night's Dream* would 'still be as fresh as paint'; he could cheerfully accept this prognosis because Ibsen's play would 'have done more work in the world', that is, would have made a greater impact on social consciousness and conscience (Shaw 1959, p. 63). An artist such as Synge was, or Chekhov for that matter, disdained such a functional view of his drama. His reaction was therefore defensive. But it need not have been, for Ibsen was himself far more of a poet than Shaw allowed himself to see, and was by no means content to be perceived as a writer of 'problem plays'. *The Wild Duck* (1884) stands as a rebuke to the utilitarian view of drama or the thesis play, and has much in common with Synge's *The Well of the Saints*: both plays celebrate the 'right' of individuals to live in and through illusion rather than according to the slide-rule of Shavian fact or socially approved reality. Moreover, Ibsen's *Peer Gynt* (1876) is nothing if not poetical; it is hard not to see it as a precursor to Synge's *Playboy*.

As to Ibsen's 'joyless and pallid words', this point is probably valid enough, given the aim of naturalism to avoid artificiality, but one would need to bear in mind also that the translations Synge had read may well have been inadequate (Archer can be very uneven, and Gissing is nowadays unreadable). It is instructive to contrast the young James Joyce's response to Ibsen in the famous review in 1900 of *When We Dead Awaken*. To Joyce at this time Ibsen was the supreme genius (in this he was at one with Shaw): 'It may be questioned whether any man has held so firm an empire over the thinking world in modern times' (Joyce 1959, p. 48). As to Ibsen's themes and language Joyce remarked:

> Ibsen has chosen the average lives in their uncompromising truth for the groundwork of all his later plays. He has abandoned the verse form, and has never sought to embellish his work after the conventional fashion. Even when his dramatic theme reached its zenith he has not sought to trick it out in gawds or tawdriness.   (1959, p. 63)

Synge, too, had begun, like Ibsen, by writing plays (or at any rate fragments) in verse – and pretty awful reading they make – before launching into prose with his own attack on conventional morality in *When the Moon Has Set*. Synge had to fight his way clear of a major writer with whom he had too much in common for his own artistic good. His way forward, unlike Joyce's, was to avoid the middle class as subject matter, and their moral and social problems, in order to focus on the people, the folk, the peasantry (always, for Joyce, merely comic because threatening). This shift (portentous word) allowed Synge to release prose into poetic, even Daedalan, flight by tapping the resources of dialect and the speech of the people, i.e. Hiberno–English. Joyce was to live to translate *Riders to the Sea* into (choice) Italian after Synge's death but there is more than a grain of mockery present when he makes Buck Mulligan in *Ulysses* describe Shakespeare as the 'chap that writes like Synge' (1960, p. 254). Synge's solution to the problem of style in the age of naturalism was to go back to the Elizabethans (as the preface to the *Playboy* proves) but for Joyce this was provincialism, a surrender to the 'rabblement'. Synge was to prove Joyce wrong in this regard, as *Finnegans*

Wake, where every phrase is as well-flavoured as a nut or an apple, may be said to illustrate; in the meantime Joyce's praise of Ibsen serves to underline how central Ibsen was to the Irish version of modernism.

After *When the Moon Has Set* Synge quit the drawing room for the open roads, banging the door on middle-class art as firmly as Ibsen's Nora Helmer had banged the door on middle-class morality. In taking to the roads like one of his own tramps, tinkers or playboys, Synge identified his aims as anti-modernist. But as Thomas Kilroy has shown, Synge was, in spite of appearances and perhaps in spite of himself, part of the modernist movement in literature.

The plays

'Modernism', says Kilroy (1972, p. 176), 'is not just a preference for one form above another, it is, in its fullest meaning, a mode of perception, of knowledge with a very definite idea of how art should express such knowledge.' *The Shadow of the Glen* is preoccupied with just such concerns of perception and knowledge. Written in the summer of 1902 this play was the first of Synge's to be staged, on 8 October 1903, when it attracted some opposition from nationalists; when it was revived in the newly opened Abbey Theatre this opposition grew to hostile proportions. Maud Gonne walked out of the opening performance and wrote against the play. Some of the actors resigned from the Irish National Theatre Society. Arthur Griffith mounted a damaging attack on *The Shadow of the Glen* in his journal *The United Irishman*. The crux of Griffith's attack was that Synge's play was not Irish at all but a dishonest recycling of the Widow of Ephesus story taken from Petronius and Boccaccio. Yeats, coming to Synge's rescue, pointed out that the source of the play was a folk version of the tale heard on Inishmaan and available in Synge's as yet unpublished prose work, *The Aran Islands* (1907). Griffith was not impressed with the tale Synge sent him: it was 'essentially different to the play he insolently calls "In a Wicklow Glen." In the Aran story the wife appears as a callous woman – in Mr. Synge's play the wife is a strumpet' (Frayne and Johnson 1975, p. 336). Unwittingly, Griffith here identifies Synge's originality; ironically, he misses the theme of freedom which Synge celebrates, a theme which actually aligns him with the nationalists (Synge wears his 'home rule' with a difference). It is necessary to refer here to the story Synge was told by Pat Dirane and quotes in *The Aran Islands*, but there is space only to quote the ending. It is told in the first person, and in outline is much as the play narrates up to the point where the husband reveals his ruse to the narrator:

> 'I've got a bad wife, stranger, and I let on to be dead the way I'd catch her goings on.'
>
> Then he got two fine sticks he had to keep down his wife, and he put them at each side of his body, and he laid himself out again as if he was dead.
>
> In half an hour his wife came back and a young man along with her.
>
> Well, she gave him his tea, and she told him he was tired, and he would do right to go and lie down in the bedroom.
>
> The young man went in and the woman sat down to watch by the dead man. A while after she got up and 'Stranger,' says she, 'I'm going in to get the candle out of the room; I'm thinking the young man will be asleep by this time.' She went into the bedroom, but the divil a bit of her came back.
>
> Then the dead man got up, and he took one stick, and he gave the other to myself. We went in and we saw them lying together with her head on his arm.
>
> The dead man hit him a blow with a stick so that the blood out of him leapt up and hit the gallery.
>
> That is my story. (1968, 2, p. 72)

Synge transformed this story radically. In the first place, he made Nora a sympathetic character. Childless, she is at an age when time seems cruelly inexorable and her own life a waste; the ache of modernism is in her every sigh for the past. The audience is allowed to contrast Nora's melancholy awareness with Michael Dara's lack of understanding. He continues to count money while she muses over the fate of the young girls of the area, Mary Brien who has passed her by to become a mother of two 'and another coming on her in three months or four' (1968, 3, p. 51), while Peggy Kavanagh (who seems once to have been a kind of housewife of the year) is now 'walking round on the roads, or sitting in a dirty old house, with no teeth in her mouth, and no sense'. Nora's consciousness of sterility informs her consciousness of her mortality. Moreover, Nora's sensibility channels the feeling to an audience required to understand her despair, grounded in her situation and the remoteness of the setting ('the last cottage' at the top of 'a long glen'). But Nora does not fully perceive Michael Dara's inadequacies and the

action brings her to full perception. Synge dramatises her discover-
ies. She already has an inkling that living with Michael Dara may not
be all that different from living with Dan Burke, but it is the Tramp
who brings her to see how much of a nonentity Michael really is
when weighed against the absent Patch Darcy. Self-preservation is
Michael's priority; when the chips are down he makes for the door.
His failure to protect Nora is a devastating indictment, at least as
revealing as Torvald Helmer's in *A Doll's House*. In the Aran folktale
the lover and the wife copulate and are killed together; by separating
them Synge isolates Nora and lets her see the treachery which has
undone her, just as Christy Mahon was later to see, appalled, the
treachery of Pegeen Mike.

In the second place, the Tramp comes to empathise with Nora,
stands up (literally, 1968, 3, p. 53) against Dan and clears a way for a
new life with Nora. To a significant degree the Tramp and Nora are
twin souls. They share a poetic awareness of the loneliness of the
glen, where 'shadow' signifies death (as in the biblical valley of the
shadow of death); they mutually admire Patch Darcy and share in
his horror of the 'back hills', a madness-inducing area. In Synge's
source there was no Tramp, only the narrator himself, an honoured
member of the community, whose point of view coincided with
that of the husband in the story. By making the visitor a tramp
Synge breaks up this collusion. He conceives the Tramp as an artist
figure. In 'The Vagrants of Wicklow', an essay written *c*. 1901–2,
Synge commented on the prevalence of gifted younger sons on the
Irish roads and on the romantic lives they led: 'In all the circumstances of this tramp life there is a certain wildness that gives it
romance and a peculiar value for those who look at life in Ireland
with an eye that is aware of the arts also' (1968, 2, p. 208). Synge was
himself a younger son and at one with the tramps he here describes.
He commonly signed his love letters to Molly Allgood, 'Ever your
Tramp', or 'Your old Tramp' (e.g., 1983–4, 1, pp. 234–47), a code
related to Molly's having played Nora at the Abbey early in 1906.
Obviously, then, Synge identified ironically with the Tramp in the
play, whose fine talk is dismissed as 'blather'. Yet although the
Tramp sees that Michael Dara is a misfit as a sheepfarmer it is left to
the audience to see that this lack of understanding undermines
Michael's status as lover. Synge's skill as playwright lies in the emancipation of the audience as well as of his main characters.

Finally, Dan reverses his view of Michael: 'I was thinking to strike you, Michael Dara, but you're a quiet man, God help you, and I don't mind you at all' (1968, 3, p. 59). In total contrast to the ending of the folktale, the two men sit down to drink together, Michael pledging Dan's health and long life, as a new collusion is formed within the establishment. The irony is deeply provocative and the nationalists were right to be shocked, although they were shocked for the wrong reasons. They missed the Ibsenist thrust of the play. Yeats saw it, for he wrote to John Quinn in New York that the fight for Synge would in future be like that 'over the first realistic plays of Ibsen' (Wade 1954, p. 448).

Synge's dramatising of perception is even more powerful in *The Well of the Saints*, his first full-length play, written 1904–5. It is a harsh, narrow-based piece with none of the colour of Synge's more popular plays. The harshness was deliberate. Synge told Willie Fay, who directed the first production on 4 February 1905, that he wanted to write 'like a monochrome painting, all in shades of one color' (Greene and Stephens 1959, p. 175). The one colour was grey. In the schematic structure of the play, with Act I set in autumn, Act II in winter and Act III in spring, there is also a triple conception of the 'well'. There is the real well on stage, used by Timmy for his forge, a holy well off-stage and far away which is the source (literally) of the Saint's holy and miraculous water. And there is the invisible well of the imagination, source of inner vision and inspiration for Martin Doul's final revolutionary action. The play provides a representation of these three forms of perception and, through a pattern of Hegelian thesis, antithesis and synthesis, arrives at an endorsement of the blind people's right to be blind. *The Well of the Saints* is thus a somewhat intellectual style of comedy, in spite of its rather folksy and medieval–farcical trappings.

In Act I Martin and Mary Doul, two beggars (Doul is a phonetic rendering of the Irish *dall*, 'blind'), are cured by an itinerant priest, the Saint. It is the community, led by Timmy the smith, which engineers this miracle, partly in a spirit of mischief: the two blind people have for years been led to believe that each is extraordinarily handsome and the truth will bring some sport. In Act II the couple have fallen out as a consequence of their discovery of each other's plainness and their own deception. Martin has now to work for Timmy for his living; the squalor and hardship quickly make him regret the gift of sight. Synge's representation of the forge and its concerns is masterly as a piece of anti-romantic writing: no horses, no glamour surround this random forge, which makes only utilitarian pothooks without beauty. It is Vulcan's stithy in an Irish setting. Yet within this sordid (naturalistic) context Martin begins to sound a romantic note when his Venus appears in the shape of Molly Byrne, Timmy's intended bride. The irony lies in the discrepant relation between setting and voice. What Martin sounds is the song of the Tramp once again, to come away and forsake the life of Puritan rule for the freedom of the open road, love and nature. 'It's queer talk you have', is Molly's initial response, 'if it's a little, old, shabby stump of a man you are itself' (1968, 3, p. 115). Martin increases his fervour and passionately insists that only those who have known blindness can see fully: he alone has 'fit eyes to look on yourself'. As he delivers this speech Martin puts his hand on Molly's shoulder, shakes her, and speaks 'with low, furious intensity'. He is the poet at full strength: not for nothing was Synge a translator of Petrarch. Elsewhere, Synge remarked that 'The artistic value of any work of art is measured by its uniqueness. Its human value is given largely by its intensity and its richness' (1968, 2, p. 350). Martin translates Molly into a work of art which he must possess. For him she is unique: 'I'm seeing you this day, seeing you, maybe, the way no man has seen you in the world' (p. 117).

When Molly calls for help and, half in terror but half fascinated, tells Timmy of Martin's mad overtures she makes a clear breach between the visionaries (denounced as ridiculous) and the decent folk of the world (incensed at being abused). The blind are now turned into a category: 'Oh, the blind is wicked people, and it's no lie' (1968, 3, p. 119). Synge makes a dichotomy which corresponds to class division. He does the same in *The Tinker's Wedding*, where, again, the tinker Sarah Byrne tries to cross over and partake of a ritual fetishised by the 'settled' community, namely marriage, and learns the folly of the attempt. From the end of Act II of *The Well of the Saints* the blind couple are in danger of being ostracised. Having lost their sight they are given one more chance in Act III to conform to the standards of vision of the community, when the Saint makes his rounds again. But it is against Martin's will that this final arrangement is made. Disillusioned, he is already outside the pale.

If in Act II the conflict lies between realism and aestheticism, the quotidian and the poetic, in Act III the conflict is between this aestheticism and the asceticism of the Saint. Yeats reported: 'He [Synge] once said to me, "We must unite asceticism, stoicism, ecstasy; two of these have often come together, but not all three"' (1961a, p. 308). In writing *The Well of the Saints* Synge dramatised this triad. Martin Doul confronts the Saint with the fruits of his spiritual power: 'What was it I seen my first day, but your own bleeding feet and they cut with the stones, and my last day, but the villainy of herself [Molly] that you're wedding, God forgive you, with Timmy the smith' (1968, 3, p. 141). These references to first and last days have a biblical ring, just as Act II undeniably concludes with an evocation of the Last Judgement. Synge is establishing a site in which to debate belief as well as art. The vision which the Saint offers is a version of coercive orthodoxy, by which the world is subordinated to divine will. It is Dante's theologically orthodox formulation: *In la sua volontade è nostra pace* (*Paradiso*, iii, 85). But what if in his will is *not* our peace? Has not the individual the right to erect or select his/her own 'Paradise within'? Martin asserts that he and Mary can look up 'in our own minds' into the sky, 'seeing lakes, and broadening rivers, and hills' (p. 141). Why should they not give allegiance to an imagined world? Rest upon a belief which is individually willed? Timmy warns that the wilful choice of blindness will meet with society's rejection of Martin and Mary. It is civilisation versus eros. Martin is determined: 'if it's a right some of you have to be working and sweating … and to be fasting and praying … it's a good right ourselves have to be sitting blind' (p. 149). And with a violent, revolutionary gesture Martin knocks over the Saint's can of holy water and ends the possibility of cure and social assimilation. 'They have chosen their lot', the Saint intones more in sorrow than in anger, as the blind couple, Synge's ironic portrayal of Adam and Eve unparadis'd, grope their way hand in hand out of conventional society and off-stage. Synge always leaves the audience in possession of the stage, while suggesting that the world off-stage (existing only in the imagination), exile or the unacceptable road, may have a lot more to be said for it, fictional though it be. Timmy knows the dangers the blind couple face and that 'the two of them will be drowned in a short while, surely' (p. 151). Thus there is nothing sentimental about the final choice; indeed, it may be seen as heroic. Like Nora's venturing forth with the Tramp at the end of *The Shadow of the Glen*, it is a wide-awake acceptance of the hardships of nature in preference over the death-in-life offered by society. It is the artist's writing of a new Ireland.

It is also the artistic option for ecstasy and death, an option given a tragic interpretation in *Riders to the Sea* and *Deirdre of the Sorrows*. In the one 'it is the life of a young man to be going on the sea', his choice as well as his fate (1968, 3, p. 11); in the other, 'it is the choice of lives we had in the clear woods, and in the grave we're safe surely' (1968, 4, pp. 267–9). In Synge's tragedies, underpinned by Nietzsche's dialectic of Apollo and Dionysus from *The Birth of Tragedy* (1872), the song of liberation has a deeper, more sombre melody, but it is still, as in the comedies, a song of deliverance. It is just that the horror of mortality is now redeemed by the sweet power of music. And music is what lay at the heart of Synge's drama from the outset, for Colm Sweeney, the hero of *When the Moon Has Set*, like Synge himself, interpreted the world in terms of symphony.

Synge's masterpiece, *The Playboy of the Western World* (1907), encompasses the full gamut of his extraordinary powers. Here all features of his art converge: the politics, the fascination with perception and perspective, the challenge to established notions of comedy and tragedy, the exploitation of language in an age of realism. The play is so rich in these and other resources that it defies satisfactory exegesis: it is the *Hamlet* of the Irish dramatic tradition. The pursuit of any one coherent reading immediately leaves exposed vast areas awaiting further excavation. Everything said about *The Playboy* must therefore be provisional. That is both the attraction of the text and its frustrating mark of plenitude. In this regard, the most significant thing Synge himself said about the play is not the oft-quoted preface but the letter to the *Irish Times* following an unfortunate interview in which he had said – referring to the riots – 'I don't care a rap how the people take it':

> 'The Playboy of the Western World' is not a play with 'a purpose' in the modern sense of the word, but although parts of it are, or are meant to be, extravagant comedy, still a great deal that is in it, and a great deal more that is behind it, is perfectly serious, when looked at in a certain light. That is often the case, I think, with comedy, and no one is quite sure to-day whether 'Shylock' and 'Alceste' should be played seriously or not. There are, it may be hinted, several sides to 'The Playboy'.
>
> (1983–4, 1, p. 286)

Upon that hint one may perhaps speak. In 1904 Bernard Shaw presented Yeats with a new play for a new theatre, *John Bull's Other Island*. It was a seminal text in modern Irish drama, a paradigm in many respects of the dream-*vs.*-mirror conflict destined to pre-occupy both content and form. Yet the play was rejected as being beyond the resources of the Abbey stage. Shaw, of course, insisted on believing that Yeats took fright at having been given rather more than he had bargained for: a representation of 'the real old Ireland' at odds with 'the whole spirit of the neo-Gaelic movement, which is bent on creating a new Ireland after its own ideal' (1963, 2, p. 443). Shaw's comedy is, indeed, satirical and debunking in style. It deconstructs the idea of the Irish peasant carefully assembled by nationalists and the Gaelic League. Synge can hardly have been unaware of the play in 1904; certainly he had no time for it when it played in Dublin in 1907: 'I do not feel the slightest inclination to go and see Shaw – I'd rather keep my money for Esposito's concert tomorrow and hear something that is really stirring and fine and beautiful' (1983–4, 2, p. 84).

As he disliked Ibsen so Synge must equally have disliked Shaw, Ibsen's champion in England. And yet they were akin in some important respects and it will be argued here that this unallowed kinship offers a fruitful means of reading *The Playboy*. As prelude to this theme it may be pointed out that in 1905 Synge wrote 'National Drama: A Farce', never finished or published (until 1968), which is quite in Shaw's satirical vein. It is Synge's revenge against those who queried his credentials as an Irish playwright and author of *The Shadow of the Glen*. (As with many writers, Synge found stimulus in the motive of revenge.) Members of a nationalist club meet to debate the question, 'What is an Irish Drama?' While waiting for others to arrive one Fogarty browses among the bookshelves:

> How to be a Genius, by a Gaelic Leaguer. The Pedigree of the Widow of Ephesus. The complete works of Petronius and Boccaccio, unabridged. The Plays for an Irish Theatre, abridged and expurgated by a Catholic critic. ... Fairy Tales for all Ages. The Dawn of the Twilight, and The Autumn of Spring. (1968, 3, p. 221).

Quite Shavian. So, too, the speech Murphy launches into:

> An Irish drama gentlemen is a Drama that embodies in a finished form the pageant of Irish life, and shines throughout with the soft light of the ideal impulses of the Gaels, a drama in short which contains the manifold and fine qualities of the Irish race, their love for the land of their forefathers, and their poetic familiarity with the glittering and unseen forms of the visionary world. ... Take Molière, for instance, is Molière a national dramatist?
> FLAHERTY. Not a bit of him, wasn't he always making fun of his own

country, till the holy bishop wouldn't take his corpse when he was dead. (1968, 3, p. 222)

We bear in mind that Shaw is sometimes regarded as the Molière of modern drama. Synge's sympathy for Molière here, and elsewhere, brings him closer to Shaw than he was prepared to acknowledge.

Yet a comparison with *John Bull's Other Island* shows how much Synge, in his anxiety to avoid the agenda of a 'problem' play, left out of his purview in writing *The Playboy*. Shaw openly confronts two issues: the ownership of the land of Ireland and the sectarian conflict between Catholics and Protestants. In Act III Shaw shows quite clearly that the Land Purchase Act (1903) failed to get to the root of the problem. Unless the weakest link in the chain, the farm labourers, were given a decent (i.e. a living) wage, then the new landlords, the small Irish famers who had purchased the leasehold, would simply perpetuate the old injustice by their self-interest. Moreover, unless it is realised that 'in Ireland the people is the [Catholic] Church and the Church the people' (1963, 2, p. 563) it is pointless to seek to change conditions: one must bring the Church into the revolution for a new, democratic state. What Shaw had to say, in his play as well as his prefaces, is still relevant to Irish–English relations today; in 1904 and in the years which followed what he had to say was both burningly topical and prophetic. Synge sidestepped the issues Shaw faced, but it may be seen that these issues nevertheless underlie *The Playboy*.

Synge's articles written in 1905 for the *Manchester Guardian* on the Congested (i.e. impoverished) Districts of the West of Ireland cover the territory which gives a local habitation and half a name to his greatest play. In those articles Synge reveals a mind critically aware of the economic factors underlying the deprivation in west Mayo. To his friend Stephen McKenna he added: 'Unluckily my commission was to write on the "Distress" so I couldn't do anything like what I would have wished to do as an interpretation of the whole life. ... There are sides of all that western life, the groggy-patriot-publican-general-shop-man who is married to the priest's half-sister and is second cousin once-removed of the dispensary doctor, that are horrible and awful. This is the type that is running the present United Irish League anti-grazier campaign' (1983–4, 1, p. 116). It was the mixture of respectability and corruption which incensed Synge. A nexus of political power is exposed. Synge translated this perception into comic terms in his play. Specific examples are the consanguinity of Pegeen and Shawn Keogh (who as cousins require a dispensation to marry, and so seem to justify a rival in Christy), and the background figures of the mad Mulrannies and the hypo-critical Marcus Quinn. More in delight than in Shavian prurience Synge parades the grotesque qualities of the Mayo peasants, not excluding the Widow Quinn. The grotesque note, as Toni Johnson (1982) has shown, gives Synge's humour a particular distinction, but in the end it is the self-interest of the Mayo community which is laid bare. As Synge later wrote to McKenna, 'The story – in its ESSENCE – is probable, given the psychic state of the locality' (1983–4, 1, p. 333).

The dramatic precedent for *The Playboy* lay in the comedies of William Boyle (1853–1923), *The Building Fund* (1905), *The Eloquent Dempsy* (1906) and *The Mineral Workers* (1906), all highly successful at the Abbey. These mocked and exposed political chicanery at the local, rural level. Synge had recommended Boyle's first play to a reluctant Yeats, and helped to re-write *The Eloquent Dempsy*. He wrote to Yeats about Boyle's characters: 'Your brother [Jack] and I saw something of these kind of people when we were away for the *Manchester Guardian*. They are colossal in their vulgarity' (Saddlemyer 1982, p. 78). The roots, in turn, of *The Eloquent Dempsy*, as Lennox Robinson observed (1951, p. 14), lay in Ibsen's *An Enemy of the People*. Therefore, what Synge's playboy finally emerges as is 'an enemy of the people'. The question is, of which people? This is where the real originality of the comedy lies, in its evasion of the easy categories of its predecessors. Boyle, as a good Catholic, was furious over *The Playboy* ('false to the verge of absurdity') and imme-diately withdrew his three money-spinning plays from the Abbey repertoire.

Politically, Aran was Synge's real social model. It gave him the standard by which to measure the flaws in Irish rural life. In the Aran scenario the landlords, agents and police were all off-stage and a classless society seemed to be on offer for Synge to join as an equal. Yet when he describes an eviction on Aran Synge can see that the police, agents, sheriffs and others who come over from the main-land represent 'the civilisation for which the homes of the island were to be desecrated' (1968, 2, p. 89). But he suppressed all such agents of 'civilisation' in his plays. Even the priest in *The Tinker's Wedding* (published after the storm over *The Playboy* but written years earlier) is made to sit and drink at night with the tinkers, which shows his humanity but discounts his class sense. In *Riders to the Sea* and in *The Playboy* alike the priest is kept carefully off stage, in addition to the police and the landlords in *The Playboy*. Where Shaw asserts in the 1906 preface to *John Bull's Other Island* that 'there can be no more sacred and urgent political duty on earth than the disruption, defeat, and suppression of the Empire' (1963, 2, p. 492), Synge holds off from any such declaration. For Shaw, Home Rule was 'a necessity not only for Ireland, but for all constituents of those Federations of Commonwealths which are now the only permanently practicable form of Empire' (p. 495). Synge wrote as if the Empire was not a problem; he had other fish to fry. And yet one of the first reviewers of *The Playboy* thought in a puzzled way that 'the parricide represents some kind of nation-killer, whom Irishmen and Irish women hasten to lionise' (*Evening Mail*, cited Kilroy, 1971, p. 13). Another reviewer (*Irish Times*) said that *The Playboy* revealed to its first audiences 'terrible truths, of our own making, which we dare not face for the present' (p. 37). Certainly, freedom is a theme in the play, even though the authority figure confronted (Old Mahon) is not overtly politicised, in spite of his broken 'crown'.

In his negotiation between actuality and art Synge at first laid stress on the documentary nature of *The Playboy*. In a programme note, which differs from the preface later published, he defended his language as taken from the speech of the people, which is a little disingenuous considering Synge's exaggerations and prose rhythms (Bliss 1972, Reynolds 1972). It is quite clear that the language of *The Playboy* is a construct, indebted to Irish (Kiberd 1993). But there was another area also in which Synge played off realism against artifice. This was in the pretence that, as he put it in his programme note, 'The central incident of *The Playboy* was suggested by an actual occurrence in the west' (Hogan and Kilroy 1978, p. 124). There were in fact two incidents he drew on as sources for his murder story. He describes in *The Aran Islands* how 'a Connaught man who killed his father with the blow of a spade when he was in passion' was smuggled away to America. Synge commented: 'This impulse to protect the criminal is universal in the west. It seems partly due to the association between justice and the hated English jurisdiction' (1968, 2, p. 95). The funny side of this social fact (for Synge took it as fact) became the starting point of *The Playboy*. The other incident was a better-known case. James Lynchehaun, a Mayo man from

Achill, was imprisoned for the attempted murder of Mrs Agnes MacDonnell, a landowner, and escaped in 1902. He was arrested in America in 1903 and there followed an extradition case which led to his release in May 1904, the year Synge first visited Mayo and heard of this colourful character. Once more, this was no laughing matter, the injuries suffered by Mrs MacDonnell being horrific, but Synge gestures jokingly to the affair in Act II where Sara Tansey is said to have driven ten miles to see 'the man bit the yellow lady's nostril on the northern shore' (p. 97). As James Carney has established (1986, p. 208), this is a reference to Lynchehaun and Mrs MacDonnell.

The joke of having an anti-heroic parricide welcomed and lauded by a village community depends firmly on the fourth-wall convention in the theatre. The audience watches in varying degrees of disbelief while the absurd situation is established. The irony demands a lack of awareness of those on stage, Christy's audience. The play develops as a play about playing. The characters stay within the confines of the established illusion in order to keep the game alive. Thus in the opening scene nobody on stage picks up on the incongruities in Christy's language. The absurdity of a law-abiding murderer is left for the audience to perceive. The greater absurdity, of course, lies in Christy's being appointed pot-boy to protect Pegeen's virtue. The only one to protest is Shawn Keogh, already disabled as witness through his laughable cowardice, neatly correlated with his religious orthodoxy. The off-stage Father Reilly, moreover, is discredited as moral arbiter through his being invoked so repeatedly by 'Shawneen' (the diminutive is scornful). Thus the audience's orthodox moral position, which would normally incline towards Shawn's, is undercut and the audience is left little choice but to rejoice with the others on stage at Christy's disclosure. A moral issue is brazenly made fun of and the audience is implicated in the conspiracy. This technique is used repeatedly.

Synge was thus elaborating a joke at the audience's expense. It happened that the first audiences (26 January 1907 and following nights for a total of eight performances) were in part gunning for Synge, but he was in any case blatantly trailing his coat. He had the courage to write what David Krause (1982) usefully calls 'profane' comedy, subversive of sacred things. In addition, as Conor Cruise O'Brien has argued (1972, pp. 72–4), *The Playboy* discovered a complex set of attitudes in Synge's audience, six groups, in fact, within the confines of the coloniser/colonised matrix, so that just about everybody had some reason to be offended. Clearly, O'Brien sees the sectarian issue, so openly acknowledged by Shaw, as at the heart of the matter. The 'people' of whom Christy ends up an enemy were the native, colonised people of rural Ireland. The protests against the play came from those Catholic nationalists who felt affronted by this representation of the 'people' with whom they identified. Doubtless, this is what Shaw meant when he said that 'The Playboy's real name was Synge; and the famous libel on Ireland (and who is Ireland that she should not be libeled as other countries are by their great comedians?) was the truth about the world' (1962, p. 84). Thus the effect of The Playboy in 1907 was, as the *Irish Times* critics noted, 'as if we looked in a mirror for the first time, and found ourselves hideous' (Kilroy 1971, p. 38). Synge held the mirror up to an incipient nation.

The Playboy ends ambiguously. The community, sheltering from 'the treachery of law,' can once again 'have peace now for our drinks' (1968, 4, p. 173). Instead of the formation of a new social nucleus symbolised through the marriage the audience has been led to expect at the end of a comedy (Frye 1957, p. 163), we have the bad marriage imminent at the beginning. The energy of the play goes out with Christy triumphant, driving his father before him like a heathen slave and destined to go Dionysiacally 'romancing through a romping lifetime'. Pegeen is left destitute; her final expression of 'grief' is closer to tragedy than to comedy. The dissonance is allowed to reverberate.

Thus the ending is ironic in the modern mode which we probably associate more with Chekhov than with Shaw. Yet *John Bull's Other Island*, too, has its dark side and its ambivalent ending. The benefits Broadbent will bring to rural Ireland will all be at the expense of dream and vision, albeit 'the dream of a madman,' Peter Keegan (Shaw 1963, 2, p. 611). The triumph of realism is at the expense of the romance of idealism. Shaw champions the former but cannot disguise the attraction of the latter. Synge shares this ironic vision but turns it around to face the other way. Out go the dreamer and madman, Christy and Old Mahon, while the realists remain holding the stage as the lights go down on Pegeen's heart-break.

In the preface to *The Tinker's Wedding* Synge said that 'The drama, like the symphony, does not teach or prove anything' (1968, 4, p. 3). Yet if a drama cannot teach it cannot offend either: both effects presuppose active audience response. One must not take what Synge says in his prefaces as gospel: apart from the tell-tale strictures on Ibsen there is the condemnation of Baudelaire's Satanic laughter and morbidity, a combination which sums up Synge's own artistic temperament very well. The final irony, therefore, may well be that Synge rather than Shaw is the great artist-as-teacher in Irish drama. After all, in a piece quaintly titled 'Can We Go Back into Our Mother's Womb?', written after the *Playboy* riots and addressed to the Gaelic League, Synge prophesied that a writer would soon appear who could 'teach Ireland again that she is part of Europe, and teach Irishmen that they have wits to think, imaginations to work miracles, and souls to possess with sanity' (1968, 2, p. 400). That man had already arrived, and his lessons were to shape the course of modern Irish drama. Alongside Yeats and Lady Gregory, Synge thus created an art form which enabled the nation to grow into violent self-discovery.

4

O'Casey: in search of a hero

> Unhappy the land that is in need of heroes
> Brecht, *The Life of Galileo* (1947)

Introduction

From the perspective of the 1990s O'Casey stands out as Ireland's greatest playwright of the century. He it was who most passionately, most powerfully and most memorably dramatised the traumatic birth of the nation. He it was who gave to the twentieth-century theatre a greater range of vivid and original characters, male and female, than any other Irish playwright. O'Casey's language, controversial though it may be in some critical circles, is a third feature of his work which for its richness, colour and vitality has won for him a lasting place in the international repertory. Because O'Casey is a great entertainer, in the style of energetic and enlivening theatre which Peter Brook (1968) has made it a compliment to call 'rough', his plays, especially the three Dublin plays (*The Shadow of a Gunman*, *Juno and the Paycock* and *The Plough and the Stars*), have steadfastly held the stage worldwide since the mid-1920s.

There are other features of O'Casey's work which go to explain his endurance. He was the first English-speaking dramatist to make the poor, the uneducated and the dispossessed the subjects of modern tragicomedy. To be sure, his art rode on the coat-tails of nineteenth-century naturalism in this regard: the plays of Hauptmann (*The Weavers*), Gorki (*The Lower Depths*) and Shaw (*Widowers' Houses*) had shown how drama might be created out of the lives and social circumstances of ordinary, socially insignificant characters. Moreover, Chekhov had shown (from *The Seagull* onwards) that the form of modern drama need not adhere to the traditional constraints of hero, plot and text-book resolution, but that form itself could reflect the desultory and random patterns of conversation and of life. Drama might be neither classically tragic nor classically comic in form but excitingly and ironically combined to express the massive shifts in consciousness and experience introduced by philosophical and social upheavals and the age of revolution dating from the 1860s.

O'Casey, of course, was an instinctive, self-taught writer, and mercifully free from academic influences. He is always closer to the popular tradition than consciously in line with intellectually accredited dramatic developments (Watt 1991). Yet it would be foolish to deny his openness to the currents of modern theatre and its wide and varied innovations. The essays collected by Ronald Ayling under the title *Blasts and Benedictions* (O'Casey 1967) give some small idea of O'Casey's osmotic powers in this regard; his *Letters*, so ably edited in four volumes by David Krause, offer further evidence of O'Casey's lively range of interests. From Strindberg to Beckett, from Gorki to Arden, from O'Neill to Osborne, he was fully aware of the trends and experiments in modern drama. The major influences, however, were Shaw, Strindberg and O'Neill in the international theatre, Boucicault, Yeats and Synge in the Irish theatre. O'Casey takes his place alongside these writers and significantly modifies not only the Irish tradition down to Friel and McGuinness but leaves a legacy from which playwrights as diverse as Clifford Odets (*Awake and Sing!, Paradise Lost*), and Arnold Wesker (*Chicken Soup and Barley, Roots, I'm Not Talking about Jerusalem*) have drawn. Thus O'Casey has stood at the centre of modern developments in the theatre.

In addition, there was always Shakespeare, whose plays O'Casey came to know in the 1890s, when he acted alongside his brother Archie in amateur productions. Next to the Bible, Shakespeare is probably the greatest literary influence on O'Casey's plays: the history plays, in particular, offered him a model for dramatising politics colourfully. His general view of Shakespeare, however, was far from idolatrous; he was quite impatient, when he lived in England, with the gentility of the productions he saw. He believed in a Shakespeare for the workers, a Shakespeare stripped of the cultural trappings which, until the 1960s, rendered the plays elitist. For to O'Casey culture was neither aestheticism nor purely a literary preoccupation. 'What is called Culture isn't just the theatre here, the other arts there, music yonder: Culture is the life we live ... always

with us in field, factory, and workshop as well as on a stage'
(O'Casey 1967, p. 77). Tyrone Guthrie, as Shakespearean director,
was the man for his money: he was the one to direct O'Casey's *The
Bishop's Bonfire* in Dublin in 1955. It was the epic, medieval-style
populism of Shakespeare's form which appealed to O'Casey, as well
as the richness of language which stayed with him always. John
Arden, whose own early plays O'Casey admired, has claimed that
the cultural basis of O'Casey's work was 'a combination of mediae-
val morality-play, Shakespeare, Bunyan, and Victorian popular
melodrama' in the service of 'a new analysis of society' (Kilroy 1975,
pp. 76, 73). This view contextualises well O'Casey's passionate regard for and influence by Shakespeare.

There is a lasting perception among critics that O'Casey's work
fell off in quality once he left Ireland in 1926. He himself fought hard
and with characteristic irony ('Tender Tears for Poor O'Casey')
against this judgement. But in spite of the championing of his later
plays by Shaw, Tyrone Guthrie and Tomás MacAnna, as well as by
fiercely loyal supporters such as George Jean Nathan and Brooks
Atkinson, the plays from *The Silver Tassie* (1929) on have not had a
worthy reception. They remain undeservedly neglected, especially
in Ireland. For not only are these plays so full of theatrical energy
and daring that they cry out for new directors to take them in hand
and (with judicious cutting) rediscover their potential, but they
stand also as powerful social and cultural critiques. Tomás MacAnna
has done well to bring onto the new Abbey stage lively productions
of *Red Roses for Me*, *The Star Turns Red*, *Purple Dust* and even *The
Drums of Father Ned*, but until the language of criticism gets away
from the old, predictable insistence on realism as the only criterion
by which to measure O'Casey, the later plays are unlikely to enter
the repertory in the same way as the three Dublin plays. In other
words, until theatre criticism becomes less literary and conventional
tender tears will continue to be shed for poor O'Casey. There may
be fresh hope, however, for a breakthrough in attitude in the new
O'Casey Theater Company founded by his daughter Shivaun in
1991 and based in Derry, which has begun to tackle the problem by
moving from the familiar, the so-called trilogy, to the strange,
O'Casey's last full-length play, *Behind the Green Curtains*.

O'Casey's lasting work had all to do with fullness of life in an Irish
context. This claim necessarily subordinates *Within the Gates* (1933)
and *Oak Leaves and Lavender* (1947), both written for and about

O'Casey: in search of a hero

England in the wake of one world war, and in the throes of another. An Irish setting was vital to the full engagement of O'Casey's imagination. The creative tension in his plays was between ideas of nationhood and international socialism; on another level this tension can be defined as that between didacticism and art. The division is crucial. O'Casey was essentially at war with himself in a complex and enriching way; enriching, that is, for his plays: the realist/satirist was at odds with the idealist/fantasist. The patriot and the apostate vied for supremacy so that the voice of the prophet might be heard. In the end, O'Casey cared too much about Ireland to be merely the comic nihilist he is sometimes taken to be. In short, O'Casey's drama embodies not only his own biography but the contradictory course of national self-definition. In his plays the coming of age of the new Irish state is graphically recorded.

In this chapter the focus is on O'Casey's search for a hero. Among the four speeches made by the Speaker outside the window in *The Plough and the Stars* (1926) is one celebrating the outbreak of World War 1: 'The last sixteen months have been the most glorious in the history of Europe. *Heroism has come back to the earth*' (1949, 1, p. 202, emphasis added) .The lines are taken from Patrick Pearse's address in 1915, 'Peace and the Gael'. The actor who first played the Speaker mimicked Pearse's voice and mannerisms; there has never, in the Abbey tradition, been an attempt to present the Speaker ironically. O'Casey allowed Pearse's words to have their full effect (although he did, in fact, omit two sentences which make a difference to the meaning), which is to celebrate bloodshed in a nationalist cause as heroic. The play itself, of course, overturns that notion. There is therefore a basic dichotomy between outside and inside the barroom window, between official ideology and individual experience. Out of that clash, variously and entertainingly represented, O'Casey created great drama. At the same time he mounted a powerful critique of 'heroism'. In order to understand the roots of that critique it is necessary to go back to O'Casey's first extant play, *The Harvest Festival*, submitted to the Abbey about 1918. It will then be possible to explore more fruitfully the three Dublin plays, and after that *Red Roses for Me* (1943), where O'Casey's notion of heroism is startlingly revised.

The Harvest Festival

That *The Harvest Festival* is not a good play need not be any embar-rassment. As the sole surviving early play among the five submitted to the Abbey before *The Shadow of a Gunman* (1923) it has its own historic importance. Its publication in 1979, in time for the O'Casey centenary in 1980, was thus something of an event; for here was a play thought lost until after O'Casey's death in 1964, when it was found among his papers and sold to the New York Public Library.

What is useful about *The Harvest Festival* is that it shows the martyrdom of a young political activist in a context which has nothing to do with nationalism. This is noteworthy because from 1913 on, the year of the Dublin General Strike and Lock-out, O'Casey was actively involved in reconciling militant republicanism with trade unionism. Because *The Harvest Festival* is set at the outbreak of a serious strike in Dublin in which there is a marked class difference between skilled and unskilled workers, the year seems to be 1913. But the national cause, Home Rule, is never mentioned. The hero, Jack Rocliffe, is a version of the O'Casey self-portrait as found in *Pictures in the Hallway* (1942). He lives with his 76-year-old mother, and is rabidly outspoken against the (Protes-tant) church. The battle is really between the church and the trade union for the possession of Jack's soul. The Rector, for his part, is just the kindly sort of liberal O'Casey celebrates in *Pictures in the Hallway* as the Rector of St Barnabas's Church, Revd E. M. Griffin, who is surrounded in parish politics by bigots and reactionaries. When Jack is killed by a 'scab' worker his body is not allowed into the Rector's church, as bigotry overrules tolerance. In disgust, Jack's mother condemns the Rector: 'You are just as bad as the rest of them; you are afraid to go again' them ... My poor, poor Jack was right – the Church is always again' the workin'-class' (O'Casey 1980, p. 63). The workers then bring the body to the trade union hall (Liberty Hall), to the strains of 'We'll keep the red flag flying here'. (All of this was to provide the raw material for *Red Roses for Me* in 1942.) This last reference indicates a date after 1917, a significant key to the way O'Casey wrote. He constantly shuffled and rearranged dates so that the point of view offered within a text was actually a revised, anachronistic one in line with his more mature reflection, but it gives the impression of sleight of hand. For by 1918, when the Bolshevik revolution converted O'Casey unequivocally to international socialism, the Irish Rising was over and Sinn Féin was about to sweep Labour aside in the general election leading to the formation of the first Dáil. In *Inishfallen, Fare Thee Well* (1949) O'Casey declared that the 'terrible beauty had been born there [in the Soviet Union], and not in Ireland', and that he, Sean, 'stood with these children, with these workers, with these Red Army Men' (O'Casey 1956, 2, p. 220). Clearly, this enthusiasm found its way into *The Harvest Festival,* as when Jack enthuses over the particular 'fight for human freedom' in which he is engaged: 'At last in Ireland the workers have begun to knit the first strands of the Red Cap, which is the only crown for the head of Graunuaile' (O'Casey 1980, p. 31). Little of this was true in 1913. O'Casey uses the interval to revise history.

Because of this internal dating, *The Harvest Festival* suggests that there was a moment *circa*1918 when a working-class revolution was about to challenge and overturn the alliance between church and bourgeoisie in Dublin. For that purpose a hero dies and offers a hero's example for the transformation of society. Apart from everything else, O'Casey's plot lacks plausibility because the church he identifies is Protestant, very much the minority one in Dublin. When he rewrote this material as *Red Roses for Me* he took good care to introduce a strong Catholic dimension. Moreover, what is implied by *The Harvest Festival* is O'Casey's need to blot out the complexities which led to James Connolly's decision in 1916 that the national question must first be solved before the labour question could properly be addressed. By airbrushing out the national question O'Casey created space for a fantasy: the elevation of a square-jawed, proletarian hero whose sacrifice was in itself a 'harvest festival', a ritual to quicken a new birth of socialism.

Moreover, as Ayling has emphasised, *The Harvest Festival* presents 'a vastly different social message from that of the Sinn Féin party which had, by 1918, obtained the foremost political role and voice in the nationalist struggle' (1980, p. 32). The symbolism is the best thing about this crude piece of agit-prop: the Rector's actual harvest festival at the church is paralleled by Jack Rocliffe's metaphorical and secular offering of himself for the *agon* in the street. The conflict is more stark than the mature O'Casey was to provide later in *Red Roses for Me*, where the Rector insists on Ayamonn Breydon's body being admitted to the church as part of the Easter celebrations. Nevertheless, stark as the conflict is in *The Harvest Festival*, it reveals the artist at work, simplifying and modifying actuality, transforming it indeed. Moreover, it was to be O'Casey's strength as playwright, as already stated above, to juxtapose two worlds as here, two realms of experience, so that their interaction created a renewal of images and symbols. He quickly learned, however, to do this with a great deal more subtlety, so that, for example, in the central scene in *Juno and the Paycock* (1924), a wild party goes on in the Boyle's apartment while Tancred's funeral, complete with hymns, simultaneously goes on outside. Out of the clash of moods and the simultaneity of rituals of life and death O'Casey came to create a form of dramatic music all his own.

The fate of *The Harvest Festival* was predictable. The Abbey supplied the verdict that '[t]his play is interestingly conceived but not well executed'. The characters were rightly condemned as conventional and stereotypical; O'Casey was advised 'to try to replace them by figures drawn as accurately as possible from his own experience' (O'Casey 1975, 1, p. 91). To do this O'Casey decentred and even severely undercut his working-class hero in the plays which followed. Jack Rocliffe disappeared, while ex-activists like Seumas Shields and the Covey took to the stage as comic figures, and Jerry Devine in *Juno* is severely criticised as '*a type, becoming very common now in the Labour Movement, of a mind knowing enough to make the mass of his associates, who know less, a power, and too little to broaden that power for the benefit of all*' (O'Casey 1949, 1, p. 8). By learning to take characterisation more seriously than sloganeering O'Casey began to show how well he understood the prioritisation of art.

The Dublin Plays

In the interpretation of O'Casey's Dublin plays it is best to take them in the order of their historical content. This means that *The Plough and the Stars*, set in 1915–16, comes first although staged last of the three plays. In this demythologising play we find O'Casey's dramatisation of the national tragedy as he saw it. It was a revisionist play before ever the term was coined. The Rising, in this account, was the fruit of vanity, demagoguery and romantic idealism, entrenching further the dispossessed into dispossession and the poor into greater poverty. By focusing on the home as central symbol, and fertility or new birth as image of natural relations, O'Casey can show the threat to hearth, home and cradle when Jack Clitheroe goes off to battle and Nora ends up simultaneously out of her mind and her home, having lost her baby as a direct result of the Rising.

Parallel to Nora's tragedy is that of little Mollser, who dies of consumption. Plainly, the text states that Mollser's fate was the one crying out for attention: 'Sure she never had any care. How could she get it, an' th' mother out day an' night lookin' for work, an' her consumptive husband leavin' her with a baby to be born before he died!' (1949, 1, p. 241). Mollser is buried along with Nora's stillborn baby, to emphasise the link between the two deaths, which the Rising did nothing to prevent. Mollser's role may be minor but her comments go to the heart of what the play has to say. At the end of Act I, frightened to be by herself, she makes her way into the Clitheroe flat to talk to Nora, whom Jack has just deserted. It is one of those delicate moments O'Casey is surprisingly good at conveying. Mollser, ignorant of the turmoil in the Clitheroe household, envies Nora her health and (from her perspective) status, and wonders 'if I'll ever be sthrong enough to be keepin' a home together for a man' (p. 190). Keeping a home together is the principal action of the play. Mollser breaks off her musings to listen to the brass band outside (a Chekhovian touch) and the Dublin Fusiliers 'lustily singing' on their way to the front, 'It's a long way to Tipperary'. At the end of the play we are reminded of this wider context of 1916 as the soldiers at a barricade off-stage sing another song from World War One, Novello's 'Keep the home fires burning'. Novello's biographer says it became and remained 'a national song' (Macqueen-Pope 1954, p. 55). Of course, he meant an *English* national song. Shaw had ended *Heartbreak House* (1921) with the same tune used ironically, as the German Zeppelins droned over Sussex. O'Casey takes Shaw's ending and reapplies it to his own 'heartbreak house', a tenement in Dublin overwhelmed not by German invaders but by a form of stupidity and delusion comparable to those attacked by Shaw. O'Casey's irony is double, however, because Dublin is at one further remove from the front and the 'home fire' at which Sergeant Tinley and Corporal Stoddart sit and sip the tea lately made by Nora in the belief that she was in her own home is that of Bessie Burgess, the loyalist whose son is, indeed, fighting at the front. All is connected. Corporal Stoddart agrees with the Covey's charge that Mollser's death is attributable to the class system but claims that although he is a socialist himself he has to do his 'dooty', and that 'a man's a man' and has to fight for his country (1949, 1, p. 249). Here the dilemma is neatly laid out in preparation for Brecht to explore further the good soldier's folly in *Mann ist Mann* (1926).

Whereas it may give the impression of arbitrariness in its plot structure, *The Plough and the Stars* is in fact unified in theme and structure to an intense degree in the modernist mode. The references just made to Chekhov, Shaw and Brecht merely indicate that O'Casey's imagination was very much in tune with the ironies and formal strategies of the greatest innovators in modern drama. But he worked through the form of a play in accordance with the pressure of his own convictions. This pressure led him to make associations on several levels at once and by that means to provide what Brecht was to call 'complex seeing' (Willett 1964, p. 44). Of course, that kind of fresh vision was to cause uproar among the first audiences of *The Plough and the Stars* in February 1926; it would have been strange had it been otherwise, since the play was an open attack on the ideology of republicanism.

Alongside the imagery of 'home' cited above, signifying its desecration in the name of protection, is the imagery of fertility. On the comic level, Uncle Peter is often referred to in the text as childish, and his soldiering no more than juvenile dressing-up: 'it's a baby's rattle he ought to have' (1949, 1, p. 167). In Act II Mrs Gogan's baby becomes the centre of a brawl in a public house, is abandoned by its [*sic*] mother and ends up abandoned in Uncle Peter's reluctant arms. Not long afterwards Rosie sings her bawdy song which delivers 'a bright bouncin' boy ... dancin' a jig in th' bed' after only one night's love-making (p. 214). These babies have a grotesque textual existence, which brings them into such contrast with the political ferment all around them (the meeting) as to make their origins a challenge to the death-wish being urged by the Speaker outside and the three uniformed men inside the public house. Nora's miscarriage in Act III extends further this metaphor of nature perverted through misguided militarism. Again, in a comic vein, the misuse of the baby carriage to facilitate the looting serves to reinforce this sequence of images. Thus the basic contradictions in the play are elaborated by means of organic imagery.

Jack Clitheroe is nominally the hero of *The Plough and the Stars*. But as he has only six lines in Act II, twenty-six in Act III, and none at all in Act IV, one is entitled to regard him as somewhat less important dramatically than, say, Fluther or Bessie or the Covey, who appear in all four acts. The focus of the play remains on the non-participants in the Rising, those who are reactive rather than proactive. The very concept of heroism is undermined through the characterisation of Jack Clitheroe, whose measure Jinny Gogan clearly gauges at the opening of the play when she pokes fun at his desire to be conspicuous. As Nora tells him when he is promoted and about to abandon domesticity, 'Your vanity'll be th' ruin of you an' me yet' (1949, 1, p. 189). Yet when he meets her in the street during the Rising Jack tells her frankly that he wishes he had never left her. He is presented here as torn between love and duty but robbed of dignity. Brennan, his subordinate, sneers openly, 'Break her hold on you, man, or go up, an' sit on her lap!' (p. 236). A more unheroic situation is hardly imaginable. The same Brennan relates Clitheroe's miserable end in Act IV and in flagrant contradiction of her condition includes the view that 'Mrs. Clitheroe's grief will be a joy when she realizes that she has had a hero for a husband' (p. 244). But, quite obviously, this hero brings home to the living no boon or community benefit as does the traditional hero, according to Joseph Campbell in *The Hero with a Thousand Faces* (1968). On the contrary, to use Nora's words in Act III, Jack is merely 'butchered as a sacrifice to th' dead!' (1949, 1, p. 220). His end was meaningless. But Jack's end was not without the context which O'Casey needed to create the central meaning of the play.

Brennan describes how, as the roof of the Imperial Hotel fell in, the flag of the Irish Citizen Army (the Plough and the Stars) collapsed with it and Clitheroe was burned alive. The role of the ICA in 1916 was not approved by O'Casey. He had been in at the beginning, as its first secretary, in March 1914; he helped formulate its constitution and wrote its history in 1919. The ICA was founded during the Dublin Lock-out: James Connolly called for it following Larkin's imprisonment in November 1913. O'Casey was, notoriously, a worshipper of Larkin and had little time for Connolly. A fellow-member of the ICA later remarked: 'O'Casey was very critical of Connolly's ideas, even to the point of hostility' (Robbins 1977, p. 77). In October 1914 Larkin left for the USA, where he remained until 1923, and Connolly took over control of the ICA as well as of the Irish Transport and General Workers' Union. By this time O'Casey had resigned as secretary, angered that the ICA was becoming involved with the Irish Volunteers, regarded by O'Casey as bourgeois opponents of the labour movement. Although Larkin himself had swung in favour of Irish nationalism in 1914, and played that card in America, he later had serious reservations about Connolly's committing the ICA to the Rising in 1916 (Larkin 1965, p. 211). Connolly linked nationalism and socialism in 1916: 'The cause of labour is the cause of Ireland, the cause of Ireland is the cause of labour' (Rumpf and Hepburn 1977, p. 12). Because O'Casey was of Larkin's party he faulted Connolly on this point, the more so as time passed. Thus we hear the Covey say in Act 1 of *The Plough and the Stars* that the ICA flag is being disgraced through its association with the Volunteers and a nationalist cause: 'It's a flag that should only be used when we're buildin' th' barricades to fight for a Workers' Republic!' (O'Casey 1949, 1, p. 181). Even though the Covey is a ridiculous character in some respects he is not ridiculous in all. On this point he speaks for O'Casey, whose analysis of 1916 can thus be seen as aggressively Larkinist. Larkin is, in effect, the absent hero, the figure who *should* have been outside the window rather than Patrick Pearse.

The collapse of flag and roof on top of Clitheroe, therefore, is something of a judgement upon the ICA. Austen Morgan says that Connolly himself raised the Plough and the Stars at the Imperial Hotel on the Wednesday morning of Easter week perhaps in retribution for 1913, when the police brutally attacked an Irish crowd addressed by Larkin from the balcony (Morgan 1988, p. 187). At 10 p.m. on that Wednesday the Imperial Hotel caught fire; nothing like the blaze, it was said, had been known since Moscow in 1812. Thus O'Casey's narrated scene of Clitheroe's end is emblematic. The Irish Citizen Army is identified with Clitheroe's folly. It is to be noted that in the play there are two members of the ICA and only one member of the Volunteers, which is, of course, hugely disproportionate since the ICA was but a small force in comparison. O'Casey designates the class difference: the two ICA men are a bricklayer and a chicken butcher, while the Volunteer is a civil servant. It is the Volunteer (Langon) who is represented as the most bloodthirsty, and he is iconic as the first casualty of 1916 seen on the stage, screaming in pain, the very embodiment of Nora's case against the fighting. Langon's terror revises Clitheroe's ideas and is an assault on the audience's complacency. When Republicans condemned the play O'Casey accused them in turn of determining 'to make of Ireland the terrible place of a land fit only for heroes to live in' (O'Casey 1975, 1, p. 175).

The major irony of the riots which erupted on the fourth night of the production (Lowery 1984), is that they were caused mainly by women. This is ironic because O'Casey's analysis of the Rising is actually gendered in favour of women. Like Shaw, O'Casey represented women in his plays as agents of 'the Life Force'. Women are elected to heroic status while men stand condemned of various forms of folly. The dedication of *The Plough and the Stars* to O'Casey's mother (who died in November 1918) is significant. If Desmond Greaves is correct, it was mainly in order to care for his mother that O'Casey did not himself participate in the Rising (Greaves 1979, pp. 79, 120). Had the cause been right, as in the scenario presented in *The Harvest Festival*, the mother might have supported Sean; at least he could thus have rationalised involvement. It was, perhaps, the energy released by the conflict within O'Casey himself on such issues which enabled him to people the stage with components of the argument for and against the Rising, from Nora's pacificism through Fluther's ambivalence, Mrs Gogan's denial of the men's cowardice and Bessie's mockery, to the commitment of Clitheroe and his two comrades. In the end it cannot be doubted that Bessie's death provides the climax of the play, activating catharsis is a way Clitheroe's death cannot rival. The power of *The Plough and the Stars*, then, resides not just in its variety of tone and mood, vigour and colour of characterisation and lyrical strangeness of language but also, and probably mainly, in its drive towards the absurdity of Bessie's violent death as she maternally protects the demented Nora. Many years ago, when I showed to my students the 16mm. film of the play made by RTE in 1966 (directed by Lelia Doolan), the college porter who was operating the projector beside me gasped audibly as Marie Kean was shot, and was much upset by her death scene. There was a lesson here about the visceral effect of tragedy.

The Shadow of a Gunman (1923) is also subtitled 'a tragedy', in spite of its often hilarious comic scenes. The tragedy is once again a woman's, who loses her life in the protection of another, the presumed gunman Donal Davoren. Minnie Powell is a surprise package, since she is perceived by male and female neighbours alike as frivolous and sexually aggressive. (Some critics, too, fall into the trap of confusing Minnie's naivety with inauthenticity.) In ironically calling her a Helen of Troy come to live in a Dublin tenement Shields means to emphasise Minnie's dangerousness; Mrs Grigson reflects upon Minnie's stylish dress as a key to her dubious morality: 'I knew she'd come to no good!' (1949, 1, p. 153). Shields warns Davoren against Minnie and adds that he himself wouldn't care to have his life depending on her, as 'she wouldn't sacrifice a jazz dance to save it' (p. 130). In the end, of course, Minnie makes the 'sacrifice' wastefully. The whole point of the play is that neither Davoren nor Shields is worth her sacrifice. Therefore it is quite appropriate that to the end Davoren remains incorrigibly the precious, priggish figure he is at the start, using language artificially and mawkishly just because he *is* artificial and mawkish. He is not a 'man', in the Dublin-speak used by Grigson of himself (less than creditably).

Davoren, the would-be hero, is ironically represented throughout. His elitist view of the artist conflicts with the image of gunman imposed on him by the tenement dwellers. His awareness of the deception, accepted through his vanity and opportunism, is at odds with Davoren's ignorance of how hollow his artistic pretensions are. The question of what is the writer's purpose when the country is engaged in a war of independence is inscribed in O'Casey's text. Shields claims that the writer's role is 'to put passion in the common people' (p. 127), but Davoren aristocratically dismisses the 'people' as too far beneath him. His invoking of Louis Dubedat's creed of 'the might of design, the mystery of colour, the redemption of all things by Beauty everlasting' places Davoren on the side of the aesthetes; he unfortunately ignores the fact that Shaw's artist (in *The Doctor's Dilemma*, 1906) is allowed to die because he is socially useless. The dilemma of the artist in society is a major theme in *The Shadow of a Gunman*. Davoren invokes Shelley's *Prometheus Unbound* (1820), a radical text for a revolutionary age, but he has no conception whatever of Shelley's social conscience. Shelley's *An Address to the Irish People* (1812) could well be taken alongside *Prometheus Unbound* (and its preface) as glosses on the action of *The Shadow of a Gunman*. In contrast to the ideal which Shelley promotes of activism and freedom based on proper notions of imitation and moral courage, Davoren is but the travesty of an artist, whose words are all rather of escape than of engagement of any kind. Three times in Act II Davoren says he must go 'on the run' out of the house. The phrase is ambiguous; Davoren uses it to mean mere escape into privacy and anonymity. His irresponsibility receives severe treatment when his cowardice is finally exposed, but before that his self-indulgence as writer is mocked by the parallel case of Mr Gallogher.

This refined but ridiculous seeker after justice prides himself in his prose, directed to the IRA. The episode where the letter is read aloud and emended by Mrs Henderson is all about style, of which Davoren is deemed the arbiter; the pretentiousness of the letter is no greater than that of Davoren's poetry, and the letter has, at least, a clear objective. Davoren's position as recipient of the letter (a source of panic later) is false; he is no more than a vacuum. In other scenes Davoren is placed on a par with two loud-mouths, Tommy Owens and Adolphus Grigson, whose language and songs reveal their bogus self-esteem. The only authentic piece of writing Davoren achieves is the typing of his name and Minnie's on the paper found on her body after she is shot. Significantly, there is no message: no verb, no conjunction. The juxtaposition of the names reveals the lack of a relationship; Minnie's blood obliterates Davoren's name, at once exonerating and shaming him. He is nothing; he is a mere shadow. O'Casey thus supplies a portrait of the artist as anti-hero, whose identity in the face of social breakdown is 'unbound', disengaged, in retreat and irredeemably guilty. The waste of Minnie's sacrifice on such a man is what makes the play tragic.

The Shadow of a Gunman inserts itself into the Irish tradition as a play making palpable the atmosphere of modern warfare when ordinary people's lives are invaded by violence and terrorism. O'Casey's play was to become paradigmatic as a tragicomic representation of political confusion ('Shot in the back to save the British Empire, an' shot in the breast to save the soul of Ireland', 1949, 1, p. 132) and danger ('You're sure of your life nowhere now; it's just as safe to go everywhere as it is to anywhere', 1949, 1, p. 142). *Juno and the Paycock* (1924) deepens those perceptions by focusing on a family struggling for survival in the midst of the civil war which literally pitted neighbour against neighbour. O'Casey again subtitles this play as a tragedy. From the start, he conceived it as the tragedy of Johnny Boyle (Fallon 1965, p. 17).

It is, of course, the case that O'Casey was not writing tragedy in the classical or neo-classical sense. There is hardly any need to argue that point further. It is clear that O'Casey wrote what we can more readily call 'tragicomedy' (Krause 1975; Kosok 1985). The *Irish Times* reviewer of *Juno* in 1924 put his finger on the spot: 'It is called a tragedy, but it simply bursts its sides with comedy. Had it been described as a comedy, its tragedy would be no less terrible. Such was life in Dublin in the year of civil "war"' (Hogan and Burnham

1992, p. 192). Yet it remains significant that O'Casey himself dubbed all three Dublin plays 'tragedies'. His notion is close to what both Dürrenmatt and Beckett had in mind a little later in the century. Dürrenmatt argued that tragedy *per se* was no longer possible in the modern age because it implied a sense of individual responsibility: 'In the Punch-and-Judy show of our century ... there are no more guilty and also, no responsible men. ... We are all collectively guilty.' In such circumstances, 'Comedy alone is suitable for us. Our world has led to the grotesque as well as to the atom bomb.' Yet 'the tragic is still possible even if pure tragedy is not. We can achieve the tragic out of comedy' (1975, p. 1028). Beckett did not theorise on the matter quite so precisely, but in his brief review of O'Casey's *Windfalls* in 1934 he commented on *Juno* in such a way as to indicate his agreement with Dürrenmatt's position. Beckett saw O'Casey as 'a master of knockabout [farce] in this very serious and honourable sense – that he discerns the principle of disintegration in even the most complacent solidities, and activates it to their explosion. This is the energy of his theatre ... mind and world come asunder in irreparable dissociation – "chassis"' (Kilroy 1975, p. 167). The first point to be noted, accordingly, in *Juno* is that Johnny Boyle is decentred, relegated to the margins of a stage on which the Falstaffian Captain Boyle and his 'butty' Joxer Daly claim the limelight. Yet Johnny's story is at the heart of the family tragedy, and central to the national tragedy which O'Casey was trying to illuminate. The second point follows: Johnny is an anti-hero rather than a hero, and a reflex of the circumstances or *mise en scène* created by the political situation.

Johnny Boyle's disability defines while it questions his heroic status. He is frightened to the point of hysteria as the result of his republican involvement. He chose to fight in 1916, though he can only have been fifteen at the time, and was wounded in the hip. He lost an arm 'in the fight in O'Connell Street' in July 1922, during the civil war. As an Irregular Boyle chose to oppose the new Free State government: this is the 'principle' for which he lost his arm. All of these choices confer tragic status, just as all this going 'through the mill' can be considered a waste stemming from the primal error of 1916. Such, at any rate, is O'Casey's perspective in 1924. He allows Juno to voice it, 'Ah, you lost your best principle, me boy, when you lost your arm; them's the only sort o' principles that's any good to a workin' man' (1949, 1, p. 31). As the play opens, however, Johnny has left the IRA and is 'On the Run', O'Casey's original title for the play. He is the obverse of Donal Davoren, who is a selfish drifter by comparison. It emerges during the course of the play that Johnny has betrayed a comrade, Tancred, shot in an ambush by Free State soldiers. His sufferings are therefore self-induced and involve him in a form of guilt manifested by superstition and hallucinations. His very life seems to depend on the trembling of a votive light, the extinction of which sends him into paroxysms of terror. If, as has been suggested by James Agate, there is a resemblance here to *Macbeth* (Ayling 1969, p. 76) then we may contrast the would-be saviour of Ireland who turns betrayer with the saviour of Scotland who also turns betrayer. Further, when Tancred's funeral takes place a neighbour declares to his sorrowing mother, 'Still an' all, he died a noble death, an' we'll bury him like a king'. The fact that Mrs Tancred can deflate the comparison ('An' I'll go on livin' like a pauper') makes O'Casey's point exactly (1949, 1, p. 54). The tragic waste of civil war changes nothing in the social conditions still awaiting revolution. In modern times, it is not possible to conceive of a single individual like Macbeth as the sole cause of a reign of terror or his removal as the guarantee of peace.

O'Casey can offer no redress, no way out of the 'chassis' into which the country, mirrored in civil war, has descended. The structure of feeling to which he gives expression corresponds with Yeats's contemporaneous lines in 'The Second Coming', 'Things fall apart; the centre cannot hold; / Mere anarchy is loosed upon the world'. But O'Casey can at least offer comedy as solvent. Captain Boyle's imperviousness to responsibility and his bogus identity born of fantasy ('Everybody callin' you "Captain", an' you only wanst on the wather, in an oul' collier from here to Liverpool', 1949, 1, p. 14) offer the audience the kind of delight such Billy Liars always command on stage. His foil Joxer, at will the parasitic straight man/ funny man, ensures a sequence of scenes where his opportunism is matched by laughable collusion in the Captain's deceptions. Between them, this comic pair suggest an attitude whereby the political dilemmas can be coped with: 'they don't affect us, an' we needn't give a damn' (1949, 1, p. 56). With half of its mind, any audience is relieved to have this assurance. With the other half, however, which O'Casey never forgets, the audience is aware of and needs to be brought back to facts rather than fantasy; Juno's role is to insist on the reality all around them. 'Hasn't the whole house, nearly, been massacreed? ... Sure, if it's not our business, I don't know whose business it is' (1949, 1, p. 56). Thus the comedy penetrates but does not displace the tragedy. The final entrance of the drunken Boyle and Daly is a superb coda in this regard. Coming as it does directly after Juno's last great, humanist speech and her exit with Mary to a new life without Captain Boyle, the final scene shoulders aside catharsis in favour of irony. The indifference of Boyle to what has happened approaches the level of parody; it is as if the sentiments of a Greek chorus were subverted. The audience cannot but laugh and be liberated by such brazen incapability to understand tragic events, and through laughter be reinforced in a sense of responsibility.

Juno and the Paycock was extraordinarily popular following its premiere at the Abbey on 3 March 1924. For the first time in years the theatre packed out and turned people away. Bankruptcy, which had been a real threat, was averted and the Abbey could seriously apply for a government subsidy in recognition of its national status. O'Casey's first two plays, then, had a lot to do with the saving of the Abbey. And there was something in them which, as the diarist Joseph Holloway noted (1967, p. 235), brought the same audiences back 'over and over again' in 1924 . It is as if O'Casey were explaining the people to themselves, providing them with the means of understanding the kind of experience they had been through, in mingled hope and despair, after the war of independence and during the civil war. When Lady Gregory came up from Galway to see *Juno* on 8 March, local atrocities were still very much on her mind. She was not likely to be taken in by a shallow representation; in fact, she was overwhelmed by *Juno*, as she confided to her *Journals*: 'A wonderful and terrible play of futility, of irony, humour, tragedy'. In the greenroom O'Casey paid tribute to her as the one who told him his gift was for characterisation. 'And so I threw over my theories and worked at characters, and this is the result' (Gregory 1978, pp. 511–12). Certainly, the distance travelled between the creation of Mrs Rocliffe in *The Harvest Festival* and *Juno* is extraordinary. Mrs Rocliffe, also a mother who loses and mourns for her son, has no language to lift her from the stereotypical. Her sympathy for 'the only son of some poor, old, heartbroken mother', when the scab is killed who killed her Jack, simply carries no weight (O'Casey 1980, p. 65). Her character, like all the characters in *The Harvest Festival*, comes ready-made and labelled; there is no expansion in feeling, no reaching out to relate to others as Juno's quotation of Mrs Tancred's lament, for example, suggests empathy which she herself can extend. And, of course, there is nothing in *The Harvest Festival* to compare with the richness of the comic characterisation in *Juno*. And yet, O'Casey's expression of indebtedness to Lady Gregory carried an implication which was to become ominous in just a few years. The success of *Juno* was actually the indirect result of the utter failure of a clever one-act piece, *Cathleen Listen In* (1923), a political satire on the new Irish Free State. It was received in deadly silence by a hostile Abbey audience, after which O'Casey decided to give them what they wanted in *Juno*. The satire and fantasy of *Cathleen Listens In* prefigure the later O'Casey and suggest that these were the areas he really wanted to develop, rather than realism (which he was later to attack). In the mean time, he was constrained, however fortuitously, to write in a certain vein. He was lucky enough to have a first-class company of actors for whom he could supply tailor-made roles, first in *Juno* and then in *The Plough*. He was moulded as an Abbey playwright. *Juno* was in some measure a well-made play in the style of (and greatly admired by) Lennox Robinson and Lady Gregory.

Then, in January 1926, O'Casey began to resist. He wrote to Lennox Robinson, who was to direct *The Plough*: 'I am sorry, but I'm not Synge; not even, I'm afraid, a reincarnation. Besides, things have happened since Synge: the war has shaken some of the respectability out of the heart of man; we have had our own changes, and the U.S.S.R. has fixed a new star in the sky' (O'Casey 1975, 1, p. 166). He had a new agenda. Following the stormy reception of *The Plough* and his departure for London, O'Casey broke away from Abbey realism. As he wrote in *Rose and Crown*, '[t]here was no importance in trying to do the same thing again, letting the second play imitate the first, and the third the second. He wanted a change' (O'Casey 1956, 2, p. 32). Here O'Casey was referring to *The Silver Tassie*, with its expression-istic second act set behind the lines in World War One. But Yeats would have none of it, and in rejecting the play revealed how far he was from understanding O'Casey's modernism: 'your great power of the past has been the creation of some unique character who dominated all about him and was himself a main impulse in some action that filled the play from beginning to end' (Wade 1954, p. 741). This is a description of Aristotelian drama complete with Aristotelian hero; it will fit the smaller compass of Yeatsian drama also, but it will not fit O'Casey's Dublin plays. O'Casey had there come to terms with heroism, which he saw as crippled, and action, which he saw as alienated from individual character.

In *The Silver Tassie* O'Casey depicts Harry Heegan at the outset as conventionally heroic, physically strong, athletic, sexually attractive, a veritable playboy of the western front. But in Act III Harry returns to Dublin in a wheelchair, permanently disabled, to represent O'Casey's now habitual image. The form of the play is likewise fragmented, diffused, at odds with itself. The result is, through the expressionist mode (not quite consistently sustained), a condemnation of the collaboration between church and state in the sacrifice of manhood to protect the status quo. Here again, as in the three Dublin plays but in a new style, O'Casey shows that political violence undertaken for a romantic or idealistic end is sheer folly, and that the necessary social revolution is sidetracked into jingoism.

Later plays

O'Casey was a disappointed nationalist. His earliest writings, articles, letters and poems were fervently republican, celebrating Irish Ireland over all other considerations. Embarrassing examples of this type of thing may be found in *Feathers from the Green Crow* (1962). Even in 1917, when he wrote *The Sacrifice of Thomas Ashe*, a brief celebration of the hunger striker who died as a result of forced feeding, O'Casey was republican in outlook, although he was no longer a member of the IRB. It was when he wrote the history of the Irish Citizen Army in 1919 that he formulated his negative view of nationalism. Here, as so often, O'Casey was influenced by Jim Larkin. Having swerved violently towards nationalist ideology in 1914 Larkin changed direction again in 1918, following Labour's capitulation to Sinn Féin, and reasserted the priority of socialism. Larkin now openly claimed (in America) that 'the Irish are with the Russians' (Larkin 1965, p. 224). He became embroiled in a struggle for power between left and right wings of the American Socialist Party and actively supported the foundation of a Communist Labour Party in 1919. In November of that year Larkin was arrested on a charge of criminal anarchy and imprisoned for five to ten years. In the course of his trial Larkin said that the socialist movement was a religion, 'a reaching up to the higher things of life, doing something or leaving something that is greater than yourself' (Larkin

1965, p. 240). All of this had its impact on O'Casey, who, back in Dublin, had placed himself on the side of Larkin's sister Delia against the Connollyites and the struggling Irish Labour Party. When Larkin returned to Dublin at the end of April 1923 he split the Labour Party and rendered it powerless in the evolution of the Free State. O'Casey's Dublin plays share Larkin's reaction against nationalism in its early consequences; they were both a lament and a mockery. The lament was basically for the lack of a hero or deliverer.

In the late 1930s, however, having tired of an unavailing attempt to intervene in British post-war politics (*Within the Gates* 1933), O'Casey returned to the Irish nationalist question and began a new, revised re-creation of its historical conflict with the labour movement. This new move began with *The Star Turns Red*, written in 1938 but not staged until 1940, i.e. when Britain was at war with Germany. On the face of it a piece of anti-Fascist propaganda, this play is actually a piece of socialist propaganda. Surprisingly, James Agate called it a masterpiece (O'Casey 1975, 1, p. 849), and yet *The Star Turns Red* is much better than propaganda usually is. It is, indeed, a fantastic and powerful yoking together of the 1913 Dublin Lock-out and the Fascism which opposed socialism (in Spain, for example) after 1936. This extravagant treatment of history supplies a key to O'Casey's later plays. *The Star Turns Red* is actually set in the future, 'Tomorrow, or the next day', thus projecting an allegory out of historical fantasy. The character of Red Jim is clearly based on Jim Larkin, whom O'Casey was to dub 'Prometheus' in *Drums under the Windows* (1945) and whose aforementioned 'religious' qualities are certainly recorded by means of the biblical language of the play (wryly noted by Shaw at the time). O'Casey now had a dramatic hero. Liberating himself from the determinism of history he could now imagine a situation where defeat was turned into victory. Thanks to the charisma of Red Jim, the workers fight for justice and turn the soldiers in their favour so that the dominant Christian ideology is transformed into (liberating) socialist ideology: the star of Bethlehem (for the play is set at Christmas) turns obligingly and yet symbolically red. Even the highly sympathetic critic Jack Mitchell (1980, pp. 175–6) balks at the 'revolutionary superman needing no collective leadership' exhibited here. And yet this play successfully turned O'Casey's imagination from a negative to a positive treatment of Irish national affairs. In *Purple Dust* (published 1940), admittedly a 'wayward' comedy set in the present, O'Casey idealised the Irish peasantry in order to mount a devastating critique of English opportunism. Outdoing Synge, O'Casey here gave the palm not just to one eloquent avatar of Celtic heroism but two: we are given, as it were, two Tramps for the price of one, and two women go off with these poet-figures while the lesser mortals are overwhelmed by a literal flood. But it was in *Red Roses for Me* (1943) that O'Casey reached the summit of his heroic post-revisionism and in the character of Ayamonn Breydon was 'able to do more justice to the real richness of a man from the Larkin mould' (Mitchell 1980, p. 176).

In *Red Roses for Me* O'Casey not only redeems history but achieves the extraordinary feat of refashioning his own early work and beliefs as dramatised in *The Harvest Festival* some twenty-five years earlier. When Hugh Hunt directed a revival of *Red Roses for Me* at the Abbey in 1980 he emphasised in a programme note that the play referred to a railwaymen's strike in 1911 and not, as commentators habitually say, to the 1913 Lock-out. Hunt based his comment on something O'Casey himself had written as a note for an American production of *Red Roses* in 1956. The point reinforces the autobiographical nature of the play. In 1911 O'Casey had worked for ten years for the Great Northern Railway when he was dismissed without explanation. David Krause says O'Casey was sacked for joining Larkin's union and for 'openly professing his socialist as well as Irish loyalties' (O'Casey 1975, 1, p. 4). In the play, Ayamonn Breydon is obviously a version of this young O'Casey: the point is put beyond dispute if the portrait of Johnny is compared in *Pictures in the Hallway* (1942), written at the same time as *Red Roses for Me*. Therefore, O'Casey is once again going back to rewrite history, and this time he inserts himself as its heroic victim.

Red Roses for Me is the story of a young man who dies for a cause. That cause is an increase in wages, a mere shilling; Ayamonn saw the shilling in the shape of a new world. That world, in turn, incorporates the city of Dublin, dramatised in Act III as a soul in need of transformation. The poor people foregrounded on the streets of this city are in '*a pathetic search for a home*' (O'Casey 1965, p. 275). They are abject and demoralised, chanting a similar song of defeat to the Chorus of Down-and-Outs in *Within the Gates*. But Ayamonn, by virtue of his energy and imagination, is empowered to regenerate the people by enabling them to see their city 'in th' grip o' God! (p. 289). To that extent Ayamonn is artist rather than activist, although it is O'Casey's point that he is both. This duality, indeed, is what distinguishes Ayamonn from his single-minded (and thus fanatic) prototype Jack Rocliffe in *The Harvest Festival*, who is likewise shot dead during a strike. The duality represents O'Casey's conviction that specialisation *per se* was a bad thing, and that advance and change are best assured through the sort of cultural wholeness for which Larkin stood. Larkin was fond of quoting the poets during his famous public addresses; he was also insistent that workers should demand flowers as well as bread on the table. O'Casey was in complete agreement. In an article published in 1923 he wrote: 'this is the silent need of the workers: loss of ignorance and acquirement of culture. However the worker may shout for an increase in his wage, or protest against a reduction, be he at work, or waiting eagerly in the Unemployment Exchange, his greatest need and most urgent claim is a share in the culture of the society of men' (O'Casey 1962, pp. 14–15). In *Red Roses for Me* O'Casey imagines a Larkinite hero capable, as Donal Davoren in *The Shadow of a Gunman* was not, of putting passion in the common people by appealing to their imaginations. Ayamonn is a lover of Shakespeare; we first meet him rehearsing from the end of *3 Henry VI*. He is convinced that the workers are 'afraid of Shakespeare' only because the cultural establishment has mystified him. The workers 'think he's beyond them, while all the time he's part of the kingdom of heaven in the nature of everyman' (O'Casey 1965, p. 229). But it is Irish mythology rather than Shakespeare – apart from the use of the red rose of Lancaster – which O'Casey uses, through Ayamonn, to awaken the people to a pride in themselves in Act III. This move, too, was related to Larkin's persona. W. P. Ryan says in *The Irish Labour Movement* (1919, p. 170) that Larkin's first association 'with the Irish mind in general was distinctly mythological. To many he is non-human and mythological still'.

During the labour dispute of 1913 Larkin made a declaration which was to form the bedrock of *Red Roses for Me* : 'living or dead, they will never break me, and dead I will be a greater force against them than alive' (Larkin 1965, p. 123). Moreover, at the Irish TUC in 1914 Larkin invoked Cathleen Ni Houlihan just as Ayamonn does in Act III. Indeed, Larkin made Yeats part of his reference (Larkin 1965, p. 172). Ayamonn, like Seumas Shields in *The Shadow of a Gunman*, sees Cathleen Ni Houlihan as ugly and dangerous rather than beautiful; she is as much in need of renewal as the people's religious statue, Our Lady of Eblana. To give force to Ayamonn's mythic status O'Casey calls for a lighting effect in the visionary scene (Act III) so that Ayamonn's head resembles 'the severed head of Dunn-Bo speaking out of the darkness' (1965, p. 287). One begins to see the eclectic nature of O'Casey's imagination at this stage in his dramatic career: an event in 1911 is combined with the Lock-out of 1913 and energised through an idealised view of Larkin, perceived as mythic so that he generates a plethora of Celtic associations. This last of the severed head of Dunn-Bo is complex. When the men of Leinster defeated Fergal Mac Maile Dúin at the battle of Allen they cut off his head and celebrated around it all night; then another head, that of the singer Dunn Bó, also killed in the battle, began to sing in praise of Fergal. 'The story demonstrates the reverence for the human head in Celtic society' (Ellis 1987, p. 29). More to the point, the reference combines battle with song and miracle. As a result of Ayamonn's poetic power in Act III the city-scape is suddenly flooded with light, the costumes of the poor people are transformed and the familiar setting is glorified. Then Ayamonn takes part in a dance with Finnoola, a street vendor, and it is as if the action had been shifted into one of Yeats's Plays for Dancers (1921): all is ritualistic and ceremonious. As soon as the dance is over, however, the moment of intense vision passes, 'and all look a little puzzled and bewildered' (1965, p. 291). One thinks not just of Yeats but of Friel's five sisters and the brief interlude of ecstasy brought into their lives through the Dionysiac dance in Dancing at Lughnasa (1990). O'Casey thus can so expand cultural horizons on all sides that he includes within his concerns the length and breadth of Irish history. The visionary moment marks the eternal moment of promise in Irish literature, in which history is emancipated and full human realisation is established. Then, as here in Act III, the scene darkens again and the hero leaves to assume again the conditions of inexorable reality: a romantic aesthetic, certainly, but endemically Irish. The artist can only provide the epiphany; its effect depends on the will of the people if the vision is to have any bearing on reality. That will is seen in Act IV of Red Roses when the strike takes place and Ayamonn's body is accepted inside the church in spite of bigoted opposition. Ayamonn has his place in the pantheon in the end, and lies in state in the church with the lights on and Brennan singing the theme song in tribute to a hero. As Carol Kleiman puts it, 'there is a sense of Ayamonn's elevation to an almost god-like role' (1982, p. 80).

O'Casey: in search of a hero

It can be claimed that in *Red Roses for Me* O'Casey revives the cultural nationalism repudiated in his three Dublin plays. He who demythologised Cathleen Ni Houlihan then re-mythologises her now, to promote a new revolution: the one which never happened but which as myth could yet generate social transformation. The fact that *Red Roses for Me* is set on the vigil of Easter relates Ayamonn's sacrifice to the 1916 Rising. Larkin merges into Connolly, who, after all, had stated in *The Re-Conquest of Ireland* that this re-conquest would be 'the victory of the working-class conception, the re-establishment of the power of the community over the conditions of life that assist or retard the development of the individual' (Connolly 1917, p. 260). O'Casey here made his peace with a lot of former enemies. Years later, in May 1962, he was to write to an old co-worker and assistant to Larkin in terms which show quite clearly the degree to which O'Casey made Larkin the centre of his heroic conception:

> Just think for a minute, Barney, on how we workers were then, living in squalid places, wretchedly paid, hard worked, not daring to say a word of protest against any of these evils. Then Jim Larkin came among us, and all became changed: the workers were on their feet, they had much to say for themselves, and they stood out to do battle. ... We, the workers, were on the march! The eloquent roaring voice of the great Jim Larkin became the trumpet of the Irish workers, ay, and of the English workers too, in his glorious Fiery Cross campaign. ... We were the Pioneers of a resurgent Labour Movement, and, now, the workers are a power in every country under the warm or the cold sun.
>
> (O'Casey 1992, 4, p. 310).

Thus the myth lived on after Larkin's death in 1947.

And yet *Red Roses* remains a play and not a manifesto. As a play it achieves a renewal of Irish drama as poetic and visionary, partly through its re-visionary tactic in making Sheila Mourneen endorse Ayamonn's sacrifice in contrast to Nora Clitheroe's pacificism in *The Plough and the Stars*. A weakness of the play, which nevertheless remains one of the best of O'Casey's later plays, is in its excessively poetic language, at times but 'a tumblin' blether o' words' (1965, p. 309). Yet this fault, too, can be excused as what John Gassner calls O'Casey's Elizabethan 'prodigality' (Ayling 1969, pp. 110–19). This play, then, fits into a Shakespearean framework, which it sustains as much by its lyricism as by its ambitious attempt to combine all the arts of the theatre. It simply requires a strong director who can find in the rich but unwieldy text the power which makes the play's shortcomings and inconsistencies irrelevant.

With *Red Roses for Me* O'Casey's search for a hero came to an end. It was not Yeats's heroic ideal (Zwerdling 1965) he was after but the heroic real, a notion of change rooted in the everyday but energised by the visionary. The plays which followed provide a third and final phase of his work. Here, in such plays as *Cock-a-Doodle Dandy* (1949) and *The Bishop's Bonfire* (1955), satire is predominant. With calm of mind, all passion spent, O'Casey looks at the ever-diminishing cultural nationalism of the Free State and the Irish Republic from the detached, amused and always ironic point of view of an outsider. It is a Fool's Paradise he observes, a world crouching in undignified submission to narrow religious and social commandments. O'Casey delights in exposing the pusillanimity of this world, its sexual timor-ousness and repression, its conformity and its hypocrisy. By means of fantasy, dance, colour symbolism and a joyousness which stands in stark contrast to the drab world he portrays, O'Casey manages to create in these last plays a strong critique of a nation demoralised. The deplorable treatment of his last comedy, *The Drums of Father Ned*, by the Archbishop of Dublin and the deferential Dublin Thea-tre Festival alike in 1958, sadly confirmed O'Casey's diagnosis of Irish society. Apart from the delightful squib *Figuro in the Night*, written in 1959, O'Casey's response to this last testimony of Ire-land's mean-spiritedness was two-fold. He withdrew his three Dublin plays from the Abbey for five years, and he wrote a blistering but in many ways unfortunate satire, *Behind the Green Curtains* (pub-lished 1961). Spleen and savage indignation here obtained the upper hand as O'Casey blasted at his old targets without his old Jonsonian wit and fantasy. It marks a sad final farewell to Inishfallen when O'Casey's second-rate working-class protagonist Beoman (=Man Alive) can only advocate exile to England as the answer to the unrelieved Fascism of Irish society. The irony is that the drums of Father Ned were, indeed, beginning to throb out in Ireland in 1958, and a new revolution, not, admittedly, the socialist one O'Casey hoped and worked for, was under way during which censorship, repression and hypocrisy would be healthily swept aside by a new generation. Of the new playwrights who would arrive to give expression to this revolution, from Behan to Friel and beyond, not one would ever disclaim the example and inspiration of Sean O'Casey. He himself became the great hero of the Irish theatre.

5

Into the twilight:
Robinson, Johnston, Carroll

I am never homesick, and I do not miss Ireland. I was glad to get
away from Ireland's ignorance and humbug, religious and political.
De Valera's 'most spiritual State in the world,' was too much for me.

O'Casey, *Letters* (1962)

Introduction

The new Free State wanted a new, free theatre. What it got in the
first instance was the national subsidisation of the old theatre in
August 1925. This symbolic as well as practical gesture was, the
Minister for Finance Ernest Blythe said, in recognition that 'the
Abbey Theatre had done work of national importance' (Hogan and
Burnham, 1992, p. 277). On 27 December (a Sunday), the Abbey
celebrated its silver jubilee with a gala performance and much self-
congratulation. The *Irish Times* in an editorial emphasised the
'national' achievement involved, and asserted that the Abbey had
'lifted Dublin from the status of a decaying provincial city to that of
one of Europe's intellectual and artistic capitals' (December 26). Its
success had been achieved because it told the truth, 'which is the
greatest of ironists'. Consequently, audiences had matured, and no
longer rioted over *The Countess Cathleen*. The gods in the wings must
have sniggered, six weeks before the riots over *The Plough and the
Stars*.

Certainly, the Abbey had once again established a first-rate
company, which facilitated O'Casey's problems as playwright: he
moulded his plays to the talents of F. J. McCormick, Barry
Fitzgerald, Arthur Shields, Gabriel Fallon, Sara Allgood, Eileen
Crowe, Maureen Delaney and others. These worked brilliantly as an
ensemble and, as Dubliners, had a special authenticity to bring to

O'Casey's plays. New audiences came flocking in because suddenly what was happening on stage related immediately to their own lives and was rendered in their own idiom and accent.

The key to the new role to be played by the Abbey in the new dispensation probably lies in this set of relations between audience, company, writers and political situation. Understandably, the public wanted diversion and, insofar as this was possible on the tiny Abbey stage, carnival. The mood of what was on offer is summed up in the title of a popular play, *The Glorious Uncertainty* (1923). Written by Brinsley MacNamara (1890–1963), better remembered as a novelist, this comedy about horse-racing and local intrigues captures well the tendency of the time to turn aside from the darker political and social realities of the civil war and revel in fantastic uncertainties. MacNamara followed up with an equally successful romantic comedy, *Look at the Heffernans!* (1926), while in the meantime George Shiels (1881–1949) provided two of his most enduring comedies in *Paul Twyning* (1922) and *Professor Tim* (1925), with *The New Gossoon* (1930) and many others to follow. Such plays offered a rollicking, good-humoured account of Irish life, very much in the peasant tradition. Yet, as MacNamara himself noted, it was not quite the same countryside which was being dramatised as in the days of Synge: 'it was being discovered that there was a town as well as a country life in the provinces. Irish life generally was becoming modernised, and this tendency was being reflected on the Abbey stage ... The play from the country did not concern itself now with the old, old subject of land-hunger, the character of the peasant half-wit had almost completely disappeared, and there was much less "poetry-talk", in imitation of Synge and Lady Gregory.' The characters from this countryside suited the players 'almost as well as those of O'Casey' (1949, pp. 17–18). A style had been found in which to bridge the gap between urban and rural; the core value in this style was amusement, laughter, rather than satire or applied judgement. In effect, this approach sanctioned evasion of serious issues. Even O'Casey's plays were played too much for laughs at this time.

Given this public mood, the fate of *The Plough and the Stars* was ominous. O'Casey challenged his audience in ways to which they were not now accustomed. But there was no apology from O'Casey, no prologue, no epilogue, no mitigating interview in the press. In the public debate which followed he stood firm, although Hanna Sheehy-Skeffington seemed to have the populist arguments in her armoury against the play. O'Casey's stand was noble, for many of the Dublin intellectuals failed to support him and the support of Yeats, the senator who had recently spoken out in favour of divorce, was a dubious asset. A lesser writer, such as Lennox Robinson (1886–1958), would have diplomatically made accommodation with the public hostility. As director of *The Plough and the Stars*, Robinson was notably silent when the flak began to fly. Accommodation was to be the central value of Robinson's own work, as we shall see. But O'Casey was trying to inject a bit of iron into the new Irish drama and this was the moment of truth. To be sure, the controversy did not damage the Abbey as the riots over *The Playboy* had in 1907. Willie Fay, who played Christy Mahon in that first production, said that for weeks after the riots the cast was playing to 'half a dozen people scattered all over the house' (1935, p. 220). Nothing like this happened in 1926. But when Yeats rejected *The Silver Tassie* two years later he unwittingly sent the wrong signal. He seemed to be denying a major playwright the right to be serious. He seemed to be offering aid and comfort to audiences who wanted no more from the national theatre than a good guffaw. Unfortunately, the trend once allowed was maintained over several decades. Writing in 1950, the astute critic Thomas Hogan remarked: 'In general, the history of the Abbey has been one of low class comedies, interspersed erratically by works of genius. The theory of the Golden Age of the Abbey ... is all my foot. The Abbey Theatre has pretty well all the time been a kind of high-class music-hall, engaged in purveying good laughs to the multitude – with, indeed, fair success' (p. 80). Had O'Casey been encouraged to stay on he would certainly not have contributed to this sad state of affairs. As will appear below, neither Denis Johnston (1901–1984) nor Paul Vincent Carroll (1899-1968) was allowed to make the impact each was capable of making on the shape of things. But the sad case of Lennox Robinson must first be inspected, in clarification of this question of the Abbey's eventual decline.

Lennox Robinson

In his lecture on 'The Rise of the Realistic Movement', delivered during the Abbey Festival in August 1938, the critic Andrew E. Malone described Lennox Robinson as 'probably the finest stage craftsman of the Irish drama' (Robinson 1939b, pp. 108–9). Even though Robinson was the organiser of the Festival and was probably seated not very far away, there is no reason to doubt the sincerity of Malone's opinion. It is, indeed, a tenable view, although Synge must be a close rival. I think, however, that Malone's emphasis contains reservations about Robinson's standing as playwright as distinct from the craftsman. Author of twenty-two plays, director of up to five times that number at the Abbey, manager and (from 1923) member of the Board of Directors, Robinson was certainly a major figure in the Irish theatre. But in the period here under review Robinson had a great subject and failed to make great drama of it.

In the earlier phase of his career at the Abbey, Robinson was identified with T. C. Murray and R. J. Ray as a Cork 'realist'. All three mirrored rural Irish life in sombre, Ibsenist terms. *The Whiteheaded Boy* (1916) marked a major shift in direction for Robinson and the revelation of a droll comic style. The stage directions in the published text seem to derive from a traditional story-teller, an acute observer but an invented persona not to be identified with Robinson himself. For example, the opening direction of this ever-popular play describes Mrs Geoghegan as follows:

> *poor* WILLIAM's *widow (that's her behind the table setting out the cups) – is a hearty woman yet, and, after all, I suppose she's not more than sixty-five years of age. A great manager she is, and, indeed, she'd need to be with three unmarried daughters under her feet all day and two big men of sons. You'd not like to deny* MRS GEOGHEGAN *anything she's such a pleasant way with her, yet you know she's not what I'd call a clever woman, I mean to say she hasn't got the book knowledge, the 'notions' her husband had or her sister* ELLEN. *But maybe she's better without them, sure what good is book knowledge to the mother of a family? She's a simple decent woman, and what more do you want?*
>
> (Robinson 1982, p. 65)

In the Abbey revival of this play in 1974 these stage directions were spoken aloud on voice over. The effect is to set up a collusion between *seanachaí* and audience, creating an intimate relationship and a tone vital to Robinson's effect. This effect is basically to lull an audience into receptiveness of a story of family intrigue, sharp practice, and self-protection. The assumptions are all declared, and this is where Robinson, sophisticated playwright that he was, enjoys himself at play with his audience. David Krause, somewhat incensed at Robinson's refusal or inability to write the rough and 'profane' comedy created by Synge, says of the stage directions that 'their sentimental aura hangs over the play like a thick syrup that will not

pour' (1982, p. 197). It is more fruitful to look for the sneer behind
the folksy narrative. For what Robinson reveals in the play is a fairly
cynical accommodation with society. The Irish regard for family
'name' was always Robinson's theme, and the desire for respectability he saw as the motive and excuse for all manner of hypocrisy.
His narrator in *The Whiteheaded Boy* actually asks us to approve of all
this chicanery. He might as well expect us to be blind to the injustice
done to Denis's sisters while Denis, the family pet, gets the lion's
share of whatever money and advantages are available. Robinson's
is a well-constructed satire of a reconstructed society. The people
had come into their own: they had land, money, status in society,
and large ambitions for their offspring. Dublin audiences were invited to laugh at the slyness of such people but to approve also of
their acumen, opportunism and ability to provide for the future.
These were among the most prized values of the new Ireland, home
of the small farmer and the go-ahead bourgeoisie. Yeats's greasy till
had become the mainstay of the new economy. It is true, as Krause
says, that 'there are no rogue heroes, no sharp ironies, no dark
shadows in the benign light comedy of Lennox Robinson' (p. 195),
but what is there is a new accommodation with the audience, asked
in turn to approve a new accommodation with reality.

Further examples may be seen in *The Far-Off Hills* (1928) and
Drama at Inish (1933), two equally accomplished and highly popular
Robinson comedies. In the latter there is a key speech in which
Robinson turns his back on the idea of drama with which he started
out after the death of Synge. Annie Twohig pays off the members of
the Hector De La Mare Theatre Company after their summer repertory has caused suicide attempts and social chaos in the seaside
community: 'Maybe they're [the plays] too good for the like of us or
we're too simple for them. ... We were all more or less happy and
comfortable, good tempered and jolly – until these plays began to
put ideas into our heads' (Robinson 1982, p. 251). Annie compares
the effect to the turning over of a big stone exposing worms and
'horrible little creepies that'd make your stomach turn': the sensible
thing is to put the stone back again. It is tempting to blame
Robinson for urging the easy option. It is more useful to respond to
the metatheatre of *Drama at Inish* in the light of the changes overtaking Ireland. A new conservatism was taking shape and with it an
anti-intellectualism, given sanction by the Censorship of Publications
Act 1929 (Lee 1989, pp. 158–60). As a Protestant, acutely conscious

of the dwindling power of Protestants in the new Free State, Robinson was not advocating opposition. As an amused observer he understood that the sensible attitude was to accept what history had delivered.

For Robinson to achieve this poise was not easy. *The Big House* (1926) reveals a more serious side to his recognition of the falling apart of the old order. Premonitions were already sounded in his earlier political play, *The Lost Leader* (1918), but in *The Big House*, set in the years 1918 to 1923, history's iron law is shown working itself out. The Alcock family is burned out by the IRA, in spite of their liberal position. Curtis Canfield, who included this play in his *Plays of the Irish Renaissance 1880–1930*, said it was 'written with the sure and delicate touch of a master of dialogue with incisive insight and sensitive understanding of both sides of a difficult question' (1929, p. 297). The press at the time actually preferred *The Big House* to *The Plough and the Stars*. But Andrew E. Malone was probably more shrewd in concluding that 'its theme is great but its characters are so petty that one cannot grieve for them' (1929, p. 183). The fact is, Robinson's allegiance was divided. He had long been a nationalist but in ending the play with young Kate Alcock's determination to rebuild the Big House Robinson was calling on the Protestant community to fight back and refuse to be driven out of Ireland. As time went by Robinson lost faith in such a possibility. The fact was that the Free State 'was intent upon the creation of an exclusively Gaelic-Catholic model' (Lyons 1979, p. 165). Hence Robinson's demoralisation in the 1930s, although alcoholism was a major factor here also. His plays came to exhibit a worldweariness. He wrote *Killycreggs in Twilight* (1937) as a riposte to *The Big House*, only now Robinson advocated assimilation at any price. He had come to accept that the old Ascendancy had no independent future in Ireland. The play was premiered in the year of de Valera's new Constitution, which formally set the agenda for a Catholic Ireland. *Killycreggs* accepts the inevitable: Judith de Lury of the Big House will marry a Catholic hotel-owner, lose her name, and assimilate with the majority. To some degree, *Killycreggs* is entitled to the comparison with *The Cherry Orchard* which Michael J. O'Neill has made (1964, p. 145). It records with a dying fall Robinson's sense of an ending.

Denis Johnston

Denis Johnston emerged out of the Dublin Drama League, forerunner of the Dublin Gate Theatre founded by Edwards and MacLiammóir in 1928. The Drama League was largely Lennox Robinson's invention. In 1918, at a time when Yeats was despondent over the nature of the Abbey's achievement (see his 'Open Letter to Lady Gregory'), Robinson tried to persuade him to expand the repertory to include European and other plays. Yeats resisted. According to its patent the Abbey was entitled to stage (in addition to Irish plays) such foreign drama as was likely to be educational to Irish audiences; this was a valuable loophole in the legal restrictions on the repertory. But apart from Lady Gregory's versions of Molière and Goldoni very few foreign plays were staged at the Abbey up to 1919. This was not from indifference but from policy. It was largely because Synge was adamantly opposed to the idea of an international repertory (Saddlemyer 1982, pp. 177–80). Thereafter Yeats felt obliged to honour this agreement, made in 1906, but he accepted Robinson's proposal to establish a new organisation, the Dublin Drama League, for the purpose of staging contemporary foreign plays at the Abbey on Sunday or Monday nights. Thus from February 1919 on the Abbey had within its doors an alternative theatre, which was eventually to spawn a new theatre outside, the Gate (Clarke and Ferrar 1979). This new theatre, the Gate, was to create for itself a position complementing the Abbey. This development represented a tactical error on Yeats's part. The opening of the Peacock Theatre in 1927 as experimental annexe was a more apparent than real solution to the Abbey's conservatism: the first production there was Kaiser's *From Morn to Midnight*, directed by none other than Denis Johnston for the New Players Theatre, an offshoot of the Dublin Drama League. The tiger was within the gates. Two years later Johnston's first play, *The Old Lady Says 'No!'*, was staged in the Peacock, now leased to the newly founded Dublin Gate Studio. In 1930 the Gate moved to its own premises within the Rotunda Buildings in Parnell Square; Johnston was appointed to the board of directors in 1931.

Denis Johnston was a brilliant and complex man. Everything about him promised success and fulfilment. Born in Dublin into an affluent, liberal Protestant family (his father William was a judge popularly known as Civil Bill), Johnston was educated in England

and graduated from Cambridge and Harvard. He abandoned a career as barrister for a varied succession of careers as stage director, playwright, scriptwriter and producer for radio and television, BBC war correspondent during World War Two, director of television programmes (BBC), and finally university teacher in the United States. In addition to his three volumes of plays and scripts for television (*Dramatic Works*), Johnston wrote a stimulating book on Jonathan Swift, a quirky autobiography (*Nine Rivers from Jordan*), and a fascinating meditation on time, physics and death (*The Brazen Horn*). A daunting figure, certainly. And yet it seems plain that Johnston did not fully realise himself in any one field. As a dramatist he was head and shoulders above any of his contemporaries apart from O'Casey: inventive, witty, diverse, profound and theatrically creative to an unusual degree. A book entitled *In Search of Denis Johnston* would make absorbing reading. It would have to take into account Johnston's lifelong practice of revising everything he wrote, from diaries and typescripts to published texts, so that there is a constant overlaying of one version of events with another. There was something philosophical in this compulsion to treat text as palimpsest, for Johnston believed in a form of 'time' which provided for two experiences simultaneously, each as real as the other. The idea permeated his plays, which often combine or superimpose two time levels or hinge upon the filmic process of a series of 'takes' of a particular scene or event. It will be seen below also that Johnston's alternation between Gate and Abbey theatres was part of this commitment to non-commitment, a shifting, revisionary attitude towards all experience. He was the complete modernist, hovering on the verges of postmodernism.

The Old Lady Says 'No!', directed by Hilton Edwards, with MacLiammóir in the starring role of Robert Emmet/Speaker, was the hit of the first Gate season when it opened on 3 July 1929. The title was purportedly a reference to Lady Gregory's rejection of the play for the Abbey, first called *Shadowdance*. Nicholas Grene has shown that Johnston later mischievously doctored the typescript of the play, now in Trinity College, Dublin, to sustain the 'evidence' that the title referred to Gregory (St Peter 1987, p. 197). This is in line with Johnston's compulsive revisionism. And it makes a good story to claim that someone at the Abbey was being insolent in 1928. Moreover, Johnston was certainly held in some suspicion there. In her *Journals* for October 1928 Lady Gregory refers to Johnston as the proposed director of *King Lear* at the Abbey. '[He] has no connection with us, and I fancy it [the production] was given to him to make up for his rejection of his impossible Emmet Play' (1987, p. 329). It is noteworthy that in his edition of the *Journals* in 1946 Robinson (p. 113) censored the word 'impossible'. He was a man who liked to please all sides; a pawn in the company of Yeats and Gregory. As a further sop to Johnston the Abbey decided to subsidise the production of the Emmet play by the Gate Studio. *King Lear* went on at the end of November 1928, the first Shakespearean production to be staged at the Abbey, and neither Yeats nor Lady Gregory liked it (Murray 1979). They decided that Johnston was too avant-garde for the Abbey. He himself believed it was Robinson who stood in his way and prevented his getting on the Abbey board, but it was Yeats who would not have him.

As a piece of expressionism, in the sense of the term derived from Strindberg's *A Dream Play* (1902), which Johnston admired alongside *The Spook Sonata* (1907), *The Old Lady Says 'No!'* is a remarkable depiction of disillusion with the Irish Free State. It emerges from the experimental work done by the Dublin Drama League, Toller's *Masses and Man*, for example, staged in January, and *The Spook Sonata* in April, 1925. Also, while in New York in 1924 Johnston was very impressed with Kaufman and Connelly's *A Beggar on Horseback* on Broadway (Barnett 1978, p. 22), which has a trial scene quite in Johnston's surrealist style and uses the framework of a dream which he favours. Josef Čapek's *Land of Many Names* (1923), which Johnston saw in 1926, was another influence (O'Brien 1989). Since Johnston and O'Casey teamed up in London in 1926 and admired the expressionist work they saw at Peter Godfrey's Gate Studio (Hickey and Smith 1972, p. 62), it may thus be taken as certain, in spite of Johnston's own disclaimers, that *The Old Lady Says 'No!'* derived from the contemporary vogue for expressionism.

Johnston's play is satirical of the nationalist ethos and tradition, by means of the literary and cultural icons and forms popularised by the Abbey Theatre. Yeats's heroic ideal, symbolised by the Old Woman's demands in *Cathleen Ni Houlihan* (1902), is irreverently debunked and his allegory travestied by Johnston's Dublin flower woman selling her four beautiful green fields. She is mistaken by the concussed actor (playing Emmet) for Sarah Curran, Emmet's romantic ideal, and the grotesque reality makes Emmet's quest appear ludicrous. The play which begins as a conventional melodrama about Emmet (cf. Robinson's *The Dreamers* (1915)) parodies many lines from nationalist Irish poets, a pastiche of forty-three passages in four pages of text (Canfield 1936, pp. 479–81). The mockery is somewhat Joycean. Joycean too is the running parody of Yeats and Synge, while O'Casey is actually guyed in the play as the loud-mouthed, working-class writer O'Cooney. A strong vein of very effective comedy pervades the play, which is certainly one quality not indebted to German expressionism and is best regarded as distinctively Irish. What is obviously expressionistic in style is the use of setting, as scenes dissolve into each other in arbitrary fashion, use of lighting, sound and musical effects to simulate the Speaker's concussed state, and the use of chanting and nonsensical exchanges which punctuate the journey of the dislocated actor around modern Dublin. By these means, as Curtis Canfield has shown (p. 25), 'We look on Dublin life through the refracted vision of a stunned actor, and it is a nightmare.'

Johnston himself called *The Old Lady Says 'No!'* a director's play: 'We were tired of the conventional three-act shape, of conversational dialogue, and of listening to the tendentious social sentiments of the stage of the 'twenties, and we wanted to know whether the emotional appeal of music could be made use of in terms of theatrical prose, and an opera constructed that did not have to be sung' (1977, 1, p. 16). The musical reference is appropriate. The play is both a fantasia and a discordant rhapsody. But where does all this virtuosity get Johnston? Into the typical Gate theatricality which enabled a stunning *Peer Gynt* and a remarkable *Faust* to gain headlines, and away from a writer's theatre.

The fact is that Johnston, while interested in theatrical experimentalism, was really an Abbey playwright *manqué*. Indeed, he gave his next play *The Moon in the Yellow River* (1931) to the Abbey and pretended to believe that the actors wanted to sabotage it (1979, 2, p.81). He returned to the Gate with *A Bride for the Unicorn* (1933), from the opening night of which Yeats stormed out (O hAodha 1990, p. 85); but Johnston gave *Blind Man's Buff*, an adaptation of a play by Ernst Toller, to the Abbey in 1936. Johnston reverted to the Gate for *The Golden Cuckoo* (1939) and his Swift play *The Dreaming Dust* (1940), after which he left Ireland. His last plays, *Strange Occurrence on Ireland's Eye* (1956) and *The Scythe and the Sunset* (1958), were staged at the Abbey. Thus Johnston oscillated between Gate and Abbey, and in the 1930s this signified a search for space in which

Robinson, Johnston, Carroll

to belong and yet to have an independent voice. He was a victim of
Yeats's strong prejudices, first against expanding horizons at the
Abbey and more directly against Johnston's 'artiness' (Yeats 1972,
p. 277).

In 1935 Sean O'Faolain wrote an open letter to Yeats (*Irish Times*,
2 March) bewailing the falling standards at the Abbey and contrasting the success of the Gate. The reservation O'Faolain had about the
Gate is revealing: 'But it is not a national theatre. It has no constant
atmosphere. One week, expressionism; another, realism; melodrama today, fantasy to-morrow; China is followed by Yorkshire;
Dublin by Scotland; antiquity by the present-day. And as a result the
one precious thing missing is that intimacy with life which is natural
to a national theatre.' It is a valid point. According to Johnston
himself, in a piece entitled 'The Making of the Theatre', the Gate
was established 'for the production of plays of unusual interest, and
for the purpose of experimenting in methods of presentation free
from the conventionalities of the commercial theatre' (Hobson
1934, p. 12). MacLiammóir summed up the difference with the
Abbey succinctly (1961, p. 355): 'whereas the Abbey set out to show
Ireland to herself and then to the world ... we in the Gate began by
attempting to show the world to Ireland.' Even a cursory study of
The Old Lady Says 'No!' would suggest that Johnston was in the
wrong shop. He clearly wanted to 'show Ireland to herself'; indeed
he wanted to rub noses in the muck of facile mythologising. He
needed a forum where questions of identity and Irish politics could
be forcibly put.

The Old Lady Says 'No!' finally made its way onto the (new) Abbey
stage in 1977, where it properly belongs. In this revived and revised
version the actor playing Emmet/Speaker, Desmond Cave, also
supplied a passable parody of MacLiammóir, so that another layer of
reference was added to Johnston's intertextuality. Looking at the
play now it is possible to regard it as a telling indictment of romantic
republicanism. At the core of the play is a death scene, that of the
young man Joe accidentally shot by the Speaker (Emmet). As he is
dying at home, in a parody of an O'Casey death scene, two men
present argue over the justification of continuing violence to fully
emancipate Ireland:

> OLDER MAN. Aw, that's all words. Nothing but bloody words. You can't
> change the world by words.
> YOUNGER MAN. That's where you fool yourself! What other way can you

change it? I tell you, we can make this country – this world – whatever we want it to be by saying so, and saying so again. I tell you it is the knowledge of this that is the genius and glory of the Gael!

(1977, 1, p. 66)

This debate on violence is the crux of the postcolonial condition. The historian Roy Foster comments in his account of Ireland in the 1920s : 'Under the cautious rule of William Cosgrave, the discourse of Free State politics remained dogmatically buried in the issues over which the civil war had been fought' (1988, pp. 520–1). Within the play Emmet, historically an ineffectual rebel responsible for the deaths of good people, is taken to task by the statue of the great parliamentarian Edward Grattan (from outside Trinity College, Dublin): 'Oh, it is an easy thing to draw a sword and raise a barricade. It saves working, it saves waiting. It saves everything but blood! And blood is the cheapest thing the good God has made' (1977, 1, pp. 32–3). Grattan accuses Emmet of prolonging the cult of bloodshed endemic in Irish history. Emmet changes in the course of the play. Although he is but an actor who cannot remember his lines he is swept into a world where even the most honoured and respectable look back in nostalgia to the days of guerrilla warfare. When Joe dies, however, Emmet comes to see that 'I am only a play-actor – unless I dare to contradict the dead! Must I do that?' (p. 68). In other words he must take issue with history and carve a new way out of the scenario of recurring violence prescribed for him. This he does. He abandons his search for Sarah and for Rathfarnham (his land of heart's desire). He may be, as the Blind Man calls him (p. 72), the 'Shadow of Ireland's Heart', but he can give substance in performance – for such is the miracle of theatre – to a new and different gospel.

Once Emmet rebels and repudiates the traditions of violence he opts out. He is free. 'I will take this earth in both my hands amd batter it into the semblance of my heart's desire!' (1977, 1, p. 73). He flings away his sword (which is only a stage property and yet assumes symbolic meaning as soon as he rejects it). Instead of the historical Speech from the Dock known to every Irish schoolgoer Emmet now forgives the strumpet city Dublin, metonymy for Ireland, adds 'There now. Let my epitaph be written', and lies down to become the concussed actor again, about to be tended by the doctor from the audience. Only seconds have passed since the incident which disrupted the play occurred. The collapsing of time has revealed how history itself may be re-dreamed and re-vised. In calling for his epitaph to be written, in contradiction of the actual Emmet's appeal that his epitaph should not be written until Ireland takes her place among the nations of the earth, Emmet the actor is giving his answer to the Younger Man quoted above. Words *can* indeed alter how a country is shaped. Shibboleths must be abandoned in favour of words imagining a new, revised and enabling history. It is the writer's responsibility to mint those words. Johnston did not shy away from that responsibility. But in order to take the argument further it was necessary for him to swop hats and cross over to the Abbey Theatre briefly in 1931.

The Moon in the Yellow River is probably Johnston's best play. It has a most unusual combination of stringent debate and relaxed, comic ease. It is the play which best challenges the moral and political bases of the new Free State. It is set in an old fort close to a large hydro-electric station which the German engineer Tausch is bringing to completion. It was a topical play in 1931, since the Shannon hydro-electric scheme, which was controversial as a national, state-owned utility, was completed in 1929 by the German firm of Siemens Schuckert. This was the beginning of the nationalised Electricity Supply Board: a mythic moment in Irish experience. In a note appropriately entitled 'Let There be Light' Johnston draws a parallel between the Shannon scheme and the politics of violence which persisted into the later 1920s and beyond :

> Although no physical assault was ever actually launched against the Shannon Hydro-electrical Power Plant, a very determined effort had been made by an armed minority to make majority government unworkable. This had been effectively stopped by the use of methods equally rough, but very practical in their results. In short, the recrudescence of murder as a political argument had been brought to a sudden stop by means of the counter-murder of prisoners in the hands of the new native Government. There was no legal or moral justification for such measures on the part of the infant Free State. But the melancholy fact remained that it had worked, and that an Irish Government had proved to be much tougher with the Irish than the English had ever dared to be. Nor did the glamour of patrioic martyrdom attach itself to the victims. This was all very sobering and disgusting. Yet it is hard to see what other answer could have been made to a continuance of underground warfare, provided of course that we were to have any government at all. (1979, 2, p. 82)

Six months after the opening of the play the government introduced the Public Safety Act to curtail the IRA, which it failed to do (Lee 1989, pp. 157, 219). Johnston's play incorporates a debate then current on progress, violence and the right to power.

Because *The Moon in the Yellow River* is a comedy of ideas, with a setting which seems metaphoric of the country's situation, critics Robert Hogan (1981) and Thomas Kilroy (1981) have usefully compared it with Shaw's *Heartbreak House* (1920). Johnston would have seen the Dublin Drama League's production in March 1926, in which Johnston's wife Shelah Richards played Ellie. Apart from resemblances in characterisation and comic style, *The Moon* incorporates a Shavian polarity between the realist Dobelle, the resident engineer, and the romantic foreigner Tausch.

The main theme is introduced when Dobelle tries to persuade Tausch to leave Ireland and return to Germany before he is destroyed by the natives. Tausch is confident in his efficiency: 'It is the change of mind that only power can bring that will be the justification for all my work here. As Schiller tells us, freedom cannot exist save when united with might. And what might can equal electrical power at one farthing a unit?' (1979, 2, p. 109). Once a character begins to quote Schiller and use a word like 'save' he has only himself to blame for what happens. On cue, as Tausch is holding forth with Dobelle, the flamboyant IRA man Darrell Blake arrives to blow up the power station. He is the kind of laughing boy who will sit down first and debate the issue with the owner. Tausch is not much of a match for the quixotic Blake, who launches into an attack on modernity. German imperialism becomes the target of Irish revolution. In Free-State Ireland, Blake argues, English imperialism has been absorbed by the native government who have employed the Germans to install an instrument symbolising their power. When Tausch tricks the simple Irish by telephoning for the army Commandant Lanigan enters to make his arrests. An old army comrade of Blake's, Lanigan calmly shoots him dead. It is the most famous *coup de théâtre* in Irish drama.

Johnston loads the dice in Act II by making Blake much more attractive than Lanigan: morally we are drawn to Blake's side, and yet Blake is a terrorist (as well as a reactionary). Lanigan has no rhetorical skill and readily concedes Blake's superiority. Yet the law must be upheld through force. Johnston isolates the dilemma facing a country which achieved independence through violence and can maintain peace only through the exercise of more violence. When the argument resumes in Act III Tausch is outraged at what he regards as Lanigan's inexcusable murder. Lanigan is the opposite of Emmet in *The Old Lady Says 'No!'*: 'I've always been taught that it's not words but deeds the country needs, so I'll go on doing what I can, no matter' (1979, 2, p. 150). After Lanigan leaves Dobelle continues the discussion with Tausch. He points out that Tausch is himself responsible: 'Lanigan is just yourself. He is your finger on the trigger' (p. 153). Moreover, there is no answer to the dilemma produced by a liberation movement: 'The birth of a nation is no immaculate conception.'

Farcically, the plant is blown up anyway through a silly accident involving the shells made by George and Captain Potts, perhaps in recollection of the absurd fate of Boss Mangan and the burglar in *Heartbreak House*. Johnston's vision of the world, while obviously fully aware of tragic suffering, was fundamentally comic. The final irony of the accidental destruction of his power plant is too much for the unfortunate Tausch: 'I think I go mad!' (1979, 2, p. 156). Dobelle, who from the start has been seen as chronically soured by life, depressed by the death of his wife in childbirth (in accordance with Catholic hospital practice), is now given a second chance. After Tausch exits Dobelle breaks through his world-weariness as he addresses the picture of his wife. 'Ah, Mary, have pity on me and on poor Tausch. No, not on Tausch. He's too great to need pity. But me. ... take away this cursed gift of laughter and give us tears instead' (p. 156). The echo of O'Casey's *Juno* seems deliberate. Just as Juno and Mary join forces against the patriarchy so does Dobelle manage to recognise and accept his daughter Blanaid, whose existence he had associated with the Catholic patriarchy which had caused his wife's death in childbirth. If such reconciliation is possible, the play seems to ask, is there not hope that Ireland's political differences might not also be solved by acceptance of the other rather than by confrontation of ideologies?

The Moon in the Yellow River is Johnston's most successful play outside Ireland, having had productions in New York in 1932, London in 1938 and New York again in 1961. In Ireland it has played second fiddle to the rather more glamorous *Old Lady*, but it has been revived in 1970 and 1983 at the Abbey. It remains 'perhaps the most interesting of all attempts to create a theatrical mode which will declare the national situation' (Edwards 1979, p. 238). It is a play which, for all its lightness of tone, involves its audience in a cultural debate with deadly implications.

The Scythe and the Sunset (1958) deals, according to Johnston himself, with 'the passing of an imperial civilization' (1977, 1, p. 92). Like Lennox Robinson, Johnston was interested in the fall from power of the Anglo-Irish Ascendancy, but unlike Robinson he had no regrets. It was both his strength and his weakness that Johnston could see both sides. He could manage a modicum of sympathy for the Anglo-Irishman 'become an invisible man' (the echo of Ralph Ellison's black hero is ironic) in the Free State and even for 'this very passé Ascendancy' (p. 86), but he had no passionate investment in their cause. But of course Johnston was not of the people either, and never could be. The fact that he had gone to university at Cambridge rather than at Trinity College, Dublin was because 'at the time a Presbyterian couldn't go to National and a Home Ruler couldn't be sent to Trinity, then a nest of Unionism' (*Irish Times*, 9 August 1984). This made him sympathetic to nationalism but nationalism itself was too emotive and destructive for Johnston to give allegiance to. He could and did endorse the 1916 Rising – hence the title of his preface, 'Up the Rebels!' – but once again in a detached, ironic manner. What Johnston wanted from drama now, after World War Two, was a balance of opposites, a 'take' on history which would offer assurance that whereas evil and good are commingled, as Dobelle says at the end of *The Moon*, and seem to depend on point of view, there is always available a script which can show that all is for the best. Not that Johnston had anything in common with Voltaire's Dr Pangloss. Far from it. He accepted the necessity of violence, just as he admired the courage of the partisans in the Balkan states when he was BBC correspondent there in the early 1940s. After Buchenwald, which he saw when it was liberated, nothing could be the same again. Johnston saw then that the victorious allies were about to be just as cruel and punitive as the enemy had been; he resolved to fight that attitude. 'If that is the law, I am going to break the law. I am going to break it as often and as openly and as ingeniously as I can; because it is a law that I am prepared to be broken for breaking, which to my Irish mind is the acid test for legitimate law-breaking' (1953, p. 347). There is a touch of old Leopold Bloom about this artist. If two wrongs did not make a right then one had to respect the first wrong, acknowledge it, and pass on 'to be happy in the facts, whatever they may be. For to be otherwise is to die twice' (*The Golden Cuckoo*, 1979, 2, p. 275). If it be asked where justice is to be found in such acceptance Johnston, a non-practising barrister, has no answer. Except to say that what happened was never the end but a version of things. Thus all is provisional. Life goes on.

In *The Brazen Horn* (1976, p. 147) Johnston says one discovers the future by free choice and one makes it happen. Negatively, the Anglo-Irish soldier Palliser in *The Scythe and the Sunset* takes his choice to die as freely as the Pearse-character Tetley, in this revision of O'Casey's revisionist play about 1916. Palliser (Johnston's spokesman) sees that imperialism is on the way out anyway: 'I know what's coming, and there's no hard feelings so long as I don't have to be part of the audience' (p. 164). The theatrical imagery reinforces Johnston's recurring point, made through the Speaker/Emmet and made again through use of the Jason myth in *A Bride for the Unicorn*, that life is not so much a dream as a performance in which, at any juncture, if one has the courage to maintain 'face' and yet really understand what 'mask' is, one may effect change. In other words, if in Beckett's phrase in *Endgame* 'something is taking its course' in history, Johnston cannot accept that this precludes individual freedom. Thus Palliser salutes Tetley even though he hates all he stands for; he chooses to die rather than be part of the new arrangements. Palliser too, as Ferrar puts it (1973, p. 129), makes his 'declaration of independence.' This is all Johnston really cared about: it is the whole story of *The Golden Cuckoo*, for instance. Movements meant nothing to him; allegiances and camps were but escape routes from individual responsibility. Identity was definable by existential revolt; national identity as such was so much essentialism and thus held no meaning for Johnston. His challenging intellect reached far beyond the 1930s; his lively brand of modernism interrogated with wit and verve the implications of those myths on which the modern Irish state was founded.

Paul Vincent Carroll

Paul Vincent Carroll was the first major Catholic playwright of post-Treaty Ireland. To use such a blunt, sectarian description requires justification. It may be claimed that up to 1922 the predominant impulse of the Irish literary renaissance was inspirational: it aimed, to a greater or lesser degree, to facilitate the emancipation of the country itself. The energies which were invested in this literary enterprise derived mostly from Protestant artists. Historically, successful marketing of writing in English tended to favour the dominant class in Ireland, and hence the dominant religious affiliation. Perhaps this explains William Carleton's turning Protestant in the 1830s, for example, after which he was able to secure a career as a popular novelist. A Catholic such as George Moore soon learned to jettison the affiliation once he was established in London, but it is not without significance that his involvement in the Irish Literary Theatre was shortlived, even though *The Bending of the Bough* (1900) can be seen to point to the realistic direction that Irish drama was destined to take, despite Yeats's resistance. This is not to argue that the Abbey was sectarian. But it is nevertheless disturbing to find Yeats writing in 1905: 'I have noticed by the by that the writers in this country ... who come from Catholic Ireland, have more reason than fantasy. It is the other way with those who come from the leisured classes. They stand above their subject and play with it, and their writing is, as it were, a victory as well as a creation. The others – Colum and Edward Martyn for instance – are dominated by their subject, with the result that their work as a whole lacks beauty of shape, the organic quality' (Wade 1954, p. 464). The management of the Abbey – Yeats, Synge, Gregory, Robinson – was Protestant. Although there were Catholic writers before 1922, in particular Colum and T. C. Murray, no Catholic was on the Board before 1925. When the Free State government first subsidised the Abbey it was thought necessary to add a representative to the Board of Directors, George O'Brien, who was surprised at his appointment: 'I possessed no obvious qualifications beyond being a Catholic, which was apparently considered desirable ... I knew nothing about the theatre' (Hussey 1993, p. 473). No Catholic writer was added to the Board until Brinsley MacNamara was appointed in 1935. The effect of all this is that there was no sustained critique of Catholicism or Catholic ideology until the 1930s; perhaps none was possible until nationalism had achieved its prior purpose in 1922. Joyce's non-relation to the Abbey probably relates in some measure to this reality.

In any case, it was not until after 1922 that Catholicism came seriously into play as a feature of culture, identity and nationalism. In the Free State the population was 93 per cent Catholic (Lee 1989, p. 206). As time went on that percentage worsened from the Protestant point of view. Consequently, let Yeats fulminate all he pleased in the Senate that 'we are no petty people' (Pearce 1960, p. 99), the dominant culture after 1922 was no longer Anglo-Protestant. Literature was more likely to be reactive than inspirational. The culture which had imagined and helped to create independence was superseded by one more critical and satirical in spirit, although it could also be infused with mysticism (as in the work of Austin Clarke or Patrick Kavanagh). The dominant literary mode in drama as in fiction was realism. Paul Vincent Carroll takes his place alongside Liam O'Flaherty.

Carroll came to prominence with *Things That Are Caesar's*, staged at the Abbey in 1932 and directed by Lennox Robinson. It was a long way from the tone of Johnston's *The Moon in the Yellow River* of the year before. But then 1932 was the year of the Eucharistic Congress in Dublin, when on 26 June a million people turned out in the Phoenix Park to give public, triumphalist testimony that Ireland was now predominantly Catholic (Boylan 1932, p. 183). The papal legate Cardinal Pacelli (himself to be Pope Pius XII), who presided over the five-day event in Dublin, later wrote to congratulate the Archbishop of Dublin: 'Your people indeed joined in the public acts of homage to Christ the King as if they were celebrating a great festival of their nation, and the whole city of Dublin – and indeed the greater part of the whole land of Ireland – was transformed into one huge temple' (Boylan 1932, p. 213). Carroll's play articulated a new protest over this Catholic hegemony. Whenever the Hardy family have a problem, which in the space of two hours' running time works out at about one every fifteen minutes, they send for Father Duffy. He is described as *'a middle-aged priest, slightly grey in the hair. His face reflects the pioneering spirit that possesses him'* (Carroll 1944, p. 143). This spirit is nothing other than to foster solidarity for mutual material benefit, a kind of Freemasonry new to the landscape. It is, of course, cloaked by a metaphysic of Christian harmony, 'and Harmony is another name for God' (p. 169). In operation, this philosophy condones 'marriage huxtering' (p. 157), the mercenary alliance of Eilish Hardy with Terry Noonan, who takes over the family hotel, bar and shop. Eilish eventually rebels against her loveless marriage, asserts herself, and walks out on husband, child, family and church. Of course this is incredible, and no more than a rhetorical two fingers raised to the power of the Catholic clergy, but it shows how far in one direction drama had come since Synge's *The Shadow of the Glen*. Carroll freely confessed his love for the plays of

Ibsen (Sitzmann 1975, p. 146), and he may here have been trying for an Irish *Doll's House*. If so, the last line of the play, given to Father Duffy, indicates how his 'Nora' figure is simply going to be written out of the script as ranks close: 'We can pray for her lost soul' (Carroll 1944, p. 196).

The priest figure in Carroll's plays is not the clichéd figure he was later to become in Irish drama. The priest is an embodiment of the feeble consciences of the ordinary people Carroll writes about. It is as if, once the weight of British political and cultural authority was lifted, the people had to create an alternative and even more oppressive super-ego. Sean O'Faolain complained in *The Irish* of the lack of room given to Catholic intellectuals: 'The Church still relies obstinately on the weapon of rigid authority' (1969, p. 118). Yet Carroll always insisted he was not opposed to Catholicism itself, which was like someone in the gulags saying he was not opposed to Stalinism. He wrote to correct Robert Hogan on this point: 'I have never at any time left the Church. Nor have I ever questioned one of her Articles of Faith or one of her established Dogmas. I have been merely anti-clerical' (Hogan 1972, p. 86). Take what you like and pay for it, says God. It is the priest as destructive figure who most excites Carroll's spleen. *Shadow and Substance* (1937), Carroll's most successful play, offers a good example. 'I decided one day to resurrect Dean Swift, make him not only a Catholic, but a learned interpreter of Catholicisms, and throw him into the modern mental turmoil in Ireland' (Fallon 1938, p. 858). Canon Skerritt is the result.

Canon Skerritt is ambiguously presented. On the one hand he is arrogant, sophisticated and intolerant of any display of vulgarity: an aristocrat of the Church, half-Spanish by birth and pining for his Spanish friends. He is out of step with his time. On the other hand he has absolutely no sympathy with the Fascist style of Catholic action favoured by his two young curates. (It is indeed a sign of the times that a parish priest in a small town in County Louth would have two curates to assist him; nowadays, he would probably have two or three parishes to minister to.) The core of the play, however, lies in Skerritt's opposition to his outspoken schoolmaster, Dermot O'Flingsley. It is still the case in Ireland that the parish priest is also the manager of the local national school and the employer of the teachers in it. In former times, and for decades after *Shadow and Substance* was first staged, this power was exercised to control what was thought as well as what was done in a community. Carroll was the first playwright to expose this form of control. In the play O'Flingsley has anonymously written a book, *I Am Sir Oracle*, attacking the church for its materialism. Skerritt, nosing the authorship, has it out with O'Flingsley, fires him from his job and gives it to a complete nonentity. The Swiftian side of Canon Skerritt's character lies in the eloquence of his contumely rather than in any regard for civil liberties, but he can blaze into anger also in a style that makes for good theatre:

> CANON (*grimly, his eye gleaming*). And I see that our educational system is the – the sewage of European culture. I'd never have thought it, O'Flingsley. Could you tell me, on what page of your teacher's Penny Catechism I could find it?
>
> O'FLINGSLEY (*with venom*). On the page, Canon, the Bishops won't add until they're made.
>
> CANON (*striking desk*). Damnation! I'll not have – *that! (He jumps up fiercely.)*
>
> O'FLINGSLEY (*also jumping up*). And hell and blazes, but you'll have to!
>
> (*They face each other on the floor, the masks now off completely. A pause as they regard each other venomously.*)　　　　　(Carroll 1938, pp. 97–8)

Meanwhile, two other developments are relevant. The Canon's housekeeper Brigid, a frail and pious young woman, sees visions of her namesake Saint Brigid, who urges her to involve the Canon in some devotional rituals. Both the Canon and O'Flingsley love and wish to protect Brigid, whose fragile, hysterical mind is combined with genuine perceptiveness and love. The theme of shadow and substance, which is, of course, central to all Irish drama, is given particular urgency in this play through the range of differences that exist between Brigid's hallucinations, the emotionalism of the people off-stage who are about to use violence against O'Flingsley, and the gulf which divides the Canon's Catholicism from that of those around him. The complexity steers the play away from dogma into the confusions which create audience involvement. Brigid's illness, for such it is, comes to a crisis on the morning of her saint's day, which is also her own birthday; it turns out also to be the day of her death. The other development, which is neatly woven into the plot, derives from the young curates' excessive zeal to foster devotionalism in the face of the Canon's rational, classical Catholicism. Thus they look with superstitious regard on Brigid's senseless instructions from above, and they work up a fury over the book *I Am Sir Oracle*. When they discover its author they allow a mob to attack

O'Flingsley. Brigid, acting on some wild premonition, arrives to protect him and is killed by the mob. In a sense Brigid is modern Ireland being destroyed in an unnecessary conflict between reason and superstition. A contrast with Lady Gregory's use of the Brigid figure (in *The Story Brought by Brigit*) would reveal the in-house nature of Carroll's drama. He is not concerned with folk materials and a vegetative goddess primed to regenerate a traumatised ex-colony. He is washing clerical linen in public. He is showing that Irish society in the post-Treaty era was built on a faultline which in due course would split the place open. The church was eager to deny or cover up this faultline, and even to legislate against its recognition. Instead of encouraging the O'Flingsleys the church insisted, with majority support or acquiescence, on censorship and silence. This was to pretend that the dialectic of shadow and substance did not exist. It was to pretend that they were identical, knowable, doctrinal and summed up in the Blessed Eucharist. When this tidy metaphysic began to fall apart in the 1960s there would be plenty of playwrights to record the upheaval, chief among them the writer who in some ways comes closest to Carroll, namely Brian Friel.

Shadow and Substance transferred to New York, where it won the Drama Critics Circle Award for the best foreign play of the 1937 season. In 1940 it had a London production. Carroll's international reputation was thus initiated. January 1939 saw the successful Broadway production of *The White Steed*, a play rejected by the Abbey board for its anti-clerical content. One can, in a sense, see why. Father Shaughnessy in *The White Steed* is of the repressive disposition one associates with the later plays of Sean O'Casey, *Cock-a-Doodle Dandy* (1949) or *The Bishop's Bonfire* (1955). Rosieanne gives a fair idea early on in *The White Steed* of Carroll's critique of clerical authority: 'If you had to hear him last night below at the pier, standin' on the promenade wall. Down with the drink, down with the dancin', down with the love-makin', a solid Catholic nation for a holy Catholic people, and a dig at the wee handful of Protestants in every line' (Carroll 1944, p. 7). The 'holy hooligans' of the earlier play had come into their own.

Religious tolerance could not be said to have improved in Ireland in the years preceding the rejection of *The White Steed*. The Censorship Act of 1929 led to the banning of virtually every reputable Irish author. The Dance Hall Act of 1935, introduced at the behest of the bishops, was a piece of social machinery which controlled the sex lives and the marriage rate of a whole generation of young people (Keogh 1994, p. 73). These were issues Carroll was to address in anger in his plays. The situation was teetering on the farcical, as Sean O'Faolain was quick to discern: his comedy *She Had to Do Something* (1937) hit back in the only way he knew, by mockery of philistinism. The fate of O'Casey's *The Silver Tassie* suggests a nastier side to what can be dubbed the cultural revolution of the 1930s. Yeats had relented and agreed to a production of O'Casey's controversial play in 1935. Before the opening Father M. H. Gaffney O.P. ominously wrote to the press to remind the Abbey that it was now subsidised at the public expense and was 'in tutelage to the Government elected by the Irish Nation [*sic*]'. Moreover, the Abbey had now to reckon with 'a vigorous intellectual force which is not alien to the authentic spirit of the Irish people. The fracas over the *Playboy* was but a flash in the pan, a child's cracker, in comparison with the hostility with which the Abbey is confronted if it persists in defying Catholic principle and flouting that reticence which is a characteristic of our people' (O'Casey 1975, 1, p. 577). Reviewers, apart from the *Irish Times*, then proceeded to condemn the *Tassie* in the narrowest moral terms. The *Evening Mail* (13 August 1935) called it 'cold-blooded obscenity and blasphemy' and singled out Act II as 'most offensive and profane. ... This kind of thing may be symbolic of something or other, but the effect would be lost on people other than Catholics, and as such, is a gross insult to Catholics.' The matter reached the pulpit after the play opened. In Galway, the Catholic Young Men's Society passed a resolution 'condemning vehemently the work of the Abbey Theatre in so far as it infringes the canons of Christian reverence or human decency, and in so far as it injures the nation's prestige at home and abroad.' The *Irish Times* in an editorial (28 August) decried the fact that, 'Any work which does not show Ireland as a land of saints and scholars, any play which ventures to attack or to satirise an aspect of Irish life, is condemned at once as a treacherous onslaught on the national prestige.' When the Abbey, through manager F. R. Higgins, agreed with this view the only Catholic member of the board of directors, Brinsley MacNamara, resigned in protest. Obviously embarrassed, the Abbey took off *The Silver Tassie* after only one week, in spite of crowded houses. Father Gaffney claimed a victory. It was a victory not for Catholic intellectualism, however, but for a new and dangerous anti-intellectualism. MacNamara made clear in a statement to the press that his resignation was partly because *The Silver Tassie* has not been censored as he presumed it would be since the majority of the cast were Catholics and might be expected to protest against 'Mr O'Casey's obscenity or insult to their religion', and partly because MacNamara objected to O'Casey's plays absolutely. As he put it: 'The audience of the Abbey Theatre has for more than ten years shown a wholly uncritical, I might say almost insane, admiration for the vulgar and worthless plays of Mr. O'Casey' (O'Casey 1975, 1, p. 584). Here, Catholic action paraded as dramatic criticism. It may be added that this anti-intellectual attitude was reinforced when the Spanish Civil War began in 1936 and Catholic Ireland went through an overt Fascist phase. It was a dangerous time. The bishops of Ireland issued a statement describing Spain as 'fighting the battle of Christendom against the subversive powers of communism' (Keogh 1994, p. 94). A national church collection netted over £40,000 for Franco's unsurgents.

There was a closing of ranks critically on what was good, wholesome Irish writing. Gabriel Fallon, O'Casey's erstwhile friend, invoked the opinion of Daniel Corkery on 'colonial' writing and concluded that Irish theatre was 'ill with a sickness that has brought it nigh unto death' (1936, p. 837). Taking note of this diagnosis, no doubt (for Fallon was eventually to be a member of the Abbey board), the Abbey rejected Yeats's *The Herne's Egg* as obscene. *Purgatory*, staged in 1938, immediately ran into clerical opposition. It was not a good time for heterodoxy.

Consequently, Carroll's *The White Steed* did not (dis)grace the Abbey stage. With its Vigilance Committee, corrupt Irish-speaking District Justice and 'the new clerical fascism' (1944, p. 40) in full battle-cry amongst a people buoyed up by 'a new Christian constitution' (p. 77), the play was certain to have stirred up trouble. The last phrase quoted refers to de Valera's new Irish constitution enacted in 1937, which accorded 'special recognition' to the Catholic Church. It is necessary also to explain that the title of the play refers to the tale of Oisin's return from the Land of Youth on a white horse only to find the Fianna all dead and the country Christianised by Saint Patrick. The debate between Oisin as poet and Saint Patrick as upholder of Christian doctrine has entered modern Irish literature at various points as a fertile means of defining the dialectic between artistic impulse and censorship. But for Carroll the myth of Oisin's return signifies only a disaster. Oisin finds Ireland 'swarming with priests and little black men', he says in a note prefacing the play, and as Oisin's feet touch the earth 'he withers miserably away.' In the text Nora Fintry, one of Carroll's most outspoken heroines, invokes the spirit of Oisin when she faces down Father Shaughnessy in Act II. He insists that she brought back her 'evil' from England, 'a pagan land' (p. 53). Her reply disclaims foreign influence. 'What I have in me that won't let me stoop I didn't get in England, for England hasn't got it to give. I got it here. It was in Aideen when she rode by Oscar's side at the battle of Garva. It was in Cu Chulainn when he tied himself to a pillar before he'd stoop to death; it was in Oisin when he rode back on Niam's [sic] white horse and found the land full of priests like you and little men like that poor schoolmaster there [Dillon]; and it's in me now, making me refuse to come to your council table and swallow the ancient draught of humility' (p. 54). She refuses to be driven out of the community either, and stays to make a man of the pusillanimous schoolteacher Dillon. It is interesting that Carroll gives to the woman the power to oppose clerical repression. Although this does not happen in *The White Steed* without the intervention of Inspector Toomey and the sudden return to vigour of the paralysed Canon Lavelle (two *dei ex machina* for the price of one), it is nevertheless a significant endorsement in Irish drama of women's empowerment. It contrasts with Denis Johnston's insistence that women are the source of violence in Irish politics.

It is generally agreed that with *The White Steed* Carroll's best work was completed. It may be, indeed, that Carroll never achieved his full potential as playwright (Doyle 1971, p. 110). Perhaps, as with other writers, Ireland so maimed Carroll emotionally that his growth was arrested. But his passionate protest against the Jansenism in Irish culture in the 1930s qualifies him as that decade's most powerful and most sincere prophet.

Carroll can hardly have known that his was a voice crying in what was soon to become a theatrical wilderness. By January 1939, when *The White Steed* was premiering on Broadway, Yeats was dead, Hugh Hunt its director had severed his links with the Abbey, and Irish theatre was poised to enter the doldrums. Peter Kavanagh exaggerated when he said in *The Story of the Abbey Theatre* (1950, p. 184) that Yeats's theatre died with him. But the exaggeration enclosed a major truth nonetheless. The Abbey was going into the twilight and Paul Vincent Carroll, more Cassandra-like than either Robinson or Johnston, had issued dire warnings that the nation was too.

6

Shades of the prison-house: Shiels, D'Alton, Molloy, Behan

Now we are the laughing-stock of the twenty-six counties. Or is it thirty-six?   Beckett, *All That Fall* (1957)

Introduction

For the most part, Irish plays of the 1940s and 1950s are now of interest predominantly as cultural documents. They reflect the values, artistic and moral as well as socio-economic and political, of a people struggling to establish firm contours of identity in a post-colonial phase. Gabriel Fallon (1953) described the playwrights of the time as the nation's ballad-makers, and this seems about right: they maintained the idiom and form of the peasant drama to narrate and give voice to primary feelings and communal anxieties. We are dealing with plays of a particular, transitional but nevertheless formative time in Irish history. It was, essentially, the de Valera era. The plays discussed below are the product of and reflect the pastoralism de Valera advocated but they also propose a critique of it, and it is the critique, the interrogation of the ideal, which is significant. The difficulty, artistically, is that virtually all of these plays fall into a conventional realistic form, whereby the critique is usually in the end accommodated to the demands of a happy ending. The major exception is Brendan Behan, a true original, whose work is on another level.

It seems best, therefore, to make a clear distinction in this chapter between the Abbey playwrights and Behan. Further, the section on the Abbey writers is merely representative. The emphasis in the first part of this chapter mainly falls on Shiels, D'Alton and Molloy.

Until 1945 Ireland was in a protracted 'emergency', as the Second World War was officially known. In a passage often since quoted the historian F. S. L. Lyons wrote (1973, pp. 557–8) that it was 'as if an entire people had been condemned to live in Plato's cave, with their backs to the fire of life and deriving their only knowledge of what went on outside from the flickering shadows thrown on the wall before their eyes by the men and women who passed to and fro behind them.' Lyons implies a wilful isolationism, costing almost everything. But other historians have demurred and have argued that honour, pride and a sense of realism were reinforced through Ireland's policy of neutrality. The social historian Terence Brown, while not blind to the deprivations and repressions which the Emergency meant for Ireland, argues (1985a, p. 180) that the period was a watershed with quite positive implications: 'the period, rather than representing a stretch of time when Ireland behaved like an historical drop-out, was in fact a period when the country's own internal historical life was entering on a crucial phase.' That crucial phase had to do with social and economic conditions as related to national identity. After all, the new Irish constitution had only been introduced in 1937; the economic war with Britain had ended only in 1938. It was time to concentrate on domestic affairs and inspection of the values in accordance with which the young nation was to live.

'Community' was a word much favoured by de Valera. He seemed to prefer it to 'society' or even 'people'. In his famous reply to Winston Churchill at the end of the war in 1945 de Valera said: 'As a community which has been mercifully spared from all the major sufferings, as well as from the blinding hates and rancours engendered by the present war, we shall endeavour to ... bind up some of the gaping wounds of suffering humanity' (Moynihan 1980, p. 476). Even de Valera's political opponents in Ireland, according to Ronan Fanning (1983, p. 128), shared his 'cultural vision'. Thus de Valera somehow managed to create within Ireland during the war years a sense of community. It was, however, a community behind metaphorical bars.

George Shiels

In August 1940 George Shiels's *The Rugged Path* set the stage at the Abbey for the new post-Yeatsian dispensation. Shiels (1881–1949) was no stranger to Abbey audiences. He had established his reputation as a popular entertainer with *Paul Twyning* (1922) and *Professor Tim* (1925). Though clever and well-made these comedies were undeniably contrived. O'Casey, writing to Lady Gregory in September 1925, was quick to spot the weakness: 'George Shiels is very fond of fashioning hearts of gold & hearts of silver, & here & there, a heart of oak, & one or two ever labouring to be deceitful above all things, & desperately wicked, but then eventually become the broken & contrite hearts that no-one dare despise, & those who do not get a crown, at least will get a palm branch. ... It's really terrible when you look into it' (1975, 1, p. 149). Andrew E. Malone commented in *The Irish Drama* that in Shiels's work there is 'no attempt to effect a contact with the life of the Ireland in which the scene is supposed to be laid' (1929, p. 239). As if to give the lie to his critics Shiels then wrote *The New Gossoon* (1930), *The Passing Day* (1936), and *The Rugged Path* (1940), each more preoccupied than the other with living conditions in Free State Ireland.

As *The Rugged Path* opens we are introduced to a peasant setting enhanced by the electricity of which Denis Johnston had made such an effective metaphor for progress in *The Moon in the Yellow River* at the Abbey in 1931. There is electric light and a radio: we are into the world to which Friel was to return in nostalgia with *Dancing at Lughnasa* (1990). For Shiels it was a harsh, joyless world, and it was to be the norm in serious Irish drama for decades. *The Rugged Path* explores rural violence and the necessity for Irish people to overturn traditional notions of law and order based on colonialist conditions. As the police sergeant says in Act I, the 'national kink' is to oppose co-operation with the police and never to 'inform' on a neighbour (Shiels 1942, p. 21). When the Dolis family – wild, mountainy people – terrorise local farmers and murder an old man for two pounds, the Tanseys (in whose farmhouse the play is set) are afraid to give evidence. The older generation, in particular, want to stay on 'the level road of safety' in community relations rather than attempt the 'rugged path' of change and confrontation (p. 83). But the young Tanseys, Sara and Sean, belong to a new generation. Sean is described as 'born free' ... the first man of his breed that never touched his cap to an alien' (p. 92). He represents the post-Treaty Irishman. Through his influence, the Tanseys give evidence against the Dolises. Unfortunately, the jury is too intimidated to convict and Peter Dolis is released rampant.

So effective in performance was *The Rugged Path* that it was given an extended run of twelve weeks, an unprecedented event at the Abbey, where the repertory system never allowed more than a two-week run. David Sears, author of *Juggernaut* (1929), a play about political violence in the 1920s, and now drama critic for the *Irish Independent*, described *The Rugged Path* as 'the most important Irish play for a long time' (6 August 1940). Shiels was encouraged to write a sequel, and *The Summit* was staged in February 1941. A reaction in the community takes place against the Dolises, as a breach is healed between the Tanseys and the Cassidys, formerly divided by 'the split' created by the civil war of 1922. A common cause is made against violence and lawlessness as a new maturity enters the social scene. Cassidy appeals to a sense of 'community' (Shiels 1942, p. 228). Given the persistence of civil-war politics in Ireland, Shiels was being didactic: we are led to believe that the old-age pensioner did not die in vain after all. Yet Shiels broke new ground with his theme, cleverly framed by news on the radio about World War Two. In a sense, we get Patrick Kavanagh's 'Epic' writ large.

As soon as it became clear that *The Rugged Path* was a hit the managing director of the Abbey, F. R. Higgins, publicly announced a new policy of providing 'nothing but new plays' (*Evening Mail*, 22 August 1940). When Higgins died suddenly in January 1941 his successor Ernest Blythe (1889–1975) continued this policy but also wanted full houses: this meant the cultivation of popular, commercial successes. Blythe also wanted to use the Abbey as an instrument to restore the Irish language, and to that end he encouraged government subsidy for the production of plays in Gaelic. He had spoken in some detail on this theme in his lecture delivered during the Abbey Theatre Festival in August 1938, concluding with the apocalyptic assertion that if the Irish language were to disappear 'distinctively Irish literature in English would soon cease to be written' (Robinson 1939b, p. 197). Now that he was in the driver's seat at the Abbey, a seat he was to occupy until 1967, Blythe was fully determined to make the theatre more authentically Irish. He changed the official name to *Amharclann na Mainistreach*, properly, as Donagh McDonagh pointed out, 'The Theatre of the Monastery' (Mikhail 1988, p. 185). In line with recent initiatives introduced by the de Valera government to make Irish central to Irish education and the civil service, Blythe decreed that Abbey actors must learn to be able to perform in both Irish and English. The director Ria Mooney was told that 'the nation was at war with the English language' and she must join the ranks or be replaced (Hunt 1979, p. 174). Blythe defended his policy in his pamphlet *The Abbey Theatre*

(1965a) and added: 'In view of the policy of the State, of the effort being made to restore Irish to wider use and of the vital need to preserve the language as *the one sure guarantee of national continuity*, failure on the part of the Abbey to get ready to work to a reasonable extent through Irish could soon have made it in reality an anti-National Theatre rather than a National Theatre' (n.p., emphasis added). The difficulty was, of course, that there were very few plays in Irish for the actors to play in. It became Blythe's mission to fill that gap. Thereafter plays in Irish were a fairly common occurrence at the Abbey: Robinson (1951) lists thirty-six by 1950. These included, besides translations and the occasional new play, the novel idea of an annual pantomime in Irish. Laudable as this cultural aim may have been, its effect was to distract from the dramatic responsibility of confronting audiences with the art which questions assumptions and reveals the gods by which people live.

Form, so long as it was form related to Irish, rather than content was Blythe's preoccupation as general manager of the Abbey. He did not really care what went on the stage in English so long as it seemed to be fulfilling the theatre's contract, viewed in traditionalist terms. In time, artistic standards fell resoundingly. A public protest was voiced within the Abbey in 1947, during a performance of *The Plough and the Stars*. Blythe was not concerned. For him the end justified the means, and the end was primarily nationalist. That end was slightly compromised once the Abbey lost its own theatre in 1951 and had to survive in commercial circumstances at the Queen's. To give Blythe his due, he kept the theatre going during those fifteen difficult years at the Queen's even though it was a thankless job. John Ryan spoke for many when he commented (1975, p. 39), 'Most of the work done was Abbey *manqué* – beside which even parody pales.' Shiels vanished into the quagmire.

Louis L'Alton

Louis D'Alton (1901–51), who toured with his own fit-up company, was a writer who found a way through this dismal prospect. His early work, such as his play about the poet Mangan, *The Man in the Cloak* (1937), had a strong vein of fantasy dramatically justified by Mangan's opium-induced dreams, and even in his realistic plays staged after 1940 this element of fantasy could not be suppressed. His characters tend to be dreamers, megalomaniacs and malcontents, characters out of step with the humdrum routines of a stable but suffocating society. *The Money Doesn't Matter* (1941) concerns the material ambitions of Tom Mannion, a powerful self-made man from a poor background, and the effects on his family. His daughter Norah, out of sympathy with the Mannion philosophy, wishes to enter a convent. The theme here is similar to that sounded at the opening of Teresa Deevy's *Katie Roche* (1936). In Deevy's play, however, it is the male authority which is thrown into question. D'Alton's play is more concerned to offer an alternative to Mannion's restless greed, and Norah is far too retiring a character to make her choice an ideological issue. She simply and quietly goes off to the African missions; Mannion does not even miss her until she is gone. Mannion ends as he began, intent on making more money to bolster his uninvestigated ego.

In the first production of *The Money Doesn't Matter* the main emphasis unfortunately fell on broad displays of vulgarity. Frank O'Connor, who walked out after two acts, wrote to *The Bell* (June 1941) deploring this vulgarity, which included a parody of Lennox Robinson as the alcoholic son Philip: 'here there was no pity, no horror, no sense of right or wrong' (p. 63). Denis Ireland posed the question in the same issue of *The Bell* (p. 68): 'Has the State-supported Irish National Theatre become simply a kind of laboratory where experts in mass-observation can test their theories about the vacuity of the twentieth-century Irish mind, counting every manufactured laugh as a hit? If it has, then does not this amount to a complete reversal of Yeats's original policy, which was to go on giving us the best until we began to like it?' It was a matter of focus, of artistic direction. The title of another comedy, *They Got What They Wanted* (1947), also based on greed, indicates D'Alton's rather cynical attitude. He was willing to exploit the Abbey's new audience and to ensure that they 'got what they wanted' while he also mocked their pretensions. The play ran for twelve weeks. While it is not possible to agree with Heinz Kosok that this later play is 'a minor comic masterpiece' (1995, p. 200), it is well focused on the Jonsonian intrigues of the central character, Bartley Murnaghan, a confidence man whose pretences bring out the hypocrisies of small-town Irish business men.

Money also forms the background of D'Alton's *Lovers Meeting* (1941), subtitled 'A Tragedy'. The first audience, however, insisted on seeing much of the play as comedy. When the Druid Theatre

Company revived *Lovers Meeting* in October 1990 its tragic as well as its sociological features were fully evident. It is a seminal play in the later Irish tradition, a play about match-making and thwarted love, which had a worthy successor in John B. Keane's ever-popular *Sive* (1959). Early on in *Lovers Meeting* the point is firmly made that marriage is a business transaction the purpose of which, from the woman's point of view, is to 'rise a step in the world' (D'Alton 1964, p. 10). This was where the deranged Hannie went wrong (p. 18), 'She refused a made match with a strong farmer. ... It was a sorry day for her. Mistress of five hundred acres she'd be to-day and the mother o' twelve children.' Her sister Jane, however, abandoned lover for security. In Ibsenist fashion, her crime against the heart returns to destroy her own child. *Lovers Meeting* may be melodrama, but it is very effective theatrically, soothing with comic rural stereo-types while also shocking the audience with a critique of arranged marriages and a sensational suicide. The mother's guilt is well charted; the greater the insistence on suppression of instinct the worse the eventual effect on the innocent daughter. It is as if D'Alton were asserting that all the protectionism and stress on moral conformity in de Valera's Ireland were but so many pretences when the power of passion is acknowledged.

In this respect D'Alton opposed the aggressively orthodox atti-tude towards evil found in the greatest theatrical success of the age, *The Righteous Are Bold* (1946), by Frank Carney (1902–78). Set on the slopes of Croagh Patrick in County Mayo, this peasant drama might have been written about one of de Valera's 'cosy homesteads', under threat from the devil himself lodged in the fair bosom of one of de Valera's 'comely maidens', returned from godless England (Moynihan 1980, p. 466). It is a cleverly coded attack on liberalism of English origin and an extraordinary vindication of the people's need for the Catholic clergy to keep 'demonism' (imported by women) from destroying family values. In *Church and State in Modern Ireland* J. H. Whyte says that even before the 1937 constitution awarded a special place to the Roman Catholic church there was 'overwhelm-ing agreement that traditional Catholic values should be main-tained, if necessary by legislation. ... The Catholic populace gave no hint of protest. The Protestant minority acquiesced' (1980, p. 60). One must accept, then, that the audiences which flocked to *The Righteous Are Bold* during its sixteen-week run approved what they saw. It was left to O'Casey to parody the famous exorcism scene in his *Cock-a-Doodle Dandy* (1949); D'Alton, a lesser writer than O'Casey but with a modicum of his intellectual independence, could only oppose such hegemony obliquely. *This Other Eden* (1953), staged posthumously, is D'Alton's finest play and the one where he most openly took issue with such complacencies of post-war Ireland.

As the title suggests, *This Other Eden* recycles Shaw's *John Bull's Other Island* to take a fresh, satirical look at Ireland–England relations. To the older generation in the small Irish town where the play is set, 'the nation's all right ... there's not a damn thing wrong with the nation' (D'Alton 1970, p. 9). But to the young people, like Maire McRoarty who drove ambulances during the blitz in London, Ireland is suffocating. The farcical side of the play concerns the arrival of an Englishman, Roger Crispin, to bid for the house and estate of a dead patriot, Carberry, who is being commemorated at the same time. It emerges that Crispin speaks Irish and is fiercely pro-Irish, even though he was Carberry's military opponent in Ireland's war of independence. When Carberry's illegitimate son Conor Heaphy burns down the memorial hall and denounces the dead hero Crispin steps in to offer to pay for a new memorial. There is an immediate attempt to cover up Conor's crime as an accident. Through Conor, D'Alton exposes hypocrisy disguised as patriotism. 'But the lie I destroyed wasn't the lie I thought. It wasn't the lie of a hypocritical Carberry who'd imposed himself on an unsuspecting community; it was the hypocrisy of a community setting up a lie in place of a man that had been, and erecting a memorial to a man who had never existed' (p. 68). Maire, in protest against her father's collusion in all of this deception, decides to return to England, 'because I like the feeling that I can go to the devil in my own way if I feel like doing that. And because I don't like the feeling that I must go to heaven someone else's way whether I like it or not. And because I like the feeling of being able to talk to a man, or even half a dozen men, without being suspected of wanting to go to bed with them!' (p. 70) This was a daring set of preferences for the year 1953 in Ireland, where sex was still a taboo topic. '*The assembly is literally paralysed by this astounding utterance*', D'Alton's stage direction reads. Her outraged father calls, with some significance for free speech at every level, for 'Silence. I tell you Silence! Silence! Silence!' One is reminded of Behan's opening stage direction in *The Quare Fellow* (1954): on the wall of the prison landing is a large notice facing the audience, 'SILENCE'. The point is exactly the same. In the new Irish

Republic there was little room for protest. If Maire goes back to godless England Irish identity as well as Irish morality is threatened, since these are equated and idealised. Unlike Shaw, D'Alton here seems unable to admit the viability of an exit to England, except as Conor naively assumes it in terms of a religious mission. But when Crispin proposes marriage to Maire the problem is paradoxically resolved. He, the irrepressible talker, will lift the ban of silence. By staying, Maire will marry a bastard and share in English values on Irish soil. In fantasy fashion, D'Alton assimilates the coloniser into a new, cynically viewed Utopia. He fails to find a place in it, however, for Devereaux, the intellectual who is the playwright's representative. Devereaux is described as *'an observer of men, who has shed the illusions of his youth, but is still at heart something of an idealist. The bitterness of a man who has witnessed, as he believes, his country fall from grace, and the disappointment of his own hopes is always with him'* (p. 6). That bitterness remains. As an 'ex-National School Teacher' he is as much an outsider as the unfrocked priest in Shaw's play, Peter Keegan. But unlike Keegan, Devereaux has nothing positive to offer, no dream. He is all the time waiting for someone else to produce the dream. And so he remains D'Alton's uncomfortable cynic, persisting in his vision of 'a people hugging to themselves a yoke that no conqueror could ever have dared to put on them' (p. 79). He sees that he is the real exile. 'I have traded the bright shadow for the bitter substance, and I'm punished for it' (p. 81). Thus D'Alton depicts Ireland in the depths of disillusion. And he assumes the only intelligent position available, that of satirist/Thersites.

M. J. Molloy

M. J. Molloy (1914–94) witnessed this moral crisis from a different perspective. Where Shiels was optimistic about the new Ireland, and D'Alton cynical, Molloy at his best was interestingly pessimistic. He was only at his best in *The Wood of the Whispering* (1953), coincidentally premiered in the same year as *This Other Eden*. Molloy is the great chronicler of the West of Ireland, its poverty, depopulation and decline in the 1940s and 1950s, who has tended to be seen as a peasant playwright very much in the style of Synge (Hogan 1968, p. 94). But Molloy's main interest was as folklorist; he wanted to capture and immortalise the manners, customs, language and people he knew intimately in County Galway. 'I found myself dramatizing aspects of rural life, which city people knew very little about and refused to believe' (Molloy 1977, p. 66). This is a danger-ous aim for a playwright, and too often Molloy simply lapsed into quaintness, the very thing the Abbey adored at this time and termed PQ or 'peasant quality'. Yet from his first play, *Old Road* (1943), Molloy showed that he had a critique to offer: that play is an early exposure of the harsh realities of poverty and emigration underlying the literary picturesque. To a far greater degree, *The Wood of the Whispering* is an effective response to de Valera's idealisation of the pastoral life. Molloy shows the misery of making do, where guests are offered tea out of jamjars or poteen out of eggshells. He shows the anxiety and loneliness of a people resolute in their stoicism but pathetic in their vulnerability to mental breakdown and institution-alisation. The young have almost all gone away; those left are in various stages of decline, madness and senility. Yet an abundant cheerfulness reigns, or rather a resignation. For this is Molloy's essential trait. He loved these people; he was one of them himself, a bachelor farmer enduring whatever the good Lord sent him and creating fun out of the most ordinary and simple events. Molloy subtitles *The Wood* 'a Comedy'. It is closer to tragicomedy. Sanbatch Daly, the main character and chorus to this Kavanagh-like drama of 'great hunger', is described as both 'haggard and worn by privation' and 'a little crazy and absurd and wild' (Molloy 1961a, p. 2). His bed is a coffin-shaped box in a clearing outside an abandoned Big House and demesne. All is in decline around him, and the play is a lament for the collapse of a community undermined by emigration and debilitated through lack of marriages. Suicide is a real danger, as of Brehoney, who 'soaped a rope and hung himself' in puritanical angst over sexual urges (p. 23). Madness is likewise a real threat for young Mark, who lives alone: 'How can a man's mind stand out for ever against misery and the badness of the night?' (p. 19). When Sanbatch turns matchmaker in a desperate attempt to counter the social malaise, farce and the grotesque colour the tragic picture. Sanbatch is the artist, the playwright, conjuring 'plots' to reorder reality. But as such he is no Prospero on the heights but the most abject of traditional shamans, who has himself eventually to feign violent madness in order to secure refuge in the Ballinasloe asylum. It is this last piece of theatre which precipitates the few surviving young couples into marriage, to make Sanbatch change his mind.

The Wood of the Whispering now begs comparison more with

Beckett than with Synge. In 1953 Beckett was unknown as a play-wright in Ireland, but he was to become the ghost at the feast of Irish drama. Beckett averted his eyes from the Irish theatre after Yeats died; yet his plays, from *Waiting from Godot* (1953) on, can be seen as engaged in a dialogue with Yeats and especially with Synge (Worth 1978). In the Beckett canon, only *All That Fall* (1957), a radio play, is at all occupied with Irish characters and society; moreover the occupation, insofar as it exists, is on the level of parody. The use of realism is jocose throughout. *All That Fall*, for all the *risus purus* it deliciously elicits, serves but to make *The Wood of the Whispering* appear doubly disturbing. Where Beckett could mock from a distance Molloy (ironically a Beckettian name) was immersed in the sociological terrain: Ireland herself was in decay. Poverty was endemic. Emigration rates for the decade 1951–61 were higher than for any comparable period in the twentieth century (Lyons, 1973, p. 625). When Sanbatch takes his broken mirror and says, 'Give me a look at my oul' withered jaws till I see am I making clay' (Molloy 1961a, p. 53), the death's head given back with a grin is an image of dying Ireland rather than of universal mortality. Clay is the word, as Kavanagh put it in *The Great Hunger* (1942); the agricultural reso-nance of 'making clay', in all its morbid irony, roots the phrase in specific Irish experience. As Sanbatch remarks to his dog, faithful auditor, 'we won't be always miserable, Leggy. We'll die at last' (Molloy 1961a, p. 27). The chord Molloy struck in *The Wood of the Whispering*, then, as opposed to the curiosity value of his historical plays such as *The King of Friday's Men* (1948) or *Petticoat Loose* (1979), was metaphysical/political, a verdict on the years of independence in Ireland leading only to neglect. 'For forty years Ireland has been free, and for forty years it has wandered in the desert under the leadership of men who freed their nation, but who could never free their own souls and minds from the ill-effects of having been born in slavery' (Molloy 1961a, preface).

Brendan Behan

It is fruitful to consider the drama of Brendan Behan in the context of what was discussed in the preceding section. He was a many-sided man, a complex and mercurial personality, and as a writer he had affinities both with the Gaelic and modern Irish literary tradi-tions. He was seriously divided against himself in the allegiances he held. There is infusing his work, especially his plays, a plangency, a 'Jackeen's Lament' not only for the Blaskets (the title of one of his best poems) but for all that history had done to make Irish politics a muddle. The song in *The Hostage* which celebrates Michael Collins as the Laughing Boy perhaps sums up the dilemma from which Behan never could escape. If only Collins had died by Pearse's side or in the GPO he could safely be revered as the lost leader, but instead he accepted the Treaty, opposed the republicans, besieged the Four Courts and saw to the execution of his former comrades: impossible to give Collins loyalty, impossible not to love and lament him. In decrying what he calls the 'civilisation' which de Valera had created in Ireland Behan comments: 'this is not what Michael Collins lived and worked for. It goes to show that if you want to make a revolution, it's as well to go and learn something about politics' (1962, pp. 87–8). Therefore Behan lived in an Ireland he could never accept, looking back to an alternative history which was itself flawed. His writing, accordingly, was from the margins of Irish society, the underground, and was radical in form and content; yet there was also in his writing a longing for a community which might have been, a counter-ideal to de Valera's dream. The tragedy for Behan was that 'this other Eden' was to be found nowhere but in his own troubled imagination.

Shortly after he was born in February 1923 Behan was taken to Kilmainham Jail and shown to his father Stephen, a republican prisoner during the civil war. He was thus initiated from birth into radical opposition to the Free State, in 1948 declared a republic. His mother Kathleen Kearney was a brave, formidable woman, to be seen as late as the 1980s on Irish television singing rebel songs without once faltering over the words. She was, in a sense, an embodiment of Cathleen Ni Houlihan, who demanded the patriotic involvement of all her sons, Brendan included: Brian Behan makes this association in *Kathleen: A Dublin Saga* (1988). It is implicit also in *Mother of All the Behans* (1984), which was turned into a one-woman show in 1987. Kathleen's brother Peadar Kearney (d. 1942) was a songwriter whose main but not inconsiderable claim to fame is as the author of *Amhrán na bhFiann* ('The Soldier's Song'), the Irish national anthem. If the anthem is embarrassing today it was doctrinal for Brendan Behan, who never lost an opportunity to remind his audience of this link with national expression. Consequently, Behan was never free. From the moment of birth he was co-opted into a

movement to continue the quixotic struggle for Ireland's total liberation from English control.

But the connection here with song is important also. Fated
though he was, Behan was brought up to know and love Ireland
through songs (with which he, no less than his mother, could regale
company endlessly). As a result all he did, all he wrote, was impelled
towards joyous song. His cousin Colbert Kearney has compared
Behan to a 'younger northside Falstaff, not only good company
himself but the inspiration of good company in others ... his whole
self ready to sing grief rather than cry it' (1993, p. 301). Even though
his material dealt with imprisonment, defeat and death, Behan's was
the art of celebration. This is why, in the end, he holds the palm over
many who were better craftsmen, harder workers, more know-
ledgeable, more intellectual and better able to sustain a theme.
Behan's art soars, free where he himself was unfree, transcending
his time, transcending the 1950s, and singing recklessly for all time.
While other writers of the 1940s and 1950s struggled to find and
shape images of the growing, unfinished nation Behan was the
nation itself, loved, lovable and forever in search of completion.

It is difficult to separate Behan the man from Behan the artist.
Most books about him, such as Jeffs's (1966) or Boyle's (1969),
chronicle the later life in tedious detail. Exceptions are Gerdes (1973)
and Kearney (1977), who concentrate on the writings. O'Connor
(1970) has supplied the definitive biography, which has stood the
test of time. But however one might wish nowadays to concentrate
on the texts and pray for the death of the author, Behan will always
rise again to shoulder aside theory and re-assert himself.

In June 1943 Behan wrote from prison to his cousin Séamus De
Búrca, 'I don't know a good deal about plays' (1992, p. 21). He was
nevertheless engaged in writing his first play, *The Landlady*, in three
acts. It has not survived, although De Búrca, more or less its mid-
wife, has given a useful summary of its contents (Boyle 1969, pp. 47–8).
According to Ulick O'Connor, Behan tried to have his fellow-
prisoners stage *The Landlady* but it proved too blasphemous and
obscene for their delicate tastes (1970, p. 74). Nevertheless Behan
sent the first act to the Abbey in May 1946, with a promise to send
two more acts. Recently, a fourteen-page fragment, entitled 'The
Rent Woman', was acquired by the National Library of Ireland (MS
29,084), and this seems to be a slightly different version from the
Abbey's Act I of *The Landlady*. From this, it is clear that Behan

always had a wonderful ear for the rhythms of Dublin speech. For example, Mag Mahon pinpoints the crawthumper Mrs Keane, thus: 'She has her two knees worn to the bone from this chapel and that chapel. One Ash Wednesday she was so long in Gardiner St., that the man who covers the statues thought she was a statue herself, and nearly choked her with four yards of purple cloth, and he thinkin' she was a new saint he hadn't noticed before.' In a letter from Arbour Hill prison dated 16 August 1943 Behan associates his dialogue with Synge (1992, p. 24). It is clear that 'talk' is the whole basis of Behan's art: he has no idea of how to move his characters (denizens of his grandmother's tenement in Russell Street) forward or to organise them in a developing plot.

In February 1947 Behan contributed a one-act play, *Gretna Green*, to a republican commemorative concert in the Queen's Theatre, Dublin, leased by his cousins the Bourkes. This play was set outside an English prison the night before two Irish men are to be hanged. The incident was based on fact (the execution of two IRA men in Birmingham in 1940) but the play was a failure and the text disappeared (De Búrca 1993, p. 20). In outline it would appear to be indebted to Lady Gregory's *The Gaol Gate*. In the mean time, while still interned in the Curragh with other IRA prisoners, to be released on general amnesty in 1946, Behan had begun *The Quare Fellow*, using the idea of an impending execution again but moving the action from outside to inside the prison. *The Quare Fellow*, however, was not conceived as a political play and was actually based on a murderer Behan got to know in Mountjoy who was executed in 1943. He began writing it in Irish, which he perfected while interned in the Curragh, and entitled it *Casadh Súgáin Eile*, or 'The Twisting of Another Rope', in parody of Douglas Hyde's whimsical folk play concerning the means taken to rid a household of an unwanted poet/outsider. In Behan's scenario a different kind of unwanted man is excluded by society through use of a more deadly kind of rope, woven by society itself. In that sense, *The Quare Fellow* is both a social accusation and a subversion of folk ritual. When Behan was later questioned by his fellow internees about the change of title he replied, according to Dominic Behan (1965, p. 102), 'Yes ... in jail the deed of hanging, the act is the enemy. Outside, yeh can think of the victim.' The answer reveals Behan's intuitive awareness of the artist's need to be at once inside and outside his material, in sympathy and yet detached. Once transferred to a theatre this idea becomes instantly dramatic: the audience is made to participate as if sharing the imprisonment and yet allowed to enjoy the pleasure of catharsis. When *The Quare Fellow* was first staged some ex-prisoners in the audience remarked that it was just like being inside again. This is the effect required, but it is also required that audiences see the stage as metaphor, the condemned man as an everyman and society itself as a prison.

Whether or not Behan was familiar with a controversial Abbey play about republican prisoners, *Design for a Headstone* (1950), by Seamus Byrne, he sent a one-act version of *The Quare Fellow* to the Abbey in 1950 or 1951. Byrne's play is set in Mountjoy and concerns IRA prisoners on hungerstrike. Byrne (1904–68) had been an activist himself and was jailed in 1940, at a time when Behan was in a Borstal institution. It seems their paths did not cross. It is unlikely, however, that Behan did not know of Byrne's play, given its subject. Byrne showed the 'futility of minority war against the state' (*Irish Times* review), but he showed too the strong opposition of the Catholic church to the IRA, a topic Behan also writes about in *Borstal Boy* (1958). In his biography of Behan, O'Connor mistakenly dates *Design for a Headstone* as 1957 and reports (p. 248) Behan's anger at it as 'an anti-I.R.A. play', which, of course, it is not. Robert Hogan, who published Byrne's play in 1967, considers it a better play than *The Quare Fellow*; in any case it has to be regarded as a significant intellectual source.

Behan had, however, been working on 'one Act of' *The Twisting of Another Rope* as early as May 1946, when he mentioned it in a letter to Blythe: 'everything is shown in the *black cell* in some prison. Two men are condemned to death and waiting for the Rope' (1992, p. 31). A one-act version was rejected by the Abbey some time after the fire of 1951. 'It just dealt with the coming of the hangman to the jail. It was a lovely little thing, written for the radio, of course, and would have lasted about half an hour. Lennox Robinson liked it. He said it would be easy to devise for the stage with very little writing, and that it didn't need to be radically changed. I wrote all this to Brendan and didn't hear anything from him for about two years' (Blythe 1965b, p. 184). Behan then re-submitted a 'bloated', three-act version. Micheál O hAodha, for whom Behan wrote his two radio plays broadcast on Radio Éireann at this time, says (1974, p. 145) that the three-act version of *The Quare Fellow* would have occupied five hours' playing time and it was sent back to be cut in half. It is therefore not true to say that the Abbey rejected *The Quare Fellow*. Behan did not submit it again at this time (it was staged at the Abbey in 1956) but tried the Gate instead, to no avail. Alan Simpson, a young director who with his wife Carolyn Swift had opened the Pike Theatre towards the end of 1953, obtained a copy of *The Quare Fellow* from Behan and decided to stage it. The premiere was thus at the 55-seater Pike on 19 November 1954. It played successfully for four weeks. The venue, which in a later decade would have been called an 'alternative theatre', was much to Behan's liking. 'I have always liked the name of this institution. Its founders and directors have been known so long to me, and I to them, that in the production of my play ... I confess to a certain intimacy of feeling with them. ... I have never got round to asking them where they got the name, "Pike," from. It doesn't matter. It brings to mind rebel memories of 'ninety-eight, and the wide breath of the French Revolution that blew round the heads – full of Continental freethinking – of Tone and Emmet. New times, new minds, new men' (Behan 1955).

Besides editing Behan's *Complete Plays* (1978), Simpson wrote an informative book on the Pike, *Beckett, Behan and a Theatre in Dublin* (1962), and seems a reliable witness for establishing the truth about Behan's texts. Simpson has this to say about the script of *The Quare Fellow* which Behan first gave him (1978, p. 7): 'While I loved the dialogue I found it somewhat repetitive and involuted and in need of some cutting. He had a lazy habit of starting off on a subject, dropping it, and then coming back to it later on, and so diminishing its dramatic impact. Brendan was most agreeable about our [*sic*] comments and with a little patient bullying but no acrimony at all we got him to assist in making the necessary alterations.' Obviously two people, Simpson and Swift, decided which were the 'necessary' alterations, and Behan's role was merely 'to assist' in this operation. In her own book, *Stage by Stage* (1985, p.139) Swift comments: 'the speeches were thick wedges of dialogue, nearly all with a minimum of four sentences, and full of subordinate clauses. As soon as we studied it, however, we realised there was pure gold waiting to be prised loose from the excessive verbiage.' This prising process meant not only cuts but rewritings. Simpson says (1962, p. 40) that Behan's 29 characters were reduced to 21. In the *Complete Plays* (p. 15) he mentions 'transpositions', which obviously means shifting dialogue around. He also says here that despite the editing done at the Pike 'and a little further tightening carried out for the Theatre Workshop productions [*sic*] in London, the text is as near to the author's manuscript as is the case with many plays published after their stage premiere.' Yes, but in other cases the author makes the alterations. Moreover, the reference to 'a little further tightening' of Behan's script for the Theatre Workshop production by Joan Littlewood in May 1956 complicates matters, since Behan gave Littlewood the script already edited by the Pike. This point is verified by the Pike prompt copy, which has survived: the cuts in this typescript correspond to the printed text (where other cuts ominously affect Behan's use of dialect and seriously alter the opening of Act III). For her part, Littlewood says that the script 'badly needed pruning: where one good story was sufficient, he's added four or five', and Behan approved of her pruning: 'Better without all that old rubbish' (Littlewood 1994, pp. 468, 470). Simpson, however, thought that Littlewood's amalgamation of some roles was a bad mistake, and he instanced (1962, p. 45) the giving of Warder Donnelly's opening lines to Warder Regan, whose character is quite different. To summarise: the text of *The Quare Fellow* in print, and the one included by Simpson in *Complete Plays*, is the one edited by Littlewood (following the Simpsons) with Behan's agreement and published in 1956 copyrighted jointly to Behan and Theatre Workshop. In a curtain speech Behan ironically claimed that Theatre Workshop had performed a better play than he had written (Bradby and Williams 1988, p. 42). Thus the 'definitive' text of *The Quare Fellow* is a long way from Behan's typescript. Even the title, it seems, was Simpson's suggestion.

At the same time, nobody doubts that *The Quare Fellow* is essentially Behan's invention. The idea of dispensing with plot, so that with one stroke attention is focused on the time process leading up to the execution, lies at the heart of the composition. The idea of keeping the condemned man anonymous and off-stage is also to be attributed solely to Behan. As Anthony Roche has shown (1994, pp. 47–70), these two ideas link Behan immediately with Beckett, the avant-garde, and the text of *Waiting for Godot*, which Simpson staged at the Pike in 1955. Simpson does not mention any perceived affinity between the two plays, however. Behan himself rather distanced himself from Beckett later on, by commenting facetiously and as it happens inaccurately: 'When Samuel Beckett was in Trinity College listening to lectures, I was in the Queen's Theatre, my uncle's music hall. That is why my plays are music hall and his are university lectures' (De Búrca 1993, p. 12). Beckett's plays are as much indebted to music-hall routines as are Behan's, but the disavowal is of interest. One is inclined to the view that they were mutually unsympathetic. O'Casey was more a model and mentor than Beckett. 'My favourite authors are Sean O'Casey and myself' (Behan 1955). Behan's characterisation, with its reliance on knockabout farce and lively Dublin speech, is very much in O'Casey's line and none the worse for that. But the balance Behan makes between sympathetic prisoners and unsympathetic, good warders and bad warders, is also crucial to the play and serves to create the sense of a world in little, a microcosm, which represents the way Behan's imagination usually worked. Above all, the spirit pervading *The Quare Fellow*, a mixture of ridicule and compassion, can be attributed only to Behan. The ridicule is of officialdom, and comes through the wit and resourcefulness of the prisoners. The compassion is mediated through the character of Warder Regan, who seems to be Behan's spokesman in the play. It is Regan who cries out against the brutality of capital punishment. And it is Regan who keeps vigil as at a wake on the night before the execution, when a prisoner sings a love song in Irish. In the final scene compassion and scorn are fused together, as the prisoners engage in a comic commentary on the condemned man's final procession surrounded by officialdom and then squabble over his letters like the soldiers after Christ's crucifixion. This mixture of death and comedy is very Irish, and links Behan closely to what Vivian Mercier (1962) calls the Irish comic tradition.

Following its London success *The Quare Fellow* was at last staged at the Abbey in October 1956. Behan had sent the script without informing the Simpsons, who failed to prove that they had the rights of the play. 'So all the Abbey could do for them was acknowledge in their programme the help they had given in the shaping of the work' (Blythe 1965b, p. 184). At the Abbey Behan was, ironically, on home ground, since the Abbey company was now playing at the Queen's Theatre, formerly leased by his uncle P. J. Bourke. In contrast to the non-realistic staging forced upon Alan Simpson in directing the play for the Pike, where the stage was only 12 feet by 12, the Abbey production attempted to present Mountjoy Jail realistically. The result, according to Gabriel Fallon in the *Evening Press* (9 October), was 'that the script, and the acting and production of the script, frequently wilt under the sheer weight of granite'. Tomás MacAnna, who designed this production, did not make the same mistake when he directed *The Quare Fellow* at the new Abbey in 1984, but ensured through the design the necessary atmosphere of containment. Fallon concluded that *The Quare Fellow* 'both gains and loses in its transition from the Pike presentation. On the whole the gains far outweigh the losses'. The credit must surely go to the director Ria Mooney, unjustly forgotten in Irish theatre history.

The Hostage, too, was to find its way onto the Abbey stage. On 14 October 1969 *An Giall* was staged at the Peacock, 'with additions from the London production by Joan Littlewood' (Hunt 1979, p. 205). Thereby hangs a tale. As is well known, *An Giall* (Irish, 'the hostage') was commissioned by the Irish language cultural body Gael-Linn in 1957 and staged at the Damer Hall, Dublin, on 16 June 1958. This play in Irish was the prototype of *The Hostage*. Behan delivered the text in instalments to Riobárd Mac Góráin of Gael-Linn, and the director Frank Dermody worked on these; Act III arrived very late. The text of *An Giall* was published by *An Comhairle Naisiúnta Dramaíochta/Conradh na Gaeilge* after Behan's death. Edited by Seán O Briain, it was true to the stage production, as Séamus Paircéar, who played Leslie, verified for me in October 1994. In effect, this is the prompt copy, with amendments created or approved by Dermody. Behan's original text has not survived. *An Giall* has been reprinted by Proinsias Ni Dhorcaí (1981) for Gallery Press and by Richard Wall (1987), who has also translated it, for Colin Smythe and CUAP (Catholic University of America Press). Behan himself was supposed to translate *An Giall* for Joan Littlewood and Theatre Workshop in 1958, but once again his 'foul papers' do not seem to have survived. It is a neat little biblio-graphical crux.

Joan Littlewood's memoirs (1994) do little to solve the textual problems which ensued when *The Hostage* was published in December 1958, following its success at Stratford East. It was copyrighted to Theatre Workshop alone. A revised edition, based on Littlewood's production in 1959, was published in 1962; this is now regarded as the definitive text of *The Hostage*. Littlewood says (1994, p. 521) that when Behan was in London to launch *Borstal Boy* she and Gerry Raffles showed him a newspaper headline announcing the death of a British soldier held hostage in Nicosia and told him, 'There's a play in it.' Behan promised to write about a hostage in Ireland. It was 17 June before they heard from him again, asking for money, but around 1 July he and Beatrice returned to London, stayed with Littlewood and had not even a scenario of the play to offer. Two things are wrong with this account: (1) The publication of *Borstal Boy* came six days *after* the opening of *The Hostage* in London on 14 October 1958. (2) *An Giall* was staged in Dublin on 16 June, and an account of the plot appeared in the review published by the *Irish Times* the following day (Behan 1992, p. 150). It is untenable, then, to suggest that in July 1958 Behan had not even a synopsis of the play. What he did not have and for some reason, which may have had to do with his knowledge of Littlewood's preferred production style, was unable to supply, was a translation of *An Giall* (Beatrice Behan 1973, pp. 138–9). Littlewood goes on in her memoirs to say (p. 529) that in default of a text the cast invented things based on Behan's 'stories of pimps and patriots, whores and social workers, IRA men and *gardai* with which he had regaled us over the years.' The most difficult part was 'holding on to the theme and sustaining the tension behind the jokes and laughter.' It is clear that this problem was of Littlewood's making. Because there was no Act III by the Saturday before opening the cast invented the raid (p. 531): 'Inspiration – a police raid. It was the only way out.' Not content with this surprising boast (since the raid, though not absurd, was part of the plot of *An Giall*), Littlewood says she supplied Teresa's last line, 'He died in a strange land [*sic*] and at home he had no one. ... The line came from the moment.' But, apart from that odd reference to 'a strange land', which suggests a London perspective, *An Giall* has a similar line: '*Ní raibh aoinne dod mhuintir féin le tú a chaoineadh, a stór*' ['You had none of your own people to mourn you, love'] (n.d., p. 37). Littlewood concedes, however, that the resurrection of Leslie and his song were Behan's invention. These comments confirm what Irish critics have said from the time *The Hostage* was first staged, namely, that Littlewood had as much to do with that text as had Behan himself. She literally picked his brains.

Taking the text of *An Giall* just quoted from, that published by An Chomhairle, one can make the following points about it in contrast with *The Hostage*. (i) *An Giall* is a straightforward naturalistic play, with no music-hall trappings. (ii) There are eight characters in all, two of them mute, as against fifteen in *The Hostage*. Those added were the homosexuals, Miss Gilchrist and Mulleady. In the original the characters were linked more firmly to the plot. (iii) The tone and mood resemble *The Quare Fellow* in that suspense predominates.

There is less emphasis on comedy. The character of Padraig (Pat) is more seriously presented, to resemble somewhat Warder Regan. (iv) The relationship between Treasa and Leslie is more purely romantic in *An Giall*. Each is depicted as naive and lonely, and they do not, of course, go to bed together. In *The Hostage* innocence is replaced with cynical sophistication. (v) No drink stronger than tea appears in *An Giall*. There is no obscenity and the whorehouse setting is not much emphasised. (vi) Local references in *An Giall* were altered to suit English audiences, and topical allusions to British royalty and to world affairs were inserted ad lib. (vii) The ending of *An Giall* is quite different. The raid, which is seriously conducted, somewhat resembles the raid in O'Casey's *Shadow of a Gunman*. Leslie is afterwards discovered suffocated in a cupboard, where he had been hidden, gagged and bound, when the raid began. It is thought that this ironic detail was based on an incident which occurred during the Suez war of 1956. In some other respects, however, Behan was indebted to Frank O'Connor's short story, 'Guests of the Nation'. (viii) The play ends with Treasa's lament over Leslie, very much in the Irish tradition, for example, of Synge's *Riders to the Sea* (1903).

The conclusion one must come to is this. Behan wrote two plays, *An Giall* and (in part) *The Hostage*. The texts published for each of these is in varying degrees a version of what Behan originally wrote. As regards the relationship of *The Hostage* to *An Giall* it is best summed up by Ulick O'Connor (1970, p. 200): 'a blown up hotchpotch compared with the original version which is a small masterpiece and the best thing Behan wrote for the theatre.' And yet it is undeniable that Behan was a willing collaborator in the staging of *The Hostage*. As he was a complex man loyalty, even to himself, was always something over which he was ambivalent. Thus he declared himself unhappy with the style in which *An Giall* had been directed by Frank Dermody, 'of the school of Abbey Theatre naturalism of which I'm not a pupil.' And he endorsed Littlewood's style instead: 'She has the same views on the theatre that I have, which is that the music hall is the thing to aim for to amuse people and any time they get bored, divert them with a song or a dance. ... While they [the audience] were laughing their heads off, you could be up to any bloody thing behind their backs; and it was what you were doing behind their bloody backs that made your play great' (1962, p. 17). In a rave review of *The Hostage* in the *Observer* Kenneth Tynan suggested that the style of production was *commedia dell' arte*. More to the point, it was Brechtian and epic, alienating and fragmented in the modernist mode. The only question worth asking after one has conceded that Littlewood did a very thorough job in co-creating a whole new play is what Behan was doing behind the audience's backs. Clearly, he was presenting the outsider as victim once again, as he did in *The Quare Fellow*. The serious genius of *The Hostage*, which remains unobscured by the interpolations, additions and Brechtian devices, lies in the use of a brothel as setting for a play with a political theme. This metaphor is there in *An Giall*. It is at the heart of Behan's intentions. It is his means of characterising the IRA border campaign of 1956–62 as absurd.

Since its premiere in 1958 *The Hostage* has been accepted world-wide as a splendid piece of theatre, entertaining, carnivalesque and irreverent. It has even, according to one German critic, become 'part of a tradition of world theatre which it shares with Shakespeare as well as Büchner, Dürrenmatt or Pinter' (Kosok 1995, p. 243). How Behan would have swaggered at the news! Sharing with Shakespeare! Or to think that *The Hostage* should run for two years in the *Deutsches Theater* in liberated East Berlin. The play has clearly assumed a life of its own.

Yet it will always be a play which disturbs Irish people, aware on the one hand of its anarchic energy and on the other of its kinship with the more serious play in Irish. The political issues seriously debated in *An Giall* are mocked in *The Hostage*; in 1958 the IRA were moribund but after 1969 and into the 1990s the IRA were no longer a laughing matter. Thus although the Abbey staged *The Hostage* in 1970 and has revived it several times (most recently in 1996), it is interesting to note that in 1990–91 it was a new version in English, by Michael Scott and Niall Toibín, using material from *An Giall*, which had Dubliners flocking to a new theatre, the Tivoli. There is a nostalgia for the original which is true to Behan's own desire for lost innocence. He was forever creating and recreating his own mythology.

Behan's only other stage play was *Richard's Cork Leg*, which he left unfinished. Alan Simpson put together a script from Behan's notes and 'additional material' which he directed at the Peacock Theatre in March 1972, casting the Dubliners group as performers on several levels. The play is mainly set in a cemetery, the location for a clash between Hero Hogan, a socialist, and the Blueshirts (or

Irish Fascists of the 1930s). But it is also the location for prostitutes, in a grotesque attempt to characterise Irish life and politics. The play is a poor thing, hardly more than self-parody on Behan's part, and redolent more of the age of Aquarius than of the age of de Valera. In the Behan canon it is no more than a parodic footnote.

To return, finally, to the idea of a community which de Valera promoted and the Abbey served in the 1940s and 1950s: it can be said that Behan was at war all his short life with this idea. He was one of those whom de Valera shut away during the war years; he found his own sense of community behind bars (pun intended). Behan was an outsider before ever Colin Wilson coined the term. Anthony Cronin writes in *Dead As Doornails* (1976, p. 111) of the effect of the war on Behan, Kavanagh and Flann O'Brien as a form of embittering provincialisation. In June 1951 Behan wrote to Sindbad Vail about 'the feeling of isolation' in terms which reveal his alienation from de Valera's ideal Ireland: 'I am a city rat. Joyce is dead and O'Casey is in Devon. The people writing here now have as much interest for me as an epic poet in Finnish or a Lapland novelist' (1992, p. 45). Peasant quality (or PQ), a commodity much promoted at the Abbey in the name of national identity, was anathema to Behan. Neither had he anything in common with the 'craw-thumpers orange and green who run the island' (p. 204). Behan was trapped by the history he so foolishly tried to change as a young man. He was pigmented by the republicanism which rejected the Republic itself. He could only turn the whole thing into a joke in the end, and yet his funeral in 1964, the biggest Dublin had seen for some time, was honoured by the IRA.

But this chapter properly comes to a close with the year 1958, the year Irish historians have decided marks the end of de Valera's dispensation and the re-birth of Ireland. A new community in Europe was soon to be the goal. In theatre history 1958 saw the death of Lennox Robinson, virtually a symbol of the old Abbey. And 1958 was the year when Behan's *Borstal Boy*, begun in prison sixteen years earlier, was finally published, and promptly banned in Ireland. Here there is no dilemma over text or authorship. *Borstal Boy* was Behan's masterpiece, and he knew it, a wonderful victory over conditioning and deprivation (Kearney 1977, p. 85). Here Behan discovers a community, which he was to spend his life looking for again. It is fitting that a dramatisation of *Borstal Boy* took Brendan

Behan's New York by storm in 1970, after it had proved 'the greatest popular success' of the new Abbey (Hunt 1979, p. 202). Resurrected like his own Hostage, Behan thus had the last laugh at a vanishing Ireland.

7

Revolutionary times:
'A Generation of Playwrights'

Robed in spattered iron
At the harbour mouth she stands, Productive Investment,
And beckons the nations through our gold half-door:
Lend me your wealth, your cunning and your drive,
Your arrogant refuse
Thomas Kinsella, 'Nightwalker' (1968)

Introduction

It is now generally agreed that with the 1960s Irish drama enjoyed a
second renaissance. Where the roots of this new growth precisely
lay is neither easy nor, I suspect, entirely profitable to determine,
but on the one hand there was the emergence of major new talent
while on the other there was the sudden and exciting set of changes
(economic, social, cultural) which the country itself underwent after
1958. The coincidence and interaction of these two factors, individual dramatic talent and national upheaval, produced a body of
work for the Irish theatre unsurpassed since the early years of the
century.

There is no question now, at the end of the twentieth century,
but that Brian Friel, Tom Murphy, Hugh Leonard, John B. Keane
and Thomas Kilroy are all major playwrights. They are all firmly
established in the Irish canon. (Perhaps Hugh Leonard's position is
less secure than that of the others, if one can judge from his omission from the *Field Day Anthology of Irish Writing* in 1991, but this
omission was, in my view, a significant error.) Each well merits a chapter here to himself. Two factors, however, inhibit that procedure.
There is now available a considerable amount of critical analysis of
the work of each of these playwrights. No fewer than six books, not
counting Marilynn J. Richtarik's book on Field Day (*Acting Between*

the Lines, 1995), have been published on Friel, by Maxwell (1973), Dantanus (1988), Pine (1990), O'Brien (1990), Peacock (1993), and Andrews (1995). Fintan O'Toole's book on Murphy, *The Politics of Magic* (1987), was accompanied in the same year by a major assessment in a special issue of *Irish University Review* and was revised and updated in 1995. Sister Marie Hubert Kealy's book on John B. Keane, *Kerry Playwright* (1993) followed the book of essays edited by John M. Feehan, *Fifty Years Young* (1979). Anthony Roche's *Contemporary Irish Drama* (1994) had individual chapters on Friel, Murphy and Kilroy. Michael Etherton's *Contemporary Irish Dramatists* (1989) focused on 'individual playwrights, rather than on groups involved in collective creation' and thus dealt with all of the writers mentioned, as, indeed, did Maxwell's authoritative study *Modern Irish Drama 1891–1980* (1984). There thus seems little need here to go over the same ground again in the same way. The other objection to individual chapters on the major playwrights of the 1960s and 1970s lies in the degree of repetition inherent in the attempt to contextualise.

The 'world' of an Irish dramatist tends to remain in an orbit reasonably adjacent to that of his fellows, writers and audience alike. The Republic of Ireland is a small and comparatively homogeneous society; experience is both shared and limited, governed by conditions well within the range of the total population of only 3.5 million, 93 per cent of whom are Roman Catholic and have uniform educational backgrounds. Since the government programme has failed to revive the Irish language, English forms the unquestioned vernacular for explorations of national identity. Moreover, this homogeneity of consciousness may be said to derive in large part from Irish literary history. Ireland's unified audience is the result of the cultural revolution which created late nineteenth-century nationalism and its consequence, national independence. The Irish literary revival, including the Abbey Theatre as instrument, created not just images of historical self-appraisal and expressions of individual experience within an invented community but also a habit of mind and a set of conventions and themes whereby the people might understand who they were. This closely-knit nexus of artist and audience is, I believe, unique in the modern literary world. It means, in effect, that whereas the imagination and indeed the voice of individual authors are sharply distinct they share a common vocabulary and may be seen as working with contemporaries in a common field. It is useful to discuss modern playwrights in this context, by following a thematic rather than strictly authorial approach. The purpose is both to show that collectively these writers addressed issues central to the developments shaping the new Ireland and that individually they felt themselves to have a role as artists in a changing society.

If one accepts Fergal Tobin's description of the 1960s as 'the best of decades' one must also pay heed to T. K. Whitaker's eventual revaluation of the 1960s and 1970s as 'a sort of Paradise Lost' (1986, p. 10). Irish writers after 1958 did not sing the new republic. On the contrary, although one of the weaknesses of the time is that there was no intellectual forum in which artists might work out anything resembling an aesthetic position *vis-à-vis* the new ideology, the tendency was for writers to resist the notion that all was for the best in the best of all possible worlds. 'Write of Ireland today, the critics scream. Show us the vodka-and-tonic society. Show us permissive Dublin. Forget about thatched cottages and soggy fields and emigration. We want the now Ireland' (Friel 1972, p. 305). The Irish theatre established in 1899, Friel argued, gave expression to a peasant people; in 1972, the Irish were still a peasant people, characterised by two main attributes, a passion for the land and a 'paranoiac individualism'. The future of Irish drama will depend on 'the slow process of development of the Irish mind, and it will shape and be shaped by political events' but cannot actually be their instrument. 'I do not believe that art is a servant of any movement.' During this period of unrest which Ireland is undergoing – Friel does not use such cant phrases as 'cultural revolution' – two allegiances which have bound the Irish imagination will be radically altered: 'loyalty to the most authoritarian church in the world and devotion to a romantic ideal we call Kathleen' (pp. 305–6). This essay provides the best guide to the directions taken by Irish drama after 1958.

The playwrights who came to prominence in the 1960s and were to run counter to the mood of the times had all been born in the later 1920s and 1930s. They had all grown up, therefore, in de Valera's Ireland and could not but see the 1960s through eyes conditioned by circumstances of penury and inhibition. Collectively, they established a kind of movement which interrogated the older, established values but could not escape their impact. As Thomas Kilroy put it in an essay entitled 'A Generation of Playwrights', 'out of this dispiriting world came the stirrings of what would be the first significant shift in sensibility in the Irish theatre since the early days of the Abbey Theatre' (1992, p. 135). But this generation was also in its own way revolutionary. The revolution was in part fuelled by the new energies released in the British theatre with the founding of the Royal Court and the impact of *Look Back in Anger* in 1956.

Indeed, when Kilroy called for a revival in the Irish theatre in an earlier essay he referred specifically to George Devine's Royal Court as model. Kilroy called for a community in the theatre, within which the writer would 'fulfil the role of commentator on current values, practising espionage for everyman' (1959, p. 195). Kilroy therefore saw the role of the Irish theatre as 'something permanent [which] absorbs some of the conflicting, topical, social issues around it and gives a public interpretation of current values' (p. 192). The search for such a model was to persist after the new Abbey was opened in 1966. (Cf. Hewison 1981, Ritchie 1988, Wardle 1978)

Emigration

Friel's assertion of two leading themes in Irish drama, cited above, is indebted to Daniel Corkery's notorious argument in *Synge and Anglo-Irish Literature* that the three great 'forces' which distinguish authentic Irish literature are religious consciousness, nationalism, and the land (1931, p. 19). Corkery did not include emigration, since his book was written before the Economic War (1932–8) and the first great exodus of Irish labour to Britain, but Friel clearly understood the theme to be part of the 'land' question. Emigration was highest in Ireland in the period 1956 to 1961, the worst record since the 1880s (Keogh 1994, p. 216). Most of this was to the United Kingdom; the Irish quota to the United States was not filled. A whole generation was siphoned off from the Irish countryside, resulting in a net population loss between 1951 and 1961 of almost half a million people. The historian J. J. Lee trenchantly refers to this evil as a 'mass eviction process', and adds that it is 'to the writers the historian must turn, as usual, for the larger truth' (1989, p. 384).

John B. Keane, rather than Friel, was the first to present on stage an angry response to this haemhorrage of emigration. Prior to this the more usual response was resignation or lament, as in M. J. Molloy's quietist *The Wood of the Whispering* (1953), or nostalgia, as in John Murphy's *The Country Boy* (1959). In Keane's *Many Young Men of Twenty* (1961b), set in a country pub where emigrants gather before taking the boat-train, the genius of the place, Danger Mulally, a sponger and ballad-singer, cries out against the politicians for neglecting a human tragedy. This protest is a new note in Irish drama, even if the play is a musical. In *Hut 42* (1962), which was staged at the Abbey, Keane set his play on a large dormitory building-site in England, where the Irish workers pine for home. One of them, the old man Root, sees clearly that even if he were to return to Ireland he would not earn enough to prevent his family from growing up thieves. A lot of social history is condensed here: Root had little education, married late, and spent a lifetime at manual work. When he is killed in a street accident there is nothing to send home to his wife except what is collected among the men. His fellow-Irishman Skylight angrily deplores the waste and the 'terrible shame' (Keane 1968, p. 37). Keane was to write better plays, but he retained this anger at the ideology which failed to provide for and keep together ordinary Irish families.

Tom Murphy's *A Whistle in the Dark* (1961) was also set in England and dealt with the lives and culture of Irish migrants there, but Murphy's purposes were less sociological than Keane's. Clearly, it is not the plight of emigrants *per se* which forms the main interest of *A Whistle in the Dark*, as it does of *Hut 42*. It is essentially a tragedy, composed of materials derived from the abuse of patriarchy. Michael Carney is interesting as the victim of what we would now call a dysfunctional family, but the roots of that dysfunction lie back in Mayo, where Mrs Carney works as a charwoman and the Carneys are regarded as tinkers. At one point in the play Michael tries to talk to Betty about his problems: 'I could have *run* years ago. Away from them. I could have been a teacher. I had the ability. ... What's wrong with me?' (Murphy 1984, p. 50). That final, plaintive question is one no hero had asked before in Irish drama. Murphy's focus is on the neurosis in the individual, related to a neurosis in Irish society itself in the post-war era. What Murphy's play explores is the pressure imposed on the individual confused by outmoded myths and unable to create a new sustainable mode of living which incorporates major cultural change. The comparison is not so much with the plays of Keane as with D'Alton's *This Other Eden* (1953). At the end of that play, Conor Heaphy, at least as confused as Michael Carney, leaves Ireland to become a missionary. The cynical Devereaux encourages him: 'What can you lose? You could stay here to be a voice crying in the wilderness. Maybe Ireland will cast out enough Irishmen to help in the saving of the world, and when that happens, maybe the world will save Ireland that couldn't save herself' (D'Alton 1970, p. 80). This was written before the EEC was even conceived. Murphy's play is a kind of sequel to *This Other Eden*. Michael Carney has no mission other than his own liberation, which he fails to establish because he remains the prisoner of his culture. Since he cannot save Des Michael cannot save himself. Murphy dramatises the anxiety and self-destructiveness attendant on the clash between tradition and change.

If emigration is the catalyst in the tragic action of *A Whistle in the Dark* it is the repudiated *deus ex machina* in the comic action of Murphy's *A Crucial Week in the Life of a Grocer's Assistant* (1969). Originally entitled *The Fooleen* (diminutive of 'fool'), this play thus has affinities with such characterisations of the misfit in rural Irish society as Patrick Kavanagh's *The Green Fool* (1938) and *Tarry Flynn* (1948), dramatised at the new Abbey in 1966. Kavanagh's text is pastoral, and concerns emigration only as a final artistic choice. As in the classic rendition of the Irish artist, Joyce's *Portrait*, emigration denotes a rejection of the values disabling growth; after Joyce, this form of exile becomes a convention in Irish literature. In more recent years that convention had been given dramatic point in Hugh Leonard's adaptation, *Stephen D* (1962). But Murphy was not sketching another portrait of the long-suffering Irish artist. To John Joe Moran emigration is ambivalent, a lure and a defeat. Its promise might lead to the kind of disgrace John Joe's brother fell into in America, where he was jailed for fourteen months for being drunk and fighting a policeman, i.e. for asserting his identity in as conventional a style as the fighting Carneys. John Joe decides to stay *in spite of* the deception and hypocrisy he discovers around him, 'the poor eating the poor' (1978, p. 80). He wants the freedom of choice to either stay or go. It is by shouting out publicly all the secrets of family and community that the 'fooleen' finally frees himself from the prison-house of respectability.

The London success of *A Whistle in the Dark* made an emigrant of Murphy himself until *A Crucial Week* was staged at the new Abbey. 'I *had* to come back,' he told an interviewer in the *Irish Times* (20 March 1972), 'because London was nothing to me – a sort of limbo where I was not English and not Irish. I had to come back, like the hero of a certain '30s play, to find the facts and face them.' To find the facts and face them is often the Oedipal task of Murphy's heroes.

Consequently, the returned emigrant (or, in *The Blue Macushla*, ex-convict) is a frequent Murphy convention. In a sense, the returned emigrant is a kind of ghost, a revenant whose incomplete knowledge acts as a device to define or re-define 'home truths'. In one of his most ambitious plays Murphy multiplied the device. Taking as subject of *The White House* (1972) the great returned emigrant John F. Kennedy, whose visit to Ireland in June 1963 was one of the decade's most defining moments (Tobin 1984, p. 94, Keogh 1994, p. 252), Murphy conceived of a look-alike, J. J. Kilkelly, whose identification with Kennedy serves to create and inspire a 'new frontier' in a small Irish town. With Kennedy's assassination the impersonator, with no stable identity of his own, collapses and with him the morale of the community. The story of this collapse is told several years later to a returned emigrant (Michael), who is still a believer in J. J. and the new frontier. By this means disillusion is powerfully dramatised. As written in 1972, part 1, 'Conversations on a Homecoming', was set in the present and part 2, 'Speeches of Farewell', returned to the year 1963. Some years later Murphy rewrote the play, cutting the idea of 'Speeches of Farewell' and retitling the long one-act *Conversations on a Homecoming* (1985), which became an enduring success and has been much imitated.

When Des Hickey and Gus Smith compiled their book of interviews under the title of *A Paler Shade of Green* (1972) they combined Brian Friel with Tom Murphy, under the chapter heading 'Two Playwrights with a Single Theme'. That theme was emigration. Yet it will surprise nobody that in speaking here of *Philadelphia* Friel quietly asserted (p. 222) that he did not 'think the play specifically concerns the question of emigration'. Indeed, in his plays, beginning with *The Enemy Within* (1962), the topos of emigration (or exile) is but the dramatic platform on which Friel could explore states of isolation and anguish. In *The Enemy Within* the future saint, Columba, is forced to come to terms with his missionary calling by turning his back on Ireland and his kinsmen; the price is heartbreak. In his short preface Friel insists (1975, p. 5) that it is not the spectacular aspects of the saint which interested him but 'the private man'. This is the key to Friel's dramatic form. In line with the modernist preoccupation with the gap between subject and object (Beckett 1983, p. 70), Friel invariably dramatises the tragic distance subsisting between consciousness (informed by memory) and experience (or history). The play which lays down the groundwork is undoubtedly

Philadelphia, Here I Come!, written after Friel's own formative exile in Minneapolis in 1963 (Dantanus, pp. 50–1). Only through the comic interventions of Private Gar can Public Gar abide the isolation he feels from those around him, particularly from his father. In a sense, Gar poses the same question as Michael in Murphy's *A Whistle in the Dark,* 'What's wrong with me?' The play is in the interrogative mood; it does not present answers. The neurosis of living in contemporary Ireland is dramatised. Although he is only poised for flight into exile Gar is an 'inner emigré', to borrow Seamus Heaney's phrase from 'Exposure' (1975, p. 73), at odds with his home. Gar is exiled already in his mind.

What was revolutionary about *Philadelphia* in 1964 was that, while using traditional materials such as a peasant setting and decor, with familiar characters such as a parish priest and a schoolmaster, it dispensed with plot and concentrated on situation or condition. The condition explored is alienation. In Gar O'Donnell Friel supplied an Irish Hamlet for his time, a character longing for contact but driven back repeatedly upon himself since the world he inhabits is no longer the stable world of authority and security it once was. As his subjective memory shows him, Gar is alone in a world of change and illusion. The rituals by which Gar lives are meaningless; he is measuring out his life in two-pound sugar bags. Katie Doogan betrayed him, like Ophelia, in response to her father's wishes. But when he opens the antiquated suitcase to do his packing Gar opens a Pandora's box of family history, and the discovery impacts on him as powerfully as the ghost on Hamlet. That is the suitcase he must take with him into exile; the past will go with him to Philadelphia. According to Friel himself, *Philadelphia* 'was an analysis of a kind of love: the love between a father and a son and between a son and his birthplace' (Hickey and Smith 1972, p. 222). Gar hopes to recover love by exiling himself and finding a surrogate family in Philadelphia, but it is clear from Private's comments (and theme song) that this is an illusion. Even Public does not really believe in exile: the last line of the play tells us he does not know why he is going. Uncertainty and agnosticism define Gar as the new anti-hero in Irish drama.

Emigration lies behind many other Friel plays as metaphor for the alienation he sees at the heart of modern life. *The Loves of Cass Maguire* (1966) concerns the disreputable returned emigrant whose illusions are painfully shattered when she ends up in a rest home, ironically called Eden House. _The Gentle Island_ (1971) begins on a conventional note of Goldsmithian lament as large numbers emigrate to England and Scotland but goes on to explode the myth of the deserted village when two outsiders become entangled in the neuroses of the one family which remains behind on the island. _Aristocrats_ (1979) presents another family poised on the brink of dissolution and dispersal while awaiting the death of its patriarchal head, Justice O'Donnell. Once again the centre cannot hold, a condition Friel sees running like a faultline through Irish society. In _Faith Healer_ (1979) Frank Hardy is an exile who may be compared with Columba in _The Enemy Within_ and whose decision to return to Ireland is presented as fatal. As late as _Molly Sweeney_ (1994), we learn that once Molly is cured of her blindness she is 'exiled' (Friel 1994, p. 59). Molly herself uses the same image when she describes her nameless dread before the operation: 'It was the dread of exile, of being sent away. It was the desolation of homesickness' (p. 31). The topos of exile is a metaphor for psychic displacement which grants access to the terrain of Frielian tragedy. Thus while Keane expressed anger at the older generation, both Murphy and Friel were more concerned to view emigration, whatever its causes, as a metaphysical condition affecting the new generation.

Sexual identity

A noted Irish politician once avowed that there was no sex in Ireland before television, i.e., before 1962 (Tobin 1984, p. 66). This is rather like Philip Larkin's famous announcement in _High Windows_ (p. 34) that sexual intercourse began in Britain in 1963, 'Between the end of the Chatterley ban / And the Beatles' first LP.' In spite of the spirit of carnival which was belatedly manifesting itself in Ireland in the early 1960s, the old puritanism was by no means 'dead and gone, / A myth of O'Connor and O'Faolain' (Montague 1982, p. 62). Censorship was still a powerful force, capable of bringing about the dismissal of the novelist John McGahern as teacher, because of the sexual frankness of _The Dark_ (1965). The papal encyclical _Humanae Vitae_ (1968) was wholly endorsed by the Irish clergy and it was not until 1979 that contraception was legally allowed, the famous 'Irish solution to an Irish problem' (Lee 1989, pp. 498–9). Other laws, not including those on divorce or abortion, were changed in the 1970s which gave more rights to women: for example, the Anti-Discrimination (Pay) Act,

1974, and the Employment Equality Act, 1977. There is a connection between the change in public attitudes towards sexual matters and the changes in legislation affecting rights and gender roles.

But it is unlikely that theatre was anything like as effective in changing attitudes to sex as was television. Although there was no official censorship in Irish theatre, as existed in Britain until 1968, the unofficial censorship was usually sufficient to maintain a conservative, not to say sanitised, stage. Resistance to this unofficial censorship was dangerous to the health of Irish theatre. The fracas over *The Ginger Man* (1959) marked the end of the valiant Globe Theatre Company. The brouhaha over O'Casey's *The Drums of Father Ned* led to the cancellation of the 1958 Theatre Festival and a ban by O'Casey himself on professional production of his plays in Ireland. But worst of all was the case of Tennessee Williams's *The Rose Tattoo* at the Pike Theatre Club in 1957, which resulted in the arrest and imprisonment of the director Alan Simpson for presenting an 'indecent and profane performance' (Swift 1985, p. 259). Although the case was not proven, this was only after Simpson fought it all the way to the Supreme Court and the vindication (without costs) was not enough to save the Pike Theatre. In effect, a puritan society had destroyed a courageous art theatre.

In rural drama prior to the 1960s there was, of course, love and marriage. Sex, however, was taboo. A classic example would be T. C. Murray's *Autumn Fire* (1924), quite a good play about an older widower who marries a sprightly young girl who then falls for the widower's son. All that occurs between Nance and Michael is one kiss, albeit delivered '*with passionate tenderness*' (1964, p. 82). It is enough to have Michael driven from the house and to destroy Nance in her husband Owen's eyes. *Autumn Fire* can be compared with Eugene O'Neill's treatment of similar material in *Desire under the Elms*, which was coincidentally staged in the same year (1924) and in which incest and infanticide are but details in a play smouldering with sexuality. Murray, however, was inhibited by his Catholicism. He ends the play with Owen taking down his rosary beads and uttering the curtain line parodied by O'Casey in *Cock-a-Doodle Dandy*, 'I've no one now but the Son o' God', even though Nance has obediently gone upstairs to bed. There had been a lot more sexuality in Synge's work twenty years earlier; now seemly reticence was the order of the day. When one skips on forty more years to McCabe's *King of the Castle* (1964) one is suddenly in a different world. The setting is still a farm, the form Irish naturalism. But now the sexual issue is frankly and even shockingly raised. The passion for the land is bound up and confused with public image and the use of fertility to reinforce male status.

John B. Keane was equally concerned to highlight ways in which sexuality is coded, traded and repressed in a rural environment. *Sive* (1959) deals with the economy of marital barter and its responsibility for the destruction of choice, love and life itself. *The Highest House on the Mountain* (1960) concerns sexual frustration and the psychological damage it can cause. Fear of sex, moreover, is projected on to the woman, identified as a prostitute, brought home from London by the son of a widowed farmer. Keane does not shirk the incestuous territory feared by Murray as in this case the father attempts to make love to his son's wife. In other plays also, violence and various kinds of physical disability signify, perhaps in rather sensational form, neuroses rooted in cultural and religious factors, for example *Sharon's Grave* (1960). With *The Year of the Hiker* (1963) one finds Keane addressing sexual needs less like an Irish Tennessee Williams and more like an updated T. C. Murray. *Big Maggie* (1969), in particular, makes a strong case for woman's sexual independence; its revival and revision for a major production in 1988 proved that Keane was ahead of his time in asserting this theme. In *The Chastitute* (1980), Keane was very frank in his assertion that sexual deprivation is a major cause of neurosis in remote rural areas; the desperation of his hero, while presented as comic, is actually suicidal. Here we find, in the later Keane, a writer with a case to make as strong as ever O'Casey made for the joys of sex, and the evil of its suppression, a case Keane made in his fiction also, especially in *The Bodhrán Makers* (1986).

The challenge to puritanism was a major feature of Irish drama in the 1960s. In terms of what was sayable on the Irish stage Tom Murphy's *The Morning after Optimism* (1971) and Hugh Leonard's *The Patrick Pearse Motel* (1971) offer contrasting modes. Where Murphy celebrates sexual experience in defiance of hegemonic idealism Leonard satirically depicts sexual innocence masquerading as sophistication. Both approaches, far from trivialising sex, asserted that older forms of reticence were dishonest.

At the same time, women were being represented in more courageous terms. In general, however, the empowerment of women in Irish drama was from a male point of view. The main focus remained on the hero. Rosie in *The Morning after Optimism* is a prostitute, and so is a special case, whose sexuality is already transgressive. Rosie's counterpart in the play is Anastasia, the quintessential virgin and fiancée of Edmund. In the virgin-whore dichotomy, which is the only one the play allows, Rosie's freedom is thus compromised. Most drama of this period falls into this pattern. A woman is given a voice of sexual independence only at the price of her status. The emphasis remains on the male, whose sense of himself is either confirmed or affronted by the woman's appearance as sexually liberated. In Thomas Kilroy's *Tea and Sex and Shakespeare* (1976) the writer-hero Brien's sanity hangs on the question (solely in his mind) of his wife's fidelity. Meanwhile he has writer's block, and at the same time his thoughts (and the stage) are inhabited with sexual encounters and guilty repercussions. On his wife's return from work, Brien is released into mental health by her presence. It is as if she existed only for his sake. In Friel's *Living Quarters* (1977), on the other hand, a play that is based on the Phaedra myth, the hero kills himself when he learns of his young wife's infidelity. Disappointingly, Friel returns us to T. C. Murray and to *Autumn Fire*: the Phaedra figure is dismissed while the Theseus figure makes his protest, which is, in effect, a protest against a male-ordained scheme of things. Thus, Irish dramatists for the most part did not challenge the conventional or traditional representation of women.

Meantime, Thomas Kilroy turned to urban society with *The Death and Resurrection of Mr Roche* (1968) and made visible a figure marginalised in Irish culture. Skilfully combining the form of Greek Old Comedy with modern naturalism Kilroy shows how the homosexual is a scapegoat in Irish society. In a spirit of drunken revelry, a group of men turn on Mr Roche and confine him in the cellar of Kelly's flat; when they open the cellar Roche seems to be dead. The focus then shifts to Kelly and the sterility of his life as hard-drinking bachelor, who confesses to a brief but guilt-ridden relationship with Roche. Thus the question posed in *A Whistle in the Dark* arises once again, 'what's wrong with me?' The play is in that sense diagnostic, less of Kelly than of the culture of which he is both product and symptom.

To put the originality of Kilroy's play into perspective, it may be pointed out that when Behan's *The Quare Fellow* was staged at the Abbey in 1956 Ernest Blythe was concerned that the homosexual should not be performed as such. 'Wisely the actor ignored the direction' (De Búrca 1993, p. 29). Ironically, when Ulick O'Connor stated in his biography that Behan himself was homosexual (1970, pp. 96–9), De Búrca (Behan's cousin) was outraged. Subsequent commentators (Ryan 1975; Cronin 1976) have supported O'Connor's contention. But in 1970 the notion was obviously too shocking to accept.

The Death and Resurrection is not a 'gay' play, in the sense in which that term is now understood (cf. de Jongh 1992). For one thing no sexual relationship is suggested between Roche and Kevin, the young man who accompanies Roche from pub to Kelly's flat but whose illness throughout much of the play conveniently makes his sexual orientation a non-issue: iconically, Kevin is not required to make a statement. For another thing, the play makes no polemic in favour of gay rights. On the contrary, it is by means of Séamus, the married friend, that the sickness of Kelly's world is first identified in the play (Kilroy 1968, p. 52) and later roundly condemned by Roche. The 'straight' or orthodox point of view is destabilised and the decent Séamus is revealed to be as great an impostor as the phoney car salesman Myles. The play invites its audience to re-read the discourse of sexuality proposed by male stereotyping. In that regard its humane defence of homosexuality is an expression of the liberal imagination. Moreover, while the play is a clever reworking of Greek Old Comedy to reinforce the resurrection motif it is also in a quiet, understated style a comedy to set alongside T. S. Eliot's more obviously poetic social critique The Cocktail Party (1949). For all that, Mr Roche is a landmark in the Irish theatre for its humane representation of homosexuality just three years after the Lord Chamberlain had rejected John Osborne's notorious A Patriot for Me in England (Findlater 1967, pp. 189–90).

Kilroy's play, which caused much discussion before and after its transfer to London, made possible a more mature attitude towards the theme of sexuality. Christopher Fitz-Simon points out (1994, p. 295) that if MacLiammóir's Prelude in Kazbek Street (1973) had been staged thirty years earlier, 'it would have caused an uproar, for the focus of the work is on the relationship between a homosexual man and an older woman.' Nevertheless, the Gay Sweatshop almost closed down the Project Arts Centre in 1977. At this time, the Project, ably led by director-playwright Jim Sheridan, presented the liveliest theatre productions in Dublin. Financially, however, the Project partly depended on an annual grant from Dublin City

Council, which refused to renew the grant in January 1977 on the basis that two plays recently staged which dealt with homosexuality were obscene. A bitter controversy ensued, during which the supporters of the Project correctly accused the Council of introducing censorship (Maher 1977).

It was not until 1993 that homosexuality was decriminalised in Ireland (Ardagh 1994, pp. 186–8). By this time, plays on gay issues, while not exactly commonplace, were being staged in experimental venues. The culmination of all this innovation was the powerful production at the Abbey Theatre in 1995 of Tony Kushner's *Angels in America*.

Religious consciousness

In the 1960s every effort was made to suggest that it was Catholic business as usual in a basically Catholic state. Questions such as abolishing the *Ne Temere* decree, which obliges Protestants in a mixed marriage to bring up their children as Catholics, or integrated education for Catholics in Northern Ireland, were dismissed out of hand. The only play on the subject of Protestant–Catholic relations at this time, Jack White's *The Last Eleven* (1968), resuming Lennox Robinson's earlier concern ruefully conceded defeat on the part of a rapidly dwindling Protestant community. (It can also be contrasted with Jim Nolan's *Moonshine*, 1991.) Although a referendum in 1972 resulted in the deletion from the Irish constitution of Article 44, according to which the state recognised the special position of the Catholic Church as 'the guardian of the Faith professed by the great majority of the citizens', no difference was made in church–state relations (Keogh 1994, p. 265). Secularism did not make the straightforward advances it made in Britain or the USA. In spite of the various crises which followed upon Vatican Two and *Humanae Vitae* church attendance remained inexplicably high. Two and a half million Irish people devotedly turned out in 1979 to greet the Pope.

Religion, according to that non-Irishman Don Cupitt, 'is just our values, expressed in our social institutions and our practices' (1984, p. 273). In that case, Irish playwrights of the 1960s and 1970s took a dim view of religion. They saw the old bonds loosening, moral and spiritual values collapsing, and the question of identity become more problematic than ever. John B. Keane treats of church and belief lightheartedly in *Moll* (1971). In comic form, the politics of

Moll predict the undermining of church control in Ireland. In *The Chastitute* Keane is more sympathetic to the plight of the church, caught in the middle of a social and sexual revolution. Behind the farcical situation in which the hero John Bosco McLaine, a bachelor in his late fifties, finds himself when he tries to appease his loneliness by joining the sexual revolution, lies a serious understanding of a crisis in rural Irish society. His confessor Father Kimmerley comments (1981, pp. 45–6): 'The Second Vatican Council should have taken parishes like this into account. ... Sometimes I think the Catholic Church is blind to the real needs of places like Tubberganban where enforced chastity is stifling life itself.' It could be said that Keane takes up O'Casey's call for a new deal, in which puritanism would be cast off and, as in *The Drums of Father Ned*, religious tolerance and sexual emancipation would go hand in hand.

Friel and Murphy, however, took a more sombre and critical view of the role of the church. The parish priest in *Philadelphia, Here I Come!* is faulted for failing to 'translate' the loneliness between father and son and to make life bearable. Otherwise, it is implied, the priest is no more than a figurehead in society. Robert Welch argues that whereas the priest fails to translate Friel succeeds, 'by making evident the gap between the realm of desire and that of necessity and by making that gap the object of our contemplation' (Peacock 1993, p. 138). In the scene under review, however, there is no confrontation: Private makes his accusation but is not seen or heard by the Canon. Yet the audience is secretly made privy to the analysis. Instead of a drama of direct confrontation, in the style of Paul Vincent Carroll (where priest and intellectual battle it out), we get the pathos of secrecy. + Gat adhering to old order of

From *Philadelphia* on Friel as playwright not only faults the res[Catholic clergy but also assumes as artist a quasi-priestly function himself. He is priest as diviner and as 'faith healer', of course. The conventional figure of priest is dismissed as a failure, as is the drunken Father Tom in *Living Quarters*. By the time he wrote *Dancing at Lughnasa* Friel had marginalised the clergy. For all his power in the community, the parish priest is kept off-stage and is replaced by Father Jack, the disgraced missionary who has discovered in Africa a religion in which formal prayer and ritual merge with community relations and celebration. Father Jack is disabled and dying, and never comes to any understanding of the tragedy overtaking the Mundy household. Here it is only the artist-narrator

Michael who has the capacity to see the whole picture and to make the audience see it too. Finally, in *Wonderful Tennessee* (1993) the church is nothing but an outworn monument, and the great Catholic occasion of the Eucharistic Congress of 1932 no more than the trigger for a horrible and senseless murder. In the background is 'a derelict church – without a roof' (Friel,1993, p. 32). Friel's insistence that the Catholic church had failed the people could not be more graphically expressed. Friel offers the theatre as an alternative sacred space.

For Tom Murphy this space is a battleground. In 1970 he was invited to join a committee of the International Commission on the use of English in the liturgy, a post-Vatican-Two attempt to find a new religious language with which lay people might feel comfortable (O'Toole 1987, p. 143). It must be one of the strangest invitations ever issued to a playwright, but it was issued to the right man. For Murphy is undoubtedly the greatest 'religious' playwright Ireland has ever produced. In a programme note Friel once wrote that Murphy's imagination was of the kind which 'inclines intuitively to the service of theatre – or religion. Both seem to offer it passing release, public consolation, and the illusion of completion' (Friel 1980b). There was something in Irish Catholicism over which Murphy's mind sat on brood. It brought a querulous note to his first outburst against the circumscriptions of small-town life, *On the Outside*, and a strong note of bitterness to its sequel *On the Inside*, where 'Self-contempt is the metaphysical key' (1974, p. 60). It could be said that all the bitterness of the disappointed believer came out in a torrent of poetic language and barely subdued violence (which finally explodes) in the aptly named *The Morning after Optimism*, staged at the Abbey in 1971. *The Sanctuary Lamp* (1975) is the culmination of a quest for a language of self-authentication on the other side of despair.

Set within a Catholic church, *The Sanctuary Lamp* uses the location and the properties in a subversive way. 'Tom Murphy rocks "cradle of genius"', announced the *Sunday Independent* (12 October 1975), thinking of Yeats's comment on *The Plough and the Stars*. There were, certainly, minor disturbances in the Abbey during the first production. Murphy was confronting secularism the way O'Casey confronted romantic republicanism. The critic for the *Observer* , covering the Dublin Theatre Festival, was bemused. 'An English dramatist who took loss of religious faith for his subject would need to work at it; he could not assume an interested audience.' Murphy presents three drifters in search of 'a common human need for belief' (Maxwell 1990a, p. 61). But orthodox Catholic belief is both mocked and repudiated in favour of a new humanism through which the Irish mind can recreate 'its own mysterious rituals' and 'heal its torn condition' (Cave 1993, p. 91).

The religious task of the 'attaining of true selfhood' (Cupitt 1984, p. 266) is in Murphy always a bloody affair. One thinks of the ending of *The Morning after Optimism* where the older brother James fights his young brother Edmund in order to kill off his own idealism and lay to rest childish things. James must be free of his former self, in spite of its innocence. So, too, Ireland must break with the childlike faith of former days and embrace new ways of knowing, new modes of moral survival. Other playwrights addressed this question of the self and authenticity in different terms. Desmond Forristal, a Catholic priest, wrote a number of plays for the Gate in the 1970s, including *The True Story of the Horrid Popish Plot* (1972), focusing on Oliver Plunkett, who was about to be canonised as a martyr, *Black Man's Country* (1974), concerning an ageing missionary priest in Biafra, and *The Seventh Sin* (1976), a play about Pope Celestine in the fourteenth century. These were all in different ways occupied with the dilemma of religious service in inauspicious times. A later play, *Captive Audience* (1979), concerns the de-briefing of a young woman recovered by her parents from a religious sect she had joined. The relationship of belief to coercion is here explored, and an attempt is made to find the roots of genuine belief. Thomas Kilroy's *Talbot's Box* (1977) dealt with similar anxieties, but in a wider context and with greater theatricality. This is a play about Matt Talbot, the Dublin worker who turned from alcoholism to a life of asceticism and prayer and who died in Dublin in 1926. Kilroy's treatment of Talbot's story, cleverly told in the manner of Brecht's epic theatre, with much use of comedy and alienation devices (such as a woman as priest), concentrates less on the idea of sanctity than on Talbot's fight to preserve a personal vision and with it his integrity. He is obsessive about this personal vision to a degree which relates him to the artist in modern society. He is depicted both in his own time and in ours, resurrected from the dead, so that his individual self is seen to be boxed in and appropriated by self-interested parties. The play discovers a sympathetic side to Talbot and finds in his struggle an image of the modern self under siege.

'A Generation of Playwrights'

It is likely that Irish television was more effective than theatre in intervening in religious as in other cultural debates in the 1960s and 1970s (cf. Sheehan 1987). In any case, the plays of major interest at this time which either embodied spiritual struggle or dramatised church authority were predominantly critical of traditional Catholicism. As a new ideology was forming in Ireland the playwrights were registering the pain of living in a world suddenly, it seemed, bereft of divine protectionism. It was less a case, perhaps, of Paradise Lost than of paradigm lost.

Politics

Even with the exclusion here of the Northern question (the subject of the next chapter) the term 'politics' is too broad to be immediately useful in a discussion of Irish drama of the 1960s and 1970s. All drama is in some way political, whether it is ideologically conscious or unconscious. But it is necessary here to break down 'nationalism' into socio-political areas urgent after 1958.

The rural–urban divide

This was no new thing in the 1960s. What was new was the sudden shift in the balance of population between town and country. In 1951, 41 per cent of the population of the Republic lived in cities and towns, with over 20 per cent in the Dublin area alone. By 1971 these figures had risen to over 52 per cent and over 33 per cent (Brown 1985a, pp. 211, 258). Dublin, indeed, has grown at a faster rate than any western European capital in modern times (Lee 1989, p. 605). Culturally there was a veritable divide in Irish society between Dublin and the rest of the country. Gearóid Ó Tuathaigh sees Ireland's access to the EEC in 1973 and the formation of a Common Agricultural Policy (the famous CAP) as 'widening still further the gap between the agriculturally more developed and the less developed regions of the country' (Kennedy 1986, p. 126). In the 1960s the 'prevailing ethos in Ireland ceased to be that of the strong farmer' and became that of 'the suburban bourgeois' (Tobin 1984, pp. 232-3).

John B. Keane's *The Field* (1965) centres on the conflict between the farmer Bull McCabe and the returned emigrant William Dee, an industrialist, for possession of the field which McCabe formerly leased but which the owner now puts up for auction. It is clear that the city dweller Dee has financial resources far beyond McCabe's capacity to outbid him at the auction. In the film version (1990), the returned emigrant is American; in the play he is English. It makes a difference to the meaning of the play, where the old Ireland–England debate is vestigially present, but the field itself is much less a republican metaphor than it was to become in the more politically conscious film version. The play's strength, indeed, rests on its ambivalence. On the one hand it clearly identifies Bull McCabe as a dangerous man, willing to kill in defence of what he regards as his right to this field. On the other hand McCabe's outrage at the despoliation of the countryside by a city slicker is couched in a feeling of injury which is calculated to evoke audience sympathy. 'I won't be wronged in my own village in my own country by an imported landgrabber' (Keane 1966, p. 44). As always, Keane grounds his play in local history, here the murder of a Kerry farmer in 1958 (Dawson 1990, p. 25). Although *The Field* in no way condones murder (for Dee's death could be called a mistake) it reveals the mechanism through which residual notions of possession and community clash with newer forces of industrial development. Bull McCabe is isolated as the victim of cultural change far beyond his control. He is a ruined autocrat, whose majestic will is defied by a woman exercising her democratic right to sell her property. Further, whereas the unwillingness of the people to give evidence against him might be compared with the situation George Shiels explored in *The Rugged Path* (1940), Keane is not dramatising the need for moral maturity and unification against lawlessness which exercised Shiels at an earlier moment in Irish history. Instead, Keane is writing a tragedy about the death of the pastoral ideal. The people remain silent. They do not 'inform', even when the bishop rebukes them for their silence. They follow an alternative code which isolates McCabe even while it protects him, so that he ends up burdened with the memory (rather than with the guilt) of Dee's death. Cosy Kerry homesteads become sites for the defence of an ancient order against the mobility and acquisitiveness of foreign investors. The landscape Keane writes about, where characters seem to step out of folklore and myth, is inevitably being overtaken by a moral order sanctioned by the metropolis.

Keane's characters embody such issues as the rural–urban divide, but he does not debate them. By coincidence, Jim Sheridan, who directed the film version of *The Field*, was a major exponent of a combative urban drama in the 1970s, particularly at the Project Arts Centre. Appointed chairman in 1976, Sheridan set about creating a politically aware theatre along lines which combined the Irish dramatic tradition (with its regard for text) and the community-style British theatre made popular by John McGrath and 7:84 (Kennedy 1977). It is significant that in 1975 Sheridan directed the six-part *Non-Stop Connolly Show*, by Arden and D'Arcy, at Liberty Hall in Dublin (Arden 1977, p. 124). Song, dance, carnival, puppets, music and an epic tale of class struggle leading to Connolly's execution after the 1916 Rising were all blended into a recreation of folk and street theatre. Indoor street theatre might be one definition of what Sheridan subsequently produced at the Project. Together with his brother Peter Sheridan, also a playwright and director, Sheridan wrote and directed a succession of working-class plays over a period of four years until the end of 1979. These were plays which attempted to come to terms with issues in a direct, sometimes agit-prop, style. Sheridan's own *Mobile Homes* (1976) offers a good example. The point is made that the exploited rural class of yesterday has become the exploiting urban class of today. Shea the agitator discovers that self-interest is as difficult a barrier to the creation of social consciousness as the more obvious enemy within bureaucracy. Most of the young people on the site want to get into council housing, and so they compromise. The play thus operates as an image of socio-political behaviour.

Sheridan was to return to this theme in his (unpublished) *Inner City Outer Space* (1979). Other issues were raised in *Liberty Suit* (1977), by Peter Sheridan and Mannix Flynn, which in a sense updates Behan's *Borstal Boy*, and especially in James Plunkett's *The Risen People* (1958), which explores in epic style the Dublin Lock-out of 1913. First staged at the Abbey in 1958, *The Risen People* in its revised form (1977) came virtually to symbolise what the Project under the Sheridans stood for. It is neither a tract nor a cosy revisitation of O'Casey's Dublin but a play about survival, about how the common people, 'Larkin's rabble of carters and dockers', fared under the worst possible conditions (Plunkett 1978, p. 47). Plunkett went on to expand the material of this play into his successful novel *Strumpet City* (1969), successfully adapted for television in 1980. In 1994 *The Risen People* was spectacularly revived by the Sheridans, thus celebrating in a post-socialist world the collaborative days of the 1970s.

Meanwhile, at another political and social remove, Hugh Leonard was holding the mirror up to Dublin's new bourgeoisie. Like Tom Murphy, Leonard was attracted back to Ireland in 1970 by the Currency Act (1969) introduced by Minister for Finance Charles J. Haughey, which exempted writers from income tax. To his credit, this particular privilege has never inhibited Leonard from not only satirising the taxpayers who were paying his bills but from repeatedly attacking Haughey and his party for their republicanism. When Haughey became Taoiseach in 1979 Leonard addressed an open letter to him acknowledging his indebtedness but avowing his unease with Haughey's ambivalence as 'a shining example of capitalistic endeavour' and an upholder of 'the ideals and ascetic republicanism of Pearse' (Leonard 1979). It is possible to read Leonard's drama in the light of this political awareness, though to do so exclusively would be unwisely to ignore some of his best work. *Da* (1973) and *A Life* (1979) transcend local and national concerns.

While living in London Leonard wrote a successful comedy of manners, *The Au Pair Man* (1968), a form which Kenneth Muir says (1970, p. 165) always requires class divisions in society as its basis. The play may be read as encoding the Ireland–England relationship. 'Class is about the only facet of English life which excites me or about which I care intensely. I certainly would not have written *The Au Pair Man* if I had stayed in Ireland.' Leonard went on to say, on the other hand, that to him 'the most interesting thing about Ireland today is the new aristocracy, which I call the Foxrock aristocracy. It has sprung up full of new business executives, all of whom seem to be called Brendan. It's a classless aristocracy' (Hickey and Smith 1972, p. 198). Having returned to Ireland Leonard settled first in Killiney and then in his native Dalkey, suburbs of Dublin (or Babylon) as populated with Brendans as nearby Foxrock, where *The Patrick Pearse Motel* (1971) is set during Act I.

Instead of being called Brendan the characters in *The Patrick Pearse Motel* are called after figures in Irish mythology. These are Dermod and Grainne, who 'might have been born for affluent living', and Niamh Kinnore, who we know must gravitate towards the television personality James Usheen. Although the plot proceeds along lines laid down by French farce, as written by Feydeau, Niamh and Usheen are never paired except by awful accident, and when the action moves in Act II to the motel it is Grainne who pursues

Usheen. This playing about with mythology makes its own commentary on modern infidelity. The setting of the motel conveys another sort of critique. Leonard was among the first playwrights to expose the potential for corruption in the new access to affluence. While maintaining good humour, he showed that the new Ireland, energised by greed but inhibited by inexperience, was sexually, socially and politically in free fall (cf. Breen 1990).

The history play

It may be said that in the 1960s the history play became once again, after an interval of some years, a useful means of dramatising political issues. Before the fiftieth anniversary of the 1916 Rising offered an occasion for revisionism, few playwrights followed in Lady Gregory's footsteps by trying to provide popular versions of Irish history (Roger McHugh and Denis Johnston would be exceptions). In 1966 the only playwrights to mark the occasion were Hugh Leonard, who scripted *Insurrection* for Irish television, and Eugene McCabe, whose *Pull Down a Horseman* was staged at the Peacock. It was, of course, a sensitive time in Irish–English relations. The IRA had just blown up Nelson's Pillar in the heart of Dublin (March 1966), and the Abbey decided against staging *The Plough and the Stars*.

A revival of the history play in England, with John Osborne's *Luther* (1961), was also influential. Osborne had used epic drama to create one more 'angry young man' in Martin Luther and in so doing sidestepped the dialectics inherent in Brecht's form. There is a general resemblance between Tom Murphy and Osborne as dramatists: the hero is usually a man of soured feelings with a gift for eloquent retaliation. *Famine* (1968), however, is different. Here Murphy achieves what Osborne (writing, after all, about a German hero) could not: a national epic. Osborne drew parallels between the new individualism of the sixteenth century and the new radicalism of the post-1956 era. But Murphy took the catastrophe of the Irish famine and showed how the seeds of violence, demoralisation and insecurity in modern Irish society had their origins in this national disaster. 'Consciously and unconsciously, in the writing of the play, while aware of the public event that was the Irish Famine in the 1840s, I was drawing on the private well and recreating moods and events, apprehensions of myself and my own times' (1992, p. xiv). This memory is in line with what F. S. L. Lyons calls the 'ultimate psychological legacy' of the famine (1973, p. 16). No answers are found in Murphy's play; no neat Brechtian argument is advanced. Instead, *Famine* dramatises horror and survival, so that the central, confused hero, John Connor, stands finally as victim and villain. The play becomes a process to be experienced traumatically. (In the year of its premiere the famine in Biafra provided a disturbing analogy.) By making an audience share that experience emotionally rather than intellectually *Famine* is closer to the Theatre of Cruelty than to epic theatre. It is a play which has often been revived in Ireland, and has become a national classic.

Thomas Kilroy's *The O'Neill* (1969), on the other hand, is an undeservedly forgotten play. It, too, has for its subject a turning point in Irish history. Hugh O'Neill, as O'Faolain saw him, was the last great hope of knitting together the Gaelic world and the modern, European consciousness. With O'Neill's defeat in 1603, Ireland was destined to endure a long period of oppression and cultural dissolution. The character of O'Neill, as Kilroy depicts him, is both image of and contributor to this collapse. At the time *The O'Neill* was staged in 1969 Ireland was about to be challenged once again by the dream of national unity, while on the other side of the equation Europe beckoned towards wider horizons as it had in O'Neill's day (O'Faolain 1942, p. 278). Kilroy's play raised contemporary issues in a stimulating and prophetic way. It also paved the way for a later treatment of the same subject by Brian Friel in *Making History* (1988), with which it should be compared.

Political allegory

In the theatre allegory, or the use of narrative to convey a specific coded meaning, is always intentional. When the allegory is foregrounded it becomes parable, as with the later plays of Brecht. History plays can sometimes be allegorical, even in the contemporary theatre. Arthur Miller's *The Crucible* (1953) is a case in point. Yeats was not above writing allegory in *Cathleen Ni Houlihan* (1902), with its coded message of recruitment. But in general allegory does not make for the best kind of drama. It narrows the horizons of audience expectation and forbids the free range of the imagination. More interesting and more satisfying drama results from a combination of allegory with other, less transparently didactic, forms.

Friel's *The Mundy Scheme* (1969) was rejected by the Abbey in 1969 and staged instead at the Olympia, a commercial theatre in

Dublin. While by no means personal, this play castigates a whole new breed of Irish politician in the Lemass-inspired economy. Friel's subtitle, 'May We Write Your Epitaph Now, Mr. Emmet?', which appeared in the theatre programme but not in the printed text, underlines Friel's satirical intent, since that question (alluding to Robert Emmet's speech from the dock in 1803) implies that Ireland may have taken her place prematurely among the nations of the earth. Lemass's ambition was 'to fashion a new national character' (Lee 1989, p. 399); Friel's was to expose its vacuity.

Friel imagines a government on the brink of bankruptcy and collapse through incompetence and over-spending, when the day is saved by the 'Mundy Scheme', brought in by the Minister for External Affairs. Irish-American millionaire Homer Mundy Jr offers to buy up large portions of the west of Ireland for use as international cemeteries, thus establishing a massive new industry with all kinds of potential for services and employment. The suave Taoiseach, the main character F. X. Ryan, addresses the Irish nation on this 'scheme' in a televised broadcast transmitted from his home, where the play is set. Friel thereby parodies the brave new world of public relations with its often absurd discourse. The play then inexorably works out the logic of the Mundy scheme, with some revelation of how Machiavellian this Taoiseach, F. X. Ryan, could be in brooking no brother near the throne, behind which is at all times a good woman: his mother. The problem is that Friel does not provide the code for the irony he employs. To the *Irish Times* reviewer (11 June 1969) *The Mundy Scheme* was not merely 'a *realpolitik* mirror of today's Ireland' but also a 'savage political satire of the most uproarious kind since the best days of ... Denis Johnston.' This is a misleading view. Like *The Communication Cord* (1982), this play, written in a realistic style, remains at the level of unsatisfactory farce.

As Friel's play provides a caustic allegory of Ireland in the swinging sixties, so Murphy's *The Blue Macushla* (1980) provides an allegory of the trouble-filled seventies. In effect, Murphy's play conceives of Ireland as a nightclub frequented by gangsters. The plot is a pot-pourri of numerous Hollywood crime films. Danny Mountjoy, just out from prison, visits his old friend Eddie O'Hara in O'Hara's nightclub, 'The Blue Macushla', there to discover a nest of crime and double-dealing. A splinter group of the IRA, here called *Erin go Bragh*, have Eddie in their power and implicate him in their violent activities. Two women (both Eddie's 'molls'), one posing as a Hungarian countess but actually working for *Erin go Bragh*, the other a chanteuse at the club who is about to fall in love with Danny, add glamour to the setting. Intrigues, violence, spying, counter-espionage and romance all contribute to the self-conscious melodrama which ensues. The whole thing is couched in wise-cracking Americanese. The public was not amused, and the play was withdrawn from the Abbey stage.

Though the form used in Hugh Leonard's *Kill* (1982) is farce the content is highly politicised. Set in a deconsecrated church, the baroque residence of Wade, never referred to as Taoiseach but always as five-year lessee of this property, *Kill* provides what Leonard calls 'a metaphor for a newly-laicised Southern Ireland' (Gallagher 1992, p. 380). Wade is something of a megalomaniac, close kin to Friel's F. X. Ryan. He will stop at nothing to remain in power. The tricks by which this feat is established all derive from Leonard's ample conjurer's bag. *Kill* was not a success. The *Irish Times* (6 October 1982) complained that 'the farce itself gets lost' in Leonard's cleverness and that his political concerns had 'cost him this play, more's the pity'. Like Friel and Murphy when they turned to political allegory, Leonard found that an extended joke is not enough to carry a play for Irish audiences conditioned to experience theatre as a thoughtful as well as an amusing experience.

In *The Politics of Performance* Baz Kershaw makes a distinction between authenticating and rhetorical conventions: 'Authenticating conventions or signs are the key to the audience's successful decoding of the event's significance to their lives.' Rhetorical conventions 'produce the signals that enable us to classify different shows as belonging to the same genre or form, and to distinguish between different genres and forms' (1992, p. 26). When playwrights get these conventions crossed the audience is confused. The allegories of Irish society offered by Friel, Murphy and Leonard, for all their satirical inventiveness, were failures. In each the very thoroughness of the application of an idea works against the imaginative freedom of the play itself. These interesting failures, however, highlight all the more the achievements of these and the other major play-wrights of this revolutionary period.

8

'A Modern Ecstasy': playing the North

Alas, poor country,
... where violent sorrow seems
A modern ecstasy. The dead man's knell
Is there scarce asked for who
Macbeth IV.iii.165–72

Introduction

In June 1969 Ernest Blythe, still (until 1972) a member of the Abbey board, delivered himself of the view that 'we are at long last nearing the end of the sticky phase in Six Counties politics which has persisted since, say, 1912'. It is a classic instance of being just as wrong about the future as you can be. Blythe had in mind on the one hand the Home Rule Bill of 1912 and on the other the election of Bernadette Devlin as MP to Westminster in 1969. Just two months later all hell broke loose in Northern Ireland.

'Most people, if asked to define the chief symptoms of the Northern Ireland troubles', according to the historian A. T. Q. Stewart (1989, p. 180), 'would say it is that the two communities cannot live together. The very essence of the Ulster question, however, is that they *do* live together, and have done for centuries. They share the same homeland, and, like it or not, the two diametrically opposed political wills must coexist on the same narrow ground. When all is said and done, Cain and Abel were brothers.' That consanguinity was not, however, acknowledged in 1969. A sense of difference, translated on one side into a sense of superiority and on the other into a sense of grievance, created what appeared to be insoluble conflict, which is the essence of tragedy. If we take Stewart's 'narrow ground' as a platform or stage it is easy to see the Northern conflict as of its very nature dramatic. In turn this means, since drama is imitation of an action, that plays about the North are drama about drama. The emphasis throughout this chapter, therefore, is on drama as 'play', and the basic argument is that what confers distinction on individual dramatisations of the Northern conflict is the writer's ability, through humour, use of fantasy, and the distancing mechanisms of form, to re-present tragic occurrence as entertainment.

In his useful article, 'Northern Ireland's Political Drama', D. E. S. Maxwell (1990) lists 24 plays which deal directly or indirectly with the Northern situation. Philomena Muinzer (1987) cites 9 additional plays in her article, 'Evacuating the Museum: The Crisis of Playwriting in Ulster'. To this total of 33 plays I would add the following 17: Tomás MacAnna's and John D. Stewart's *A State of Chassis* (1970), John Boyd's *The Flats* (1971), Graham Reid's *Dorothy* (1980), *The Hidden Curriculum* (1982), *Remembrance* (1985) and *Callers* (1987), Martin Lynch's *Castles in the Air* (1983), Christina Reid's *Joyriders* (1986), Frank McGuinness's *The Bread Man* (1990), Tom Murphy's *The Patriot Game* (1991), Vincent Woods's *At the Black Pig's Dyke* (1992), Bill Morrison's trilogy *A Love Song for Ulster* (1993), Michael Harding's *Hubert Murray's Widow* (1993), Anne Devlin's *After Easter* (1994), and Marie Jones's *A Night in November* (1994). Most of these plays have been published. In addition there are television plays on the North, which it is beyond the scope of this study to include. Des Cranston (1985) refers to 20 television plays on Northern Ireland, a figure he doubles six years later (1991, p. 33).

In what follows three areas will be distinguished: drama staged in the North, drama staged in the South, and drama staged by the Field Day Theatre Company North and South. The partition is deliberate. My account is based on the acceptance of two states within the island of Ireland.

The North

The theatre in the North is, historically, a mirror image of the political relationship between North and South. When the Ulster Literary Theatre was founded in 1902 it was with the ambition of establishing in Belfast a Northern version of Yeats's Irish Literary Theatre in Dublin. It was at once a form of imitation and a gesture of independence. The new plays which followed, by such noteworthy dramatists as Rutherford Mayne (pseudonym of Samuel Waddell, 1878-1967), Gerald McNamara (pseudonym of Harry C.

Morrow, 1866–1938), and St. John Ervine (1883–1971), had much in common with the Abbey repertory but were also distinguished by use of a local dialect and a satiric point of view. The Ulster Theatre had a long history as a mainly amateur association; in 1940 it developed into the professional Group Theatre, which thrived over the next two decades (Bell 1972). When the Group management refused to stage Sam Thompson's *Over the Bridge* (1960) without cuts unacceptable to author and director, the Group was seen to support the unionist government of Northern Ireland. Thompson's play, a hard-hitting investigation of sectarianism in the Belfast shipyards, was then staged independently in Belfast. To a significant degree Thompson (1916-65), a Protestant working-class socialist, prefigured in his work the journey Northern society and drama alike had to go after the outbreak of sectarian hostilities in 1968–69. He saw in advance the need not only to break down fanaticism and bigotry in the workplace but also to create a theatre independent of unionist hegemony. Had he lived Thompson would probably have applauded Mary O'Malley's Lyric Players Theatre, which from its humble beginnings in the O'Malley household in 1951, acquired a professional theatre in 1968 dedicated to poetic drama in its widest sense. The Lyric entered Northern life at a critical time and aspired, according to Conor O'Malley (the founder's son) 'to become an artistic conscience in the community' (1988, p. 55). The use of the singular here is interesting. It was natural for those overcoming what John Wilson Foster calls 'the voicelessness of Ulster unionist culture' (1992, p. 171) to find common cause with those in another tradition, even one mapped out south of the border. The ultimate question for the diverse playwrights so thrown together in the North to express 'an artistic conscience' must be one of identity. After Sam Thompson writers both Catholic and Protestant could inspect the turmoil from different spheres of cultural experience, which intersecting might yet provide space for that 'narrow ground' where players could set their scene and meet an audience productively.

The O'Casey model

The Flats (1971), by John Boyd (b. 1912), was the first play at the Lyric about the modern violence in the North. It is set in Belfast in the summer of 1969. The location is a block of flats in which Protestants and Catholics live together but which is now under attack by Protestants seeking to drive out the Catholics. In that regard the play is both metaphor and prophecy. Skip twelve years to Christina Reid's *Tea in a China Cup* (1983) and one finds the other side of the coin: the mixed area in which Sarah lives is being taken over by Catholics and the Protestant Defence Committee urge her to get out, and burn the house. The atmosphere in Reid's play, with 'bin lids bangin' and riots in the streets' (Reid 1987, p. 29), derives from internment without trial, which mainly affected Catholics; the atmosphere in *The Flats*, which was staged five months before internment, is quite different. Interestingly, both authors are Protestant. *The Flats* represents the British army as a well-meaning and cheerful buffer between the two Northern factions because that was the perception in 1969. The emphasis throughout the play is that the sectarian difference is but a smokescreen for what is essentially a class struggle (Boyd 1971, p. 82). It is the Protestant Monica who is killed by the (Protestant) mob attacking the flats and not, as might have been expected, her Catholic friend Brid. This ironic twist, reminiscent of the ending of *Over the Bridge*, underlines the irrationality of the violence.

As the pioneer play on the Northern troubles *The Flats* deserves attention. It is a hinge play, in that being written by a product of Belfast's Protestant working class it links up with Thompson and lays the basis for the plays of social conscience which followed. Yet the larger hinge on which *The Flats* depends extends behind Thompson to Sean O'Casey. Monica's death in *The Flats* recalls Minnie Powell's in *The Shadow of a Gunman*; work-shy Joe Donellan with his weakness for drink recalls Captain Boyle, while his wife Kathleen recalls Juno; the British soldier repeatedly echoes Corporal Stoddart in *The Plough and the Stars*, a Cockney at sea in the Irish troubles and clinging to the wreckage of his 'duty' (Boyd 1971, pp. 75-6). It is unlikely that Boyd was himself unaware of the O'Casey echoes in *The Flats*, which act as deliberate alienation devices prompting reassessment of the basis of conflict.

In an essay in *Threshold* at this time Seamus Deane argued that O'Casey was in fact a bad example: 'it would be wrong, especially in present conditions, to take him as our paradigm of a dramatist who made political preoccupation central to his work' (1973, p. 11). The intellectuals were suspicious of O'Casey's treatment of politics in his drama. They saw his plays as dangerously 'simple-minded and sentimental' in regard to nationalism (Watson 1994, p. 265), because O'Casey debunked militant republicanism. But what O'Casey's

Dublin plays actually do is to highlight, through comedy and ironic juxtaposition, the absurdity as well as the horror of war. That viewpoint, together with O'Casey's technical ability to make audiences see behind political posturing, made him an excellent model for Northern dramatists. And they instinctively knew this. Besides Boyd, Wilson John Haire (b. 1932) and Martin Lynch (b. 1951) adapted O'Casey's methods to Belfast conditions. Indeed, the fruitfulness of the O'Casey model (his combination of tragedy and comedy, his use of melodrama, colourful characters and heightened speech based on local usage, all in the service of political comment), is discernible as late as *Joyriders* (1986), by Christina Reid (b. 1942).

Reid opens *Joyriders* in a theatre where O'Casey's *The Shadow of a Gunman* is reaching its tragic climax. Minnie Powell is shot in the street to save the neck of the anti-hero Donal Davoren. As the voice-overs die away to applause (off) Reid's play begins with the reactions of a group of young people whose lives in some respects bear resemblance to O'Casey's tenement dwellers. The idea for this play came to Reid when she was writer-in-residence at the Lyric in 1983–4 and met just such a group of teenagers when they came to see *The Shadow of a Gunman*. They were on a Youth Training Scheme and had little knowledge of theatre but their reactions attracted Reid, who befriended them. In the resultant play, Maureen, the sweetest but most naive of the group, gets pregnant by a university student, and steals clothes to rescue her self-esteem. In the end Maureen is killed in the street when she rushes out of the workshop to help her young brother, who has stolen a police car while 'coked to the gills' (Reid 1993, p. 61). Like Minnie Powell, Maureen is caught in the crossfire: 'she run between the car an' the army' (p. 63). Sandra, the most intelligent of the whole group, refuses to see Maureen's death as romantic in any way: 'It's not lovely, an' it's not romantic like in stupid friggin' plays!' (p. 63). O'Casey's text is used, therefore, as an ironic frame of reference. Audiences are forced to confront the socio-economic reasons behind the Northern situation (McMullan 1993, p. 121). The O'Casey model constantly bore fruit in this way. In his Dublin plays O'Casey had shown through a simple private/ public interaction of ordinary citizens and state apparatus how ideology initiates urban warfare, which is indiscriminate, and how the cost condemns justification. It is a paradigm which allows the emphasis to fall on waste of life, and thus has universal tragic application.

The Romeo and Juliet *typos*

There is another exemplar whose style and emphasis also made a significant mark on modern Northern drama. St John Ervine had a long and varied career in the Irish and English theatre, and even influenced the modern American theatre through his powerful tragedy *John Ferguson* (1915), staged by the Theatre Guild in New York in 1919. Ervine's *Mixed Marriage* (1911) is a seminal play in the development of drama in Northern Ireland. As the title suggests, the play explores the tensions arising from a love affair between a Catholic and a Protestant. It is the perennial Romeo-and-Juliet situation. But in Shakespeare's play the malevolent stars, as much as the family feud, destroy the lovers. A modern writer cannot use this idea. Naturalism is based on the premise that material conditions govern the happiness or otherwise of individuals. Ervine, writing in the naturalistic mode which was to dominate Irish drama after Synge, provided a persuasive analysis of sectarianism in Belfast. His play is primarily about labour relations at a specific time, 1911, when Home Rule was in the air and Sir Edward Carson was organising trade-union opposition. Carson argued that if Home Rule came about partition was a necessity; trade-union solidarity, therefore, was to be avoided. Moreover, the Protestant workers had too much to lose to make alliance with their Catholic counterparts. This dilemma is introduced early into *Mixed Marriage* and is combined with a love story which divides a Protestant labourer (Rainey) from his son Hugh and sparks off violence causing the death of Hugh's Catholic girlfriend Nora. Sectarianism proves fatal. Old Rainey's point of view, voiced in Act I, is borne out: 'A don't like Cathliks an' Prodesans mixin' thegither. No good ivir comes o' the like o' that' (Ervine 1988, p. 20).

Ervine was himself a unionist and an opponent of Home Rule but as a playwright he was able to present with sharp definition the two sides of the Northern conflict. He could offset the humanism of Mrs Rainey, a Juno before her time, with the realistic intransigence of her husband who, even after Nora's death, insists he was right. The point made by the ending is that reconciliation is deliberately made impossible by special interests. The Shakespearean solution to tribalism is sabotaged. Difference is manipulated by forces working to prevent a working-class 'marriage' of interests.

Ervine's analysis could be applied to a great deal of Northern drama after 1969. The plays of John Wilson Haire, himself a product of a 'mixed marriage', are examples. *Bloom of the Diamond Stone* (1973), in particular, reveals the impossibility of any Romeo-and-Juliet union, since militant tribalisms forbid it. Whereas the material of the play is grimly naturalistic, Haire prefaces it with two short mummers' plays mocking both the nationalist and unionist traditions. The element of 'play' is here used for ironic and farcical purposes. In other plays love across the sectarian divide is more obviously the means of asserting the absurdity as well as the pity of the Northern tragedy. Graham Reid's *Remembrance* (1984) is a case in point. Like Ervine, Boyd and Haire, Reid (b. 1945) is a Belfast Protestant. His early work was not accepted in Belfast, however, and as it was staged in Dublin it will be described below. By the time he wrote *Remembrance* for the Lyric Reid had acquired a considerable reputation as an unblinking witness of violence and its dehumanising effects. Compared with the general grimness of Reid's material, *Remembrance* is a mellow play. Bert, a widowed Protestant aged 68, meets Theresa, a widowed Catholic aged 63, in a Belfast cemetery, where they fall in love. They visit the cemetery daily where the graves of their sons, each murdered by the other side, are ironically adjacent. The difficulty for the lovers lies in the sectarian bitterness of their surviving children. This, of course, is to invert the Romeo-and-Juliet pattern. Psychologically, the younger generation cannot endure the alliance of Bert and Theresa, and the irony provides its own wry comment on sectarianism.

Examples could be multiplied. Christina Reid's first play, *Did You Hear the One About the Irishman?* is subtitled *A Love Story* in the 1989 edition. Brian, a Catholic, and Allison, a Protestant, are lovers who are warned to stop seeing each other and then are executed by paramilitaries. These lovers are not star-crossed. They are caught up in internecine strife, which in turn is bound up with stereotyping which is culturally condoned. The ending makes the point that sectarian violence has its roots in racial insult. Anne Devlin's *Ourselves Alone* (1985) also adopts the form of a love story for political purposes. Devlin's subject, essentially, is women, the Nora Clitheroes broken by the war or the Mary Boyles betrayed and yet surviving to begin afresh elsewhere. *Ourselves Alone,* the title of which is an ironic translation of *Sinn Féin,* tells the story of Josie, who is involved with the IRA, falls in love with an Englishman who infiltrates the organisation, and is carrying his child when he is

revealed as a traitor. The play enacts a drama of individual liberation. Josie's love affair is delusory: her Romeo is a double agent. Joe
Conran really was from an unacceptable tribe, though she had not
suspected this fact. Josie is a pathetic failure; her betrayal delivers her
back into the power of men. It is not Josie who experiences liberation but her flighty sister Frieda. Shaking off all the pressures imposed by her republican environment Frieda leaves for England (of
all places). 'I'd rather be lonely than suffocate', she decides (Devlin
1986, p. 90). Thus 'ourselves alone' takes on a new meaning.

Devlin's later play *After Easter* (1994), while containing familiar
material on the Northern war, is also not quite what it seems. This is
in many respects a dream play (the title of which conjures up
Strindberg's *Easter*), which goes further into the territory opened up
by *Ourselves Alone*, namely the female psyche and the traumas which
stand in the way of realising selfhood. Here Devlin is occupied with
the spiritual breakdown of her main character Greta, attributable in
part to her experience as a child of a misalliance between a Communist father and an ultra-Catholic mother, and in part to her mixed
marriage in Oxford. Yet this is but an outline for a play which
combines politics, a search for self-knowledge, and what Devlin
herself calls 'the mystery of the personality' (Devlin 1994b, p. 3).
After Easter is about the healing process, a search for an alternative
language and a new narrative other than the deadly ones
bequeathed by *Mixed Marriage*. In short, much of Northern drama
plays variations on Ervine's original theme but in recent years a
socialist gloss has given way to a feminist/humanist revision.

The Theatre of hope

The theatre of hope endorses 'play' and builds hope on the fanciful.
It reinforces the idea that humour is essential today for the successful dramatisation of horror. What is remarkable in Martin Lynch's
work, for example, is his inclusion of comedy and the comic spirit in
his depictions of even the most appalling accounts of misery among
the poor and underprivileged in Belfast. Thus *The Interrogation of
Ambrose Fogarty* (Lynch 1982b) is adept at combining a grim topic
with humour so as to deconstruct stereotyped attitudes. On the day
that Fogarty is arrested for interrogation, Willie Lagan is also arrested for 'taking part' (theatrical term) in a riot (1982b, p. 3). Lagan
is a clown, a half-wit with a guitar whose jests subvert the seriousness of the interrogation process. Whereas Lynch clearly wishes to

address issues of police brutality and bias in the aftermath of the hunger-strike period he also, like Friel in *The Freedom of the City* (1973), suggests that the victims' weapons include humour and the ability to distance themselves through fantasy from the conditions imposed. It is ironic and yet appropriate (since he is the embodiment of the comic spirit) that it is Willie Lagan who is detained for further questioning while Fogarty is released. Certainly, Fogarty is brutalised while in custody. That aspect of the play is to an extent propagandistic, and links it to Ron Hutchinson's powerful but humourless *Rat in the Skull* (1984). What lives dramatically is what escapes from and raises the audience above prejudice. Lynch is at his best when he gives zaniness utterance.

Lynch subsequently wrote for a new women's community theatre company, Charabanc, to produce *Lay Up Your Ends* (1983), a social documentary on the Belfast linen mills at the start of the century, and *Oul' Delf and False Teeth* (1984), a social history centering on the election year of 1949. The style of this company was from the outset remarkably vital. Charabanc led Lynch back into community theatre where his heart seems to lie. He is perhaps the most committed playwright the North has produced since Sam Thompson, and his work deserves more attention than can be accorded it here. The publication of *Three Plays* (1996), with introduction by Damian Smyth, is a step in the right direction. Charabanc, however, deserves attention in its own right (cf. Bort 1995). It produced at least one significant playwright from among its dedicated collaborators in Marie Jones (e.g. *A Night in November*, 1994). And whereas it addressed social issues in *Somewhere Over the Balcony*, according to the director Pam Brighton (1990, p. 42) Charabanc remained politically neutral. In the North, that is no mean theatrical trick. In Charabanc's case the neutrality left energy for documentary or community drama which concentrated on survival and therefore accentuated hope (Coyle 1993). Its demise in 1995 was surely premature.

There is also the kind of play which only obliquely expresses hope. One of these is *We Do It for Love* (1975), by the poet Patrick Galvin (b. 1927), who was writer-in-residence at the Lyric in the early 1970s. This was a highly successful revue-style play, with songs, using as central image a child's merry-go-round, manned by Moses Docker, the master of ceremonies. The merry-go-round itself is not real, but it works as an effective metaphor for the cycle of Northern violence and retaliation. Perhaps it is more a conceit than a metaphor, since it is ironic also in its misapplication as a source of amusement. The roots of Galvin's technique are, no doubt, Brechtian. There are traces, too, of Joan Littlewood's production of *Oh, What a Lovely War!* (1963), which presented the horrors of World War One in terms of music-hall. And, inevitably, O'Casey is in the background. But Galvin has a voice of his own, strong, compassionate and ironic. He knows how to juxtapose the serious and the music-hall to highlight the outrageousness of exploitation masquerading as idealism. In an earlier play, *Nightfall to Belfast* (1973) he had a prologue in which three men play cards, one man representing the church, one representing the law and one the business community, while sounds of bombing and gunfire are heard all around and a young masked man lies dying unattended on the floor. This juxtaposition is the key to the style of *We Do It for Love*. There is a similar scene where three British soldiers are gunned down in a public house while bystanders go on playing cards unperturbed. By showing two bombers doing a song-and-dance routine to the refrain, 'We do it for love', a certain degree of ambivalence in response to terrorism is mocked. But Galvin also emphasises the necessity to destroy the merry-go-round, which Moses Docker burns down as the cast sing of liberation. Moses brings together two women from either side of the divide, each of whom has had a son murdered in the conflict. Such unison was wishful thinking in 1975, but it marks an effective use of fantasy to create an image of hope.

Another writer who understood this imaginative imperative and had the genius to apply it to the horrors of the Northern situation was Stewart Parker (1941–88). Looking at Parker's tragically short career (for the cancer which caused him to lose a leg at age nineteen finally cut him off at the height of his powers) one is struck by that combination of commitment to a just society and a zany sense of the ridiculous which gives warmth to his plays. His eight television plays lie outside the scope of this study, but they too emanate a warmth and a love of whimsy. It is ironic that Parker, an ardent admirer of Sam Thompson, whose Belfast family background he to some extent shared and whose controversial play *Over the Bridge* he edited after Thompson's death, should himself experience rejection in Belfast when he tried to have *Spokesong* staged there. It received its première instead in Dublin, where it was the hit of the 1975 Theatre Festival, and proved an international success. *Spokesong* is a light-hearted story about Frank Stock, fighting to hold onto the small family bicycle business in a part of Belfast under the twin attacks of political violence and urban redevelopment (cf. Kurdi 1993). Where Galvin used the merry-go-round Parker uses the bicycle as theatrical conceit. Using these simple narrative ingredients Parker constructs a whimsical comedy which is at once a love story between Frank Stock and schoolteacher Daisy Bell (a useful cue for songs) and a story of resistance to paramilitary pressures to take over the shop under cover of urban development. The whole story, which might be described as freewheeling romance, is from time to time undercut by flashbacks to remind Frank of the 'stock' from which he comes and by the intrusions of the Trick Cyclist, a narrator on a unicycle, who is a trickster with deep roots in Irish culture (Harrison 1989). Parker was considerably less radical than Galvin; indeed, his politics in *Spokesong* are highly conservative. In effect, he wanted to replace politics with theatre. Parker's whole dramatic aesthetic was bound up with a concept of play. He aimed to create a 'ludic theatre', understood as performing 'a crucial function in our society' (1981, p. 10). In *Spokesong* Parker stops the action one millimetre short of the saccharine, with a screech of brakes exuding the whiff of boulevard theatre. Daisy agrees to stay with Frank and save the shop. Thus the happy ending is a joyous, fantastic rebuff to the revolutionary times rather than a serious engagement with the political situation.

Northern Star is a different matter. The Lyric Theatre expected this play to make a political difference in Northern Ireland, 'because it would show a time when Catholics and Protestants worked together for reform' (Harris 1991, p. 237). Parker's title is a pun on the name of the radical newspaper founded by the United Irishmen in 1791, *The Northern Star*. As the play opens, following the defeat of 1798, Henry Joy McCracken is on the run and rehearsing not only the past seven years in memory but also in reality his speech from the gallows. He is thus introduced as the 'Northern star' addressing the audience on his 'positively last appearance' (Parker 1989, p. 18). The play then takes the form of flashbacks through the period 1791–8, interspersed with moments in McCracken's present situation as he hides out. What makes the whole affair ironic and histrionic is the nature of the rebellion itself. As may be recalled from *Translations* (1980), the Catholics did not turn out in any force to support the republican dream of the Protestants (Friel 1984, p. 445). The historian J. C. Beckett comments (1966, p. 265) that it is perhaps for this reason that the insurrection 'is remembered by Ulster protestants without any of the rancour commonly associated with Irish historical events'. It was essentially an interlude.

Parker seizes upon the events's histrionic quality and exploits it to the full. To each of the seven 'ages' which McCracken identifies when he rehearses the course of the United Irishmen in Belfast, Parker ascribes a specific dramatic style. Thus the early days in 1791 are dubbed the 'Age of Innocence' and are written in the style of the first professional Irish playwright, George Farquhar (1677–1707). The 'Age of Idealism' follows, in the style of Dion Boucicault (1820–90). Then comes the 'Age of Cleverness', in the style of Oscar Wilde (1856-1900). Next in order come the 'Age of Dialectics' (Shaw), the 'Age of Heroism' (Synge), the 'Age of Compromise' (O'Casey) and the 'Age of Knowledge' (Behan and Beckett). Parker called this literary device 'pastiche' and told an interviewer that the association with Joyce's technique in the 'Oxen of the Sun' episode in *Ulysses* was deliberate. It was a risky undertaking in the theatre. As audiences were amused at the style of a particular episode they were automatically coaxed into an awareness of the political content of the dialogue in use. Everything becomes 'play'. And play in turn becomes what Parker calls 'a workable model of wholeness' (Andrews 1990, p. 239). In other words, the imitation breaks down barriers between then and now and involves an audience in seeing the historical and the actual as sharing the same space. McCracken muses on his failure. 'We never made a nation. ... We botched the birth.' And he leaves the unresolved problem with the audience. 'So what if the English do bequeath us to one another some day? What then? When there's nobody else to blame except ourselves?' (Parker 1989, p. 75). Without either scapegoats or the stereotypes of history, how will a divided people find wholeness? The hope remains to be literally acted upon.

Parker's work for the Belfast stage sums up what was best in the plays on the Northern situation staged in the North. They established a perspective by means of which the horror and the waste could be registered not as numbing and overwhelming but, as art dictates, as liberating and enabling. *Pentecost* (1987), which as a Field Day production will be explored below, took a huge risk in asking the audience to believe in the instrumentality of hope. Parker worked, it has to be remembered, while despair was the common response to events in the North. With the IRA ceasefire in August

1994 hope flickeringly alighted on the North at last. Subsequently, Parker's *Pentecost*, revived in both Belfast and Dublin, has shown how history itself may be transcended and division healed.

The South

In Tom Murphy's *The White House* (1972) there was a passage in which the auctioneer Liam let the returned emigrant Michael know how seriously Liam and his friends took the situation up North. Although *The White House* remains unpublished this passage was retained in *Conversations on a Homecoming* (1985):

> MICHAEL (*joking*): You didn't consider taking up the gun and marching on the North?
> JUNIOR: We thought about it.
> MICHAEL *laughs*
> [JUNIOR:] Serious.
> MICHAEL: What?
> JUNIOR: We did.
> LIAM: We nearly did.   (Murphy 1993, p. 13)

They 'nearly' took up arms to sort things out, but not quite. Some time later in the evening Liam defends the Irish Catholic state. A little the worse for drink, he musters up a fine range of political clichés, 'A minority Catholic group being oppressed!', 'A gerrymandering majority' (p. 48), and so forth, culminating in, 'No border, boy! And cultural heritage inex-inextricably bound with our Faith and Hope and Hope and Faith and *Truth!*' Liam is an updated Tommy Owens (*The Shadow of a Gunman*) but with status in society as one of the rising rural middle class. Murphy captures with delicious accuracy the tones of ludicrous outrage with which this class spluttered over the Northern situation in the early years after 1969. The phrase, 'No border, boy!', referring to the nationalist claim that the partition of Ireland was the root of the problem in the North, virtually sets the headline for Clare O'Halloran's sharp attack on Southern rhetoric, *Partition and the Limits of Irish Nationalism* (1987). Murphy's irony obviously spoke for the majority of his fellow-playwrights at this time, for we hear no more of Liam's facile republicanism in Irish drama hereafter, whatever about the rhetoric heard at Ireland's annual party political conferences. The fact is that in the South, after some initial confusion on the subject, aggravated by the serious national crisis known as the Arms Trial in May 1970, people soon began to detach themselves from the Northern troubles in a mixture of apathy, guilt and frustration. The sight on television of daily carnage reinforced the partitionist mentalities of a people 'few of whom would contemplate venturing north of the border' (Fanning 1983, p. 212). Murphy the playwright made the point eleven years before the historian Fanning.

It follows that plays written in the South about the Northern situation were few. The first was actually a revue, *A State of Chassis* (1970), written by Tomás MacAnna, John D. Stewart and Eoghan Ó Tuairisc. The title was derived from Captain Boyle's all-Ireland refrain in *Juno and the Paycock* but applied to the chaos in the North after 1968. Although the text has not survived the production, directed by MacAnna, made a big impact because the satire of Bernadette Devlin (in particular) was resented. Eamonn McCann jumped onto the stage and took loud exception to the attitudes 'down here' to the conflict 'up there'. He can hardly have known how prophetic his remarks were. Whether he was justified in asserting that 'the people here are total hypocrites' (Hunt 1979, p. 211) is another matter.

Brian Friel's *The Freedom of the City* (1973) was the first major new Northern play to be staged at the Abbey. It also marked Friel's return to the national theatre, for a play relating to Bloody Sunday, 30 January 1972. As Eamonn McCann emphasised, 'After Bloody Sunday the most powerful feeling in the area was the desire for revenge' (1974, p. 102). But it was more the palpable injustice of the *Widgery Report* (1972) which exercised Friel. He later confessed that he wrote *The Freedom of the City* too soon after Bloody Sunday, 'out of some kind of heat and some kind of immediate passion that I would want to have quieted a bit before I did it' (O'Toole 1982, p. 22). Still, the play is by no means a polemic, nor is the anger out of control. Indeed, the expected feelings of pity, anger and terror are tightly reigned in and defused by the form. Time, place and action, the good old unities, are shuffled with such mastery that conventional outlets for audience response are blocked, and one is forced to think and feel in broken sequences, arrested and incomplete. As to time, the play begins with three bodies on the stage and then moves forward to the tribunal of enquiry before going backward to introduce Lily, Michael and Skinner as they find refuge in the Guildhall. From this point on, the scenes in which these three appear are in the present tense, and are intercut with scenes which jump days to their funerals and weeks to the tribunal of enquiry and a vaguer time span when a sociologist conducts his own enquiry into the culture of poverty. The effect every time we return to the main characters is a compound of pathos, irony and shock. As to space, the stage is like a cobweb with the Mayor's Parlour (the interior of the Guildhall) at the centre, surrounded by concentric rings occupied by officials and commentators of various kinds. As to action, Friel is here probably most daring of all. After all, in Brechtian drama, which Friel's techniques here recall, action is always taken and then reviewed, assessed and put into social and/or political context. In Brecht we always have to see the 'hero' (the term becomes problematic) in actions which are contradictory and thus capable of revealing how things are done, how history is constructed as opposed to just happening in nature. Friel takes the opposite line in *The Freedom of the City*. His three central characters are clearly seen to take no action. Like characters more out of Beckett than out of Brecht they merely pass the time. It is important, in order to establish their 'innocence' (another problematic term) that their time in the Mayor's Parlour be no more than an interlude, in parenthesis between participating in a civil rights march and going home to tea. The action is thus non-action. Friel increases the poignancy of the central situation by setting up a contrast between the playfulness of the three characters and the formality and seriousness of those surrounding them. This recklessness is orchestrated by Skinner, the trickster figure and comic subversive. As mock Lord Mayor he confers the freedom of the city on the other two, and we need no sociologist to point up the irony. Lily can see it. 'Sure that means nothing' (Friel 1984, p. 165). Before he leaves, Skinner uses the ceremonial sword on the portrait of Sir Joshua, icon of the Ascendancy, and insists on its remaining: 'Allow me my gesture'. After all, 'It's only a picture. And a ceremonial sword'. It's all only play, a dance, as it happens, of death. Skinner's consciousness thus holds *The Freedom of the City* together as a tragicomedy.

The Freedom of the City had what is called a mixed reception. In effect, the ironic, hard-hitting elements of the play were not appreciated, largely because of the conservatism of Dublin audiences. Although it was subsequently dismissed in New York as politically biased, *The Freedom of the City* has since 'gained greatly in stature' as its theatrical skilfulness has been better appreciated (Zach 1989, p. 432). Yet it has never been revived at the Abbey, and its reception underlines the antipathy in the South to plays about Northern politics. The same point can be made even more emphatically about Friel's next play for the Abbey, *Volunteers* (1975). Audiences obviously expected a play about internment, a serious Northern issue. Instead Friel offered more irony by setting his play in the South (transparently in Dublin) and by bringing together two quite distinct fields of reference: the subject of IRA prisoners and the contemporary subject of an archaeological dig on a Viking site (Bradley 1984). The result was sardonic attack on Southern complacency. Dublin audiences were not amused and, in spite of an eloquent defence by Seamus Heaney (*TLS*, 21 March 1975), *Volunteers* did poor business. It marked Friel's last attempt to interest Abbey audiences in political matters. When next he had something political to say he set up his own company to say it. Moreover, *Volunteers* put paid for a considerable time to plays about the North on the Abbey's main stage. The subject was relegated to the Peacock annexe, surely a telling development.

Perhaps the most interesting playwrights to cope with this situation were Graham Reid (b. 1945) and Frank McGuinness (b. 1953). Reid came down in 1979 from his native Belfast to the Peacock, where he learned his trade through the workshop atmosphere created by Seán McCarthy and Patrick Mason. Eventually, Reid was to go off to London and into television, for which he wrote some very successful plays about the North, including the ground-breaking three *Billy* plays (1982-4), adapted for the stage in 1990. In 1995 he returned to the stage with two new plays, *Love*, staged at the West Yorkshire Playhouse, and *Lengthening Shadows*, staged with Martin Lynch at the Lyric in Belfast.

Reid was at first determined to write about urban violence without overtly referring to the Northern situation. *The Death of Humpty Dumpty* (1979) tells the story of a man shot on his own doorstep and crippled for the rest of his life. Although the location is clearly Belfast, Reid deliberately tried to avoid 'the troubles' as theme (Gillespie 1979). The avoidance leaves a vacuum. In subsequent plays avoidance begins to look like evasion. We never know who the dark forces in an early Reid play are, or why they commit violence. *The Closed Door* (1980) and *Dorothy* (1980) end up as crude melodramas just because Reid wanted, by eliding the coded, tribalist geography of Belfast, to avoid sectarian issues. But if the grounds of violence are, in fact, sectarian it robs drama of meaning to keep it out of the analysis. Therefore, although Reid's early plays are strong stuff (reminiscent of Edward Bond) they actually disguise rather than illuminate the politics of the North. A fresh development comes, however, with *The Hidden Curriculum* (1982), Reid's best play.

This play is given a specific Northern location, a Protestant secondary school in West Belfast, where Reid finds a model for the politics of culture. The teacher of English, Tony Cairns, discovers painfully that many of his former pupils of the 1970s are involved with paramilitaries and that one is actually serving four life sentences for murder. This time Reid discloses the politics behind the violence: one of Cairns's ex-pupils says, 'We're just loyalist extremists' (Reid 1982, p. 134). The school serving this loyalist district has failed to prevent violence based on sectarianism. Cairns discovers that 'the pupils were our victims' (p. 155). In an attempt to instil a love of poetry in his students, on the humanistic assumption that poetry is a moral force in society, Cairns is in the habit of teaching the war poets and of reminding his students that a lot of Ulstermen died in World War One. But his language is itself sectarian. 'Thousands of Protestants, UVF men and Orangemen. Many of them went over the top wearing their sashes, singing orange songs or shouting "No Surrender". ... This is about *your* history, *your* backgrounds' (p. 103). This hidden curriculum, the English teacher comes to understand, may have contributed to the contemporary violence; it certainly did not prevent it. In his plot, Reid exposes the nexus of class, culture and social breakdown and shows how education is implicated with the moral and political collapse of a community.

As mentioned earlier, *Remembrance* (1984) is a version of the Romeo and Juliet story, but reversed so that the lovers are elderly and the opposition comes from the young people, on both sides of the sectarian divide. Here also Reid displays considerable insight into the psychological plight of the RUC officer, living on the brink and by his hysteria manifesting better than any scene of violence the destructive effects of sectarianism. *Callers* (1985) tried to show the brutalising process on both sides, by using a split stage to present the IRA plan its attack on the home of a RUC man. The poor reception of this graphically brutal play may well have decided Reid to abandon the stage for television. Looked at now in hindsight, Reid's output records the struggle of an artist to be truthful without becoming the prisoner of a restricted political vocabulary. The path was not a straight one, but it led to television, where Reid emancipated himself from the fear of partisanship.

Frank McGuinness's development forms a contrast to Reid, in that far from having to struggle to find a form to accommodate his own background, McGuinness manifests a chameleon ability to switch points of view, in gender and in politics. Born in Buncrana, in north-east Donegal, McGuinness grew up in traditional nationalist territory. Yet his earliest play, *Factory Girls* (1982), while set in this territory avoids nationalist issues to concentrate on women, power, and solidarity. Then as the tide of opinion in the South turned more against old-style republicanism McGuinness's *Observe the Sons of Ulster Marching Towards the Somme* (1985) was staged at the Peacock. This history play is narrated altogether from the unionist point of view. Its ramifications include the whole question of unionism and the Empire, and the fate of the Ulster Division at Thiepval on the Somme on 1 July 1916 when that division lost 6000 men in one day (White 1976). The play has the simplicity of epic. No extraneous characters are admitted; no representatives of church, state or even officer class. All is concentrated on the intimate relations between eight volunteers, as they form friendships which enable their identities to clarify and then coalesce into a collective consciousness of their specific Irishness, defined as the battle of the Somme begins. *Observe* was first seen as an 'attack on the trappings and tribalism of Ulster Protestantism' because of the link between constructed identity and death (*Irish Times*, 19 February 1985). Although that link is there, it is not necessarily forged as a critique of 'tribalism'; it is difficult to see the play as an attack on Ulster Protestantism. Indeed, as Barry Sloan has pointed out, 'in this play anti-Catholicism is not viewed merely as a negative posture. It is also an essential mark of Protestant identity, a sign of God's chosen people' (1993, p. 40).

Graham Reid had exposed in *The Hidden Curriculum* the link between the educational system, which promotes war poetry as a means of creating a shared consciousness, and sectarian violence. McGuinness shows the ambivalence inherent in the very process of national self-definition. It is as if the play were negotiating a passage between O'Casey's *The Silver Tassie* and Shakespeare's *Henry V*. The horror and destructiveness of war, while not shown as O'Casey showed them, permeate and inform the thoughts and tones of the men, and yet in the final scene when they exchange Orange sashes and Pyper addresses his friends before the battle quite a different structure of feeling is created, a fellowship reminiscent of St

Crispin's Day.

Observe is neither condescending towards unionism nor a covert attack on its possibly jingoist elements. It is about transformation and change. Moreover, Pyper, the artist figure, manages to focus the diffused and confused loyalties of the men at the end. Part 3 of the play, subtitled 'Pairing', is the key to this process. Here the eight men are home from the front on leave, located in pairs at distinctive 'habitats' in the Northern landscape. The simultaneity of the staging is all-important; the intercutting between the four areas heightens the sense of isolation. The fourth location is the climactic one, 'Holiest spot in Ulster' (McGuinness 1986, p. 43). This is the Field at Finaghy, outside Belfast, where the annual Orange parade has its destination and full celebration. When Anderson and McIlwaine visit the Field they are alone, for the Twelfth of July has passed. The emptiness of the big field anticipates 'this deserted temple of the Lord' (p. 80) which Ulster is to become. Miserable and depressed, Anderson and McIlwaine go through the rituals of the Twelfth, beating the lambeg drum, drinking and making a speech about the Boyne as a river of blood. But the year being 1916, Anderson focuses on the threat from the South: 'And this blood will not be drained into the sewers of an Irish republic. We will not recognise this republic. We will fight this republic' (p. 59). He goes on to say they will fight and die in answer to the 'call to freedom'. In 1913 Sir Edward Carson had formed the Ulster Volunteer Force (UVF) from 100,000 men who had signed the Covenant (Lucy 1989, p. 89) to oppose Home Rule. When the 1914 war broke out the UVF became the 36th (Ulster) Division, the one to which McGuinness's men belong. In answering the king's call the UVF were thus indirectly fighting Home Rule (Orr 1987). Therefore, Pyper links the Boyne and the Somme when he prays for and with the men (McGuinness 1986, p. 80). With an incantatory rhetoric, Pyper overcomes his deathwish and declares instead his love for life, for the men, and for Ulster. The men pick up the last word and turn it into a battle-cry. 'Ulster' is used twenty-one times in that final page of text. The irony is that Home Rule was destined to create an independent 'Ulster'.

The omission of the phrase 'Home Rule' from the text maintains the focus on a form of patriotism more acceptable in the South in 1985. The New Ireland Forum had just sat and brought in its *Report*. McGuinness's contribution to the debate is to assert that unionist 'loyalty' is primarily to 'Ulster', for at the time in which the play is set the province had not been divided; unionist identity is represented in opposition to the dreaded 'republic', a reality only since 1949. The play asks the audience to 'observe' these men at the moment of self-definition marching in the wrong direction, perhaps, but marching together in solidarity nonetheless. To observe them is to understand what it is they will die for. The key speech by Anderson in the field, in imitation of the Grand Master, assumes an 'audience' of Orangemen. The real audience in the Peacock might have taken offence but they did not. Anderson breaks down as soon as he finishes the speech and cancels it: 'It's all lies. We're going to die. It's all lies. We're going to die for nothing' (McGuinness 1986, p. 59). That contradiction stands, until Pyper dissolves it in the final prayer to which the audience as 'observer' assents. In effect, the play recognises and celebrates partition.

In the South the reception of *Observe* was mainly positive. The play was elevated to the Abbey's main stage in December 1985, which speaks volumes, and it won many awards, including, appropriately, the Ewart-Biggs Prize in memory of the British ambassador assassinated by the IRA in 1976. It seemed to call forth the generosity of Southerners towards much-maligned unionism. It was seen as such when revived in October 1994 at the time of the UVF ceasefire. Edna Longley has noted that *Observe* was as popular in Dublin as Stewart Parker's *Northern Star* was in Belfast: 'This may help to change something, if not any results' (1994, p. 157). It may be noted that Dublin audiences could admire McGuinness's play because it cost them nothing to do so: it did not press upon feelings either of guilt or grievance, the twin forces which for long had made plays about the North unpalatable.

Observe the Sons of Ulster represents a triumph of the imagination. It sympathises profoundly with an alien point of view. *Carthaginians* (1988), while a very interesting pendant to the earlier play, lacks this quality. The most interesting feature of the play, so far as the general argument of this chapter is concerned, is the way in which it makes use of 'play' in the service of a drama about the Northern trauma. The central device, a parodic play-within-the-play, occurs half-way through the extended ritual of remembrance. Dido, the homosexual master of ceremonies, brings in the text of *The Burning Balaclava*, a play he has written under the pseudonym Fionnuala McGonigle. The dramatic effect of this diversion is to galvanise the six characters, now that they have found their author, into energetic reappraisal of their individual disabilities. Their response, 'Well, that was crack' (McGuinness 1988, p. 44), is reminiscent of Lily's summation of the time spent in the Mayor's Parlour in Friel's *The Freedom of the City*. In Friel the 'crack' exists in a world tragically separated from the avenging world of responsibility; in McGuinness the 'crack' creates a bridge to the world of responsibility. All now focus on Bloody Sunday and realise, 'in a way we all died' (p. 66). Like the characters in the parodic play they can rise again, once they share the sense that the space is holy. 'Carthage has not been destroyed' (p. 70). More Dionysus than drag queen, Dido creates the possibility for renewal through art. His last word, and the last word of *Carthaginians*, is 'play'.

By the time the 75th anniversary of the Easter Rising occurred the general antipathy towards republicanism was very marked. It was decided to hold no public commemoration of 1916 in Dublin. For the most part, the playwrights were silent. There were a few telling exceptions, for example, Peter Sheridan's bilingual version of *Diary of a Hunger Strike* (1987), Tom Murphy's *The Patriot Game* (1991), Vincent Woods' *At the Black Pig's Dyke* (1992), and Michael Harding's *Hubert Murray's Widow* (1993). In 'Staging the Troubles', Ian Hill has validly claimed: 'In Dublin there is a comfortable society which, though its Government claims in its constitution to possess the northern six counties, certainly does not want to possess its violent troubles' (1993, p. 45). Almost ten years earlier Fergal Tobin (1984, p. 231) had commented in similar vein. The validity of the charge is reflected in the reception in the South of plays on the Northern question after 1969.

North and South: Field Day

The Field Day Theatre Company was founded in Derry in 1980 by Brian Friel and the actor Stephen Rea. Four other directors were soon added, the poets Seamus Heaney and Tom Paulin, the critic and professor of English and American literature at University College Dublin Seamus Deane, and the musician David Hammond. The board was balanced between three Protestants and three Catholics, all from the North. In 1986, however, the novelist and playwright Thomas Kilroy was added to the board from the South. Between 1980 and 1993, when Field Day announced suspension of its activities, twelve plays were staged, as follows: Friel's *Translations*

(1980), his version of *Three Sisters* (1981) and his *Communication Cord* (1982); Fugard's *Boesman and Lena* (1983); Paulin's version of Sophocles' *Antigone*, *The Riot Act* (1984); Derek Mahon's version of Molière's *L'École des maris*, *High Time* (1984); Kilroy's *Double Cross* (1986); Stewart Parker's *Pentecost* (1987); Friel's *Making History* (1988); Terry Eagleton's *Saint Oscar* (1989); Heaney's version of Sophocles' *Philoctetes*, *The Cure at Troy* (1990); and Kilroy's *The Madame MacAdam Travelling Theatre* (1991). Only one production a year was undertaken, which toured for about ten weeks, with the exception of the year 1985, when there was no production, McGuinness's *Carthaginians* having been rejected that year.

From 1983 on Field Day began to publish pamphlets on language, myth, law and the interrelation of literature and colonialism, all with specific reference to the Ireland–England question. Between 1983 and 1988 fifteen such pamphlets were published. In 1991 three volumes of the *Field Day Anthology of Irish Writing* were also published, under the general editorship of Seamus Deane. A fourth volume, on Irish women's writing, was later added after much controversy. In addition, Field Day published Heaney's *Sweeney Astray* (1983), co-published with Faber his *Cure at Troy* (1990), and published a volume of essays on 1916, *Revising the Rising* (1991), edited by Máirín Ní Dhonnchadha and Theo Dorgan.

The definition of Field Day which appeared in the programme for the first production, *Translations*, whether ironic or not, is primarily a military one: 'a day on which troops are drawn up for exercise in field evolution; a military review …', but Friel's own comment is simpler. That is, that Field Day was derived from 'Friel' and 'Rea', 'because it was the only way to get money from the Northern Ireland Arts Council to perform "Translations". They only fund existing establishments so we had to become an establishment' (Carty 1980, p. 16). During its dozen years of somewhat radical existence Field Day, while having a base in Derry, was mainly a cross-border touring company with no permanent theatre, company or artistic director. It received assistance from the two Arts Councils, North and South, as well as a grant from Derry City Council, in contrast to the Irish Theatre Company, a national touring company founded in the South in 1974 but soon (in 1982) to be disgracefully dissolved by the Arts Council in Dublin. Field Day also defined itself in relation to the Lyric Theatre in Belfast and the Abbey in Dublin.

In relating Field Day's statements of aims and policy to the dramatic productions staged one must bear in mind Friel's earlier assertion, 'I do not believe that art is a servant of any movement' (1972, p. 306). That precept did not alter. When Fintan O'Toole asked if the 'whole Field Day project' didn't depend on a united Ireland Friel replied: 'I don't think it should be read in those terms. I think it should lead to a cultural state, not a political state. And I think out of that cultural state, a possibility of a political state follows. That is always the sequence' (1982, p. 23). It was because Friel felt he was being 'categorised' as a political playwright with *Translations* that he wrote its dramatic critique, *Communication Cord* (1982), in which the 'pieties' of Irish culture are sharply satirised. He needed to stay free within an enterprise which was occupied with re-defining Irish freedom. Moreover, distinctions have to be made between the aims of Field Day *as a whole* and the aims of the Field Day *Theatre Company*. The pamphlets did not begin to appear until 1983, after which their content tended to complicate the cultural politics of Field Day. In its extra-theatrical guise Field Day had, indeed, a political aim, which was to contribute to the solution of the Northern political crisis 'by producing analyses of the established opinions, myths and stereotypes which had become both a symptom and a cause of the current situation' (*Ireland's Field Day*, 1985, p. vii). In a later collection of pamphlets Seamus Deane defined the Northern crisis as 'a colonial crisis' (1990, p. 6). The theatre company, however, was concerned with the creation, distribution and reception of plays. Stephen Rea not only acted in most of these but also directed from time to time and was a major force in maintaining artistic standards (Hadfield 1993). For Rea the purpose of the touring company was to disseminate ideas and give hope of change by helping people to 'choose the history that is enabling to you rather than one that holds you back' (Worth 1993, p. 76). That notion may be qualified by Friel's earlier assertion, 'we don't go to art for meaning. We go to it for perceptions of new adjustments and new arrangements' (1980, p. 43). In a word, 'transformation' is what Field Day as a theatre company laboured to produce (cf. Burke 1991).

In a programme note for *Three Sisters* in 1981 Seamus Deane asserted that Field Day was in search of an audience and would avoid both the example of the Lyric in Belfast and the example of community drama, which comprised 'the plebification of drama' and 'spurious "relevance".' Deane went on to both align the Field

Day theatre with and distance it from the Abbey. 'It is like the Abbey in its origin in that it has within it the idea of a culture which has not yet come to be in political terms. It is unlike the Abbey in that it can no longer subscribe to a simple nationalism as the basis for its existence.' What Field Day subscribed to instead was what was elsewhere termed 'the fifth province' and the idea of a theatre which might imaginatively make it perceptible. None of these ideas was ever properly worked out as part of a programme for theatre production.

Friel considered that Field Day was trying to create 'a fifth province to which artistic and cultural loyalty can be offered' (O'Toole 1982, p. 21). Ireland has but four provinces. The old Irish word for 'province', however, meant 'a fifth', giving rise to a debate about the possible location of a lost province. Its symbolic agency was invoked in the first issue of *Crane Bag,* and the restoration of 'this second centre of gravity' to contemporary Ireland demanded (Hederman and Kearney 1977, p. 4). The notion resembles what Seamus Heaney calls the 'omphalos' or 'a country of the mind' (1980, pp. 17, 132). It implies a space made and an allegiance won: an expansion of the 'narrow ground' inhabited by Catholics and Protestants in Northern Ireland and its transformation into what Thomas Kilroy called 'a platform for the life of the mind, of whatever persuasion, at a time when mindlessness threatens to engulf us all' (1986, p. 7).

In any examination of the twelve plays staged by Field Day up to 1991 two broad areas or themes, covering the ideas and issues just summarised, come prominently into discussion: language/identity and history/mythology/vision. Each of these areas will briefly be explored.

Language and identity

The impact of Friel's *Translations* in production, during the first tour from Derry all around Ireland, was momentous (Zach 1988, pp. 74-5). In Dublin extra performances had to be put on to cope with the numbers unable to obtain admission. The atmosphere at the Gate Theatre was quite extraordinary. People applauded frequently and with vigour, as if the play stirred something special in their hearts. Strangely enough, the play is old-fashioned melodrama up to a point, as its three-act structure and a landscape reminiscent of Boucicault's Irish plays testify. There is also the simple mode of the love relationship that grows between the English soldier Yolland and the Irish girl Máire, which is on the level of the Indian girl (Pocohontas) and the enemy soldier (Smith) in early nineteenth-century melodrama, and the use of a mute girl, Sarah, devoted to the rival of the soldier, Manus, who tries to teach her to speak. Sarah's tears evoke those of the audience when she observes how Máire falls for Yolland, thereby betraying Manus, and goes dumb again under interrogation. From Holcroft's *A Tale of Mystery* (1802) on, a dumb innocent was part of the formula of melodrama, what has been termed the 'theme of picturesque affliction' (Davies 1975, p. 207). Given all this, 'a recipe for some kind of instant death' in the modern theatre, Friel understandably said that the success of *Translations* astonished him (*Irish Times*, 15 January 1981).

The significant thing is how Friel modified the melodrama and used it as frame for his multivalent tale. As all great plays have roots in the simplest and most popular of forms, *Translations* has the courage of its own basic naivety. The firm structure can thereafter support any number of ideas. Because the love story is allowed to seep into the larger texture of a community suddenly split apart by the might of an angered soldiery (after Yolland is presumed murdered) the pathos in the situation is not evoked in the service of plot but of ideas. These are mainly cultural and anthropological. Friel, very much like Heaney, is exploring the significance of place to sensibility and also the nature of change, the action of growth, its effect on experience measured primarily by language. The device of having two languages on stage although only one (English) is spoken brilliantly exposes two areas of experience, two cultures, but as Hugh the hedge-school master puts it in the end, learning a common language will not help 'to interpret between privacies' (Friel 1984, p. 446). Old Hugh, O'Caseyan Paycock though he in part is, seems to be the guide to what Friel is saying. That is, to use Hugh's own style, (a) native culture is a fine and noble thing but one must also welcome what is new, otherwise 'a civilization can be imprisoned in a linguistic contour which no longer matches the landscape of ... fact' (p. 419). One must be prepared to change and to grow, as replacing Irish with English placenames implies. And (b) culture does not necessarily lead to an ennoblement of the individual or to national greatness. Hugh is quite willing to take up the position of National schoolmaster, although the position would mean teaching through English and the abandonment of Irish; his failure to get the job is received as a lost opportunity. Hugh tends to despise Daniel O'Connell, whose attitude towards the people's learning English was positive and influential, but speaks of no alternative. Culture and politics have no interrelationship. (Compare Hugh's comments on 1798.) Perhaps this point is also suggested by Manus's foolish departure from Ballybeg, leaving the mysterious Donnelly twins to fill the vacuum left by the abdication and (in Hugh's case) the collapse of learning.

As the historian J. J. Lee has remarked, 'but for the loss of the [Irish] language, there would be little discussion about identity in the Republic' (1989, p. 662). Friel hit upon a central nerve in the contemporary body politic. He wrote a play in which language is both the subject and the medium and which therefore reflects back upon itself in interrogation of national identity. Unlike Pinter's *Mountain Language* (1988), which invites comparison, *Translations* does not present on stage a facile reflex between totalitarianism and the denial of a peasant language. Pinter's is melodrama of a far cruder kind. Friel, while not denying the imperialist content of the educational and mapping projects of the 1830s, does not fall into the artistic trap of opposing villains and heroes (for where would such a strategy leave the ambidexterous Owen?). *Translations* ends with a trio on stage. There is the Greek 'student', Jimmy Jack, fantasising over marrying Athene (for companionship!) and yet aware as Yolland was not of the dangers of 'exogamy' (Friel 1984, p. 446). There is Máire, her mind broadened by Yolland to admit placenames and a rough map of his native Norfolk, seriously disturbed by the foreigner's disappearance (she never mentions Manus's). And there is Hugh, sitting on the stairs of a ruined and obsolete schoolhouse, quoting with hesitancy from Virgil's *Aeneid* about the fated fall of Carthage. This depleted community signals loss and decline at some future curve of history intersecting with our present. Hugh's final act of translation has been seen as ironic (McGrath 1990, p. 247) and as underlining uncertainty (Pilkington 1990, p. 291). But it is its seeming irrelevance which strikes home with pathos. Hugh is translating for an 'audience' on stage who do not need it and for whom it encodes only doom. All that they are and have been will be swept away. A contemporary audience, aware that they have already lost contact with Hugh's Irish language, can only be struck with recognition of an embodied source of contemporary fracture, division and alienation.

Playing the North

Field Day followed *Translations* with a 'translation' of Chekhov's *Three Sisters*, but Friel actually worked on both texts at the same time (Agnew 1980, p. 59). A key source of inspiration for both was George Steiner's *After Babel: Aspects of Language and Translation* (1975). The gap Friel felt between the available English translations of *Three Sisters* and the language/syntax of modern Irish-English impelled him not only to search for a version more true to the English spoken in Ireland but to reflect on the relation of translation to human communication. On the first point he came to the conclusion that 'apart from Synge, all our dramatists have pitched their voice for English acceptance and recognition' (Agnew 1980, p. 60). It was time once again to consolidate a more authentic speech on the Irish stage. *Three Sisters* is an exercise in this direction. (In later years versions of Turgenev's *Fathers and Sons*, 1987, and *A Month in the Country*, 1992, provided other exercises.) It is less a matter of vocabulary than of rhythm. Placing Chekhov in this Irish context, while less radical than Thomas Kilroy's transfer of *The Seagull* to an Irish setting for the Irish Theatre Company's production earlier in 1981, invited audiences to consider further the link between language and identity. On the limits of translation, Steiner had commented, 'inside or between languages, human communication equals translation' (1975, p. 47). This was already familiar Friel territory, the sense that 'an essential part of all natural language is private' and untranslatable (Steiner 1975, p. 198). Working on Chekhov, an author with whom Friel had always shown affinity, reinforced for Friel the division which exists between public and private discourse. *Three Sisters*, then, lay down a marker for the style of Field Day translations, which was mainly to affect those poets who tried their hands at versions of the classics, Paulin, Mahon and Heaney.

The Communication Cord, a farce set in modern-day Donegal, was called an 'antidote' to *Translations* in the Field Day programme. This is a term Friel accepted (O'Toole 1982, p. 21). It implies something poisonous in *Translations*, or at any rate in the nature of the public response to that play. The sequel is a send-up of misplaced worship of Ireland's past. It is also a rather acerbic satire of the whole relationship of language to national identity. Friel was determined to demolish a sentimental rhetoric rendering sacred all that belonged to tradition. *Communication Cord* also poked fun at Field Day itself: where Deane had lauded Field Day as 'the idea of a theatre without a roof over its head' in his programme note for *Three Sisters*, Friel's farce ends with the roof falling in on the linguistics expert Tim Gallagher, made up and played by Stephen Rea to resemble Seamus Deane: Field Day was not a humourless enterprise. At the same time, Friel's farce brought his own work to a sudden and unexplained halt. He did not write another play for six years, when *Making History* might well be read as a play about a leader surrounded by ideologues inhibiting the full expression of his personality. After 1983, the Field Day pamphlets sidelined Friel.

Tom Paulin's pamphlet *A New Look at the Language Question* (1983) consolidated some of the ideas on language and identity so far raised in production. Deane's two pamphlets, *Civilians and Barbarians* (1983) and *Heroic Styles: The Tradition of an Idea* (1984), called for a deconstruction of the language which imprisoned attitudes in Northern Ireland and called also forth a dissolution of the mystique of 'Irishness'. In a sense Deane was here clearing the ground for the eventual production of the *Field Day Anthology*. Paulin's breezy advocacy of dialect in his pamphlet, as a neglected but rich resource in Irish speech, paved the way for its use in his own and Mahon's versions of two classical texts staged together in 1984. Paulin thus radicalised the emphasis Friel had laid on the need for an authentic language.

As a commentary on the contemporary political situation in Northern Ireland *The Riot Act* was only partially successful, although the relevance of *Antigone* to Northern Ireland was peculiarly apt. As Richard Kearney (1988, p. 232) has said, the British 'have repeatedly assumed the role of the magistrate Creon before the Republican Antigone.' In Paulin's version the setting is decked with Masonic symbols, which identify the power structure with Presbyterianism; Antigone's insistence on burial rites for her brother smacks of Catholic preoccupations. Characters and Chorus unmistakably locate the play in Belfast. The language Paulin uses is steeped in Northern speech, with copious use of dialect words. But all style is lowered to such a common level that the tragedy dwindles into provincial simplicities. Paulin merely reinforces political stereotypes.

Derek Mahon's *High Time* is equally problematic. Freely adapted from Molière's harmless comedy about paternalist discipline and the danger of running too strict a 'school' in the home, it was first conceived as a political comment on the student revolts of 1968. Dissuaded from this idea Mahon created a modernised, spectacular but non-political entertainment, a 'pure romp', according to the *Irish Times* (20 September). With this description Mahon was content (1985, p. 7). Why Field Day should spend their time on 'romp' nobody seems to have enquired. In any case, Mahon does not use dialect to the degree that Paulin does, but rather follows Friel's example of a supple, natural style of speech using Irish rhythms and only occasional phrases with an Irish flavour.

In another version of a classical text, Heaney's *The Cure at Troy*, the Field Day production in 1990, the impetus of Friel's *Translations* is once again registered. In a review of Friel's play for the *TLS* (24 October 1980) Heaney had related this struggle with a fractured language to Friel's critique of 'the need we have to create enabling myths of ourselves'. The play Heaney now chose to 'translate' for Field Day was itself a myth of the artist, as Edmund Wilson had shown in an essay on *Philoctetes* in *The Wound and the Bow* (1961). This myth asserts that society may not have the necessary powers of the artist without enduring his/her disagreeable personality: one may not have the benefit of the magic bow without having to put up with the stench of its owner's wound. For Heaney, who had in *Sweeney Astray* (1983) already viewed Ireland from the point of view of the mythic mad Sweeney in another 'version' (of the Middle Irish romance *Buile Suibhne*), Philoctetes was another alienated artist, 'displaced, guilty, assuaging himself by his utterance' (Heaney 1983, p. viii). In *The Cure at Troy* that utterance is a prolonged cry of pain and outrage which finds its register in a language often recognisably Northern. The use of dialect words such as 'hagged', 'clouts' and 'throughother' make possible, if not entirely defensible, the sudden evocation by the Chorus of hunger strikers and terrorist activities in Northern Ireland of the 1980s: 'The innocent in gaols/Beat on their bars together', etc. (Heaney 1990, p. 77). The question of language and the actuality of politics were found to be inseparable (Meir 1991). Field Day had by this time been ten years on the road, during which the war in the North had stretched on, Troy-like and seemingly without cure. Like all of the playwrights sponsored by Field Day Heaney's ambition was not to suggest a cure for the Northern conflict: 'I'm not a political writer and I don't see literature as a way of solving political problems' (Battersby 1990). But there was no way language could remain uncontaminated.

History, myth and vision

As is well known, Friel insisted that *Translations* 'has to do with language and only language' (1985, p. 58). Of course, no play is about *only* language, and *Translations* is a history play. Some critics, such as Edna Longley, would argue that it is bad history. Longley is supported in this view by a few historians, notably J. H. Andrews, whose *A Paper Landscape* (1975) was a major source for Friel's play. Yet the uses of history on stage have more to do with images and symbols than with documentary facts. Whereas it must be of interest to have Andrews's 'Notes for a Future Edition of Brian Friel's *Translations*' (1992–93), his 'corrections' do not have much significance. Friel's own view on the matter was given in his programme note to *Making History* (1988): 'history and fiction are related and comparable forms of discourse and ... an historical text is a kind of literary artifact.' He was pleased to have 'kept faith with the narrative'. This defines the ethic as well as the aesthetic of the history play.

However, a more benign understanding of myth/history must be established. Richard Kearney offers a way forward in his Field Day pamphlet *Myth and Motherland*. Following Eliade, Kearney defends myth from the charge of escapism or easy pastoralism: myth narrates a sacred history which is exemplary and imitable (1984, p. 6). Two forms of time emerge, the sacred and the secular. A polarisation is discerned between mythic and anti-mythic discourse: 'Myth is a two way street' (p. 23). It could be said that *Translations* gains its power from its fluent direction of the traffic along this two-way street. Nothing is resolved in the play: the forces of possible change and of decay are balanced to authorise the very debate which has arisen. In *Making History* Friel plays with the conflict between 'mythologising' and 'demythologising' forms as Kearney describes them (p. 13) by establishing a debate over the process by which history re-creates and distorts. Historiography is ironically dramatised. A play about the failure of Hugh O'Neill and the collapse of the old Gaelic order is simultaneously an interrogation of myth as incarceration. The link with *Translations* is obvious: the two-way street is extended back in time from 1833 to 1603.

Yet for Field Day in general, myth as grand narrative was not fruitful dramatic terrain. Neither Paulin's version of *Antigone* nor Heaney's version of *Philoctetes* is more than a curiosity. In each case the traffic between myth and contemporary Northern Ireland is only one-way. At the same time, Heaney's desire in *The Cure at Troy* to make 'hope and history rhyme' (1990, p. 77) defines succinctly Field Day's motive so far as its theatrical productions were concerned. The 'golden' world of suffering transcended (art) was to replace in the minds of audiences the 'brazen' world of dissension (fact). In that way the despair created by the impasse in the North might be lifted. For if poetry makes nothing happen the same is not true of drama. Kearney calls this kind of motive *re*-mythologising: 'If we need to demythologize, we need also to remythologize' (1984, p. 23). This process is what one finds in the best plays which followed *Translations*, namely *Double Cross* and *Pentecost*.

Double Cross explores the ambiguities of loyalty and treason by putting back-to-back the careers of Brendan Bracken, Churchill's Minister of Information, and William Joyce, 'Lord Haw-Haw'. As it is set in the early 1940s *Double Cross* is a history play. But as Kilroy is a playwright for whom theatricality is a primary value (compare *Talbot's Box*, 1977), the play is also preoccupied with 'doubleness' and 'doubling', the very basis of performance itself (Kilroy 1986, p. 6). That fertile text Antonin Artaud's *Le Théâtre et son double* (1938), translated as *The Theater and its Double* (1958), is thus acknowledged. Bracken and Joyce were played by the same actor, Stephen Rea, in the Field Day production: the performances thus ironically intersected as 'traitor' and 'trickster' (Kilroy 1986, p. 19). Opposites, these two are also mirror images. Towards the end of Part 1 Bracken disrobes on stage and becomes Joyce addressing a Fascist audience in 1933. His subject is 'the serpent of history' (p. 48) and as it ends the real audience conventionally applauds for the end of Part 1, even though the speech addressed to them is virulently anti-Semitic. Thus Kilroy implicates the audience in the action.

Under the guise of a history play enacting the conflict between England and Germany *Double Cross* is essentially a play about Ireland's relations with England. In his Field Day pamphlet Declan Kiberd had paved the way for Kilroy's dramatisation of this issue. Having explored plays by Wilde, Shaw and Behan, Kiberd commented: 'In all of the plays discussed, opposites turn out to be doubles; cliches employed at the start by one side are appropriated by the other; and each time an Irishman meets an Englishman, he simply encounters an alternative version of himself. The Irish Question is really the English Question, and *vice-versa*' (1984, p. 15).

Kilroy thus addresses an historical/traditional idea. Both Bracken and Joyce are Irish and the identity of each is defined through denial of his history. Bracken's Fenian roots break through conspicuously when he is terror-stricken during the London blitz: his breakdown admits a language, an accent and a family history which he had persistently suppressed and creates one of the best scenes in the play. Joyce, on the other hand, dates his Fascism from childhood identification with the murderous Black and Tans in Galway. His determination to 'serve' an idea of English order led to his support of Hitler's war on England, a perversity to match Bracken's perversions. Joyce's complex psychology, in particular his passionate sexual jealousy, gives much scope for gripping theatre in Part 2 of *Double Cross* and we see also how it is his obsession with language which, as with Bracken, both defines and undermines him. Joyce's self-destruction shows how the 'serpent of history' can indeed bite off its own head in pursuit of an unattainable ideal. The application to internecine strife in Northern Ireland may be inferred. It is a colonial issue: an investigation of the meaning(s) of loyalty. In Northern Ireland one person's loyalty is another's treason. Doubleness is built into the political system.

Parker's *Pentecost* is less cerebral and more didactic than *Double Cross*, but it too is a form of history play. The background to the play is the Ulster Workers' Council strike in Northern Ireland in May 1974. Following Bloody Sunday the unionist-dominated Parliament at Stormont was prorogued and from the end of March 1972 Northern Ireland was ruled directly from Westminster. In December 1973 a power-sharing Executive Assembly was established by agreement among the various political parties in Northern Ireland and a new dawn was predicted. It was, alas, a false dawn. A wave of opposition to sharing power with (Catholic) nationalists gathered force in the early months of 1974 and crashed down upon the Executive in May. The Ulster Workers' Council organised a general strike in key installations; the new Labour government in Britain refused to move against the strikers. The Executive resigned two weeks into the strike on 28 May and direct rule from London was resumed. It was a key moment in the history of modern Northern Ireland (Lee 1989, pp. 445–8). The intransigence of popular unionism was spectacularly manifested.

Parker gathers together four ordinary characters in the last occupied house in a Belfast terrace. Two are Catholic, the estranged couple Marian and Lenny, and two Protestant, Peter, a college friend home from Birmingham to get a sense of 'Historic days in Lilliput', and Ruth, a battered wife escaping from her husband (Parker 1989, p. 171). *Pentecost* links up with *Double Cross* in a key sequence in Act II when Prime Minister Wilson makes a speech on radio concerning the 'gravest crisis' in the history of Northern Ireland. Wilson attacks the strikers as 'sponging on Westminster and British democracy' (pp. 182-3). Ruth is incensed at the insult but Peter queries: 'Can you not see, this whole tribe, so-called Protestants, we both of us grew up in it, all that endless mindless marching ... straight up a dead-end one-way blind alley, self-destroying, *the head's eating the tail now*, it's a lingering tribal suicide going on out there' (p. 184, emphasis added). The serpent of history has recoiled upon itself as Joyce accused Jewish expansionism of doing in *Double Cross*. In a reverse procedure from Kilroy's, Parker sees unionist fanaticism as fascist. He then goes on to draw a parallel with white supremacy over blacks in the United States, as Peter (representing Parker's point of view) describes an experience he had in America, when white liberals acted as buffers between 'armed blacks behind us and armed cops in front'. The point of the story is in its resolution. Although the confrontation was violent, 'there was playacting involved too', which ended with blacks and whites on a stage together, hugging each other. As Peter drily concludes: 'I don't quite see that happening here' (Parker 1989, p. 185). The emphasis on 'playacting' is crucial. Only thus can the serpent of history become the serpent of myth, like Shaw's wise Serpent who says to Eve: 'You see things; and you say "Why?" But I dream things that never were; and I say "Why not?"' (1963, 2, p. 7).

The action, against the background of the political events off-stage, then takes a deeply spiritual turn. It is Whit Sunday, the Feast of Pentecost, when the Holy Spirit descended in tongues of flame on the frightened disciples gathered like Parker's characters in a room. In his Field Day pamphlet Terence Brown declared: 'What T. S. Eliot in *Four Quartets* termed "the communication Of the dead ... tongued with fire beyond the language of the living" is simply not heard in Ulster. With its messages of social complexity, that communication hints at a richer kind of cultural inclusiveness than the myth of besieged solidarity can possibly allow' (1985b, p. 20). Parker's achievement was to establish that 'cultural inclusiveness' in the theatre between audience and stage.

Not without placing a strain on a contemporary audience Parker allows his four beleaguered characters to read from the Bible about Pentecost. This allows Marian to talk openly for the first time of her dead baby, 'a kind of Christ to me' (Parker 1989, p. 207). Here much depends on the atmosphere already created of frustration trembling on the brink of release. It marks a critical point in production, like that magical moment towards the end of *The Winter's Tale* when the statue of Hermione seems to come to life. Marian's confession of her pain and anger at the loss of her child banishes hostility between self and world, 'us' and 'them', wife and husband, mother and the innocent dead. At last, pity like a new-born babe is striding the Northern blast. 'We have got to love that in ourselves. In ourselves first and then in them. That's the only future there is' (Parker 1989, p. 207). Elsewhere Parker said that the challenge for the Northern playwright was 'to find a belief in the future and to express it with due defiance' so as 'to assert the primacy of the play-impulse over the deathwish' (1986, p. 20).

Pentecost is thus a play about reconciliation; like all of Parker's work it is in the optative mood. It calls for change in the form of miracle. The scenario might well seem merely fanciful were it not strangely replicated in the work of a serious political scientist, who concludes his study of northern Ireland with the argument that 'faith' in the 'miracle' of the Resurrection provides the only hope of reconciliation: 'The miracle of the Resurrection makes visible to us, who live in the world of "effectiveness", that which is "not effective". But then the blindness of our worship of effectiveness plays its last trick. Christ risen from the dead becomes a subject of "debate" about whether he was mega-effective, a spiritual superpower or a fraud (according to ideological disposition). The "debate" destroys the miracle and allows us to forget that we are tempted to worship the "effective". So long as we are trapped in this worship we shall not see Christ's disciples, whether they be Christian or non-Christian' (Wright 1987, p. 290). Parker's analysis is astonishingly similar.

Thomas Kilroy's *The Madame MacAdam Travelling Theatre* (1991), which was the last full Field Day production at this time, calls for a miracle also, but in a more sophisticated way. Kilroy's play was not successful and drew some venomous reviews in Dublin, but it contains within it much that was most imaginative and theatrical about Field Day's work. As always Kilroy is in search of a model for a regenerated society, and he here locates it somewhere between the

[**220**]

players (barely holding together as English people stranded in Ireland during World War Two) and a society where a stolen child and a disguised greyhound provide signs of unfulfilled longing. This history play is less a looking back in nostalgia to the innocent days of the 1940s than a critique of those times when a pastoral ideology disguised repression. In his refashioning of history Kilroy clears a space for a new community. The theatre itself is raised here into revolutionary status. As Rabe says of Madame MacAdam: 'She made it sound as if theatre could heal everything, make it whole again' (Kilroy 1991, p. 18). Kilroy wants a redemption rather than a mirroring of history.

When audiences and critics expressed lack of interest in such ideas, Field Day began to call it a day. Morale was severely dented by the poor reception of *Madame MacAdam* and also by Friel's giving *Dancing at Lughnasa* to the Abbey. Kilroy resigned from the board in October 1992, Friel in January 1994. Although a separate company was producing the *Anthology*, the work-load involved and the controversy when the three volumes were published in November 1991 were borne by the same board members as oversaw the theatre company. The controversy was only in part related to the perceived nationalistic emphasis on the *Anthology* and was mainly centred on the neglected representation of women writers: 'It was as if the all-male editorial board had simply forgotten their existence. ... Because of the general condemnation from women, and many men, a fourth volume is in preparation entirely devoted to the work of Irish-women' (Hussey 1993, p. 486). This public outcry exacerbated the crisis within the Field Day Theatre Company, which had more personal origins. Stephen Rea's film career demanded more time; Seamus Deane accepted a professorship in the USA; Friel and Kilroy wished to find fuller expression for their writing elsewhere. Although it did not dissolve, and recommenced production with a version of *Uncle Vanya* in 1995, a significant phase in Field Day's history had come to an end.

To sum up on Field Day, it may be said first that the aim of establishing a theatre company with deep roots in Derry was never fully realised (Woodworth 1993). A permanent theatre was always lacking, without which any rivalry with the Lyric or the Abbey was simply unrealistic. Moreover, Field Day as travelling 'fit-up' goes against the founding of a theatre of ideas, for which a place, an artistic director, a unified style of production and a regular audience are essential components. But Field Day generated excitement and hope in Ireland at a time of political and indeed theatrical uncertainty. Of the twelve plays staged by 1991 at least three, *Translations*, *Double Cross* and *Pentecost*, stand out among the best Irish plays of the past twenty-five years, while several of the other productions are crucial to any study of modern Irish drama. All Field Day plays insist that the problem of identity is best understood theatrically, involving audiences in the process of redefinition. According to Seamus Heaney, the best work to come out of the North has been 'writing that is a mode of integration, of redistributing the whole field of cultural and political force into a tolerable order' (1995, p. 189). At its best, Field Day achieved this kind of integration. Thus Field Day made cultural nationalism a live issue once again in Ireland, North and South, and turned the 'narrow ground' of factionalism into an imaginative playground.

9

'A National Dream-life':
the contemporary drama

We respond to a drama to that extent to which it corresponds to our
dream life.   David Mamet, *Writing in Restaurants* (1988)

Introduction

Fittingly enough in some ways, the State of Emergency declared in
1939 was not declared officially over until 1995. All through the
1980s the country was beset by changes of government, ever-rising
unemployment, a new wave of emigration and a strong sense of
entropy. The bright lights of Europe seemed at times to be no more
than will o' the wisps, and yet focused national needs and hope in an
ambiguous, tantalising way. Where twenty years earlier the poet
Thomas Kinsella could refer to Dublin as 'this untiring, crumbling
place of growth' (1973, p. 61), now both the crumbling and the
growth appeared even more oxymoronic. Things continued to
change but change itself now seemed haphazard, aleatory, entirely
unpredictable. In the North the violence continued relentlessly, and
yet the All-Ireland Forum (1984) followed by the Hillsborough
Agreement (1985) seemed to promise a solution which faded with
the decade itself. The moral life in the South appeared equally
contradictory. On the one hand referenda over abortion (1983) and
divorce (1986) resulted in conservative victories. On the other hand
scandals hit the headlines which proved that the established
Catholic mores were no defence against cruelty and victimisation
(Ardagh 1994; Keogh 1994). The spirit of the age was unsettlingly
ambiguous. It became common to hear quoted the line from Friel's
Translations, 'confusion is not an ignoble condition' (1984, p. 446).
The intermittent Taoiseach Charles J. Haughey used the phrase
'grotesque, unbelievable, bizarre and unprecedented' to describe a

murder case which strangely touched on but did not implicate the Attorney General in 1982 and the phrase was seized on with delight, turned into an acronym by Conor Cruise O'Brien and as GUBU given currency to express political confusion throughout the 1980s and into the following decade. Metaphysical 'crumbling' began to seem more meaningful than economic 'growth'. Paradoxically, this climate was more hospitable to the creation of good drama (in the theatre) than had been the climate of stagnation in the age of de Valera. In the land of GUBU the Irish imagination is very much at home. Freud is reported to have said that the Irish are the only race that cannot be psychoanalysed since they are too ready to invent dreams or to invent lies more interesting than the truth (Hussey 1993, p. 470). One may be sure Shaw felt exactly the same, as he defined the Irish imagination in *John Bull's Other Island* (1904): 'Oh, the dreaming! the dreaming! the torturing, heart-scalding, never satisfying dreaming, dreaming, dreaming, dreaming! ... An Irishman's imagination never lets him [*sic*] alone, never convinces him, never satisfies him; but it makes him that he cant face reality nor deal with it nor handle it nor conquer it: he can only sneer at them that do, and ... "be agreeable to strangers," like a good-for-nothing woman on the streets' (1963, 2, p. 517).

Irish drama oscillates always between tradition and innovation. It never occupies either pole for long, but invariably registers the tension. Irish drama is a long, energetic dispute with a changing audience over the same basic issues: where we come from, where we are now, and where we are headed. Alternatively, these questions comprise history, identity, home or a sense of place, and visionary imagination or what Shaw above called dreaming, or myth-making. The questions renew themselves urgently yet creatively. All such questions emanate from a passion for language, a determination by Irish writers to find the words which will act like a spell, tap roots, release the hidden, real world within and establish a new realm. Thus it is that in their mature work Friel, Murphy and Leonard all converge on a set of questions on origin and destination which keep faith with what Yeats demanded of Irish playwrights at the beginning of the century: 'A play to be suitable for performance at the Abbey should contain some criticism of life, founded on the experience or personal observation of the writer, or some vision of life, of Irish life by preference, important from its beauty or from some excellence of style' (Gregory 1972, p. 62). These three playwrights, together with Keane and Kilroy, now occupy a classic status; their work is on a par with that of Yeats, Synge and O'Casey. It is a body of work which maps out and defines the uncertain moral climate of modern Ireland. The first part of this chapter attempts to assess their contribution from this perspective.

In turn, these writers are being succeeded by playwrights whose status is as yet uncertain. A long list could be made, ranging alphabetically from Sebastian Barry to Michael West (see Bort 1996, pp. 9–23). Since it is not practicable to examine their work in any comprehensive way here I shall focus on two categories, those who are arguably avant-garde and those more obviously traditional. As will be seen, the distinction is but provisional and is employed only to emphasise the oscillation mentioned above.

Murphy, Friel, Leonard

The unease and powerful resistance shown to the new Ireland of the 1960s by Murphy, Friel, Kilroy and others gave way in the 1980s and after to a less angry and more philosophical response to social change. Murphy's *The Gigli Concert* (1983) best encapsulates the frustrated aspirations of the time. It is significant that the setting is no longer a house or home but an office, a refuge for that lost soul J. P. W. King, a quack scientologist living on the margins of law and psychology. From this point on the home is no longer a credible paradigm of order in Irish drama. The plays of Billy Roche, for example, tend to be set in such refuges as a pool hall or a betting shop or even a belfry (*The Wexford Trilogy*). Such plays, like so many of this period, are concerned with redefinition of self and aims in a society where old structures are disintegrating. Murphy's King is likewise decentred, if not dethroned, living in his shabby office, a man of uncertain identity. Yet he is a man capable of growth in a crumbling world of brute force and material ambition. That world comes bursting through his door in the shape of the Irish Man, a self-made businessman suffering a breakdown and in search of help. He wants to sing like Gigli. Interviewing him King, eyes alight at the prospect of a rich loony, thinks he means 'to sing, like Gigli, inverted commas' (Murphy 1994, p. 175). But the Irish Man means just what he says, old style, 'No inverted commas.' His mad ambition provides a frightening portrait of a soul in torment. The association here with Eugene O'Neill's tragic vision suggested in the title of

Richard Kearney's essay on *The Gigli Concert*, 'Tom Murphy's Long Night's Journey into Night', is quite appropriate (1988, pp. 161–71). O'Neill himself said of *The Iceman Cometh* (1946) that there were moments in it 'that suddenly strip the secret soul of a man stark naked, not in cruelty or moral superiority, but with an understanding compassion which sees him as a victim of the ironies of life and of himself. These moments are to me the depth of tragedy, with nothing more that can possibly be said' (Sheaffer 1974, p. 504). Although Murphy has denied influence by O'Neill (Shaughnessy 1988, p. 114) there is a strong affinity between them. It is *The Iceman Cometh* rather than *Long Day's Journey into Night* (1956) which supplies the basis for this view. The yearning for purity in a context of squalor and failure lends to Murphy's work an intensity defining his attitude towards Ireland as akin to that of O'Neill's towards the American dream. As a metaphor for Ireland in the 1980s *The Gigli Concert* not only charts the spiritual impasse reached but also, by sidestepping orthodox religious teaching, establishes a new mode of relating to experience: through a combination of compassion and an ethic derived from music. It was King's triumph over tragic circumstance which had Irish audiences on their feet in a standing ovation when *The Gigli Concert* had its première at the Abbey. The irrationality of the triumph was no matter, may even have been the source of the empathy felt. In this Faust/Houdini figure is an image of transcendence, of an alternative to the new Irish culture of success. A national dream is challenged.

Conversations on a Homecoming and *Bailegangaire* (1985) traverse similar terrain. In both plays contemporary Ireland is contrasted with vanished ideals. In the former the pub as talk-shop, symbol of so much that is at once spontaneous and confessional in Irish culture, is presented as microcosm, with disillusion as the main theme. Many a play of the 1980s and 1990s followed Murphy's model here, for example Declan Hughes's *Playing with Fire* (1991). In *Bailegangaire*, which was to be the swan-song of the great Siobhán McKenna, it is easy to see Mommo as Ireland herself caught in a time warp and perpetually rehearsing her misfortunes while the new world of modern technology whizzes by outside. There is a conflict between morality, Mommo's responsibility for what happened during and as a result of the famous laughing contest, and modernity, the off-stage industrial dispute at the Japanese factory. 'I'll come to grips with my life': Dolly's motive underlies the whole action of *Bailegangaire* (Murphy 1993, p. 152). It is a story of the possibility of characters, old and young alike, being able to come to terms with the chaos of experience. Mommo, with Mary's help, finishes her tale at last and its sorrow acts as if in her own private theatre: Mary as audience is drawn in and acknowledged, tears flow, and a current of feeling unites three isolated women into a family 'of strangers' given 'another chance' (p. 170). The real audience is brought to share this sense of communion. The last word in the play is 'home', marking a destination along a moral journey rather than a ready-made institution. The strength of Murphy's drama lies in the persuasion that this destination is available (cf. Richards 1989).

Friel's *Dancing at Lughnasa* (1990) reverses Murphy's telescope and inspects the dysfunctional family from a distance. In looking back to the 1930s and interrogating at source the breakup of the traditional order in Irish society, Friel is at his subtle, terrifying best. Everything flickers into intense life for a moment and then is gone, like the music on the unreliable radio. The most obvious example is the dance of the five sisters, so wonderful in its abandon and expression of defiance at the unfairness in their lives, which is cut short when *'the music stops abruptly in mid-phrase'* (Friel 1990, p. 22). But awareness of artificiality is built into the performance here. In the extended stage directions (pp. 21–2) Friel uses such words as 'caricatured', 'grotesque' and 'parodic'. The dance is not, cannot be allowed to be, simply natural. Its meaning is filtered through the mind of Michael, who knows how much conflict there is between the image of the dance as joyous and the actuality of the sisters' doomed lives. It is in that gap that the poignancy of the play lies, and it is in his adept use of the narrator/actor that Friel allows the audience to feel it keenly as a kind of tragic knowledge. From the vantage point of 1990 the pastoral life of the 1930s may appear idyllic and its passing a reason to grieve; on closer inspection and against the background of ritual and rival theologies this pastoral life contains within itself frustration, repression and the signs of a terrible fall. The balance between the two responses, nostalgia and tragic awareness, is all. The final tableau in the play is significantly seen *'almost, but not quite, in a haze'* (p. 70). Our whole experience of the play is in some respects a dream: almost, but not quite. For it is a dream of wholeness, of integrity, and only in the artistic consciousness can Ireland now be imagined as anything other than fragmented, fragmenting and in disarray.

Wonderful Tennessee (1993) is a lesser play not because there is less in it that is visionary but because there is too much that floats on the surface artistically unabsorbed. But it is a fine play in the sense that it is a significant meditation on the Irish dream at the end of the twentieth century. It harks back to and as it were revises *The Gentle Island* (1971), that ironic allegory which exposes the violence born of fear which underlies the stereotyped, utopian image of Ireland (Lanters 1996). *Wonderful Tennessee* depicts through its six 'lost' characters a diagnosis of the spiritual illness of contemporary Ireland. The deserted pier they arrive at looks onto *Oileán Draíochta*, the destination they fail even to see clearly, much less visit. Its location in the auditorium (as Frank, who claims to have bought the island, indicates) implicates the audience in the quest. It is a quest for identity via history: medieval Ireland is superimposed on de Valera's Ireland of 1932 and the Eucharistic Congress, perceived now as a travesty of religious culture. The history of the 'magic island' incorporates a murder which debases sacred ritual just as surely as the residual *lughnasa* rituals offer a critique of contemporary religion in Friel's preceding play. None of this is exactly Broadway material, and it is surprising that it was ever thought to be. (It was withdrawn after nine performances.) But *Wonderful Tennessee* is no less a play for that. It marks a significant expression of a rapidly secularising society still hungering for 'what is beyond language. The inexpressible. The ineffable' (Friel 1993, p. 52). *Molly Sweeney* (1994), while a beautiful dramatisation of the theme of blindness last explored in Synge's *The Well of the Saints* (1905), is less ambitious, although it has paradoxically been far more successful internationally than *Wonderful Tennessee*. *Molly Sweeney* can be understood as a variation on a theme in *Faith Healer* (1979), even though its immediate source is a case history recorded by Oliver Sacks, 'To See and Not See' (1995). It is to a significant degree a dream play, a play within a play, in which Molly's inner life recedes from us and establishes its own brittle autonomy. This is Frielian tragic discourse at its most lyrical. Yet *Wonderful Tennessee* throws down a greater challenge to Irish audiences on the urgency of finding the means to live with some sort of rootedness among the ruins of a collapsed tradition.

Hugh Leonard, the last of the 'old guard' of Irish playwrights to be considered here, obstinately insisted in the 1980s that drama has no

The contemporary drama

priority higher than entertainment. In a diary written around the staging of *The Mask of Moriarty* (1985), his seventeenth play for the Dublin Theatre Festival, Leonard defensively claimed he was in his work 'saying something, if with a small "s", and it is this. If you care to come in out of the rain for a couple of hours, I shall attempt to entertain you and send you out again feeling as if you have had a good meal' (1987, p. 16). Leonard deliberately embraced the 'culinary' form of theatre which fifty years earlier Brecht had warred upon (Willett 1964, pp. 40, 89). It is a defensible notion. In the theatre, as in God's house, there are many mansions. Nevertheless, there has historically been a positive discrimination in favour of drama which 'says something' rather than gives one a sense of having had a good meal. Underlying Leonard's insistence on self-reflexive fun, in *Time Was* (1976) and in *The Mask of Moriarty*, is a form of dissent. He is taking a political position while claiming the opposite. *The Mask of Moriarty* is a farce about Sherlock Holmes and his old antagonist Moriarty, imagined to have undergone a facelift so that he looks identical to Holmes. The thing runs about as one would expect, amusingly, and then it stops. In the mode of travesty of Conan Doyle or pastiche of the detective form it lacks the necessary cerebral power which by contrast raises Stoppard's *The Real Inspector Hound* (1968) into a philosophical critique of truth and reality.

Returning to theatre in 1992 after a gap of several years Leonard was less insistent on his right to omit social comment from his plays (something he did not do, of course, in much of his earlier work). But the *Irish Times* described his new play *Moving* at the Abbey as 'dangerously subtle, socially provocative, and most skilfully constructed' (22 April 1992). The *Sunday Tribune* (26 April) went further and said *Moving* 'like Irish culture, is so loaded with comic, emotional and social subtleties that you need a very alert ear and eye to catch all the drift of what is said and to read between the lines of what is not.' Leonard himself had expected that the critics would say, 'here's a lightweight who's trying to get into the heavyweight territory' (O'Byrne 1992). There has to be a lesson in that last comment, where the 'mask of Hugh Leonard' slips a mite. It is clear, at any rate, that Leonard recognised the hierarchy mentioned above, though he speaks here in terms of boxing divisions. It is equally clear, however, if rather surprising to note, that he – the author of the *Au Pair Man* and *Da*, to go no further – should be apprehensive of making the weight at the Abbey. Be that as it may, it is good to note

[229]

Leonard's late victory in *Moving*. The play is, in the manner of a playwright Leonard admires, Denis Johnston, a palimpsest. It concerns a Dublin family's moving house twice over, once in 1957 and again in 1987. Leonard adds a necessary note to the published text: 'Although there is a 30 year gap between the two parts of the play, the characters do not age in the slightest. These are basically the same people and at the same age' (Leonard 1994). Thus the subject matter of Part 1 is rewritten as Part 2. This is 'back to the future' Irish style. It provides a mechanism for revealing changes in fashion, attitude and values. Leonard began it as an Irish version of *Our Town*, and the Wilder emphasis is well absorbed. For what *Moving* communicates is something of what Friel's *Dancing at Lughnasa* also communicates: a sense of foreboding percolating through a loving portrait of an Irish family. The contrast between the 1950s and 1980s is particularly interesting in two areas. One is the way in which the character of the schoolteacher friend of the Noone family, John Turvey (nicknamed 'Topsy'), changes from the uptight, nationalist puritan in Part 1 to a likeable homosexual who has lost his job because he has 'come out' in Part 2. A lesser writer might have waved a banner here; Leonard prefers to show how Ellie Noone, so warm and friendly in Part 1, turns firmly against John in Part 2 because she fears his influence over her teenage son. The other area is in the way each Part ends. In 1957 Tom Noone really loved Ellie's sister, who died of consumption, more than Ellie; having moved into the new home Tom thinks of this sister and we realise he has settled for less than romance. In Part 2 this sister is very much alive and a thorn in Tom's side; Tom and Ellie have a row about her before moving on to the more serious difference between them over John, whom Ellie does not want in the new house any more. Ellie wins her point and, escaping, John turns on the television as he prates about the good times coming: 'The important thing is to follow your star' (Leonard 1994, p. 80). The irony here is very effective. Given a second chance, as it were, people will end up making much the same kind of mistake, and still look to the future to deliver them from evil. Framing the play Leonard has a Removals Man and his Assistant, who form a chorus to the two parts. They also ensure the self-conscious theatricality of the whole play, since the Removals Man is in charge of the setting as well as the story. He thinks the two parts end up the same, which is what he is aiming for, but the point of the play is that they do not. The Ireland of the 1980s is a lot less certain of itself and of its destination, although constantly 'moving' and changing.

The avant-garde

It can be claimed that the modern Irish drama is rooted in the avant-garde. It may be fashionable in some quarters to deride Yeats's politics as conservative, but the fact remains that his founding idea of a theatre was radical and revolutionary. If the concept of tradition is in itself conservative, so be it. This simply means that the Irish drama is radically conservative; so long as the emphasis remains radical the tradition will renew itself in the avant-garde. It will not do this automatically, however, and so each generation must begin anew to reinvent and restore the savagery of the 'savage god' Dionysus. Christopher Innes has argued in *Modern British Drama* (1993, p. 3) that the avant-garde has two main features: (1) exploration of dream states or the instinctive and subconscious levels of the psyche; (2) a quasi-religious focus on myth and magic involving ritualistic patterns of performance. These are certainly two main features of the Irish drama from Yeats and Synge on. It is obvious, however, that for a long time after Yeats's death the avant-garde impulse was suppressed, and writers such as George Fitzmaurice, Austin Clarke and Donagh McDonagh (not to mention Jack B. Yeats) were shunted to the margins of the Peacock, while it lasted, and to the Lyric in Belfast thereafter. But 'in every era the attempt must be made anew to wrest tradition away from a conformism that is about to overpower it' (Benjamin 1992, p. 247). The poetic impulse was all but quenched until it blazed up again in the work of Friel, Murphy and their generation. As the need for such incendiarism was less acute in the 1980s the contribution of the poets and experimentalists was less emphatic. Minimalist though it may be it is nevertheless vital. Of all those who might be included in this category, from Frank McGuinness in prose to Brendan Kennelly in verse, none is more significant than Tom MacIntyre (b. 1933).

In the 1980s MacIntyre was no newcomer to the Irish literary scene. He had been around as poet and man of letters from the mid-1960s and had a political play at the Peacock in 1972, *Eye-Winker Tom Tinker*. In the later 1970s four experimental pieces were presented in Dublin; the *Irish Times* was bemused. There was nothing specifically Irish about this early work, which was influenced by modern dance and film. But with the collaborative creation of *The Great Hunger* in 1983, based on Patrick Kavanagh's poem, MacIntyre began at the Peacock a series of explorations of the hidden Ireland. These plays, or events, used as starting points Irish stories, folklore and myth to provide on stage by means of images, movement and mime new ventures into dream territory.

The Great Hunger, first staged at the Peacock in 1983 but with far greater impact in the revised production of 1986, provides the best example. The primary text is a long poem, *The Great Hunger*, published by Patrick Kavanagh in 1942. It is the classic Irish anti-pastoral, a dark and metaphysical rendition of 'Religion, the fields and the fear of the Lord' (Kavanagh 1964, p. 40). MacIntyre, in collaboration with actor Tom Hickey and director Patrick Mason, recreated Kavanagh's poem as a piece of theatre where text is of less importance than mime, stage properties and use of space. The twenty-one scenes, played without an interval, comprise improvisations on the key motifs in the lonely life of the archetypal, middle-aged, unmarried farmer, Patrick Maguire. These scenes are often very funny, turning bored repetition into comic ritual. Scenes in the home are lightened by the presence of a large wooden totem figure representing Maguire's mother, constantly deferred to by him and his sister Mary Anne but occasionally the centre of a real psycho-logical storm, as in Scene Eleven, where Mary Anne tries to goad Maguire into liberating himself from his mother's oppressive power. The wooden totem has a drawer, in which all manner of household effects are kept. The scene, mostly mime, builds from Maguire's 'shamelessly infantile' tantrums on the kitchen floor to his mumbling the word 'mother' (MacIntyre 1988, pp. 55–6).

In other scenes the power of the church over conscience and thought itself is illustrated. But instead of recreating the grinding conditions of the 1940s and 1950s, about which Kavanagh was merely bleakly critical, MacIntyre builds into his version the joy and sexual release which in Kavanagh is everywhere suppressed. There-fore MacIntyre's play provides a critique of the culture by means of a balancing out of the poem's pessimism. The perspective is from the 1980s, when the plenitude of sex is a resource to be celebrated rather than a sin to be expunged.

At the same time, *The Great Hunger* as avant-garde drama reveals a significant paradox. While it explodes the naturalistic form and releases copious energy on stage the play simultaneously deals with traditional materials. Its surrealism was rooted in Irish soil. Indeed, it was quite appropriate that *The Great Hunger* was chosen in 1988 to accompany John B. Keane's *The Field* as the double bill to represent the Abbey's work on its first tour to Russia (Hosey 1988). Each complements the other, although on the tour there was some resistance to MacIntyre's play. In New York the play was perceived by Clive Barnes as 'a nightmare of curious and intriguing resonance'. But, as Robert Hughes claims in *Culture of Complaint* (1994, p. 163), the avant-garde no longer has any validity in America, which 'is addicted to progress; it loves the new as impartially as it loves the old.' Not so in Ireland; hence the complex response to MacIntyre's work. In Ireland the past is still acknowledged and yet furiously contended: debates over historical revisionism raged in the 1980s. At the same time, postmodernism is not congenial to Irish audiences, whose sense of history remains too strong for it to be shredded as *mise en scène*. Thus in Dublin MacIntyre is at once both loved and hated.

Dublin audiences are well attuned to folklore and myth, and it is in these areas that MacIntyre is archaeological. In digging into the past MacIntyre is revivifying myth and releasing its language of psychological power. *The Bearded Lady* (1984) went to Swift's *Gulliver's Travels* to put on stage the madness that can arise from an over-insistence on the rational at the expense of the sexual in human relations. *Rise up Lovely Sweeney* (1985), in a most inventive montage of images, adapted the mythic mad Sweeney as a late twentieth-century outcast and ex-IRA man. *Dance for Your Daddy* (1987), a lament for lost innocence, explored Freudian territory in a surrealistic, zany collection of styles, including dance. Until the failure of *Snow White* (1988), the collaborative work of Mason, Hickey and MacIntyre thus continued to radicalise tradition at the Abbey. But when Patrick Mason took over as artistic director at the Abbey in 1993 he asserted its historic role as a protector and promoter of 'the word and the writer' (pp. 13–14). This seemed to place MacIntyre within a literary tradition, a position firmly challenged by his latest work, the folkloric *Sheep's Milk on the Boil* (1994) and the historical *Good Evening, Mr. Collins* (1995), each of which boldly explores Irish puritanism in an experimental fashion.

The savage god also has other disciples. One of these is Michael Harding (b. 1953). *Strawboys* (1987), directed by Tom Hickey at the Peacock, transformed the benevolent tradition of mummers (strawboys) into a malevolent expression of nightmare images (rather as Vincent Woods was later to do in a more political context in *At the Black Pig's Dyke*). These strawboys are products of a misogynistic society, threatening women in a variety of ways. They operate on male fears of women and excite violence against them. Using song, dance and rhyme Harding thus portrays an aspect of Irish life rarely exhibited. Tom MacIntyre hailed the experiment in a programme note: 'A scorching theme, the deepest hurt of the male soul these days of confusion. ... He names the cancer' (MacIntyre 1987). Once again, traditional materials and the stuff of popular, community diversion are pressed into service in a disturbing way which turns celebration into menace. The main character, Jackson, in failing to confront the strawboys suffers the loss of his wife Tahenny, a Juno figure who deserts him, and is finally strung up on high dressed as a woman: a fascistic image of contempt.

In other plays, *Una Pooka* (1989), *Misogynist* (1990) and *Hubert Murray's Widow* (1993), Harding has continued to use folklore materials together with images of Catholic liturgy and belief (Harding was formerly a priest). In an interview on *Hubert Murray's Widow*, a play on Northern violence cited in the last chapter, Harding said that his preoccupations as a writer are war, sex and God (Grant 1991, p. 46). Although it is difficult to estimate the value of this work collectively it may be said that unlike MacIntyre Harding is essentially a melodramatist. He likes to build a play, by whatever experimental means, to a sensational image or disclosure. Moreover, he appears to use the theatre to vent his pro-feminist and anti-clerical views: there is an air of opportunism about this side of his work which goes against the avant-garde mode. *Misogynist*, unsuitably placed on the main stage of the Abbey during the 1990 Theatre Festival, is certainly an avant-garde piece, set in a church, using a good deal of fantasy, a chorus and only two characters, Him and She. Its rather wilful obscurity and strident tone condemned it to spectacular failure in that production (White 1990–1, p. 41), although it was later more successfully played as a one-man show (by Tom Hickey). *Una Pooka*, a psychodrama, remains Harding's most successful play. But while it is a clever and absorbing piece of theatre it is doubtful whether it makes the transition to being the sort of religious mystery Harding had in mind when he wrote in a programme note: 'It is this dream in which Palm Sunday meets Good Friday that finds implicit remembrance in UNA POOKA. Just as the church constantly reaffirms its identity in remembering the Truth of its original Event, so Theatre, at certain times can have no higher function than to be faithful, both actors and audience, in remembering the interior truth of specific historical events which bear upon the ground of our being, and touch upon the ground of our anxieties, even in the present. The play ... attempts to catch in some small way, that interior dream, that moment of human frailty when we look for signs and certainties, only to end up discovering that all the while, we were looking in the wrong direction' (Harding 1989). From this note one would hardly expect a play about marriage difficulties in Dublin, a mysterious death, and a visiting priest who may or not be what he claims to be. There are shades of J. B. Priestley's *An Inspector Calls* (1946) here, combined with a dash of Ira Levin's *Deathtrap* (1978), and it was on such a level that it had its justified success. As to the 'interior dream' Harding speaks of, that is the heart of the mystery: a terrain where the Pooka from Irish folklore holds dangerous sway. Decoding, one might say that for Harding the Pope's visit to Ireland (the background to the play) was a step in the wrong direction for the Irish, who need to listen instead to the Unas of this world, and, in Beckett's phrase, all the dead voices.

Marina Carr (b. 1964) has also much in common with the avant-garde theatre of Tom MacIntyre. In an enthusiastic programme note for her *Ullaloo* (1991) at the Peacock MacIntyre said her theme is 'love, sex, the erotic, the harmonies and discords attendant. ... She's pointing to the furnace (heeded or unheeded) at the centre of our lives.' Carr had already had three plays staged in Dublin: *Low in the Dark* (1989), *The Deer's Surrender* (1990) at Andrew's Lane Studio, and *This Love Thing* (1991) at the Project. Of *The Deer's Surrender* the poet/critic Mary O'Donnell (1990) wrote: "The play is flawed in places, the conclusion irresolute, yet it sparkles with unashamed energy, with feminist guff, and succeeds hilariously in presenting a potted history of the world which includes the story of womb-envy and a new reply to the old catechism question "Who Made The World?"'. *Low in the Dark*, the first of Carr's plays to be published, is a witty, absurdist play subverting the patriarchal view of women. It is a play in which men get pregnant and 'Great men always sound like women' (Carr 1990, p. 121). The absurdism is given a satiric thrust, as Irish Catholic attitudes are parodied through a language recognisably traditional. The influence of Beckett is well absorbed

(Roche 1994, p. 287). Bender, a quintessential wife and prolific mother, calls for the baby she calls the Pope (a doll) and as she feeds him dreams of the future: 'We'll have tea in the palace and I'll learn Italian and the pair of us side by side, launching crusades, banning divorce, denying evolution, destroying the pill, canonising witches. Oh, a great time we'll have' (Carr 1990, p. 104).

This irreverent note is continued into *This Love Thing*. Here Carr brings together Jesus, Da Vinci and Michelangelo and the women in their lives, Magdalene, Mona Lisa and Eve, to explore representations of women in culture. A choric figure, Love Doctor, does his best to hold the Monty Pythonesque proceedings in thematic order by insisting that love is definable by a willingness to face death: 'I bury you' must replace 'I love you' as a meaningful declaration. As an exploration of man–woman relations the play stops short of any radical statement, and in stopping short it rather sells short the feminist project which, according to Lizbeth Goodman, is 'to achieve positive re-evaluation of women's roles and/or to effect social change' (1993, pp. 36–7). In that regard *Low in the Dark* was more progressive. Carr was certainly being careful not to be pigeon-holed as a feminist playwright. It is not easy for a woman writer to be avant-garde and not feminist in contemporary Ireland. One obvious reason for this is the lack of women playwrights whose work gets staged in Ireland. The general rule in the Republic is that plays by women may be heard, i.e., given a reading, but not seen, i.e., staged. There are exceptions and Carr is one of them. But she is an individualist and does not write for any feminist group. Carr's *Ullaloo* (1991) conspicuously took its stand on absurdism rather than on a feminist issue. The man–woman relationship was presented as played out, reduced to fetishes and absurd obsessions, offset by a dream of a unisex future. As the dramatisation of an impasse it was a noted flop, and sadly shows how Beckett can sometimes be bad for a rising young playwright.

The Mai (1994) is a happier and more assured play. *Ullaloo* alienated audiences; *The Mai* drew them to its heart. It was a hit at the 1994 Theatre Festival. When Michael Coveney (1994) saw it as 'a feminist riposte to Brian Friel' presumably he had *Dancing at Lughnasa* in mind. *The Mai* is certainly about a houseful of women and a recalcitrant husband; the narrator, Mai's daughter, is likewise an actor within the story. But thereafter Carr's play has nothing in common with Friel; it is a development of Carr's art to date. Like

The contemporary drama

Ullaloo, The Mai is a play about modern marriage, but 'this love thing' now both defines and is the Achilles heel of the woman's role. The eponymous Mai has just reconstructed her life after her husband Robert's desertion, building the house she always wanted by her favourite lake ('the kind of house you build to keep out neuroses, stave off nightmares'), coping with an extended family and having a career as a teacher (Carr 1995, p. 51). Then Robert, as the saying goes, walks back into her life and wrecks everything. The basis of the play is thus quite realistic, as is the setting. The characterisation is no longer absurdist but grounded in realism, although with much room left for fantasy and eccentricity. In particular, the portrait of Grandma Fraochlain, aged 100, is a mixture of the naturalistic and the *cailleach* from folklore: her stories of love and fidelity carry a mythic power and yet she remains a Falstaffian rogue. The portraits of Mai's two aunts, Agnes and Julia, are parodies of traditional Abbey types, as well as women with very specific views on marriage and divorce. Carr seems to want to bring together the mythic and the trite. The action releases raw suffering on stage, as the Mai is humiliated in her marriage; yet the romantic, if inevitable, outcome seems disappointing. Technically, Mai's suicide is a return to the nineteenth-century drama, to *Hedda Gabler* or *Rosmersholm*, and so is anything but avant-garde.

Whether *The Mai* is feminist is more debatable. The audiences it attracted in Dublin were predominantly female, and the play was a major success. Does this make it feminist? As a 'riposte to Brian Friel' *The Mai* certainly mobilises a woman's point of view on a family tragedy. It seems likely that Carr sees pathos as more important than polemics; she is not interested in dramatising 'issues' on stage. Like so many Irish playwrights (Teresa Deevey and Maura Laverty spring to mind), she is too protective of her individualism to employ political analysis dramatically. Myth rather than politics shapes her narrative. She tends to fetishise the 'story' as access to the wellsprings of passion and wisdom. It is an approach which contains the danger of closing down rather than opening up the possibilities of dramatic conflict.

Carr's latest play *Portia Coughlan* (1996) gives even more point to the paradox that in the Irish theatre the avant-garde is conservative while it is revolutionary. What lends extraordinary power to this play is the frank characterisation of a discontented, sexually-liberated married woman capable of articulating in violent language her disillusion with men ('ah jus' want ta castrate thim'), children and marital responsibilities. Portia Coughlan bids fair to be the Medea of contemporary drama. Moreover, she thinks mythically; she is wedded to a river in the Irish midlands just as fatally as a legendary mermaid to the sea or Keane's princess to the whirlpool in *Sharon's Grave*. And Portia's true being, her suffering self, is bound up in dreams: she is haunted by the loss of her twin brother, her alter ego. The play thus creates a modern psychological myth. It narrates in tragic form the kind of nightmare which MacIntyre's plays rehearse with comic buoyancy. At the same time, Portia is rooted in a naturalistic landscape that recalls the deterministic strain of the Abbey tradition (e.g., early Lennox Robinson), here put under scrutiny by the dramatic form. Carr's use of dialect seems at first reactionary, a whimsical throwback to peasant drama, until its strangeness and bluntness are registered. The whole process is a making strange, a dramatisation of alienation. *Portia Coughlan* is a more focused feminist protest than anything Carr has so far attempted, thrusting into audiences's faces a radical rewriting of Irish women's writing (e.g., Deevy's *Katie Roche*).

The avant-garde *per se* is always only a transitional moment in the Irish theatre. Fairly quickly, the necessary work done by the experimentalist is either rejected (Fitzmaurice's plays) or absorbed (O'Casey). So it is that the current avant-garde in Ireland is rapidly being assimilated into the establishment. MacIntyre, no longer writing wild, intertextual theatre of image, had a major success at the Peacock with his history play on Collins; Carr is writer-in-association at the Abbey (1995–96); only Harding is as yet marginalised. All three could readily be described as 'new voices' and yet the distinction made here seems worthwhile: these are pioneers whose work represents the occasional and necessary reinvestigation of the whole purpose of theatre.

New voices

A noteworthy development in the Irish theatre since the 1970s is decentralisation. The Druid Theatre Company, founded by Garry Hynes and others in Galway in 1975, gave the lead in establishing dynamic regional theatre. Other successful companies grew in Waterford (Red Kettle), Kilkenny (Bickerstaffe), Clonmel (Galloglass), Cork (Meridian), Limerick (Island), Ballina (Yew Tree), and Sligo

(Red Raincoat). This development was part of a general change in relationship between Dublin and the rest of the country, and for the first time the Arts Council was obliged to recognise the claims of good artistic work in areas remote from Dublin. No doubt, the master model for all these theatres was the Abbey, the voice of the nation. That being so, the impulse of the new writing to emerge from the regional theatres shared the traditional concerns with self, community, and national identity. This is not to say that the plays, by Ken Bourke in Galway or Jim Nolan in Waterford, were imitative or even ostentatiously preoccupied with anything resembling an agreed ideology. But in retrospect these plays may be seen to parallel in technique and direction the ambitions of Irish drama produced in Dublin. They are plays sharply engaged with traditional styles, themes, and issues. Bourke's *Wild Harvest* (1989) confronts life on the land in modern times, and thereby cannot avoid confronting also the drama of John B. Keane and T. C. Murray while its main preoccupation is with identity. Jim Nolan's *Moonshine* (1991) deals with the fate of a dwindling Protestant community in a small Irish town and finds potent connection with the work of Lennox Robinson as well as, more obviously, with *A Midsummer Night's Dream*. The intertextuality of such work lends them a voice in the ongoing debates on the Irish tradition.

A comparable decentralisation, if it is not an Irish bull to say so, took place in Dublin. From Joe Dowling's landmark production of *Juno and the Paycock* at the Gate Theatre in 1986 the Abbey no longer had supreme claim to Irish classics. Ben Barnes's productions of the plays of John B. Keane at the Gaiety reinforced this move. Dowling's defection from the Abbey, where he had been influential in nourishing new playwriting talent, including Neil Donnelly, Graham Reid, Bernard Farrell and Frank McGuinness, redirected new plays elsewhere. Not only was McGuinness writing for the Gate – *Innocence* (1986), and *The Bread Man* (1990) – but the new young companies such as Rough Magic, Passion Machine, Wet Paint and Pigsback all produced their own new writers. These included Declan Hughes, Paul Mercier, Dermot Bolger and Gavin Kostick. Belonging to no one group but a frequent 'Project' playwright in the 1990s is Gerard Stembridge. In so far as these writers are 'alternative' they exhibit a brash and refreshing opposition to the Abbey's traditionalism; but insofar as they are Irish writers they perforce worry in updated fashion about the issues which exercised their predecessors. But they are attracting new, young audiences and it is heartening to see a whole new generation finding theatre the medium through which, alongside vibrant popular music, they can best define themselves in their time. These writers are not at all interested in an Ireland–England opposition; the quarrel is now internalised so that new voices are sounding from *within* a national discourse. One does not see these writers as mirroring 'reality' in any naive sense; they are reflecting *upon* that complex web of experience which is in part man-made and in part linguistically produced.

There is room here for consideration of only a few contrasting playwrights. A good place to begin is with the plays of Bernard Farrell (b. 1940). In the past fifteen years Farrell has established himself as the author of twelve stage plays and the most consistently popular Irish comic playwright. He is often compared with Hugh Leonard as a chronicler and mild satirist of Ireland's *nouveaux riches*. But Farrell has always tried to embody a minor nightmare in his comedies. The goal is an awakening. Farrell's plays are an unmasking, a stripping away of pretence and dishonesty, and there is usually a catalyst who brings about this development. In *All the Way Back* (1985) it is Sheila, Brendan's no-nonsense wife. In Farrell's first play, *We Do Not Like Thee, Dr Fell* (1979) it is Joe Fell.

Dr Fell ironically describes the process: drama as pleasant therapy. It is thus metatheatre. Five characters are locked into a room for a weekend encounter session and required to talk out their psychological problems. Amongst them is Joe Fell, who seems crazier than any of them but whose motive is revenge for his sister's suicide as a result of such a session. The comedy builds to Joe's exposure of the American group leader as a fraud. Farrell's point is that people with emotional problems are vulnerable and if exploited by sham encounter groups may be plunged deeper into nightmare rather than released. The popularity of *Dr Fell* suggests that there is something at the core of this play which answers to the anxieties of many Irish people.

One sees a similar technique at work in three plays from his mature period, *Forty-Four Sycamore* (1992), *The Last Apache Reunion* (1993) and *Happy Birthday, Dear Alice* (1994). In each of these a pretence is being kept up, of social grandeur, or success, or family happiness, which a catalystic figure, usually scapegoated like Joe Fell as undesirable, shows to be based on lies. The catalyst figure can be an ambiguous figure, an Irish 'joker' playing on others' insecurity. In that sense, audience insecurity is played with before it is allayed: use of violence in *Forty-Four Sycamore* (ironically set in the house of a 'security engineer') is instructive here. As a writer of comedy Farrell plays with quite dangerous material: *The Last Apache Reunion*, for example, forces a group of 'old boys' to recognise their responsibility for the suicide of a boy they have all conveniently forgotten. Farrell raises to consciousness certain guilts and fears (such as, in *Happy Birthday, Dear Alice*, fears of what to do with an ageing mother living alone) and provides a comic catharsis. He thus resembles Alan Ayckbourn's 'delight in the *play* aspect of playwriting and at the same time a sense of ... the daily hurts we inflict on each other as we go about our business' (Billington 1983, p. 171).

Paul Mercier (b. 1958) is co-founder and driving force behind Passion Machine, a highly successful community theatre established in 1984. Its most famous author now is Roddy Doyle, who wrote two plays for Passion Machine, *Brownbread* (1986) and *War* (1989), before turning to fiction and its greater rewards. Mercier's plays, however, have from the beginning been the mainstay of Passion Machine and are frequently revived. They are usually premiered in a northside community hall and then move into one of the big commercial theatres in the city, where they pack out with young, enthusiastic audiences. The plays reflect their lives, for example, *Drowning* (1984), *Wasters* (1985), *Studs* (1986), *Spacers* (1986), where the titles alone indicate the nature of the material. 'I am trying to create a theatre that reflects, celebrates and comments on everyday life as it is. It is indigenous in every respect, from ourselves, about ourselves, for ourselves' (Mercier 1990). They reflect working-class life in much the same way as does Roddy Doyle's *The Commitments* (1988), with great energy but without social commentary. They ritualise dreams of order. *Home* (1988) recalls the Dublin plays of Sean O'Casey, for the setting is a large apartment building inhabited by a rich variety of types. Mercier's hero, Michael Sheehy, is an innocent country boy trying to resist the tug of home and to make a career in hotel management; he is largely at the mercy of the city slickers all around (and often in) his bedsit. He is befriended, however, by a likeable labourer, Valentine, who teaches him valuable survival techniques. But Valentine leaves for London when unemployment bites; he had only stayed, he says, 'Cos I thought it was home. I wanted home. Ye won't find it here' (Mercier 1988, p. 80). But Michael decides to stay, even though he has failed in his bid to enter hotel management. This apartment house becomes a micro-cosm of Ireland, and lonely though his final situation is, Michael is at home here. It is this sense of home, nostalgic but problematic, which unites Mercier's work with that of many of his young con-temporaries. There is a search for re-definition of place, a destina-tion for a new kind of pilgrim in Irish society. Still very much in development, Mercier captures the mood and tone of a new urban generation. *Buddleia* (1995), a hit at the Dublin Theatre Festival, provides in epic style a series of insights into the changes overtaking the city, as crime, drugs and cynical exploitation take root like weeds.

Dermot Bolger (b. 1959), who is a poet and novelist as well as a playwright, writes far less positively about working-class Dublin life than Mercier. *The Lament for Arthur Cleary* (1989) began as a poem, a remaking of a famous eighteenth-century Irish poem, which a Dublin community theatre, Wet Paint, and director David Byrne helped Bolger to transform into a most successful play. In the eight-eenth-century version, Arthur O'Leary is a young (Catholic) captain of the Hungarian Hussars who is killed under the Penal Laws when he returns to Ireland: it is a favourite nationalist text as well as being a powerful love poem. Bolger's is a motor-cycling hero returned to Dublin after fifteen years in the factories of Denmark. He has come back because 'Here, at least, I know who I am' (Bolger 1992, p. 51). But the Dublin to which Cleary returns is changed utterly, and he runs foul of a moneylender who enforces a new set of 'penal laws'. Cleary is inevitably killed, and is lamented by the young woman who befriended him. It emerges that this is a dream play and that Cleary is 'trapped in her grief' (p. 67) and must let her go. Although the play in its harsh urban realism can be compared with Heno Magee's ground-breaking *Hatchet* (1972) it also has distant echoes of Yeats's *Purgatory* (1938) in its emphasis on dream and spiritual release. The shadow of Yeats thus falls silently on contemporary Irish drama, in spite of its trans-European mobility.

Here and in *One Last White Horse* (1991), commissioned by the Abbey, Bolger exposes the raw side of contemporary Dublin, violent, drug-infested, careless of all tradition. Significantly, Bolger's best-known novel is entitled *The Journey Home* (1991), since this quest for a metaphysical place which could be called 'home' is Bolger's most urgent theme. He is, as well as poet, an angry young man one generation after Osborne. The monologue *In High Germany*

(1990), set in Hamburg, looks at this question of home from a different angle. Here the young man is an exile, whose sense of home is recreated by the Irish soccer team playing against Holland; although the eleven are themselves expatriates (all being English league players) they are able to represent Ireland in the narrator Eoin's mind: 'this was the only country I still owned, those eleven figures in green shirts' (Bolger 1992, p. 106). Eoin is able finally to occupy this international sense of home. To Bolger's generation, local habitation, being torn between urban anonymity and unrecognised rural and historical roots, is no longer a key to self-definition: the old theme of 'the land' has been bulldozed into unacceptability. Thus national identity is more an idea, a rootless desire, something to be able to cheer for. As the tragic hero of *One Last White Horse* puts it, 'All I ever wanted was just to fill this hole in my heart, to belong, not to be haunted by this unease' (Bolger 1992, p. 195).

Sebastian Barry (b. 1955) takes it from there. 'In 1985 I landed back in Ireland after a few years of restlessness in Europe. I was at home, homesick for abroad. ... Since I was now to be an Irishman, it seemed I would have to make myself up as I went' (Barry 1991, p. v). Like Bolger, Barry is essentially a poet and comes to the theatre as a relative outsider. Although he does not write his plays in verse there is an indefinable poetic quality there which makes his work unique in the contemporary Irish theatre. *Boss Grady's Boys* (1988) is about two old bachelors living on an isolated farm, a strange choice of play for a modern city boy like Barry to write. It is the total opposite of Bolger's world: a version of pastoral lovingly imagined. The lifestyle of the two brothers, one simple-minded, the other his patient keeper, is created in all its loneliness, warmth and eccentricity. In an Ireland where attacks on such old people are a frequent occurrence this intimate recreation of hidden but vulnerable Ireland is extraordinarily moving, with the dreams of the old men conjuring up dead parents, friends and even animals. Thus Barry is imagining 'another Ireland altogether' (1991, p. 93). *Prayers of Sherkin* (1990) goes further. It depicts a Quaker community on a small island off the south-west of Ireland in 1890. In a poem entitled 'Fanny Hawke Goes to the Mainland Forever' Barry had already written of his Quaker ancestor who left Sherkin Island 'to marry/a Catholic lithographer in Cork City' (1989, p. 54). In the play no trace of disapproval surrounds Fanny's decision to leave the dying community.

This is a prelapsarian society. Fanny says to her brother: 'we are not from here and I have such a sense of home. ... I think it is the site of our new Jerusalem' (1991, p. 13). Yet time, history, decrees otherwise and in a dream Fanny is given approval of her decision to marry Patrick and leave for the mainland. Her future children call her. 'They wait for you up the years, and you must go. All about them lies a cruel century of disasters and wars that I did not foresee. I steer you back into the mess of life because I was blinder than I knew' (Barry 1991, p. 57). Thus speaks the dead founder of the community to Fanny in a dream. The play celebrates Fanny's courage and the transition to a new home, Ireland in the twentieth century, from the end of which we look back as to a brave new world, an island imagined without a Caliban, pluralist, free of violence, a prayerful place.

White Woman Street (1992), set in Ohio in 1916, dramatises a dream of home by an outlaw emigrant from Sligo. It is really a romantic myth of expiation and redemption poetically proposed. In *The Steward of Christendom* (1995) the historical is better integrated with the spiritual, to create a moving sense of confusion and breakdown in post-1922 Ireland. The technique both resembles Beckett's and demarcates contemporary Irish drama from Beckett's. The main character, Thomas Dunne, uses monologue to recall and in some sense justify his life as a police officer before 1922; the poetic quality of these monologues recalls Beckett's trilogy and *Company* (1980). But Beckett invariably avoids Irish history; his voices derive from characters preoccupied only with being. Barry's character, as is more usual in Irish drama, is rooted in particularities of time, place and event. If one were seeking for a literary counterpart to *The Steward of Christendom* it would not be in Beckett but in John McGahern, whose novel *Amongst Women* (1990) provides a useful contrast. Barry, like McGahern, portrays an old man struggling to make sense of a life spent in devotion to an ideal of public order which abruptly came to nought, a man isolated in age and mind but surrounded by love. The power of Barry's play is bound up in this interweaving of love and history, seen again in *The Only True History of Lizzie Finn* (1995), where the Big House theme is interestingly combined with the world of the music-hall, two contrasting forms of community. Barry thus addresses the past in order to redeem it.

Conclusion

In the 1990s the fortunes of Irish theatre look set to improve greatly. The efforts of a dynamic Minister for Arts and Culture have found worthy compliance in Arts Council initiatives which have resulted in new plans and new resources for theatre. There is now an air of newfound confidence which augurs well for the future of Irish drama as the centenary of the foundation of the Irish Literary Theatre falls due.

From 1990 to 1993 Garry Hynes was a controversial artistic director at the Abbey. She spoke a language impatient with older notions of cultural nationalism: 'This theatre itself is an act of the imagination, for God's sake ... founded in 1904 by a group of people in an effort to invent a national identity for a nation that did not exist. So the nation then was a fiction. And regardless of constitutions and borders, and all the things that came afterwards, it still is – at best – a collection of fictions. And you cannot arbitrate between fictions. You can only hope to experience them and, arising from those experiences, perhaps begin to sense something of yourself as part of a community. ... It is in the multiplicity of experience that we find the only possible meaning of our national identity and finally, too, the only possible value' (Hynes 1993). Hynes thus served during her term of office to challenge the whole idea of a national theatre in Ireland today. Her successor Patrick Mason has taken up this challenge, as his three policy documents testify, and has reinstated the Abbey's role as 'the making of the national soul' (1995, p. 5). At the same time there is a clear danger that the national theatre is being taken for granted.

It seems fairly clear that in Ireland in the 1990s it is not possible to invoke the 'nation' in the same terms as obtained even a generation, much less a century, ago. The country has undergone massive changes which are still causing moral and social upheaval. In *Ireland Today*, Gemma Hussey puts these in perspective: 'Irish society has changed more in the two decades leading up to the 1990s than in the whole of the previous one hundred years. ... An inward-looking, rural, deeply conservative, nearly 100 per cent Roman Catholic and impoverished country has become urbanized, industrialized, and Europeanized. ... And still the hunger for change is there' (1993, p. 1). The consciousness has mutated; it is probably only in metropolitan centres abroad (among the diaspora) that the metaphysical

Ireland, the *patria* claiming urgent allegiance, has a claim now. At home, human rights, sexual equality, access to information at every level, and the breaking down of old hierarchies of power and privilege are the dominant concerns. The success of the Divorce Referendum in November 1995 marked a major, if belated, shift in Irish society: seventy years after Yeats's appeal for divorce to accommodate the Protestant minority a pluralist Ireland has voted to set aside Catholic narrow-mindedness. This is not a simple matter: the strain shows in an urban–rural division on the divorce issue. Change is proving painful. But there is a momentum which is carrying the country firmly beyond the old parameters. The present generation of young Irish people, wanting nothing to do with the ideals of either Pearse or de Valera, has found its preferred liberty in secularism, tolerance, and a new, very appealing, humanism. Ireland is rapidly becoming European, its culture cosmopolitan; yet there is a new-found passion for the arts as a means of articulating and celebrating home-based experience. A new kind of awareness is being forged. The landscape is breaking out in interpretative centres. Heaney's winning of the Nobel Prize has reasserted national pride, which is bound to have new and lasting effects.

The theatre is beginning to reflect this new ethos, not only in dramatic forms but in a reaching out to devised forms and in a hospitality to different voices within the old structures. Generating 'a national dream-life', to appropriate the title of a Mamet essay (1988), amounts to creating through theatre images, rhythms and especially stories which fully and powerfully give expression to a people's experience. Without photographs, Benedict Anderson insists, we cannot remember our childhood: these provide an apparent continuity of identity, as we look and discover, 'yes, you and that naked baby are identical' (1991, p. 204). So it is with theatre: it provides at communal level the records and representations (the photographs and mirrors) which enable self-discovery. The history of Irish drama in the twentieth century is thus based on a need for a narrative of identity. Nowadays, as Denis Donoghue asserts in *Warrenpoint*, 'Ireland without its story is merely a member of the EC, the begging bowl our symbol' (1991, p. 172). The more problematic and fragmented identity becomes the greater the need for imagery of wholeness.

This national need to rephrase, however obliquely or symbolically, this Beckett-like obligation to express, is not just a mark of the garrulous Irish swopping yarns in the pub or within earshot of earnest American scholars. It persists as a mode of being. It is the material of performance, of enacting assurances that we are alive and can survive in spite of our unshakable memory of defeat. It is the stuff, in short, of theatre, that obsessive dream factory. For Yeats (1950, p. 392), 'It was the dream itself enchanted me', and so it has always been. The dream is always waiting to be fulfilled; the nation is always awaiting completion. It has been the assumption of this book that mirror and dream are two sides of the same mimetic process. Irish drama both records cultural conditions and generates fresh possibilities. As the century draws to a close and with it one hundred years of native Irish theatre, the enabling mirror on the other side of dream shines brightly still.

References

Note: Dates of plays are dates of publication; in the text, dates of plays are of first production

Adams, Hazard (1973), *Lady Gregory*, Lewisburg: Bucknell University Press

Agnew, Paddy (1980), 'Talking to Ourselves: Brian Friel talks to Paddy Agnew', *Magill*, Dec. 1980, pp. 59–61

Anderson, Benedict (1991), *Imagined Communities: Reflections on the Origin and Spread of Nationalism*, rev. edn, London and New York: Verso

Andrews, Elmer (1990), 'The Will to Freedom: Politics and Play in the Theatre of Stewart Parker', in *Irish Writers and Politics*, ed. Okifumi Komesu and Masaru Sekine, Gerrards Cross: Colin Smythe, Savage, Maryland: Barnes & Noble, pp. 237–69

Andrews, Elmer (1995), *The Art of Brian Friel: Neither Reality Nor Dreams*, Basingstoke: Macmillan, New York: St Martin's Press

Andrews, J. H. (1983), '*Translations* and *A Paper Landscape*: Between Fiction and History: Brian Friel, John Andrews and Kevin Barry', *Crane Bag*, 7.2, pp. 118–24

(1992–93), 'Notes for a Future Edition of Brian Friel's *Translations*, *Irish Review*, 13, pp. 93–106

Ardagh, John (1994), *Ireland and the Irish: Portrait of a Changing Society*, London: Hamish Hamilton

Arden, John (1977), 'A Socialist Hero on the Stage', in *To Present the Pretence: Essays on the Theatre and its Public*, including Two Essays Written in Collaboration with Margaretta D'Arcy, London: Eyre Methuen, pp. 92–138

Ayling, Ronald (1969), ed., *Sean O'Casey: Modern Judgements*, London: Macmillan; Nashville: Aurora, 1970

(1980), 'Seeds for Future Harvest: Propaganda and Art in O'Casey's Earliest Play', *Irish University Review*, 10, pp. 25–40

Barnett, Gene A. (1978), *Denis Johnston*, Boston: Twayne

Barry, Sebastian (1989), *Fanny Hawke Goes to the Mainland Forever*, Dublin: Raven Arts

(1991), *Prayers of Sherkin [and] Boss Grady's Boys: Two Plays*, London: Methuen

(1995), *The Only True History of Lizzie Finn / The Steward of Christendom / White Woman Street*, London: Methuen

Battersby, Eileen (1990), 'Sometimes a great notion' [interview with Seamus Heaney], *Irish Times*, 29 September (*Weekend*, p. 5)

References

Beckett, J. C. (1966), *The Making of Modern Ireland 1603–1923*, London: Faber

Beckett, Samuel (1957), *All That Fall: A Play for Radio*, London: Faber

(1958), *Endgame: A Play in One Act*, New York: Grove

(1965), *Waiting for Godot: A Tragicomedy in Two Acts*, 2nd edn, London: Faber

(1983), *Disjecta: Miscellaneous Writings and a Dramatic Fragment*, ed. Ruby Cohn, London: Calder

Behan, Beatrice (1973), with Des Hickey and Gus Smith, *My Life with Brendan*, London: Leslie Frewin

Behan, Brendan (1955), 'The Pike and I', *Pike Theatre Club* [illustrated programme], Dublin

(1958), *Borstal Boy*, London: Hutchinson

(1962), *Brendan Behan's Island: An Irish Sketch-Book*, London: Hutchinson, repr. Corgi, 1965 [quotation from 1965 edn]

[1964], *An Giall: Dráma Trí Gníomh*, Dublin: An Chomhairle Náisiúnta Dramaíochta, n.d.

(1978), *The Complete Plays*, ed. Alan Simpson, London: Methuen

(1992), *The Letters of Brendan Behan*, ed. E. H. Mikhail, Basingstoke: Macmillan

Behan, Brian (1988), *Kathleen: A Dublin Saga*, London: Century

Behan, Dominic (1965), *My Brother Brendan*, London: Leslie Frewin, repr. Four Square, 1966 [quotation from 1966 edn]

Behan, Kathleen (1984), *Mother of All the Behans: The Story of Kathleen Behan as Told to Brian Behan*, London: Hutchinson

Bell, Sam Hanna (1972), *The Theatre in Ulster: A Survey of the Dramatic Movement in Ulster from 1902 until the Present Day*, Dublin: Gill and Macmillan

Benjamin, Walter (1992), *Illuminations*, ed. with intro. by Hannah Arendt, trans. Harry Zohn, London: Fontana

Bentley, Eric (1969), *What is Theatre?*, London: Methuen

Bhabha, Homi K. (1990), ed., *Nation and Narration*, London and New York: Routledge

Billington, Michael (1983), *Alan Ayckbourn*, London and Basingstoke: Macmillan; New York: Grove Press, 1984

Bliss, Alan J. (1972), 'The Language of Synge', *J. M. Synge Centenary Papers 1971*, ed. Maurice Harmon, Dublin: Dolmen, pp. 35–62

Bloom, Harold (1970), *Yeats*, New York: Oxford University Press

(1973), *The Anxiety of Influence*, New York: Oxford University Press

Blythe, Ernest [1965a], *The Abbey Theatre*, Dublin: The National Theatre Society Ltd., n.d.

(1965b),'The Behan We Knew', in *The World of Brendan Behan*, ed. Sean McCann, London: New English Library, pp. 182–5

(1969) 'Mid-Ulster and After, 1: Dawn of New Political Era in Northern Ireland', *Irish Times*, 30 June, p. 8

Boal, Augusto (1979), *Theater of the Oppressed*, trans. Charles and Maria-Odilia Leal McBride, London: Pluto

Bolger, Dermot (1992), *A Dublin Quartet*, Harmondsworth: Penguin

Bort, Eberhard (1995), 'Staging the Troubles: Civil Conflict and Drama in Northern Ireland', *Journal for the Study of British Cultures*, 2.2., pp. 141–60

(1996), ed., *The State of Play: Irish Theatre in the 'Nineties*, Trier: Wissenschaftlicher Verlag Trier

References

Boyce, D. George (1995), *Nationalism in Ireland*, 3rd edn, London and New York: Routledge

Boyd, Ernest (1922), *Ireland's Literary Renaissance*, rev. edn, New York: Knopf

Boyd, John (1973), *The Flats: A Play in Three Acts*, Belfast: Blackstaff
(1981), *Guests*, in *Collected Plays 1*, Belfast: Blackstaff

Boylan, Very Revd. P. Canon (1932), ed., *The Book of the Congress*, Dublin: Governing Committee of the Congress and Archbishop of Dublin

Boyle, Ted E. (1969), *Brendan Behan*, New York: Twayne

Bradby, David and David Williams (1988), *Directors' Theatre*, Basingstoke: Macmillan

Bradley, John (1984), ed., *Viking Dublin Exposed: The Wood Quay Saga*, Dublin: O'Brien

Bramsbäck, Birgit (1984), *Folklore and W. B. Yeats: The Function of Folklore Elements in Three Early Plays*, Uppsala: University of Uppsala

Brecht, Bertolt (1963), *The Life of Galileo*, trans. Desmond I. Vesey, London: Methuen
(1964), *Brecht on Theatre*, ed. John Willett, London: Methuen

Breen, Richard (1990), Damian F. Hannan, David B. Rottman, Christopher T. Whelan, *Understanding Contemporary Ireland: State, Class and Development in the Republic of Ireland*, Basingstoke: Macmillan

Brighton, Pam (1990), 'Charabanc', *Theatre Ireland*, 23, pp. 41–2

Brook, Peter (1968), *The Empty Space*, London: MacGibbon and Kee; New York: Avon Books

Brown, Terence (1985a), *Ireland: A Social and Cultural History 1922–1985*, London: Fontana
(1985b), *The Whole Protestant Community: The Making of a Historical Myth*, Derry: Field Day

Burke, Patrick (1991), 'Field Day's Fables of Identity', *Perspectives of Irish Drama and Theatre*, ed. Jacqueline Genet and Richard Allen Cave, Gerrards Cross: Smythe, pp. 140–4

Byrne, Seamus (1950), *Design for a Headstone*, in *Seven Irish Plays 1946–1964*, ed. Robert Hogan, Minneapolis: University of Minnesota Press, 1967, pp. 97–181

Cairns, David and Shaun Richards (1988), *Writing Ireland: Colonialism, Nationalism and Culture*, Manchester, Manchester University Press

Campbell, Joseph (1968), *The Hero with a Thousand Faces*, 2nd edn, Princeton: Princeton University Press

Canfield Curtis (1929), ed., *Plays of the Irish Renaissance 1880–1930*, New York: Ives Washburn
(1936), ed., *Plays of Changing Ireland*, New York: Macmillan

Carney, Frank (1951), *The Righteous are Bold*, Dublin: James Duffy

Carney, James (1986), *The Playboy & The Yellow Lady*, Dublin: Poolbeg

Carpenter, Andrew (1974), ed., *My Uncle John: Edward Stephens's Life of J. M. Synge*, London: Oxford University Press

Carr, Marina (1990), *Low in the Dark*, in *The Crack in the Emerald: New Irish Plays*, selected and introduced by David Grant, London: Nick Hern
(1995), *The Mai*, Loughcrew, Oldcastle: Gallery
(1996), *Portia Coughlan*, in *The Dazzling Dark: New Irish Plays*, selected and introduced by Frank McGuinness, London and Boston: Faber

References

Carroll, Paul Vincent (1938), *Shadow and Substance: A Play in Four Acts*, London: Macmillan
(1944), *Three Plays: The White Steed, Things That Are Caesar's, The Strings, My Lord, Are False*, London: Macmillan
Carty, Ciaran (1980), 'Finding voice in a language not our own' [interview with Brian Friel], *Sunday Independent*, 5 October, p. 16
Cave, Richard Allen (1993), 'Tom Murphy: Acts of Faith in a Godless World', *British and Irish Drama since 1960*, ed. James Acheson, Basingstoke: Macmillan, New York: St Martin's Press, pp. 88–102
Clarke, Brenna Katz and Harold Ferrar (1979), *The Dublin Drama League 1918–1941*, Dublin: Dolmen
Colum, Padraic (1963), *Three Plays*, Dublin: Allen Figgis
Connolly, James (1917), *Labour in Ireland: Labour in Irish History: The Re-Conquest of Ireland*, Dublin and London: Maunsel
Corkery, Daniel (1931), *Synge and Anglo-Irish Literature: A Study*, Dublin and Cork: Cork University Press; London: Longmans, Cork: Mercier, repr. 1966
Coveney, Michael (1994), 'Theatre: Finest slices of Irish life', *Observer* Review, 9 October, p. 12
Coxhead, Elizabeth (1966), *Lady Gregory: A Literary Portrait*, 2nd edn, London: Secker and Warburg
Coyle, Jane (1993), 'Now we are 10: Jane Coyle talks to Charabanc', *Theatre Ireland*, 30, pp. 16–18
Cranston, Des (1985), 'Conflict and Censorship', *Theatre Ireland*, 11, pp. 30–31
(1991), 'Skimmers, Spaghetti and the Boiler House', *Theatre Ireland*, 25, pp. 32–4
Cronin, Anthony (1976), *Dead as Doornails*, Dublin: Dolmen
Cupitt, Don (1984), *The Sea of Faith*, London: BBC
D'Alton, Louis (1960), *They Got What They Wanted: A Three-Act Comedy*, Dundalk: Dundalgan Press
(1964), *Lovers Meeting: A Tragedy*, Dublin: P. J. Bourke
(1970), *This Other Eden: A Play in Three Acts*, 3rd edn, Dublin [1954]: repr. P. J. Bourke
(1980), *The Money Doesn't Matter: A Play in Three Acts*, Dublin: [1942], repr. P. J. Bourke
Dantanus, Ulf (1988), *Brian Friel: A Study*, London and Boston: Faber
Davies, Robertson (1975), 'Playwrights and Plays', in *The 'Revels' History of Drama in English*, vol. IV *1750–1880*, ed. Michael Booth *et al.*, London: Methuen, pp. 147–269
Dawson, Kevin (1990), 'The Field Killing', in 'People', *Sunday Tribune*, 23 September, p. 25
De Búrca, Séamus (1993), *Brendan Behan: A Memoir*, 3rd edn, Dublin: P. J. Bourke
De Jongh, Nicholas (1992), *Not in Front of the Audience: Homosexuality on Stage*, London and New York: Routledge
Deane, Seamus (1973), 'Irish Politics and O'Casey's Theatre', *Threshold*, 24, pp. 5–16
(1977), 'Unhappy and at Home: Interview with Seamus Heaney', *Crane Bag*, 1.1, pp. 61–7
(1983), *Civilians and Barbarians*, Derry: Field Day
(1984), *Heroic Styles: The Tradition of an Idea*, Derry: Field Day
(1985a), *Celtic Revivals: Essays in Modern Irish Literature 1880–1980*, London and

References

Boston: Faber

(1985b), 'Preface', *Ireland's Field Day: Field Day Theatre Company*, London: Hutchinson

(1990), 'Introduction', *Nationalism, Colonialism, and Literature: Terry Eagleton, Fredric Jameson, Edward W. Said: A Field Day Company Book*, Minneapolis: University of Minnesota

(1991), ed., *The Field Day Anthology of Irish Writing*, 3 vols, Derry: Field Day

Deevy, Teresa (1939), *Katie Roche*, in *Three Plays*, London: Macmillan

Devlin, Anne (1986), *Ourselves Alone: with The Long March and A Woman Calling*, London and Boston: Faber

(1994a), *After Easter*, London and Boston: Faber

(1994b), 'Pride of Belfast' [interview with Jane Coyle], *Irish Times*, Supplement, 2 November, pp. 2–3

Dolan, T. P. (1990), ed., *The English of the Irish: Special Issue, Irish University Review*, 20.1

Donoghue, Denis (1974), 'The Politics of Yeats's Theatre', *Threshold*, 25, pp. 27–33

(1991), *Warrenpoint*, London: Cape

Dorn, Karen (1984), *Players and Painted Stage: The Theatre of W. B. Yeats*, Brighton: Harvester; Totowa: Barnes & Noble

Doyle, Paul A. (1971), *Paul Vincent Carroll*, Lewisburg: Bucknell

Dürrenmatt, Friedrich (1975), 'Preface to *Four Plays*', in *The Reader's Encyclopedia of World Drama*, ed. John Gassner and Edward Quinn, London: Methuen, pp. 1027–30

Dunleavy, Janet Egleson (1991) and Gareth W. Dunleavy, *Douglas Hyde: A Maker of Modern Ireland*, Berkeley and Los Angeles: UCLA Press

Edwards, Hilton (1958), *The Mantle of Harlequin*, Dublin: Progress House

Edwards, Philip (1979), *Threshold of a Nation: A Study in English and Irish Drama*, Cambridge: Cambridge University Press

Edwards, Ruth Dudley (1977), *Patrick Pearse: The Triumph of Failure*, London: Gollancz

Eliot, T. S. (1960), 'Tradition and the Individual Talent', in *The Sacred Wood: Essays on Poetry and Criticism*, London: Methuen, pp. 47–59

Ellis, Peter Berresford (1987), *A Dictionary of Irish Mythology*, London: Constable

Ellis, Sylvia C. (1994), *Yeats and the Dancer*, London: Macmillan, New York: St. Martin's Press, 1995

Ellis-Fermor, Una (1954), *The Irish Dramatic Movement*, 2nd edn, London: Methuen

Ellmann, Richard (1948), *Yeats: The Man and the Masks*, London: Macmillan

(1982), *James Joyce: New and Revised Edition*, Oxford: Oxford University Press

Empson, William (1935), *Some Versions of Pastoral*, London: Chatto and Windus

Ervine, St John (1988), *Selected Plays*, ed. John Cronin, Gerrards Cross: Smythe; Washington, DC: Catholic University of America Press

Esslin, Martin (1978), *An Anatomy of Drama*, London: Sphere/Abacus

Etherton, Michael (1989), *Contemporary Irish Dramatists*, Macmillan Modern Dramatists, Basingstoke: Macmillan

Fallon, Gabriel (1936), 'This Catholic Theatre Business,' *Irish Monthly*, LXIV, pp. 77–80, 837

(1938), 'Mr. Caroll's "Shadow and Substance",' *Irish Monthly*, LXVI, 858

(1953), review of Louis D'Alton's *This Other Eden*, in *The Standard*, 12 June, p. 4

References

(1965), *Sean O'Casey: The Man I Knew*, London: Routledge and Kegan Paul; Boston: Little, Brown

Fanning, Ronan (1983), *Independent Ireland*, Dublin: Helicon

Fay, W. G. and Catherine Carswell (1935), *The Fays of the Abbey Theatre*, London: Rich and Cowan

Feehan, John M. (1979) ed., *Fifty Years Young: A Tribute to John B. Keane*, Dublin and Cork: Mercier

Ferrar, Harold (1973), *Denis Johnston's Irish Theatre*, Dublin: Dolmen

Findlater, Richard (1967), *Banned! A Review of Theatrical Censorship in Britain*, London: Macgibbon and Kee

FitzGerald, Mary (1987), 'Four French Comedies: Lady Gregory's Translations of Molière', in *Lady Gregory Fifty Years After*, ed. Ann Saddlemyer and Colin Smythe, Gerrards Cross: Smythe, pp. 277–90

Fitz-Simon, Christopher (1994), *The Boys: A Double Biography* [of Micheál MacLiammóir and Hilton Edwards], London: Nick Hern

Flannery, James W. (1976), *W. B. Yeats and the Idea of a Theatre: The Early Abbey Theatre in Theory and Practice*, New Haven and London: Yale

Forristal, Desmond (1975), *Black Man's Country: A Play in Two Acts*, The Society of Irish Playwrights Series, no. 3, Newark: Proscenium

(1976), *The True Story of the Horrid Popish Plot*, Dublin: Veritas

Foster, John Wilson (1992), 'Culture and Colonization: A Northern Perspective', in *Irish Literature and Culture*, ed. Michael Kenneally, Irish Literary Studies 35, Gerrards Cross: Smythe, pp. 158–72

Foster, R. F. (1988), *Modern Ireland 1600–1972*, London: Allen Lane/Penguin

(1993), *Paddy and Mr Punch: Connections in Irish and English History*, London: Allen Lane/Penguin

Frazier, Adrian (1990), *Behind the Scenes: Yeats, Horniman, and the Struggle for the Abbey Theatre*, Berkeley: University of California Press

Friel, Brian (1968), 'The Theatre of Hope and Despair', *Everyman: An Annual Religio-Cultural Review*, 1.1, pp. 17–22

(1970), *The Mundy Scheme: A Play in Three Acts*, New York: Samuel French

(1972), 'Plays Peasant and Unpeasant', *TLS*, 17 March, pp. 305–06

(1975), *The Enemy Within: A Play in Three Acts*, The Irish Play Series, no. 7, Newark, DE: Proscenium

(1979), *Volunteers*, London and Boston: Faber

(1980a), 'Extracts from a Sporadic Diary', in *The Writers: A Sense of Ireland*, ed. Andrew Carpenter and Peter Fallon, Dublin: O'Brien, pp. 39–43

(1980b), 'Exiles', programme note, *The Blue Macushla*, by Thomas Murphy, Abbey Theatre, 6 March

(1981), *Anton Chekhov's Three Sisters: A Translation*, Dublin: Gallery

(1983), *The Communication Cord*, London and Boston: Faber

(1984), *Selected Plays*, London and Boston: Faber & Faber

[1985], 'Extracts from a Sporadic Diary', in *Ireland and the Arts*, ed. Tim Pat Coogan, *A Special Issue of Literary Review*, London: Namara [n.d.]

(1989), *Making History*, London and Boston: Faber

(1990), *Dancing at Lughnasa*, London and Boston: Faber

(1993), *Wonderful Tennessee*, Loughcrew, Oldcastle: Gallery

(1994), *Molly Sweeney*, Loughcrew, Oldcastle: Gallery

References

Frye, Northrop (1957) *Anatomy of Criticism: Four Essays*, Princeton: Princeton University Press

Fugard, Athol (1987), *Boesman and Lena*, in *Selected Plays*, Oxford and Cape Town: Oxford University Press

Gallagher, S. F. (1992), ed., *Selected Plays of Hugh Leonard*, Irish Drama Selections 9, Gerrards Cross: Smythe, Washington, DC: Catholic University of America Press

Galvin, Patrick (1976), *We Do it for Love*, in *Three Plays*, no. 27 issue of *Threshold*, Belfast: Lyric Players Theatre

Gerdes, Peter Rene (1973), *The Major Works of Brendan Behan*, Bern and Frankfurt: Lang

Gillespie, Elgy (1979), 'Elgy Gillespie talks to ... J. Graham Reid', *Irish Times*, 21 August, p. 8

Goldring, Maurice (1993), *Pleasant the Scholar's Life: Irish Intellectuals and the Construction of the Nation State*, London: Serif

Goodman, Lizbeth (1993), *Contemporary Feminist Theatres: To Each Her Own*, London and New York: Routledge

Grant, David (1991), 'War Sex God: David Grant Talks to Playwright Michael Harding about the Major Preoccupations of his Work', *Theatre Ireland*, 25, pp. 46–7

Greaves, C. Desmond (1979), *Sean O'Casey: Politics and Art*, London: Lawrence and Wishart

Greene, David H. and Edward M. Stephens (1959), *J. M. Synge*, New York: Macmillan

Gregory, Augusta (1970a), *Gods and Fighting Men: The Story of the Tuatha De Danaan and of the Fianna of Ireland, Arranged and Put into English by Lady Gregory*, Gerrards Cross: Irish University Press in association with Colin Smythe

(1970b), *Cuchulain of Muirthemne: The Story of the Men of the Red Branch of Ulster...*, Gerrards Cross: Irish University Press/Smythe

(1970–1), *Collected Plays*, ed. Ann Saddlemyer, 4 vols, Gerrards Cross: Irish University Press/Smythe

(1972), *Our Irish Theatre: A Chapter of Autobiography* [1913], 3rd edn., Gerrards Cross: Smythe

(1974a), *Seventy Years: Being the Autobiography of Lady Gregory*, ed. Colin Smythe, Gerrards Cross: Smythe

(1974b), *Poets and Dreamers: Studies and Translations from the Irish by Lady Gregory including Nine Plays by Douglas Hyde*, Gerrards Cross: Smythe

(1978), *Lady Gregory's Journals*, vol. 1 [1916–1925] ed. Daniel J. Murphy, Gerrards Cross: Smythe

(1987), *Lady Gregory's Journals*, vol. 2 [1925–1932], ed. Daniel J. Murphy, Gerrards Cross: Smythe

(1995), *Selected Writings*, ed. Lucy McDiarmid and Maureen Waters, Harmondsworth: Penguin

(1996), *Lady Gregory's Diaries 1892–1902*, ed. James Pethica, Gerrards Cross: Smythe

Grene, Nicholas (1975), *Synge: A Critical Study of the Plays*, London: Macmillan

(1982), ed., *The Well of the Saints: By J. M. Synge*, Washington, DC: Catholic University of America Press, Gerrards Cross: Smythe

Griffith, Arthur (1916), ed., *Thomas Davis: The Thinker & Teacher: The Essence of his Writings in Prose and Poetry*, Dublin: M. H. Gill

References

Hadfield, Paul (1993), 'Field Day: Over but Not Out', *Theatre Ireland*, 31, pp. 47–50

Haire, Wilson John (1973), *Within Two Shadows*, London: Davis-Poynter

(1979), *Bloom of the Diamond Stone*, London: Pluto

Harding, Michael (1989), 'Calling to mind: a few notes written in Holy Week', programme note for *Una Pooka*, Michael Harding, Abbey Theatre, 17 April

(1990a), *Misogynist*, in *The Crack in the Emerald: New Irish Plays*, selected and introduced by David Grant, London: Nick Hern

(1990b), *Una Pooka*, in *First Run 2: New Plays by New Writers*, London: Nick Hern

Harris, Claudia (1991), 'From Pastness to Wholeness: Stewart Parker's Reinventing Theatre', *Colby Quarterly*, 27.4, pp. 233–41

Harrison, Alan (1989), *The Irish Trickster*, Sheffield: Sheffield Academic Press

Hawkins, Maureen S. G. (1990), 'Ascendancy Nationalism, Feminist Nationalism, and Stagecraft in Lady Gregory's Revision of *Kincora*', in *Irish Writers and Politics*, ed. Okifumi Komesu and Masaru Sekine, Gerrards Cross: Smythe, Savage, Maryland: Barnes & Noble, pp. 94–108

Hayley, Barbara (1991), 'Self-Denial and Self-Assertion in Some Plays of Thomas Kilroy: *The Madame MacAdam Travelling Theatre*', in *Studies on the Contemporary Irish Theatre*, ed. Jacqueline Genet and Elisabeth Hellegouarc'h, Caen: Université de Caen

Heaney, Seamus (1975), *North*, London: Faber

(1980), *Preoccupations: Selected Prose 1968–1978*, London and Boston: Faber

(1983), *Sweeney Astray: A Version from the Irish*, Derry: Field Day

(1990), *The Cure at Troy: A Version of Sophocles' Philoctetes*, London: Faber / Field Day

(1995), *The Redress of Poetry: Oxford Lectures*, London and Boston: Faber

Hederman, Mark Patrick and Richard Kearney (1977), 'Editorial 1 / Endodermis', *Crane Bag*, I.1, pp. 3–5

Herr, Cheryl (1991), ed., *For the Land They Loved: Irish Political Melodramas, 1890–1925*, Syracuse: Syracuse University Press

Hewison, Robert (1981), *In Anger: British Culture in the Cold War*, New York: Oxford University Press

Hickey, Des and Gus Smith (1972), *A Paler Shade of Green*, London: Leslie Frewin, [American edn. entitled *Flight from the Celtic Twilight*, Indianapolis: Bobbs-Merrill, 1973]

Hill, Ian (1993), 'Staging the Troubles', *Theatre Ireland*, 31, pp. 42–46

Hobson, Bulmer (1934), ed., *The Gate Theatre Dublin*, Dublin: Gate Theatre

Hogan, Robert (1968), *After the Irish Renaissance: A Critical History of the Irish Drama since 'The Plough and the Stars'*, Minneapolis: University of Minnesota Press, 1967; London: Macmillan

(1970), ed., *Towards a National Theatre: The Dramatic Criticism of Frank J. Fay*, Dublin: Dolmen

(1972), ed., *Journal of Irish Literature*, 1.1, special issue on Paul Vincent Carroll

(1981), 'Denis Johnston's Horse Laugh' [*The Moon In the Yellow River*], in *Denis Johnston: A Retrospective*, ed. Joseph Ronsley, Gerrards Cross: Smythe; Totowa: Barnes & Noble, pp. 59–77

and James Kilroy (1978), *The Abbey Theatre: The Years of Synge 1905–1909*, vol. 3, *The Modern Irish Drama: A Documentary History*, Dublin: Dolmen Press, Atlantic Highlands: Humanities Press

References

and Richard Burnham (1992), *The Years of O'Casey, 1921–1926: A Documentary History*, Gerrards Cross: Smythe; Newark: University of Delaware Press;

Hogan, Thomas (1950), 'Theatre', *Envoy*, 2.6, pp. 80–84

Holland, Jack (1976), 'The Writer and the North', *Irish Times*, Arts and Studies, 29 June, p. 10

Holloway, Joseph (1967), *Joseph Holloway's Abbey Theatre: A Selection from his Unpublished Journal Impressions of a Dublin Playgoer*, ed. Robert Hogan and Michael J. O'Neill, London: Feffer and Simons; Carbondale and Edwardsville: Southern Illinois UP

Hosey, Seamus (1988), 'The Abbey in Russia', *Theatre Ireland*, 15, pp. 14–17

Hughes, Robert (1994), *Culture of Complaint: The Fraying of America*, rev. edn, London: Harrill/Harper Collins

Hunt, Hugh (1979), *The Abbey: Ireland's National Theatre 1904–1979*, Dublin: Gill and Macmillan

Hussey, Gemma (1993), *Ireland Today: Anatomy of a Changing State*, Dublin: Townhouse/Viking

Hutchinson, John (1987), *The Dynamics of Cultural Nationalism: The Gaelic Revival and the Creation of the Irish Nation State*, London: Allen and Unwin

Hyde, Douglas (1894), 'The Necessity for De-Anglicising Ireland', in *The Revival of Irish Literature*, London: Fisher Unwin, pp.117–61

Hynes, Garry (1993), 'Accepting the Fiction of being "National"', *Irish Times*, 3 May, p. 12

Innes, Christopher (1992), *Modern British Drama 1890–1990*, Cambridge: Cambridge University Press

—— (1993), *Avant-Garde Theatre 1892–1992*, London and New York: Routledge

Ireland, Denis (1941), 'The Abbey Theatre', *The Bell*, 2.3, pp. 67–8

Jeffares, A. N. (1988), *W. B. Yeats: A New Biography*, London: Hutchinson

Jeffs, Rae (1966), *Brendan Behan: Man and Showman*, London: Hutchinson

Johnson, Toni O'Brien (1982), *Synge: The Medieval and the Grotesque*, Gerrards Cross: Smythe

Johnston, Denis (1953), *Nine Rivers from Jordan: The Chronicle of a Journey and a Search*, London: Verschoyle

—— (1959), *In Search of Swift*, Dublin: Hodges Figgis

—— (1976), *The Brazen Horn: A Non-Book for Those Who, in Revolt Today, Could be in Command Tomorrow*, Dublin: Dolmen

—— (1977), *The Dramatic Works of Denis Johnston: Volume 1*, Gerrards Cross: Smythe

—— (1979), *The Dramatic Works of Denis Johnston: Volume 2*, Gerrards Cross: Smythe

—— (1992a), *The Dramatic Works of Denis Johnston: Volume 3*, ed. Joseph Ronsley, Gerrards Cross: Smythe

—— (1992b), *Orders and Desecrations: The Life of the Playwright Denis Johnston*, ed. Rory Johnston, Dublin: Lilliput

Joyce, James (1959), *The Critical Writings of James Joyce*, ed. Ellsworth Mason and Richard Ellmann, London: Faber

—— (1960) *Ulysses*, London: Bodley Head

Joyce, P. W. (1910), *English As We Speak it in Ireland*, Dublin: Gill, London: Longmans; repr. with an introduction by Terence Dolan, Dublin: Wolfhound Press, 1979

Kavanagh, Patrick (1964), *Collected Poems*, London: Macgibbon & Kee

References

(1977), *Patrick Kavanagh's Tarry Flynn: A Play in Two Acts*, adapted by P. J. O'Connor, New Abbey Theatre Series, vol. 1, n.p.: Proscenium

Kavanagh, Peter (1950), *The Story of the Abbey Theatre*, New York: Devin-Adair; repr. Orono: University of Maine at Orono, 1984

Kealy, Sister Marie Hubert (1993), *Kerry Playwright: Sense of Place in the Plays of John B. Keane*, Selinsgrove: Susquehanna University Press, London and Toronto: Associated University Press

Keane, John B. (1959), *Sive: A Play in Three Acts*, Dublin: Progress House

(1960), *Sharon's Grave: A Folk Play in Two Acts*, Dublin: Progress House

(1961a), *The Highest House on the Mountain: A Play in Three Acts*, Dublin: Progress House

(1961b), *Many Young Men of Twenty: A Play with Music*, Dublin: Progress House

(1963), *The Year of the Hiker: A Play in Three Acts*, Cork: Mercier

(1966), *The Field: A Play in Three Acts*, Cork: Mercier

(1968), *Hut 42*, 'Irish Play' series, no. 2, Dixon, California: Proscenium

(1969), *Big Maggie: A Play in Three Acts*, Dublin and Cork: Mercier

(1971), *Moll: A Comedy in Three Acts*, Cork: Mercier

(1981), *The Chastitute: A Play in Two Acts*, Dublin and Cork: Mercier

(1986), *The Bodhrán Makers*, Dingle: Brandon

(1990), *Three Plays: Sive, The Field, Big Maggie: New Revised Texts*, ed. Ben Barnes, Dublin and Cork: Mercier

Kearney, Colbert (1977), *The Writings of Brendan Behan*, Dublin: Gill and Macmillan

(1993), *The Consequence*, Belfast: Blackstaff

Kearney, Richard (1984), *Myth and Motherland*, Derry: Field Day

(1985), 'Language Play: Brian Friel and Ireland's Verbal Theatre', *Studies*, 72, pp. 20–56

(1988), *Transitions: Narratives in Modern Irish Culture*, Dublin; Wolfhound

Kelly, John and Ronald Schuchard (1994), eds, *The Collected Letters of W. B. Yeats*, vol. 3: *1901–1904*, Oxford: Clarendon

Kennedy, Kieran A. (1986), ed., *Ireland in Transition*, Cork and Dublin: Mercier

Kennedy, Maeve (1977), 'Saturday Profile: Jim Sheridan Chairman of the Project Arts Centre', *Irish Times*, (Weekend, p. 4)

Kenner, Hugh (1983), *A Colder Eye: The Modern Irish Writers*, London: Allen Lane; New York: Knopf

Keogh, Dermot (1994), *Twentieth-Century Ireland: Nation and State*, Dublin: Gill and Macmillan

Kermode, Frank (1975), ed., *Selected Prose of T. S. Eliot*, London: Faber

Kershaw, Baz (1992), *The Politics of Performance: Radical Theatre as Cultural Intervention*, London and New York: Routledge

Kiberd, Declan (1984), *Anglo-Irish Attitudes*, Derry: Field Day

(1993), *Synge and the Irish Language*, 2nd edn, Basingstoke: Macmillan

(1995), *Inventing Ireland*, London: Cape

Kilroy, James (1971), *The 'Playboy' Riots*, Irish Theatre Series 4, Dublin: Dolmen

Kilroy, Thomas (1959), 'Groundwork for an Irish Theatre', *Studies*, 48, pp. 192–8

(1969), *The Death and Resurrection of Mr Roche: A Comedy in Three Acts*, London: Faber

(1972), 'Synge and Modernism', *J. M. Synge Centenary Papers 1971*, ed. Maurice Harmon, Dublin: Dolmen, pp. 167–79

References

(1975), ed., *Sean O'Casey: A Collection of Critical Essays*, Englewood Cliffs, New Jersey: Prentice-Hall

(1979), *Talbot's Box: A Play in Two Acts*, Dublin: Gallery

(1981), 'The Moon in the Yellow River: Denis Johnston's Shavianism', *Denis Johnston: A Retrospective*, ed. Joseph Ronsley, Gerrards Cross: Smythe; Totowa: Barnes & Noble. pp. 49–58

(1986), *Double Cross*, London and Boston: Faber

(1991), *The Madame MacAdam Travelling Theatre: A Play*, London: Methuen

(1992), 'A Generation of Playwrights', *Irish University Review*, 22.1, pp. 135–41

(1995), *The O'Neill*, Loughcrew, Oldcastle: Gallery

King, Mary C. (1985), *The Drama of J. M. Synge*, Syracuse: Syracuse University Press

Kinsella, Thomas (1973), *Selected Poems 1956–1968*, Dublin: Dolmen

Kleiman, Carol (1982), *Sean O'Casey's Bridge of Vision: Four Essays on Structure and Perspective*, Toronto: University of Toronto Press

Knapp, James F. (1987), 'History against Myth: Lady Gregory and Cultural Discourse', *Éire-Ireland*, XXII.3, pp. 30–42

Knowland, A. S. (1983), *W. B. Yeats: Dramatist of Vision*, Gerrards Cross: Smythe; Totowa: Barnes & Noble

Kohfeldt, Mary Lou (1985) *Lady Gregory: The Woman Behind the Irish Renaissance*, London: Andre Deutsch

Kopper, Edward A., Jr. (1976), *Lady Isabella Persse Gregory*, Boston: Twayne

Kosok, Heinz (1982), 'Louis D'Alton', in *Dictionary of Literary Biography*, vol. 10, *Part 1: Modern British Dramatists, 1900–1945*, ed. Stanley Weintraub, Detroit: Gale, pp. 129–33

(1985); *O'Casey: The Dramatist*, Irish Literary Studies 19, Gerrards Cross: Smythe; Totowa: Barnes & Noble

(1995), *Plays and Playwrights from Ireland in International Perspective*, Trier: Wissenschaftlicher Verlag Trier

Krause, David (1975), *Sean O'Casey: The Man and His Work: An Enlarged Edition*, London: Collier Macmillan; New York: Macmillan,

(1982), *The Profane Book of Irish Comedy*, Ithaca: Cornell University Press

Kurdi, Mária (1993), 'The Ways of Twoness: Pairs, Parallels and Contrasts in Stewart Parker's *Spokesong*', *A Small Nation's Contribution to the World: Essays on Anglo-Irish Literature and Language*, ed. Donald E. Morse, Csilla Bertha and István Palffy, Gerrards Cross: Smythe; Debrecen: Lajos Kossuth University, pp. 61–9

Lamb, Charles (1964), 'On the Artificial Comedy of the Last Century (1822)', in *Theories of Comedy*, ed. Paul Lauter, New York: Doubleday / Anchor, pp. 295–302

Lanters, José (1996), 'Violence and Sacrifice in Brian Friel's *The Gentle Island* and *Wonderful Tennessee*', *Irish University Review*, 26, pp. 163–76

Larkin, Emmett (1965), *James Larkin: Irish Labour Leader 1876–1947*, London: Routledge

Larkin, Philip (1974), *High Windows*, London: Faber

Laurence, Dan and Nicholas Grene (1993), eds, *Shaw, Lady Gregory and the Abbey: A Correspondence and a Record*, Gerrards Cross: Smythe

Lee, J. J. (1989), *Ireland 1912–1985: Politics and Society*, Cambridge: Cambridge University Press

Leonard, Hugh (1964), *Stephen D*, London and New York: Evans

(1971), *The Patrick Pearse Motel: A Comedy*, London: French

References

(1979), 'An Open Letter to Mr. Haughey', *Sunday Independent*, 16 December

(1981), *Da, A Life, and Time Was*, Harmondsworth: Penguin

(1987), 'A Playwright's Diary', in *The Mask of Moriarty*, Dublin and London: Brophy Books, pp. 5–22

(1988), 'Introduction', *Summer*, Dublin and London: Brophy Books, pp. 5–7

(1992), *Kill*, in *Selected Plays*, ed. S. F. Gallagher, Gerrards Cross: Smythe; Washington, DC: Catholic University of America Press

(1994), *Moving: A Play*, London and New York: Samuel French

Littlewood, Joan (1994), *Joan's Book: Joan Littlewood's Peculiar History as She Tells It*, London: Methuen

Longley, Edna (1985), 'Poetry and Politics in Northern Ireland', *Crane Bag*, 9.1, pp. 26–40

(1994), *The Living Stream: Literature & Revisionism in Ireland*, Newcastle upon Tyne: Bloodaxe

Lowery, Robert G. (1984), ed., *A Whirlwind in Dublin: The Plough and the Stars' Riots*, Westport, Connecticut: Greenwood

Lucy, Gordon (1989), *The Ulster Covenant: A Pictorial History of the 1912 Home Rule Crisis*, Craigavon: New Ulster Publications

Luke, Peter (1978), ed., *Enter Certain Players: Edwards-MacLiammoir and the Gate 1928–1978*, Dublin: Dolmen

Lukács, Georg (1976), 'The Sociology of Modern Drama', in *The Theory of the Modern Stage*, ed. Eric Bentley, Harmondsworth: Penguin, rev. edn, pp. 425–50

Lynch, Martin (1982a), *Dockers*, Belfast: Farset Co-Operative Press

(1982b), *The Interrogation of Ambrose Fogarty: A Play in Three Acts*, Dundonald, Belfast: Blackstaff

Lyons, F. S. L. (1973), *Ireland Since the Famine*, rev. edn, Glasgow: Collins/Fontana

(1979), *Culture and Anarchy in Ireland 1890–1939*, Oxford: Oxford University Press

MacAnna, Tomás (1976), 'How Stands the Abbey? … Elgy Gillespie talks with Tomás MacAnna, the Theatre's Artistic Director', *Irish Times*, 4 November, p. 10

McCabe, Eugene (1978), *King of the Castle: A Play in Two Acts*, Dublin: Gallery

(1979), *Pull Down a Horseman/Gale Day*, Dublin: Gallery

McCann, Eamonn (1974), *War and an Irish Town*, Harmondsworth: Penguin

McDiarmid, Lucy (1994), 'Augusta Gregory, Bernard Shaw, and the Shewing-Up of Dublin Castle', *Publications of the Modern Language Association*, 109.1, pp. 26–44

(1995) and Maureen Waters (1995), eds, *Lady Gregory: Selected Writings*, Harmondsworth: Penguin

McGrath, F. C. (1990), 'Brian Friel and the Politics of the Anglo-Irish Language', *Colby Quarterly*, XXVI.4, pp. 241–8

McGuinness, Frank (1986), *Observe the Sons of Ulster Marching Towards the Somme*, London and Boston: Faber

(1987), 'We Are All Children of Enniskillen Now', *Irish Times*, 13 November, p. 8

(1988), *Carthaginians and Baglady*, London and Boston: Faber

(1991), 'An Irishman's Theatre', in *Studies on the Contemporary Irish Theatre*, ed. Jacqueleine Genet and Elisabeth Hellegouarc'h, Caen: Université de Caen, pp. 57–66

McHugh, Roger (1946), 'Dublin Theatre', *The Bell*, XIII. 3, p. 59

MacIntyre, Tom (1987), 'The Winter's In', programme note for *Strawboys*, by Michael Harding, Abbey Theatre, 4 August

References

(1988) and Patrick Kavanagh, *The Great Hunger: Poem into Play*, Dublin: Lilliput

(1991), Untitled programme note for *Ullaloo*, by Marina Carr, Abbey Theatre, 25 March

(1994), 'Where Your Treasure Is', programme note for *The Mai*, by Marina Carr, Abbey Theatre, 5 October

MacKenna, Stephen (1982), 'Stephen MacKenna on Synge: A Lost Memoir', ed. Nicholas Grene and Ann Saddlemyer, *Irish University Review*, 12, pp. 141–51

MacLiammóir, Micheál (1961), *All for Hecuba: An Irish Theatrical Autobiography* [1946], rev. edn, Dublin: Progress House

(1964), *Theatre in Ireland*, 2nd edn, Dublin: Cultural Relations Committee of Ireland

McMahon, Frank (1971), *Brendan Behan's Borstal Boy: Adapted for the Stage*, Dublin: Four Master

McMullan, Anna (1993), 'Irish Women Playwrights since 1958', in *British and Irish Women Dramatists since 1958*, ed. Trevor Griffiths and Margaret Llewellyn-Jones, Buckingham: Open University, pp. 110–23

MacNamara, Brinsley [n.d.] (1949), *Abbey Plays 1899–1948*, Dublin: Three Candles

Macqueen-Pope, W. (1954), *Ivor: The Story of an Achievement: A Biography of Ivor Novello*, London: Hutchinson

Magee, Heno (1978), *Hatchet*, Dublin: Gallery

Maher, Mary (1977), 'The Challenge of the Project', *Irish Times*, 26 January, p. 8

Mahon, Derek (1985), *High Time: A Comedy in One Act Based on Molière's 'The School for Husbands'*, Dublin: Gallery

Malone, Andrew E. (1929), *The Irish Drama*, London: Constable, rpt New York: Blom, 1965

Mamet, David (1988), 'A National Dream-life', in *Writing in Restaurants*, London and Boston: Faber, pp. 8–11

Martyn, Edward (1991), *The Heather Field*, in *The Field Day Anthology of Irish Writing*, vol. 2, ed. Seamus Deane, Derry: Field Day, pp. 568–97

Mason, Patrick (1993), '"A High Ambition": The Work of the National Theatre Society', in *Application to the Arts Council for a Grant-in-Aid to the National Theatre Society Ltd. for Year Ending 31st December 1994*, Dublin: Abbey Theatre, pp. 1–18

(1995), 'Artistic Policy', in *A Statement of Needs of the National Theatre Society Limited For Year Ending 31 December 1996*, pp. 1–17

Maxwell, D. E. S. (1973), *Brian Friel*, Lewisburg: Bucknell University Press

(1984), *A Critical History of Modern Irish Drama 1891–1980*, Cambridge: Cambridge University Press

(1990a), 'New Lamps for Old: The Theatre of Tom Murphy', *Theatre Research International*, 15.1, pp. 57–66

(1990b), 'Northern Ireland's Political Drama', *Modern Drama*, 33.1, pp. 1–14

Meir, Colin (1991), 'Irish Poetic Drama: Seamus Heaney's *The Cure at Troy*', in *Studies on the Contemporary Irish Theatre*, ed. Jacqueline Genet and Elisabeth Hellegouarc'h, Caen: Université de Caen, pp. 67–78

Mercier, Paul (1988), *Home*, Dublin: Passion Machine

(1990), 'A Man's Passion for a People's Theatre: Paul Mercier ... Talks to Francine Cunningham', *Irish Times*, 25 April, p. 8

Mercier, Vivian (1962), *The Irish Comic Tradition*, London and New York: Oxford University Press

References

(1994), *Modern Irish Literature: Sources and Founders*, ed. and presented by Eilis Dillon, Oxford: Clarendon

Meyer, Michael (1974), *Ibsen: A Biography*, Harmondsworth: Penguin

Mikhail, E. H. (1988), ed., *The Abbey Theatre: Interviews and Recollections*, Basingstoke: Macmillan

Miller, Liam (1977), *The Noble Drama of W. B. Yeats*. Dublin: Dolmen

Mitchell, Jack (1980), *The Essential O'Casey: A Study of the Twelve Major Plays of Sean O'Casey*, Berlin: Seven Seas

Molloy, M. J. (1953), *The King of Friday's Men; A Play in Three Acts*, Dublin: James Duffy

(1961a), *Old Road; A Comedy in Three Acts*, Dublin: Progress House

(1961b),*The Wood of the Whispering: A Comedy in Three Acts*, Dublin: Progress House

(1977), 'The Making of Folk-plays', in *Literature and Folk Culture: Ireland and Newfoundland*, ed. Alison Feder and Bernice Schrank, St John's: Memorial University of Newfoundland, pp. 59–80

Montague, John (1982), *Selected Poems*, Mountrath, Portlaoise: Dolmen

Moore, John Rees (1971), *Masks of Love and Death: Yeats as Dramatist*, Ithaca: Cornell University Press

Morgan, Austen (1988), *James Connolly: A Political Biography*, Manchester: Manchester University Press

Motion, Andrew (1993), *Philip Larkin: A Writer's Life*, London: Faber

Moynihan, Maurice (1980), ed., *Speeches and Statements by Eamon de Valera 1917–73*, Dublin: Gill and Macmillan, New York: St. Martin's

Muinzer, Philomena (1987), 'Evacuating the Museum: The Crisis of Playwriting in Ulster', *New Theatre Quarterly*, 3.9, pp. 44–63

Muir, Kenneth (1970), *The Comedy of Manners*, London: Hutchinson

Murphy, John (1963), *The Country Boy*, Dublin: Progress House

Murphy, Thomas [Tom] (1976) *On the Outside/On the Inside*, Dublin: Gallery

(1978), *A Crucial Week in the Life of a Grocer's Assistant*, Dublin: Gallery

(1980), 'Back to Broad Strokes: John Boland Talks to Playwright Tom Murphy', *Hibernia*, 6 March, p. 21

(1984), *A Whistle in the Dark*, Dublin: Gallery

(1992), *Plays: One: Famine, The Patriot Game, The Blue Macushla*, London: Methuen

(1993), *Plays: Two: Conversations on a Homecoming, Bailegangaire, A Thief of a Christmas*, London: Methuen

(1994), *Plays: Three: The Morning after Optimism, The Sanctuary Lamp, The Gigli Concert*, London: Methuen

Murray, Christopher (1979), 'Early Shakespearean Productions by the Abbey Theatre', *Theatre Notebook*, XXXIII, pp. 66–79

(1986), 'Lennox Robinson: The Abbey's Anti-hero', in *Irish Writers and the Theatre*, ed. Masaru Sekine, Gerrards Cross: Smythe; Totowa: Barnes & Noble, pp. 114–34

(1994), 'Billy Roche's *Wexford Trilogy*: Setting, Place, Critique', in *L'Irlande Aujourd'hui / Ireland Today*, ed. Adolphe Haberer, Lyon: Presses Universitaires de Lyon, pp. 11–24

(1995), 'Introduction: The Stifled Voice', *Irish University Review*, 25.1, *Jubilee Issue: Teresa Deevy and Irish Women Playwrights*, pp. 1–10

Murray, T. C. (1964), *Autumn Fire: A Play in Three Acts*, Dublin: Duffy

References

Mursi, Waffia (1987), 'Molière and the Abbey Theatre', in *Literary Interrelations: Ireland, England and the World*, ed. Wolfgang Zach and Heinz Kosok, 1 *Reception and Translation*,Tübingen: Gunter Narr, pp. 69–74.

Nagler, A. M. (1952), *A Source Book in Theatrical History*, New York: Dover

Nairn, Tom (1977), *The Break-Up of Britain: Crisis and Neo-Nationalism*, London: NLB

Nathan, Leonard E. (1965), *The Tragic Drama of William Butler Yeats: Figures in a Dance*, New York: Columbia University Press

Ní Dhonnchadha, Máirín and Theo Dorgan (1991), eds, *Revising the Rising*, Derry: Field Day

Ní Dhorchaí, Proinsias (1981), ed., *Brendan Behan: Poems and a Play in Irish*, with an introduction by Declan Kiberd, Dublin: Gallery

Nic Shiubhlaigh, Maire (1955), *The Splendid Years: Recollections of Maire Nic Shiubhlaigh, as Told to Edward Kenny*, Dublin: Duffy

Nietzsche, Friedrich (1956), *The Birth of Tragedy and The Genealogy of Morals*, trans. Francis Golffing, New York: Doubleday

Nowlan, David (1985), '"Observe the Sons of Ulster Marching Towards the Somme" at the Peacock', *Irish Times*, 19 February, p. 10

O'Brien, Conor Cruise (1972), *States of Ireland*, London: Hutchinson

(1994), *Ancestral Voices: Religion and Nationalism in Ireland*, Dublin: Poolbeg

O'Brien, George (1990), *Brian Friel*, Boston: Twayne

O'Brien, John (1989), 'Expressionism and the Formative Years: Insights from the Early Diaries of Denis Johnston', *Canadian Journal of Irish Studies*, XV.1, pp. 34–57

O'Byrne, Robert (1992), 'A Life of Drama: Robert O'Byrne Talks to Hugh Leonard', *Irish Times*, 20 April, p. 8

O'Casey, Sean (1949–51), *Collected Plays*, 4 vols., London: Macmillan

(1955), *The Bishop's Bonfire: A Sad Play Within the Tune of a Polka*, London: Macmillan

(1956), *Mirror in My House: The Autobiographies of Sean O'Casey*, 2 vols., New York: Macmillan

(1960), *The Drums of Father Ned: A Mickrocosm of Ireland*, London: St Martin's

(1961), *Behind the Green Curtains, Figuro in the Night, The Moon Shines on Kylenamoe: Three Plays*, London: Macmillan; New York: St Martin's

(1962), *Feathers from the Green Crow: Sean O'Casey, 1905 1925*, ed. Robert Hogan, Columbia: University of Missouri Press; London: Macmillan, 1963

(1965), *Three More Plays: The Silver Tassie, Purple Dust, Red Roses for Me*, London: Macmillan, New York: St Martin's. Quotations from *Red Roses from Me* are from this edition, O'Casey's final, approved version

(1967), *Blasts and Benedictions: Articles and Stories*, selected and introduced by Ronald Ayling, London: Macmillan, New York: St Martin's

(1975–92), *The Letters of Sean O'Casey*, ed. David Krause, 4 vols., vol. 1, London: Macmillan/Cassell, vol. 2, New York: Macmillan, vols. 3 and 4, Washington, DC: Catholic University of America Press

(1980), *The Harvest Festival: A Play in Three Acts*, with a foreword by Eileen O'Casey and introduction by John O'Riordan, Gerrards Cross: Smythe

(1991), *Cock-a-Doodle Dandy*, ed. David Krause, Washington, DC: Catholic University of America Press; Gerrards Cross: Smythe

Ó Catháin, Séamus (1995), *The Festival of Brigit: Celtic Goddess and Holy Woman*, Blackrock, Co. Dublin: DBA Publications

[263]

References

O'Connor, Frank (1941), 'Public Opinion: The Stone Dolls', *The Bell*, 2.3, pp. 61–68
  (1971), *My Father's Son*, London: Pan, repr. Belfast: Blackstaff, 1994
O'Connor, Ulick (1970), *Brendan Behan*, London: Hamish Hamilton
Ó Crohan, Tomás (1937), *The Islandman*, trans. from the Irish by Robin Flower,
  Dublin: Talbot Press; London: Chatto and Windus
O'Donnell, Mary (1990), 'Putting a Misogynistic World to Right', *Sunday Tribune*,
  10 June, Arts, p. 27
O'Faolain, Sean (1942), *The Great O'Neill: A Biography of Hugh O'Neill Earl of Tyrone,
  1550–1616*, London: Longmans, repr. Cork: Mercier, 1970
  (1969), *The Irish*, revised edn, Harmondsworth: Penguin
O'Halloran, Clare (1987), *Partition and the Limits of Irish Nationalism: An Ideology
  under Stress*, Dublin: Gill & Macmillan
Ó hAodha, Micheál (1974), *Theatre in Ireland*, Oxford: Blackwell
  (1990), *The Importance of Being Micheál*, Cooleen, Dingle: Brandon Books
O'Malley, Conor (1988), *A Poets' Theatre*, Dublin: Elo Press
O'Neill, Michael (1964), *Lennox Robinson*, New York: Twayne
O'Sullivan, Maurice (1953), *Twenty Years A-Growing: Rendered from the Original Irish
  with a Preface* by Moya Llewelyn Davies and George Thomson, Oxford: Oxford
  University Press
O'Sullivan, Seumas (1946), *The Rose and Bottle and Other Essays*, Dublin: Talbot Press
O'Toole, Fintan (1982), 'The Man from God Knows Where: An Interview with
  Brian Friel', *In Dublin*, 28 October, pp. 20–3
  (1987), *The Politics of Magic: The Work and Times of Tom Murphy*, Dublin: Raven
  Arts, revised edn, Dublin: New Island Books/London: Nick Hern Books 1995
Ó Tuathaigh, M. A. G. [Gearóid] (1986), 'The Regional Dimension', in *Ireland in
  Transition*, ed. Kieran A. Kennedy, Cork and Dublin: Mercier, pp. 120–32
Orr, Philip (1987), *The Road to the Somme: Men of the Ulster Division Tell Their Story*,
  Dundonald, Belfast: Blackstaff
Parker, Stewart (1980), *Spokesong*, New York: French
  (1981), 'State of Play', *Canadian Journal of Irish Studies*, 7.1, pp. 5–11
  (1986), *Dramatis Personae: A John Malone Memorial Lecture*, Belfast: Queen's University
  (1989), *Three Plays for Ireland: Northern Star, Heavenly Bodies, Pentecost*, Birmingham: Oberon
Parkin, Andrew (1978), *The Dramatic Imagination of W. B. Yeats*, Dublin: Gill and
  Macmillan
Paulin, Tom (1983), *A New Look at the Language Question*, Derry: Field Day
  (1985), *The Riot Act: A Version of Sophocles' 'Antigone'*, London and Boston: Faber
Peacock, Alan J. (1993), ed., *The Achievement of Brian Friel*, Gerrards Cross: Smythe
Pearce, Donald R. (1960), ed., *The Senate Speches of W. B. Yeats*, Bloomington,
  Indiana: Indiana University Press
Pierce, David (1995), *Yeats's Worlds: Ireland, England and the Poetic Imagination*, New
  Haven and London: Yale University Press
Pilkington, Lionel (1990), 'Language and Politics in Brian Friel's *Translations*', *Irish
  University Review*, 20, pp. 282–98
Pine, Richard (1990), *Brian Friel and Ireland's Drama*, London and New York:
  Routledge
Plunkett, James (1978), *The Risen People*, Dublin: The Irish Writers' Cooperative

References

Reid, Christina (1987), *Joyriders & Tea in a China Cup: Two Belfast Plays*, London: Methuen

(1989), *The Belle of the Belfast City [and] Did You Hear the One About the Irishman ...?: Two Plays*, London: Methuen

(1993), *Joyriders and Did You Hear the One About the Irishman?*, London: Heinemann Educational

Reid, J. Graham (1980a), *The Death of Humpty Dumpty*, Dublin: Co-Op Books

(1980b), *The Closed Door*, Dublin: Co-Op Books

(1982), *The Plays of Graham Reid: Too Late to Talk to Billy, Dorothy, The Hidden Curriculum*, Dublin: Co-Op Books

(1985), *Remembrance*, London and Boston: Faber

Reynolds, Lorna (1972), 'The Rhythms of Synge's Dramatic Prose', *Yeats Studies*, 2, pp. 52–65

Richards, Shaun (1989), 'Refiguring Lost Narratives – Prefiguring New Ones: The Theatre of Tom Murphy, *Canadian Journal of Irish Studies*, 15.1, pp. 80–100

Richtarik, Marilynn J. (1994), *Acting Between the Lines: The Field Day Theatre Company and Irish Cultural Politics 1980–1984*, Oxford: Clarendon

Ritchie, Harry (1988), *Success Stories: Literature and the Media in England, 1950–1959*, London and Boston: Faber

Robbins, Frank (1977), *Under the Starry Plough: Recollections of the Irish Citizen Army*, Dublin: Academy Press

Robinson, Lennox (1911),*The Clancy Name*, in *Two Plays: Harvest: The Clancy Name*, Dublin: Maunsel

(1918), *The Lost Leader: A Play in Three Acts*, Dublin: Eiglas Press

(1931), *The Far-Off Hills: A Comedy in Three Acts*, London: Chatto

(1939a), *Killycreggs in Twilight & Other Plays*, London: Macmillan

(1939b), ed., *The Irish Theatre: Lectures Delivered during the Abbey Theatre Festival Held in Dublin in August 1938*, London: Macmillan, repr. New York: Haskell, 1971

(1942), *Curtain Up: An Autobiography*, London: Michael Joseph

(1946), ed., *Lady Gregory's Journals 1916–1930*, London: Putnam

(1951), *Ireland's Abbey Theatre: A History 1899–1951*, London: Sidgwick and Jackson

(1982), *The Big House*, in *Selected Plays of Lennox Robinson*, ed. Christopher Murray, Gerrards Cross: Smythe; Washington, DC: Catholic University of America Press

Roche, Anthony (1994), *Contemporary Irish Drama: From Beckett to McGuinness*, Gill's Studies in Irish Literature, Dublin: Gill and Macmillan

Roche, Billy (1992), *The Wexford Trilogy*, London: Nick Hern

Rumpf, E. and A. C. Hepburn (1977), *Nationalism and Socialism in Twentieth-Century Ireland*, Liverpool: Liverpool University Press

Ryan, John (1975), *Remembering How We Stood: Bohemian Dublin at the Mid-Century*, Dublin: Gill and Macmillan

Ryan, W. P. (1919), *The Irish Labour Movement: From the 'Twenties to Our Own Day*, Dublin: Talbot Press; London: Fisher Unwin

Sacks, Oliver (1995), 'To See and Not See', in *An Anthropologist on Mars: Seven Paradoxical Tales*, London: Picador, pp. 102–44

Saddlemyer, Ann (1966), *In Defence of Lady Gregory, Playwright*, Dublin: Dolmen

(1977), 'Augusta Gregory, Irish Nationalist: "After all, What is Wanted but a

References

Hag and a Voice?"', in *Myth and Reality in Irish Literature*, ed. Joseph Ronsley, Waterloo Ontario: Wilfrid Laurier University Press, pp. 29–40

(1982), ed., *Theatre Business: The Correspondence of the First Abbey Directors: William Butler Yeats, Lady Gregory and J. M. Synge*, Gerrards Cross: Smythe and Colin Smythe (1987), eds., *Lady Gregory, Fifty Years After*, Irish Literary Studies 13, Gerrards Cross: Smythe, Totowa: Barnes & Noble

Said, Edward W. (1993), *Culture & Imperialism*, London: Chatto

Sekine, Masaru and Christopher Murray (1990), *Yeats and the Noh: A Comparative Study*, Irish Literary Studies 38, Gerrards Cross: Smythe

Setterquist, Jan (1951), *Ibsen and the Beginnings of Anglo-Irish Drama, 1, John Millington Synge*, Uppsala and Dublin

Shaughnessy, Edward L. (1988), *Eugene O'Neill in Ireland: The Critical Reception*, Westport, Connecticut: Greenwood

Shaw, Bernard (1957), *The Quintessence of Ibsenism* [1891], 3rd edn repr., New York: Hill and Wang

(1959), *Shaw on Theatre*, ed. E. J. West, New York: Hill and Wang

(1962), *The Matter with Ireland*, ed. David H. Greene and Dan H. Laurence, London: Hart-Davis

(1963), *Complete Plays with Prefaces*, 6 vols, New York: Dodd Mead

Sheaffer, Louis (1974), *O'Neill: Son and Artist*, London: Elek

Sheehan, Helena (1987), *Irish Television Drama: A Society and its Stories*, Dublin: Radio Telefis Eireann

Sheridan, Jim, *Mobile Homes* (1978), Dublin: Irish Writers' Cooperative

Shiels, George (1942), *The Rugged Path & The Summit: Plays in Three Acts*, London: Macmillan

Simpson, Alan (1962), *Beckett and Behan and a Theatre in Dublin*, London: Routledge

(1978), ed., *Brendan Behan: The Complete Plays*, London, Methuen

Sitzmann, Fr. Marion OSB (1975), *Indomitable Irishery [sic]: Paul Vincent Carroll: Study and Interview*, Salzburg: Institut für Englische Sprache und Literatur

Sloan, Barry (1993), 'Sectarianism and the Protestant Mind: Some Approaches to a Current Theme in Irish Drama', *Études Irlandaises*, 18.2, pp. 33–43

Smith, Peter Alderson (1987), *W. B. Yeats and the Tribes of Danu: Three Views of Ireland's Fairies*, Gerrards Cross: Smythe, Totowa: Barnes & Noble

St Peter, Christine (1987) 'Denis Johnston, the Abbey and the Spirit of the Age', *Irish University Review*, 17, pp. 187–206

Steiner, George (1975), *After Babel: Aspects of Language and Translation*, Oxford: Oxford University Press

Stewart, A. T. Q. (1989), *The Narrow Ground: The Roots of Conflict in Ulster*, rev. edn, London and Boston: Faber

Styan, J. L. (1981), *Modern Drama in Theory and Practice*, vol.1: *Realism and Naturalism*, Cambridge: Cambridge University Press

Swift, Carolyn (1985), *Stage by Stage*, Dublin: Poolbeg

Synge, J. M. (1962–8), *Collected Works*, 4 vols., general ed. Robin Skelton, *Plays Book 1* and *Plays Book 2*, ed. Ann Saddlemyer, *Prose* ed. Alan Price, Oxford: Oxford University Press, new edn, Gerrards Cross: Smythe, 1982

(1982), *When the Moon Has Set*, ed. Mary C. King, in *Long Room*, 24 & 25, pp. 9–40

(1983–4), *The Collected Letters of John Millington Synge*, ed. Ann Saddlemyer, 2 vols., Oxford: Clarendon.

References

Taylor, Richard (1976), *The Drama of W. B. Yeats: Irish Myth and the Japanese Nō*, New Haven and London: Yale University Press

Taylor, Ronald (1980), trans., ed., *Aesthetics and Politics: Ernst Bloch, Georg Lukács, Bertolt Brecht, Walter Benjamin, Theodor Adorno*, London and New York: Verso

Thompson, Sam (1970), *Over the Bridge*, ed. Stewart Parker, Dublin: Gill and Macmillan

Tobin, Fergal (1984), *The Best of Decades: Ireland in the Nineteen Sixties*, Dublin: Gill and Macmillan

Torchiana, Donald T. (1966), *W. B. Yeats & Georgian Ireland*, London: Oxford University Press; Evanston: Northwestern University Press

Trench, Richard Chenevix (1898), *English Past and Present*, 19th edn, London: Kegan Paul

Ure, Peter (1963), *Yeats the Playwright: A Commentary on Character and Design in the Major Plays*, London: Routledge and Kegan Paul; New York: Barnes & Noble

Wade, Allan (1954), ed., *The Letters of W. B. Yeats*, London: Rupert-Davis

Wall, Richard (1987), ed., trans., *An Giall: The Hostage*, Gerrards Cross: Smythe; Washington, DC: Catholic University of America Press

Wardle, Irving (1978), *The Theatres of George Devine*, London: Cape

Waters, Maureen (1995), 'Lady Gregory's *Grania*: a feminist voice', *Irish University Review*, 25, pp. 11–24

Watson, G. J. (1994), *Irish Identity and the Literary Revival: Synge, Yeats, Joyce and O'Casey*, 2nd edn, Critical Studies in Irish Literature, vol. 4, Washington, DC: Catholic University of America Press

Watt, Stephen (1991), *Joyce, O'Casey, and the Irish Popular Theater*, Syracuse: Syracuse University Press

Welch, Robert (1993a), ed., *W. B. Yeats: Writings on Irish Folklore, Legend and Myth*, Harmondsworth: Penguin

(1993b), '"Isn't This Your Job? – To Translate?": Brian Friel's Languages', in *The Achievement of Brian Friel*, ed. Alan J. Peacock, Gerrards Cross: Smythe, pp. 134–48

Weygandt, Cornelius (1913), *Irish Plays and Playwrights*, London: Constable; Boston and New York: Houghton Mifflin

[Whitaker, T. K.] (1958), *Economic Development*, Dublin: Stationery Office

(1986), 'Economic Development 1958–1985', in *Ireland in Transition*, ed. Kieran A. Kennedy, Cork and Dublin: Mercier, pp. 10–18

White, Anna MacBride, and A. Norman Jeffares (1992), eds., *The Gonne-Yeats Letters 1893–1938: Always Your Friend*, London: Hutchinson

White, Jack (1976), 'Battle of the Somme: How 6,000 Familes Heard of "Thiepvall"', *Irish Times*, 1 July, p. 5

(1978), *The Last Eleven: A Play in Three Acts*, n.p.: Proscenium Press

White, Victoria (1990–1), 'Review of *Misogynist*', in *Theatre Ireland* 24, p. 41

Whyte, J. H. (1980), *Church and State in Modern Ireland 1923–1979*, 2nd edn, Dublin: Gill and Macmillan, Totowa, NJ: Barnes & Noble

Widgery, The Rt Hon. Lord (1972), *Report of the Tribunal Appointed to Inquire into the Events on Sunday, 30th January 1972*, London: Her Majesty's Stationery Office

Willett, John (1964), ed., trans., *Brecht on Theatre: The Development of an Aesthetic*, New York: Hill and Wang

Williams, Raymond (1968), *Drama from Ibsen to Brecht*, London: Chatto

Wilson, Edmund (1961), 'Philoctetes: The Wound and the Bow', in *The Wound and*

References

the Bow: Seven Studies in Literature, London: Methuen, pp. 244–64

Woodworth, Paddy (1993), 'Straight from the Arts; Field Day Calls it a Night', *Irish Times*, 29 April, p. 8

Worth, Katharine (1978) *The Irish Drama of Europe from Yeats to Beckett*, London: Athlone

—— (1993), 'Translations of History: Story-telling in Brian Friel's Theatre', in *British and Irish Drama since 1960*, ed. James Acheson, Basingstoke: Macmillan, pp. 73–87

Wright, Frank (1987), *Northern Ireland: A Comparative Analysis*, Dublin: Gill and Macmillan; Totowa: Barnes and Noble

Yeats, W. B. (1900), 'Edward Martyn's *Maeve*', *Beltaine*, no. 2, February, p. 3

—— (1921), *Four Plays for Dancers*, London: Macmillan

—— (1950), *The Collected Poems of W. B. Yeats*, 2nd edn, London: Macmillan

—— (1952) *The Collected Plays of W. B. Yeats*, London: Macmillan

—— (1959), *Mythologies*, London: Macmillan

—— (1961a) *Essays and Introductions*, London: Macmillan

—— (1961b), *Autobiographies*, London: Macmillan

—— (1962a), *Explorations*, selected by Mrs W. B. Yeats, London: Macmillan

—— (1962b), *A Vision*, London: Macmillan

—— (1966) *The Variorum Edition of the Plays of W. B. Yeats*, ed. Russell K. Alspach, London: Macmillan

—— (1972), *Memoirs: Autobiography – First Draft: Journal*, transcribed and edited Denis Donoghue, London: Macmillan

—— (1975), *Uncollected Prose*, vol. 2, ed. John P. Frayne and Colton Johnson, London: Macmillan

Young, Lorna D. (1987), 'In Retrospect: Lady Gregory's Plays Fifty Years Later', in *Lady Gregory, Fifty Years After*, ed. Ann Saddlemyer and Colin Smythe, Gerrards Cross: Smythe, Totowa : Barnes & Noble, pp. 291–306

Zach, Wolfgang (1988), 'Brian Friel's *Translations*: National and Universal Dimensions', in *Medieval and Modern Ireland*, ed. Richard Wall, Gerrards Cross: Smythe, pp. 74–90

—— (1989), 'Criticism, Theatre, and Politics: Brian Friel's *The Freedom of the City* and its Early Reception', in *Kunstgriffe: Auskunfte zur Reichweite von Literaturtheorie und Literaturkritik: Festschrift für Herbert Mainusch*, ed. Ulrich Horstmann and Wolfgang Zach, Frankfurt-on-Main: Lang, pp. 418–34, rpr in *Irish Literature and Culture* (1992), ed. Michael Kenneally, Gerrards Cross: Smythe, pp. 112–26

Zwerdling, Alex (1965), *Yeats and the Heroic Ideal*, New York: New York University Press

Index

Note: page numbers in **bold** refer to main entries. Plays are listed under playwrights' names

Abbey Theatre, 4, 7, 13, 14, 15, 22, 24, 25, 28, 29, 31, 37, 38, 39, 43, 50, 52, 53, 54, 56, 62, 64, 74, 81, 83, 87, 91, 104, 105, 113, 114, 115, 119, 120, 127, 130, 131, 134, 135, 136, 137, 140, 141, 142, 143, 150, 152, 153, 155, 156, 158, 160, 163, 165, 166, 173, 175, 181, 183, 184, 186, 200, 201, 206, 208, 210, 226, 229, 232, 233, 238, 239, 242, 245
Adams, Hazard, 58, 61
Agate, James, 103, 107
Agnew, Paddy, 213
Allgood, Molly (1887–1952), 65, 72
Allgood, Sara (1883–1950), 56, 113
Anderson, Benedict, 246
Andrews, Elmer, 163, 198
Andrews, J. H. (John), 216
Antoine, André (1858–1943), 17, 70
Ardagh, John, 175, 223
Arden, John, 90, 181
    Non-Stop Connolly Show, 181
Artaud, Antonin (1896–1948), 217
avant-garde, 154, **231–8**
Ayling, Ronald, 89, 103

Banville, John, 5
Barnes, Ben, 239
Barnes, Clive, 233
Barry, Sebastian, 36, 225, **243–4**
    Boss Grady's Boys, 243
    Only True History, 244

Prayers of Sherkin, 243–4
Steward of Chistendom, 244
White Woman Street, 244
and Beckett, 244
and McGahern, 244
Basterot, Florimond Jacques (1836–1904), Comte de, 2
Battersby, Eileen, 215
Beckett, J. C., 197–8
Beckett, Samuel, 6, 12, 31, 35, 51, 89, 102, 129, 138, 148, 154, 155, 168, 198, 201, 235, 236, 244, 246
    All That Fall, 138, 148
    Disjecta, 168
    Endgame, 129
    Waiting for Godot, 148, 154, 235
Behan, Beatrice, 157
Behan, Brendan, 43, 112, 138, 145, **148–61**, 173, 174, 181, 198, 217
    Borstal Boy, 152, 156, 157, 160, 181
    An Giall, 156–8, 159
    Hostage, 149, 156, 157–9
    Landlady, 150–1
    Letters, 150, 151, 157, 160
    Richard's Cork Leg, 159–60
Behan, Brian, 149
Behan, Dominic, 151
Bell, Sam Hanna, 189
Benjamin, Walter, 231
Bentley, Eric, 32
Bhabba, Homi, 5
Big House theme, 31, 32, 118, 147, 244

Index

and Sebastian Barry, 244
and M. J. Molloy, 147
and Robinson, 118
and Yeats, 31–2
Billington, Michael, 241
Bloom, Harold, 26, 69
Blunt, Wilfrid Scawen, 41, 59
Blythe, Ernest, 113, 141, 142, 152, 155,
    173, 187
Boal, Augusto, 54
Bolger, Dermot, 239, **242–3**
    In High Germany , 242–3
    Lament for Arthur Cleary, 242
    One Last White Horse, 242
    and Yeats, 242
Bort, Eberhard, 195, 225
Boucicault, Dion, 89, 198
Bourke, Ken, 239
    Wild Harvest, 239
Bourke, P. J., 154, 155
Boyd, Ernest, 11
Boyd, John, 188, 189, 190, 193
    The Flats, 188, 189–90
Boyle, William, 83
Bond, Edward, 203
Boyle, Ted E., 150
Brecht, Bertolt, 88, 96, 159, 178, 183,
    184, 201, 229
Brook, Peter, 88
Brown, Terence, 139, 179, 219
Brighton, Pam, 195
Büchner, Georg (1813–37), 159
Burke, Patrick, 209
Byrne, David (director), 242
Byrne, Seamus, 152

Carney, Frank, 10, 144
Carr, Marina, **235–8**
    Low in the Dark, 235
    This Love Thing, 235, 236
    The Mai, 236–7
    Portia Coughlan, 237–8
    Ullaloo, 236, 237
    and Beckett, 235, 236
    and feminism, 235–8
Carroll, Paul Vincent, 9, 115, **129–37**,
    176
    Shadow and Substance, 132–4

White Steed, 134, 136–7
Campbell, Joseph, 97
Canfield, Curtis, 12, 118
Carson, Sir Edward, 192, 205
Carty, Ciaran, 208
Cave, Desmond, 123
Cave, Richard Allen, 178
Charabanc, 195
Chekhov, Anton, 58, 86, 88, 95, 96,
    213, 221
Clarke, Austin, 36, 131, 231
Collins, Michael, 149, 233
Colum, Padraic, 8, 69, 130
    The Land, 8–9
Connolly, James, 93, 97, 98, 111, 181
Corkery, Daniel, 136, 165
Coveney, Michael, 236
Coxhead, Elizabeth, 55, 58, 62
Coyle, Jane, 195
Craig, May, 30
Cranston, Des, 188
Cronin, Anthony, 160, 174
cultural nationalism, 3, 4, 6, 8, 42, 111,
    164, 222, 245
Cupitt, Don, 175, 178

D'Alton, Louis, 138, **142–6**, 166, 167
    Lovers Meeting, 143–4
    Man in the Cloak, 142
    Money Doesn't Matter, 143
    They Got What They Wanted, 143
    This Other Eden, 145, 146, 149, 166–7
Dantanus, Ulf, 169
D'Arcy, Margaretta, 181
Davis, Thomas, 3, 4
Deane, Seamus, 190, 207, 209, 214, 221
De Búrca, Séamus, 150, 155, 174
Deevy, Teresa, 143, 237, 238
    Katie Roche, 143, 238
de Jongh, Nicholas, 174
Dermody, Frank, 156
de Valera, Éamon, 10, 118, 138, 139,
    141, 144, 149, 160, 224, 246
de Valois, Ninette, 28
Devine, George, 165
Devlin, Anne, 188, 193, 194
Devlin, Bernadette, 187, 200
Donnelly, Neil, 239

Index

Donoghue, Denis, 29, 246
Dowling, Joe, 239
Doyle, Roddy, 46, 241
Druid Theatre Company, 143–4, 238
Dublin Drama League, 119
Dublin Theatre Festival, 112, 177, 196, 229, 242
Dürrenmatt, Friedrich, 102, 159

Eagleton, Terry, 208
Edwards, Hilton, 7, 29, 119, 120
Edwards, Philip, 15, 127
Ellis-Fermor, Una, 12, 13, 40, 49, 55
Eliot, T. S., 23, 26, 35, 174, 219
Ellmann, Richard, 23
Ervine, St John, 8, 189, 192, 193
Etherton, Michael, 163
Ewart-Biggs, Christopher, 206
expressionism, 106, 121, 123

Fallon, Gabriel, 101, 113, 132, 136, 138, 155, 156
Fanning, Ronan, 139, 200
Farquhar, George (1677?–1707), 198
Farrell, Bernard, 239, **240–1**
Fay, Frank (1870–1931) , 20
Fay, William George (1872–1947), 49, 77, 115
Field Day Anthology of Irish Writing, 162, 208, 214, 221
Field Day Theatre Company, 10, 188, 198, **207–22**
    aims, 209
    definition, 208
    directors, 207
    pamphlets, 208, 209, 214, 216, 217
    productions, 207–8
        and Abbey, 208, 210, 221
        and fifth province, 210
        and history, myth, vision, 216–21
        and language, identity, 210–15
Findlater, Richard, 174
Fitzgerald, Barry (William Joseph Shields), 55, 113
Fitzmaurice, George, 231, 238
Fitz–Simon, Christopher, 174
Flannery, James W., 13, 14, 16
Flynn, Mannix, 181

Forristal, Desmond, 178
Foster, John Wilson, 189
Foster, Roy, 65, 66, 67, 124
Frazier, Adrian, 21
Friel, Brian, 6, 7, 10, 16, 42, 89, 110, 112, 134, 140, 162, 163, 164, 168, 173, 176, 177, 184, 185, 195, 197, **207–13**, 221, 223, 224, 236, 237
    Aristocrats, 170
    Communication Cord, 185, 208, 209, 213
    Dancing at Lughnasa, 110, 140, 176, 221, 227–8
    The Enemy Within, 168
    Faith Healer, 16, 170, 176, 228
    The Freedom of the City, 195, 200–2, 207
    The Gentle Island, 170, 228
    Living Quarters, 173, 176
    The Loves of Cass Maguire, 169
    Making History, 184, 208, 214, 216
    Molly Sweeney, 170, 228
    The Mundy Scheme, 184–5
    Philadelphia, 168–9, 176
    Three Sisters, 208, 213
    Translations, 197, 208, 209, 210–12, 213, 215, 223
        and Chekhov, 213
        and Heaney, 211, 215
        and history, 216
        and language, 210–12, 216
        and melodrama, 211
        and myth, 217
        and Turgenev, 213
    Volunteers, 202
    Wonderful Tennessee, 177, 228
    and cultural nationalism, 164, 227–8
    and emigration/exile, 168–70
    and farce, 185, 214
    and history play, 184
    and Northern drama, 195, 197, 200, 201
    and political allegory, 184–5
    and religious consciousness, 176–7
Frye, Northrop, 86
Fugard, Athol, 208

Gael-Linn, 156

Index

Gaelic League, 42, 81
Gallagher, S. F. (Sean Finbarr), 254
Galvin, Patrick, 195–6
Gate Theatre, 7, 119, 120, 122, 123, 153, 178, 210, 239
Gillespie, Elgy, 202
Gogarty, Oliver St John, 40
Gonne, Maud, 4, 20, 21, 37, 56, 67, 74
Goodman, Lizbeth, 236
Grant, David, 234
Greaves, C. Desmond, 99
Gregory, Isabella Augusta, Lady (née Persse), 1, 2, 3, 5, 6, 9, 14, 19, 25, 27, 32, **37–63**, 64, 104,105, 114, 119, 120, 121, 130, 134, 140, 151, 183, 224
  Aristotle's Bellows, 60
  Bogie Men, 48
  Book of Saints and Wonders, 44
  Canavans, 53, 57
  Cuchulain of Muirthemne, 44
  Dave, 62
  Dervorgilla, 27, 53, 58
  Diaries, 2
  Full Moon, 50, 56
  Gaol Gate, 46, 50, 56, 151
  Gods and Fighting Men, 44, 58, 59
  Golden Apple, 60
  Grania, 50, 58–9
  Hyacinth Halvey, 50
  Image, 51–2, 57, 63
  Jackdaw, 50
  Journals, 39, 61, 62, 104, 120–1
  Kincora, 57, 61
  Our Irish Theatre, 38, 42, 44, 47, 53, 54, 224
  Poets and Dreamers, 43, 53
  Rising of the Moon, 50–1, 62
  Sancho's Master, 55
  Seventy Years, 37, 38, 42, 44, 47, 54, 56
  Shanwalla, 49, 60
  Spreading the News, 47, 49, 56
  Story Brought by Brigit, 61, 134
  Twenty–Five, 48
  Visions and Beliefs, 61
  Workhouse Ward, 46, 47, 56
Grene, Nicholas, 67, 120

Griffith, Arthur, 3, 4, 74
Guthrie, Tyrone, 90

Hadfield, Paul, 209
Haire, Wilson John, 191, 193
Hammond, David, 207
Harding, Michael, 188, 207, **233–5**, 238
  Hubert Murray's Widow, 188, 207, 234
  Misogynist, 234
  Strawboys, 233–4
  Una Pooka, 234
Harris, Claudia, 197
Harrison, Alan, 54, 197
Haughey, Charles J., 182, 223
Heaney, Seamus, 7–8, 202, 207, 208, 210, 211, 213, 216, 222, 246
  The Cure at Troy, 208, 215, 216–17
  Sweeney Astray, 208, 215
  and Field Day, 207–8, 215
Hederman, Mark Patrick, 210
Herr, Cheryl, 52
Hewison, Robert, 165
Hickey, Des, 168, 169, 182
Hickey, Tom, 232, 233, 234
Higgins, F. R. (Frederick Robert), 135, 141
Hill, Ian, 207
Hogan, Robert, 11, 12, 84, 101, 113, 126, 132, 146, 152
Holcroft, Thomas (1744–1809), 211
Holloway, Joseph, 104
Horniman, Annie, 4, 21, 22, 56
Hosey, Seamus, 233
Hughes, Declan, 226, 239
Hunt, Hugh, 29, 108, 137, 141, 156, 161, 200
Hussey, Gemma, 130, 221, 224, 245
Hutchinson, John, 6–7, 8
Hutchinson, Ron, 195
Hyde, Douglas, 17, 42, 43, 53, 151
  Casadh an tSúgáin, 43
Hynes, Garry, 238, 245

Ibsen, Henrik, 15, 17, 18, 33, 69, 70, 72, 73, 74, 81, 83, 132, 237
  Brand, 69
  Doll's House, 17, 71, 74, 76, 132

Index

Enemy of the People, 83
Ghosts, 70, 72
Hedda Gabler, 72, 237
Peer Gynt, 73
Rosmersholm, 237
When We Dead Awaken, 33, 73
Wild Duck, 72
Innes, Christopher, 18, 231
Ireland, Denis, 143
Irish literary revival, 163
Irish Literary Theatre, 1, 2, 188, 245
Irish National Theatre Society, 2, 4,
    49, 74, 143
    see also Abbey Theatre
Irish Theatre Company, 208, 213

Jeffares, A. Norman, 26, 37
Jeffs, Rae, 150
Johnston, Denis, 9, 115, **119–29**, 137,
    140, 183, 185, 230
    Blind Man's Buff, 122
    Brazen Horn, 120, 129
    Bride for the Unicorn, 122, 129
    Dreaming Dust, 122
    Golden Cuckoo, 122, 129
    Moon in the Yellow River, 122, 125–8,
    131, 140
    Nine Rivers from Jordan, 120, 128
    Scythe and the Sunset, 122, 128, 129
    Strange Occurrence, 122
Jones, Marie, 188, 195
Jonson, Ben (1572–1637), 49–50, 143
Joyce, James, 5, 9, 34, 40, 64, 71, 73,
    128, 130, 160, 167, 198

Kaiser, Georg (1878–1945), 119
Kavanagh, Patrick, 131, 141, 147, 148,
    160, 167, 232
    The Great Hunger, 147, 148, 232
    see also MacIntyre, Tom, 232
Kavanagh, Peter, 12, 137
Kealy, Sister Marie Hubert, 163
Keane, John B., 10, 144, 162, 163, 165–
    6, 172, 175, 225, 233, 238, 239
    Big Maggie, 172
    Bodhrán Makers, 172
    Chastitute, 172, 176
    The Field, 179–80, 233

Highest House on the Mountain, 172
Hut 42, 166
Many Young Men, 165–6
Moll, 175–6
Sharon's Grave, 172, 238
Sive, 144
Year of the Hiker, 172
and emigration, 165–6
and religious consciousness, 175–6
and rural–urban divide, 179–80
and sexual identity, 172

Kearney, Colbert, 150, 160
Kearney, Richard, 210, 214, 216, 217,
    226
Kennelly, Brendan, 231
Kenner, Hugh, 44, 72
Keogh, Dermot, 135, 136, 165, 175, 223
Kershaw, Baz, 186
Kiberd, Declan, 21–2, 84, 217
Kilroy, Thomas, 10, 74, 102, 126, 162,
    163, 164, 172, 207, 208, 210, 217,
    218, 219, 220, 221, 225
    Death and Resurrection, 173, 174
    Double Cross, 208, 217–18, 219, 222
    Madame MacAdam, 208, 220–1
    O'Neill, 184
    Seagull, 213
    Talbot's Box, 178, 217
    Tea and Sex, 173
    and Field Day, 207, 210
    and history play, 184
    and religious identity, 178
    and sexual identity, 173–4
Kinsella, Thomas, 162, 223
Kohfeldt, Mary Lou, 48, 55, 56, 58, 62
Kosok, Heinz, 101, 143, 159
Kostik, Gavin, 239
Krause, David, 85, 89, 101, 108, 116,
    117
Kurdi, Mária, 197

language, 43–8, 84, 88, 141–2, 212
Lanters, José, 228
Larkin, James, 97, 98, 106, 107, 108,
    109, 111
Larkin, Philip, 10–11, 170
Laverty, Maura, 237

Index

Lee, J. J. (Joseph), 117, 165, 185, 212, 218
Lemass, Seán, 185
Leonard, Hugh (John Keyes Byrne), 7,
    10, 162, 167, 172, **182–3**, 186,
    224, **228–31**, 240
  Au Pair Man, 182, 229
  Da, 182, 229
  Kill, 186
  A Life, 182
  Mask of Moriarty, 229
  Moving, 229–31
  Patrick Pearse Motel, 172, 182–3
  Stephen D, 167
  and class, 182
  and farce, 182
  and political allegory, 186
Littlewood, Joan, 154, 156, 157, 158,
    159, 196
Longley, Edna, 206, 216
Lowery, Robert, 99
Lucy, Gordon, 205
Lukács, Georg, 6
Lynch, Martin, 188, 191, 194
  Castles in the Air, 188
  Interrogation of Ambrose Fogarty,
    194–5
Lyons, F. S. L., 118, 139, 148, 183
Lyric Players Theatre (Belfast), 189,
    191, 193, 202, 208, 209, 221, 231

MacAnna, Tomás, 90, 155, 188, 200
McCabe, Eugene, 171, 183
  King of the Castle, 171–2
  Pull Down a Horseman, 183
McCarthy, Seán, 202
McCann, Eamonn, 200
McCormick, F. J. (Peter Judge), 113
McDiarmid, Lucy, 38, 55
McDonagh, Donagh, 36, 141, 231
McGahern, John, 5, 170, 244
Mac Góráin, Riobárd, 156
McGrath, F. C., 212
McGrath, John, 181
McGuinness, Frank, 89, 188, 202, **204–
    7**, 208, 231, 239
  Bread Man, 188, 239
  Carthaginians, 206–7, 208
  Factory Girls, 204

Innocence, 239
Observe the Sons of Ulster, 204–5
McHugh, Roger, 10, 183
MacIntyre, Tom, 16, 36, **231–3**, 234,
    235, 238
  Bearded Lady, 233
  Dance for Your Daddy, 233
  Eye–Winker, Tom Tinker, 231
  Good Evening, Mr Collins, 233, 238
  Great Hunger, 232
  and Kavanagh, 232
  and Yeats, 16, 231
McKenna, Siobhán, 226
McKenna, Stephen, 66, 82, 83
MacLiammóir, Micheál, 7, 10, 29, 119,
    120, 123, 174
MacNamara, Brinsley (John Weldon),
    114, 130, 135, 136
McNamara, Gerald (Harry C. Mor-
    row), 188
Magee, Heno, 242
Mahon, Derek, 208, 213, 214
Malone, Andrew E., 12, 115, 116, 118,
    140
Mamet, David, 223, 246
Martyn, Edward, 2, 3, 5, 37, 69, 130
Mason, Patrick, 202, 232, 233, 245
Mayne, Rutherford (Samuel Waddell),
    188
Maxwell, D. E. S. (Desmond), 12, 163,
    178, 188
Meir, Colin, 215
Mercier, Paul, 239, **241–2**
  Buddleia, 242
  Home, 241–2
Mercier, Vivian, 70, 155
Mikhail, E. H. (Edward), 11, 141
Miller, Arthur, 184
Molière (Jean–Baptiste Poquelin, 1622–
    73), 53–4, 55, 81, 82, 119, 208
Molloy, M. J. (Michael Joseph), 138,
    146–8, 165
  King of Friday's Men, 148
  Old Road, 147
  Petticoat Loose, 148
  Wood of the Whispering, 146, 147–8,
    165
Montague, John, 170

Index

Mooney, Ria, 141, 156
Moore, George, 3, 5, 40, 69, 130
Morrison, Bill, 188
Muinzer, Philomena, 188
Murphy, John, 165
Murphy, Thomas (Tom), 7, 10, 16,
    162, 163, **166–8**, 169, 172–3, 182,
    183, 186, 188, 207, 224, **225–7**
  Bailegangaire, 226–7
  Blue Macushla, 168, 185–6
  Conversations, 168, 199, 226
  A Crucial Week, 167
  Famine, 183–4
  Gigli Concert, 225–6
  Morning After Optimism, 172, 177,
    178
  On the Outside/Inside, 177
  Patriot Game, 188, 207
  Sanctuary Lamp, 177–8
  Whistle in the Dark, 166–7, 169, 173
  White House, 168, 199
  and emigration, 167
  and Eugene O'Neill, 226
  and history play, 183–4
  and religious consciousness, 177–8
  and sexual identity, 172–3
  and political allegory, 185–6
Murray, T. C. (Thomas Cornelius),
    116, 130, 170, 172, 173, 239

Nairn, Tom, 6
naturalism, 69, 73, 158, 192
Nic Shiubhlaigh, Maire, 21, 25, 56
Nietzsche, Friedrich, 24, 80
New Ireland Forum, 205
Noh drama, 16, 25, 31
Nolan, Jim, 175, 239
Northern drama, **186–222**
  and Field Day, 207–22
  and O'Casey, 189–91
  and Romeo and Juliet, 192–4
  and theatre of hope, 194–9
  and Yeats, 188
Northern Ireland, 10, 179, 187, 189,
    192, 198, 199, 200, 205, 206, 209,
    215, 218, 219, 223, 234
  drama, 10–11, **186–222**
  theatre, 188–9

Novello, Ivor, 95
Nowlan, David, 204

O Briain, Seán, 156
O'Brien, Conor Cruise, 22, 85, 86, 224
O'Brien, George (1892–1974), 130
O'Brien, George (b. 1945), 163
O'Casey, Sean, 6, 8, 9, 12, 16, 41, **88–
    112**, 114, 115, 120, 121, 122, 123,
    127, 129, 134, 136, 140, 144, 145,
    155, 158, 160, 171, 172, 176, 177,
    181, 189, 190, 191, 193, 196, 198,
    204, 211, 225, 238, 239, 241
  Autobiographies, 92, 93, 105, 108
  Behind the Green Curtains, 90, 112
  Bishop's Bonfire, 90, 112, 134
  Blasts and Benedictions, 89
  Cock-a-Doodle Dandy, 112, 134,
    144–5, 171
  Drums of Father Ned, 90, 112, 171,
    176
  Feathers from the Green Crow, 106
  Figuro in the Night, 112
  Harvest Festival, 91, 92–4, 104, 108,
    109
  Juno and the Paycock, 88, 94, 101–4,
    127, 190, 192, 211, 239
  Letters, 41, 94, 98, 108, 111, 113,
    135, 136, 140
  Oak Leaves and Lavender, 90
  Plough and the Stars, 29, 39, 88, 91,
    94–9, 111, 113, 114, 115, 142,
    177, 183, 190
  Purple Dust, 90, 107–8
  Red Roses for Me, 90, 91, 92, 108–12
  Sacrifice of Thomas Ashe, 106
  Shadow of a Gunman, 88, 92, 93, 99–
    101, 109, 158, 190, 191, 199, 200
  Silver Tassie, 105, 106, 115, 135, 204
  Star Turns Red, 90
  Within the Gates, 90, 107, 108
  and Northern drama, 189–91, 193,
    196, 198, 211
  and Shakespeare, 89, 90, 102, 103,
    109
O'Connor, Frank, 29, 143, 158, 170
O'Connor, Ulick, 150, 152, 158, 174
O'Donnell, Frank Hugh, 19

Index

O'Faolain, Sean, 123, 132, 135, 170, 184
O hAodha, Micheál, 122, 152
O'Flaherty, Liam, 131
O'Malley, Conor, 189
O'Neill, Eugene, 39, 89, 171, 225–6
   and Tom Murphy, 226
   and T. C. Murray, 171
Osborne, John, 165, 174, 183, 242
   Look Back in Anger, 165
   Luther, 183
   Patriot for Me, 174
O'Toole, Fintan, 163, 177, 200, 209, 210

Pacelli, Eugenio (1876–1958), Cardinal, 131
Paircéar, Séamus, 156
Parker, Stewart, **196–99,** 206, 208, **218–20**
   Dramatis Personae, 220
   Northern Star, 197, 206
   Pentecost, 198, 199, 208, 217, 218–20, 222
   Spokesong, 196–7
   'State of Play', 197
Paulin, Tom, 207, 208, 213, 214, 215, 216
   director Field Day, 207
   Riot Act, 208, 214
Peacock, Alan J., 163, 176
Peacock Theatre, 29, 119, 156, 159, 183, 202, 204, 231, 232, 233, 235, 238
Pearse, Patrick, 91, 149, 182, 246
Pike Theatre, 153, 154, 156, 171
Pilkington, Lionel, 212
Pinter, Harold, 159, 212
Plunkett, Horace, 22
Plunkett, James, 181
Pound, Ezra, 25, 26
Project Arts Centre, 174, 175, 180, 181

Queen's Theatre, 142, 151, 154, 155
Quinn, John, 39, 68, 77

Reid, Christina, 188, 191, 193
   Did You Hear the One, 193
   Joyriders, 188, 191

Tea in a China Cup, 190
Reid Graham, 188, 193, **202–4**, 239
   Billy plays, 202
   Callers, 88, 203
   Closed Door, 202
   Death of Humpty Dumpty, 202
   Dorothy, 188, 202
   Hidden Curriculum, 188, 203, 204
   Lengthening Shadows, 202
   Love, 202
   Remembrance, 188, 193, 203
Rea, Stephen, 207, 209, 214, 217, 221
Renan, Ernest, 5
Richtarik, Marilynn J., 162
Robinson, Lennox, 9, 14, 24, 32, 49, 62, 83, 105, **115–18**, 121, 122, 128, 130, 131, 137, 141, 142, 143, 152, 160, 175, 238
   Big House, 118
   Drama at Inish, 117
   Far-Off Hills, 117
   Lost Leader, 118
   Killycreggs in Twilight, 118
   Whiteheaded Boy, 116
Roche, Anthony, 12, 154, 163, 236
Roche, Billy, 227
Royal Court Theatre, 165
Ryan, John, 142, 174

Sacks, Oliver, 228
   and Friel, 228
Saddlemyer, Ann, 38, 41, 48, 50, 54, 55, 69, 119
Said, Edward, 41
Scott, Michael (director), 159
Sears, David, 141
Sekine, Masaru, 25
Shakespeare, William, 15, 29, 89, 90, 109, 111, 121, 159, 169, 173, 187, 192, 204, 220, 237, 239
Shaughnessy, Edward L., 226
Shaw, George Bernard, 9, 17, 22, 38, 56, 60, 62, 64, 69, 72, 73, 80, 81, 82, 83, 84, 86, 87, 88, 89, 95, 96, 100, 126, 145, 146, 198, 217, 219, 224
   Back to Methuselah, 219
   Doctor's Dilemma, 100

Index

Fanny's First Play, 62
Heartbreak House, 95, 126, 127
John Bull's Other Island, 65, 80, 81,
    82, 86, 145, 146, 224
Matter with Ireland, 86
Shewing–Up of Blanco Posnet, 38, 87
Widowers' Houses, 88
Sheaffer, Louis, 226
Sheehan, Helena, 179
Shelley, Percy Bysshe, 100
Sheridan, Jim, 174, 180–1
Sheridan Peter, 181, 207
Shiels, George, 114, 138, **139–42**, 180
    New Gossoon, 114, 140
    Paul Twyning, 114, 139
    Professor Tim, 114, 139
    Passing Day, 140
    Rugged Path, 139, 140–1, 180
    Summit, 141
    and Friel, 140
    and Keane, 180
Simpson, Alan, 153, 154, 155, 159, 171
Sinclair, Arthur, 54
Sloan, Barry, 204
Smith, Gus, 168, 169, 182
Sophocles, 28, 208, 215
Stephens, Edward, 66, 67, 69, 77
Steiner, George, 213
Stembridge, Gerard, 239
Stewart, A. T. Q., 187
Stoppard, Tom, 229
Strindberg, August, 89, 121, 194
Swift, Carolyn, 153, 155, 171
Swift, Jonathan, 30, 122, 132, 133, 233
    and Carroll, 132, 133
    and Johnston, 122
    and MacIntyre, 233
    and Yeats, 30
Synge, John Millington, 4, 5, 9, 17, 37,
    38, 39, 43, 44, 45, 46, 54, 59, 64–
    87, 89, 105, 114, 115, 116, 117,
    119, 122, 130, 131, 146, 148, 151,
    158, 165, 171, 192, 198, 213,
    225, 228, 231
    Aran Islands, 65, 71, 74–5
    Autobiography, 66, 69
    Deirdre of the Sorrows, 59, 72, 79
    Letters, 76

Playboy, 4, 29, 38, 57, 64, 68, 71, 72,
    73, 76, 80–6, 87, 115
    riots, 57, 86, 115
Riders to the Sea, 64, 73, 79, 83, 84,
    158
Shadow of the Glen, 4, 17, 71, 74–6,
    79, 81, 131
Tinker's Wedding, 72, 78, 86
Well of the Saints, 70, 72, 77–9, 228
When the Moon Has Set, 69–72, 80
    and Ibsen, 69–74

Theatre Workshop, 154, 156
Theatre of Cruelty, 184
Thompson, Sam, 189, 190, 195, 196
Tobin, Fergal, 164, 170
Tóibín, Niall, 159
Toller, Ernst (1893–1939), 121, 122
Torchiana, Donald, 31
Tynan, Kenneth, 158

Ulster Literary Theatre, 188

Wade, Allan, 21, 27, 28, 33, 34, 68, 77,
    105
Wall, Richard, 156
Wardle, Irving, 165
Waters, Maureen, 55
Watson, George J., 190
Welch, Robert, 18, 176
West, Michael, 225
Weygandt, Cornelius, 11
Whitaker, T. K., 164
White, Jack, 175, 204
White, Victoria, 234
Widgery, Rt. Hon. Lord, 200
Wilde, Oscar, 198, 217
Wilder, Thornton, 230
Willett, John, 229
Williams, Tennessee, 171, 172
Wilson, Colin, 160
Wilson, Edmund, 215
Woods, Vincent, 188, 207, 234
Woodworth, Paddy, 221
Worth, Katharine, 12, 13, 14, 16
Wright, Frank, 220

Yeats, Jack B., 68, 83, 231

Index

Yeats, William Butler, 1, 2, 3, 4, 5, 7,
9, **13–36**, 37, 38, 39, 40, 41, 45,
55, 56, 64, 65, 67, 69, 70, 81, 89,
103, 105, 109, 110, 115, 117, 119,
121, 122, 123, 130, 136, 137, 139,
143, 177, 184, 188, 224, 225, 231,
242, 246, 247
At the Hawk's Well, 26
Cat and the Moon, 14
Cathleen Ni Houlihan, 3, 20–2, 27,
56, 109, 121, 184
Countess Cathleen, 2, 18–20, 39, 113
Death of Cuchulain, 33–5
Deirdre, 20, 24
Dreaming of the Bones, 26–8, 30, 58
Four Plays for Dancers, 26, 34, 110
Herne's Egg, 14, 29, 33, 136
Hour Glass, 20

King's Threshold, 13, 22, 33
Land of Heart's Desire, 17, 25
Oedipus the King, 24, 28
On Baile's Strand, 20, 22–4, 26, 32
Only Jealousy of Emer, 14, 26
Player Queen, 14, 30, 57
Pot of Broth, 39
Purgatory, 31–2, 33, 136, 242
Resurrection, 28
Shadowy Waters, 14, 23
Unicorn from the Stars, 14
Vision, 14, 64–5
Where There is Nothing, 14, 39
Words upon the Window-Pane, 28,
30–1, 32

Zach, 201, 210